The Color-Blind
Constitution

The
Color-Blind
Constitution

Andrew Kull

Harvard University Press

Cambridge, Massachusetts

London, England

Copyright © 1992 by the President and Fellows of Harvard College
All rights reserved
Printed in the United States of America
Second printing, 1994

First Harvard University Press paperback edition, 1994

Library of Congress Cataloging-in-Publication Data

Kull, Andrew, 1947–
    The color-blind constitution / Andrew Kull.
        p. cm.
    Includes bibliographical references (p.) and index.
    ISBN 0-674-14292-6 (acid-free paper) (cloth)
    ISBN 0-674-14293-4 (pbk.)
    1. Equality before the law—United States—History. 2. Race discrimination—Law and
legislation—United States—History. 3. Afro-Americans—Legal status, laws, etc.—United
States—History. 4. Affirmative action programs—Law and legislation—United
States—History. I. Title.
KF4755.5.K85   1992
342.73′0873—dc20
[347.302873]

91-43317

To Dana Kull

Preface

My object in this book is to discover the history of the argument that the United States Constitution prohibits (or should prohibit) racial classification by the agencies of government. That history inevitably implicates, in its most recent episodes, the modern debate over government-sponsored racial preferences; indeed, the perspective it affords on the affirmative-action dilemma accounts in part for the story's compelling interest. But I will discuss affirmative action in order to complete the account of color blindness, not the other way around. While I believe that the history of the color-blind contention illuminates the affirmative-action debate at a number of points, I make no claim that it decides that issue. Short of a demonstration that the Fourteenth Amendment was intended by its framers to require color blindness on the part of government—and the evidence I adduce tends strongly to refute any such contention—it is difficult to imagine how one could hope, by an analysis of what was thought and argued in the past, to conclude the profoundly political question of what we should do *now;* and I shall not attempt to do so.

I offer this disclaimer because a number of people to whom I described this project while working on it plainly assumed that the only reason to write a history of the color-blind Constitution would be to develop history-based arguments against affirmative action. When I responded that my purpose was not so much to advance a thesis as to tell a story, they were visibly skeptical. The reader may share their skepticism. It seems unlikely that anyone would bother to write a history of the color-blind Constitution unless he found the idea an attractive one; and the ideal of nondiscrimination epitomized by the color-blind proposition is obviously antithetical to a policy that recognizes proportional entitlements for racial and ethnic groups. The fact remains that the best arguments against affirmative action are not to be found in the history of the color-blind idea. Its relative lack of utility for partisan purposes is surely one of the reasons why this interesting history has not previously been explored.

But while history cannot decide the issues, it can illuminate the ongoing (if covert) debate over the policy of racial preferences. The story that follows is rich in "implications," one way and another. Let me suggest two.

Most obviously, perhaps, the history of the color-blind Constitution gives the lie to those who would explain the idea away: who deny the reality of any "color-blind" constitutional tradition, disparaging "race neutralism" as merely a self-regarding strategy devised to resist policies of redistribution. The unavoidable fact is that over a period of some 125 years ending only in the late 1960s, the American civil rights movement first elaborated, then held as its unvarying political objective a rule of law requiring the color-blind treatment of individuals. Not only did nondiscrimination hold out the promise of black social and economic advancement, but the right of the individual to be treated without regard to race was strenuously defended as a moral and political end in itself. The extraordinary shift of a generation ago, in which "civil rights" became associated with a demand for compensatory racial preferences, has yet to be openly avowed. It is the older civil rights, not the new, that prevails in public opinion; and if the public debate over the conditions of racial equality is one day reopened, the adversary with which the modern civil rights movement may ultimately be forced to compromise will be not the old enemy of racism but its own liberal tradition.

From the same history one might draw contrasting lessons. The color-blind proposition was first discovered, and was employed throughout the classical civil rights movement, in the pursuit of a more nearly perfect equality for black Americans. At a time when the law frequently imposed explicit disabilities on racial grounds, the natural starting point was to demand "equality before the law." Antebellum civil rights lawyers, whose claim to legal "equality" was conceded by the courts in a state like Massachusetts, derived the color-blind argument as the means to defend their clients against the inequality that resulted when supposedly equal treatment was provided in segregated facilities. A rule of color blindness, as men like Charles Sumner and Wendell Phillips correctly perceived, was the only means to ensure a perfect legal equality. But it took the nation more than a century to reach the point at which "equality before the law" could reasonably be thought to have been achieved; and only then could we finally perceive the extent to which a purely legal equality was equality in inadequate measure. It does not follow that policies of racial preference are an appropriate response: liberal egalitarians including Bayard Rustin and William Julius Wilson have argued that they are not. But there is an undeniable irony, which close attention to the color-blind history will only underscore, in applying a rule of nondiscrimination to frustrate measures designed (however imperfectly) to promote equality of condition for black Americans as a group.

I place these observations here, outside my text, because of my conviction that such considerations are largely extraneous to the interest of the story that follows. The history of the color-blind Constitution offers, I believe, a new, rewarding, and frequently surprising perspective on the development of the American constitutional law of race. Its relevance to present-day policy choices lies in the familiar premise that we can better understand what we are doing if we understand how we got here. Whether these claims are made good the reader must decide.

For their kindness in reading all or part of this work at different stages, and for the helpful comments and corrections they offered, I am grateful to Jennifer Arlen, Harold J. Berman, George Forgie, John P. Frank, Richard W. Hulbert, Marc L. Miller, Robert C. Post, Geoffrey R. Stone, Nathan S. Tarcov, and Timothy P. Terrell, as well as to several anonymous readers for Harvard University Press. William Marshall and his colleagues at a Case Western Reserve University Law School faculty seminar gave me many useful suggestions as well as a cordial reception. John F. Burleigh, Jonathan Entin, Jack Greenberg, James Lindgren, Charles A. Lofgren, Phil C. Neal, LaDean Sypher, and Alan F. Westin provided valuable information and assistance in various forms, for which I thank each of them sincerely. I am indebted to Aida Donald and Ann Hawthorne for their perceptive and bracing editorial guidance.

The following narrative incorporates, at two points, the fruits of others' unpublished research. The correspondence in 1829 between Mayor Williams of Savannah and Governor Gilmer of Georgia on the subject of *David Walker's Appeal*, with the governor's subsequent communication to the legislature (reproduced in notes to Chapter 1), were discovered through the tireless efforts of Rhonda Philopoulos, Emory Law School J.D. 1991. Philip Hamburger very kindly brought to my attention the Ohio House and Senate reports of 1834 (discussed in notes to Chapter 2), rejecting petitions that sought the repeal of state laws making a distinction between persons on the basis of color. My own research has benefited from the assistance of Daniel Conaway, Mary Lynn Hawkins, Sung Hui Kim, Matthew Minelli, Lisa Mantz, and Daniel P. Rader, and from the financial support of the Emory Law School.

Extracts from letters in the collections of the Boston Public Library, the Houghton Library, the Massachusetts Historical Society, and the Yale University Library are published by the kind permission of those institutions.

The unfailing help and encouragement provided in connection with this work by Robert Dawidoff are but a small part of what I owe to his generosity and friendship.

Atlanta, Georgia
December 1991

Contents

The Color-Blind
Constitution

Introduction

The notion of a Constitution that is "color-blind" is recognizable, even familiar, thanks to the majestic language of John Marshall Harlan's famous dissenting opinion in *Plessy v. Ferguson.* In that 1896 decision, the Supreme Court of the United States upheld the constitutionality of a Louisiana statute requiring that railway passengers be segregated by race. The other Justices found such a regulation reasonable under the circumstances. Harlan, the sole dissenter, denied that reasonableness was the proper standard:

> In respect of civil rights, common to all citizens, the Constitution of the United States does not, I think, permit any public authority to know the race of those entitled to be protected in the enjoyment of such rights.
> . . . There is no caste here. Our Constitution is color-blind, and neither knows nor tolerates classes among citizens.

The comfortable metaphor stands for an austere proposition: that American government is, or ought to be, denied the power to distinguish between its citizens on the basis of race. A blanket prohibition of racial classifications is impossible to locate in a literal reading of the constitutional text, and it has never been acknowledged by the Supreme Court as a requirement of the "equal protection of the laws" guaranteed by the Fourteenth Amendment. Yet the color-blind idea persists nevertheless, forming a seemingly indispensable theme in the constitutional law of race.

The moral and political attractiveness of a rule of nondiscrimination made it for approximately 125 years the ultimate legal objective of the American civil rights movement. From the 1840s to the 1960s, the profoundest claim of those who fought the institution of racial segregation was that the government had no business sorting people by the color of their skin, regardless of the equality with which they were treated. By some point in the mid-1960s—the enactment of the Civil Rights Act of 1964 makes a convenient benchmark—this once-radical idea had become part of the governing liberal consensus of American political life. But the achievement at long last of "equality before the law" revealed a harsh truth that the long struggle for civil rights had tended to obscure: the fact that guarantees of legal equality would be inadequate to redress the inequality of condition afflicting black Americans as a group. Almost at once, the field of debate shifted; and the older civil rights ideal has since stood as the most widely voiced objection to the race-conscious methods by which, in the post–civil rights era, a fuller measure of equality has generally been sought.

The arguments for and against affirmative action, except as they may be illuminated by legal history, are not the subject of this book. Its purpose is to explore the history of a legal argument: to locate the sources of the constitutional argument for radical nondiscrimination, "color blindness," and to trace its subsequent manifestations. The events of the last quarter-century are an important part of that story, but they comprise—in the perspective here adopted—only its most recent chapter.

The color-blind argument was a product of the struggle for legal equality for black Americans—"equality before the law," in Charles Sumner's phrase—and it was discovered nearly at the outset. The Massachusetts constitution of 1780 contained, in effect, the guarantee of legal equality that was added to the U.S. Constitution only in 1868. In consequence, issues of racial discrimination that would occupy the nation during the hundred years following the Civil War were addressed in Massachusetts during the twenty years that preceded it. Massachusetts did not exclude free Negroes from coming within her borders, as did Indiana; nor provide public schools for white children only, as did Ohio; nor restrict her black citizens' exercise of the franchise, as did New York. Some cities in Massachusetts, however, provided education for black and white children in separate schools; and a state statute forbade interracial marriage. The arguments that proved significant for the future were developed in the context of the school segregation controversy. Because the Massachusetts constitution promised "equality," the familiar task facing the nation's first civil rights lawyers was to explain that racially segregated schools with theoretically equal facilities nevertheless denied equality of treatment; and that racial segregation had this effect although segregation by age or sex did not.

Seen in retrospect, the exploration of this question by Charles Sumner (as attorney for the plaintiff) and Chief Justice Lemuel Shaw in *Roberts v. City of Boston*, a school desegregation case decided in 1850, established a number of points that are still being rediscovered. The implications of Sumner's argument and Shaw's decision introduce the principal themes of the color-blind history.

Sumner (and the other lawyers, like Wendell Phillips, on whose ideas he drew) had discovered that a perfect legal equality between persons might require that they not be separately classified at all. The reason lay in the adverse consequences, under certain circumstances, of the bare fact of classification. But such an argument was bound in subtleties, and it was a weak answer to the inevitable rejoinder that "equality" did not mean "identity."

Even more awkward was the fact that segregation of schoolchildren by age and sex was evidently unobjectionable. There is, as Shaw pointed out, scarcely an act of government that does not make or depend on some classification of persons; yet it could not be the case that all citizens of the commonwealth were thereby denied the equality of treatment to which all were admittedly entitled. Simply stated, the right to equal treatment cannot mean a right to the same treatment accorded one's neighbor. Shaw solved this problem in the context of *Roberts* by declaring, in effect, that legal equality consists in affording like treatment to those situated alike. A constitutional guarantee of "equality" becomes therefore, and necessarily, a guarantee of reasonable classification. Shaw found segregation of Boston's primary schools a reasonable policy.

These conclusions (save the last) are among the fundamental elements of the constitutional law of "equal protection"; they were worked out sixteen years before the Fourteenth Amendment was written. For the opponents of segregation, the natural if paradoxical lesson of *Roberts* was that true legal equality was only weakly protected by an explicit guarantee of equal treatment; while the constitutional rule that would best secure an unqualified legal equality was, by contrast, a guarantee of nondiscrimination. At the close of the Civil War, when the nation briefly debated the terms on which civil rights for the Negro would be brought under federal protection, Wendell Phillips and Thaddeus Stevens campaigned strenuously for precisely the latter guarantee. (The vast literature on the framing of the Fourteenth Amendment—the most thoroughly worked ground in American constitutional history—entirely ignores Phillips's efforts to promote an amendment based on nondiscrimination.) Phillips's views, at the time, were as widely publicized as those of any Republican leader; and the rejection of his ideas in favor of John Bingham's "privileges and immunities," "due process," and "equal protection" carries unmistakable implications for the "original understanding" of the words ultimately adopted.

The Phillips/Stevens Fourteenth Amendment would have prohibited state and federal governments from distinguishing between persons on the basis of race, no more and no less: it would thus have made the Constitution color-blind in so many words. Bingham's sibylline phrases were the conservative alternative: since Bingham's proposal, whatever it meant, promised less interference with those forms of racial discrimination with which the Republicans of the Thirty-ninth Congress felt comfortable. Phillips and Stevens would have prohibited all racial classifications; Bingham wished to prohibit only the unreasonable ones. The difference has dominated our constitutional law of race ever since.

A constitutional standard of "reasonableness" gives the final say to judges. The real choice made by the Thirty-ninth Congress thus lay between a rule permitting the legislature to employ racial classifications in its discretion, subject to judicial veto; and a rule forbidding such classifications altogether. Once the Fourteenth Amendment had been ratified, and its meaning entrusted to the judiciary, proponents of color blindness were in the anomalous position (whether they realized it or not) of asking judges to declare that the judges' own determination of the reasonable uses of race afforded an inadequate safeguard. They had to argue, in other words, that an arbitrary, prophylactic rule was preferable to a wise and flexible judicial discretion that would strike down the bad uses of race while allowing the good ones. Precisely that self-denying assertion forms the heart of Harlan's opinion in *Plessy v. Ferguson,* though it is not usually so understood. Harlan's argument is the more noteworthy, especially from the perspective of the present day, because he nowhere asserts that the use of racial classifications must in every instance be bad policy.

It is not surprising that few judges have wished to relinquish the ultimate power to rule on policy, in this or any other area of their competence. During the 1950s and early 1960s, it is highly doubtful that the members of the Supreme Court foresaw any use of racial classifications that would be thereafter upheld against a claim of unconstitutional discrimination. In an era when the NAACP Legal Defense Fund never lost a case before the Supreme Court, its lawyers repeatedly argued to the justices that the Constitution was already color-blind—as the Court's decisions seemed to indicate—and urged them to declare that politically and historically gratifying fact. What restrained the Court from doing so, well before the advent of what it would later consider to be "benign" uses of race, was a political reflex that counseled against the gratuitous relinquishment of power.

The Supreme Court today exercises an unconstrained discretion in determining the permissible and impermissible uses of race. By a well-known irony, the rule of constitutional law that grants this authority is the direct legacy of *Plessy v. Ferguson:* a rule that those racial classifications are permissible that a majority of the justices find to be reasonable and appropriate under the circumstances. That rule decided *Plessy v. Ferguson* in 1896, *Brown v. Board of Education* in 1954, the most recent affirmative action cases, and everything in between; with equal authority, it could justify a return to color blindness should the Court someday be persuaded of its advantages. From *Plessy* onward, in fact, it is impossible to identify in the opinions of the Supreme Court of the United States a constitutional law of racial classifications that may usefully be distinguished from the ad hoc policy preferences of a majority of the Court. The chance to establish a rule that would constrain judges, instead of merely authorizing them, died in the Joint Committee on Reconstruction of the Thirty-ninth Congress.

In the era of affirmative action as in the era of segregation, the idea of color blindness stands in radical contradistinction to a constitutional orthodoxy that at every stage of our history has permitted the government to classify by race so long as—by contemporary standards—it classified reasonably. The benefits to be gained from one or another form of racial discrimination have usually appeared self-evident to those who write and administer laws, and the renunciation of this powerful tool of government has accordingly been favored only by a relative few. The conventional view reflects an optimistic political conception: that legislators, subject to the oversight of wise judges, may be trusted to govern in accordance with standards of equality, reasonableness, and justice. Contemporary arguments for affirmative action are politically optimistic—in this sense among others. The color-blind proposition, in Phillips's as in Harlan's version, is the product instead of a radical skepticism about our political capabilities where race is concerned. Because neither legislators nor judges may be trusted to choose wisely in this vexed area, and because we know that racial classifications are often highly injurious, our only safety lies in foreclosing altogether a power of government we cannot trust ourselves to use for good. Such an argument may yet have force; but it must await the outcome of a political debate, still far from resolution, over the utility of the race-conscious policies currently being employed.

The history that follows is legal history, and the story to be told is largely preoccupied with lawyers and lawyers' arguments. The emphasis on a legal and judicial perspective is not intended to suggest that the history of American ideas about racial equality is best understood in legal terms. The law can be the instrument, but never the source, of social change; the most momentous legal judgments only give effect to conclusions that others have already reached. As it happens, however, the color-blind conception is notably the work of lawyers, and the characteristic product of a lawyer's effort to obtain a result for a client. Like every other appeal to constitutionally protected rights, the argument attempts to prevail over an adverse political consensus by reading the law to deny to those who exercise power the discretion to act as they see fit. The party that dominates the consensus, by contrast, has no interest in constitutional constraints; so it is hardly surprising, from this point of view, that the adoption of civil rights objectives as federal policy in the 1960s was followed so quickly by the repudiation of the color-blind ideal. An argument designed to restrict the power of government to harm one's client loses its attraction when one's client begins to govern.

Even within the narrow perspective of a legal history, the recurring argument for color blindness has been only one strand of a broader argument for racial equality. The present attempt to isolate the color-blind argument is new, and until relatively recently it might not have been comprehensible. So long as black citizens were denied a simple legal equality, it would not have occurred to many people to distinguish an argument against racial classifications from an argument in favor of equal treatment. Both sought the same practical ends, and the former could usually be seen (correctly) as a tactical variation on the latter. So long as enforcement of the antidiscrimination principle served to correct the nation's historic racial inequality, the contours of this particular contention could not, in fact, be accurately distinguished from the surrounding argument for racial justice. The advent of affirmative action, by contrast, has caused the old argument for color blindness to stand forth in sharp relief, while inviting new attention to its historical rationale.

A Glorious Liberty Document | 1

The usual starting point of the legal argument for nondiscrimination was the idea of equality as a cornerstone of American institutions; but the idea of equality does not appear in the Constitution of 1787. It was not only the federal Constitutional Convention that neglected to reaffirm Jefferson's paradoxical, self-evident truth. Among state constitutions of the revolutionary period, only the Massachusetts Declaration of Rights asserted boldly that "All men are born free and equal."[1] Other states went no further than the statement of the Virginia Declaration that "all men are by nature equally free and independent"[2]—avoiding, with this more cautious formula, the suggestion that men had any inherent claim to civic equality. Of the many reasons why a recognizable constitutional argument for the antidiscrimination principle first appeared in Massachusetts in the 1840s, not the least important is that Wendell Phillips and Charles Sumner had at their disposal a constitutional text on which the argument might readily be constructed.

The argument that the federal Constitution restricted the power of government to classify by race had therefore to be based, prior to the adoption of the Fourteenth Amendment, on close attention to what had not been said. A constitution that admitted Negro slavery did not make a promising charter of nondiscrimination; yet it had unmistakably been written to accommodate, not only the compromise of the present moment, but also a future in which the institution of slavery would somehow have been abolished.[3] The framers' refusal to speak the name of slavery made it possible to argue, with Frederick Douglass, that the Constitution embodied more fundamental values with which slavery was ultimately incompatible:

Fellow-citizens! there is no matter in respect to which, the people of the North have allowed themselves to be so ruinously imposed upon, as that of the pro-slavery character of the Constitution. In *that* instrument

> I hold there is neither warrant, license, nor sanction of the hateful thing; but, interpreted as it *ought* to be interpreted, the Constitution is a GLORIOUS LIBERTY DOCUMENT. Read its preamble, consider its purposes. Is slavery among them? Is it at the gateway? or is it in the temple? It is neither. While I do not intend to argue this question on the present occasion, let me ask, if it be not somewhat singular that, if the Constitution were intended to be, by its framers and adopters, a slave-holding instrument, why neither *slavery, slaveholding,* nor *slave* can anywhere be found in it.[4]

This was generous toward the framers, but it is a view of the Constitution that the people of the North came shortly to adopt.

The studied absence of any reference to "black" or "white," and the framers' apparent preference for securing the rights of "persons," carried significant negative implications. The careful neutrality of the language implied that race and sex were, in some measure at least, disfavored grounds of legal distinctions. Charles Sumner successfully resisted the plan of the Republican leadership in the Thirty-ninth Congress for adjusting the basis of federal representation—namely, to reduce a state's representation in Congress "whenever the elective franchise shall be denied or abridged on account of race or color"—in part because of the "discord and defilement" that would be introduced into the text of the Constitution by an amendment acknowledging even the possibility of a racial distinction:

> It was wrong to admit in the Constitution the idea that man could hold property in man. Accordingly, in this spirit the Constitution was framed. This offensive idea was not admitted. The text at least was kept blameless. And now, after generations have passed, surrounded by the light of Christian truth and in the very blaze of Human Freedom, it is proposed to admit in the Constitution the twin idea of Inequality in Rights, and thus openly set at naught the first principles of the Declaration of Independence and the guarantee of a republican government itself, while you blot out a whole race politically. For some time we have been carefully expunging from the statute-book the word "white," and now it is proposed to insert in the Constitution itself a distinction of color.[5]

In the House, where an attempt was made to avoid this difficulty by an amendment that would base national representation on the number of male electors in the several states, Thaddeus Stevens raised a similar objection:

> But I have another objection to the amendment of my friend from Ohio. His proposition is to apportion representation according to the

male citizens of the States. Why has he put in that word "male?" It was never in the Constitution of the United States before. . . . I do not think we ought to disfigure the Constitution with such a provision. . . . I certainly shall never vote to insert the word "male" or the word "white" in the national Constitution. Let these things be attended to by the States.[6]

It required an ambitious further step to argue that the neutral wording of any of the constitutional provisions might of its own force restrict the freedom of the states to distinguish between citizens on the basis of race. Yet with respect to one highly significant provision—the comity clause of article IV, providing that "[t]he Citizens of each State shall be entitled to all Privileges and Immunities of Citizens in the several States"—a striking piece of legislative history supported precisely that contention. The clause was directly derived from the fourth article of the Articles of Confederation, which had secured "all the privileges and immunities of free citizens in the several States" to "the free inhabitants of each of these States."[7] The racial inclusiveness of the phrase "free inhabitants" was not inadvertent. In 1778, in the course of a debate over proposed amendments to the Articles, delegates to the Continental Congress from South Carolina and Georgia had tried to restrict this grant of privileges and immunities—already limited by a clause excluding "paupers, vagabonds and fugitives from justice"—to free *white* inhabitants. The amendment was defeated by a vote of eight to two, with one delegation divided.[8]

To regard this vote as evidence of a "majoritarian devotion to interracial equality" would undoubtedly be to overstate the case, as Don E. Fehrenbacher has pointed out: "Congress, hoping to avoid the necessity of resubmitting the Articles to the states, rejected *all* proposed amendments, including one that would have *removed* the word 'white' from the apportionment of militia quotas."[9] But in the intense controversy to which the episode later became relevant, the issue was not interracial equality but race as a qualification of constitutional citizenship. It is to this effect that the action of the Continental Congress was cited by Justice Benjamin Curtis, in his celebrated dissenting opinion in the *Dred Scott* case:

The fact that free persons of color were citizens of some of the several States, and the consequence, that this fourth article of the Confederation would have the effect to confer on such persons the privileges and immunities of general citizenship, were not only known to those who framed and adopted those articles, but the evidence is decisive, that the fourth article was intended to have that effect, and that more restricted language, which would have excluded such persons, was deliberately and purposely rejected.

. . . The language of the article stood unchanged, and [by its terms] it is clear, that under the Confederation, and at the time of the adoption of the Constitution, free colored persons of African descent might be, and, by reason of their citizenship in certain States, were entitled to the privileges and immunities of general citizenship of the United States.[10]

At a minimum, the rejection of the amendment made it appreciably more difficult to maintain—as the southern states sought to do during the forty years preceding the Civil War—that the comity clause of article IV, section 2 could never have been intended to protect state citizens who happened to be black. Sympathetically observed, the episode demonstrated something more: that by a conscious decision, the framers of our first national charter had refused to qualify with a racial distinction the one provision in the document dealing directly and immediately with the rights of citizens.

The fact of the episode and the availability of this favorable interpretation were not lost on the abolitionists. At the close of 1832 William Lloyd Garrison would memorably pronounce the U.S. Constitution to be "the most bloody and heaven-daring arrangement ever made by men for the continuance and protection of a system of the most atrocious villany ever exhibited on earth."[11] A year and a half earlier, however, addressing the Philadelphia convention of the Free People of Color in June 1831, Garrison had praised the Constitution as an engine of nondiscrimination that had only to be harnessed. Garrison's reference to "free inhabitants," a phrase not appearing in the Constitution itself, recalled the color-blind comity clause of the Articles of Confederation:

The Constitution of the United States knows nothing of white or black men; it makes no invidious distinction with regard to the color or condition of free inhabitants; it is broad enough to cover your persons; it has power enough to vindicate your rights. Thanks be to God that we have such a Constitution!

I say . . . that those State Laws which disfranchise and degrade you, are unconstitutional. I say that if they fall upon the Constitution, they will be dashed in pieces. I say that it is your duty to carry this question up to the Supreme Court of the United States, and have it settled forever. . . . Once get yourselves acknowledged, by that august tribunal, as citizens of the United States, and you may walk abroad in majesty and strength, free as the air of heaven, sacred as the persons of kings.[12]

Garrison's sense of the constitutional issue anticipated, from a contrary perspective, Chief Justice Roger B. Taney's 1857 opinion in *Dred Scott*. The question was whether free people of color, citizens by the laws of the several states, might be acknowledged to be "citizens" as that term was used in the Constitution. From Garrison's point of view as from Taney's, the clause that made U.S. citizenship significant was the color-blind comity clause of article IV.

The Constitution that "knew nothing of white or black men" scarcely touched the duties of the states to persons within their jurisdictions. Yet at the one point where the Constitution of 1787 directly constrained the authority of the states to grant or withhold civil rights, it had undeniably omitted any racial qualification. This simple fact about the comity clause offered a narrow but substantial basis for the original argument that the Constitution prohibited some forms of racial discrimination. The rule such an argument could support was naturally limited in scope, extending no further than the relations between a state and the handful of black citizens of other states who might choose to sojourn within it. Still, the assertion of an antidiscrimination claim on the basis of the comity clause, confined though it was to this narrow range of circumstances, provoked repeated and bitter sectional controversy. The idea that the Constitution could conceivably restrict a state's freedom to enforce racial distinctions came to be as intolerable to the South as the fugitive slave clause had become to the North.

Events combined to lend substance to what must originally have seemed a largely hypothetical question. In 1822, in the panic that followed the discovery at Charleston of a slave insurrection plot organized by a free Negro, Denmark Vesey, South Carolina moved to restrict her free black population with increasingly repressive laws. The most visible of these was the Negro Seamen Act, providing that free black sailors aboard out-of-state or foreign vessels calling at South Carolina's ports should be seized and imprisoned until their ships were ready to depart. If at that point the ship's captain (whose employers would be indebted to the seamen for wages) neglected or refused to pay the expenses of their detention and remove them from the state, the prisoners would be sold into slavery.[13] Variations of the law were adopted by other slaveholding states, inspired by the same concern that free Negroes (particularly those from northern states) carried the contagion of rebellion.[14]

The Negro Seamen Acts were at least intermittently enforced, notwithstanding a prompt decision by Justice William Johnson of the U.S. Supreme Court, sitting on circuit in *Elkison v. Deliesseline,* that the South Carolina statute was an unconstitutional infringement of the exclusive federal commerce and treaty powers.[15] Because the seaman arrested in *Elkison* was a British subject, an argument based on the comity clause did not arise. But if black citizens of northern states were included by the words "the citizens of each State" as used in article IV, section 2, then southern laws restricting their immigration or sojourn were plainly unconstitutional on that basis as well.

During this initial phase of the controversy over the comity clause, the reply of the southern states to the charge that their laws were unconstitutional tended implicitly to concede the point: they proposed either to change the Constitution or to ignore it. In the legislative session following Justice Johnson's decision in *Elkison,* the Georgia legislature resolved to *amend* the Constitution to provide "[t]hat no part of the Constitution of the United States, ought to be construed, or shall be construed to authorise the importation or ingress of any person of color into any one of the United States, contrary to the laws of such state."[16] The Senate of South Carolina was meanwhile asserting that its Negro Seamen Act was justified by considerations transcending the issue of constitutionality:

> (4) Resolved that it is as much the duty of the State, to guard against insubordination or insurrection among our colored population, or to control and regulate any cause which might excite or produce it, as to guard against any other evil, political or physical, which might assail us. This duty is paramount to all *laws,* all *treaties,* all *constitutions:*—it arises from the supreme and permanent law of nature, the law of self-preservation; and will never by this State be renounced, compromised, controlled or participated with any power whatever.[17]

Twenty years later, when greater political importance attached to having the better of the constitutional argument, the South defended the constitutionality of the same laws by denying that a black person could be a citizen of the United States within the meaning of the Constitution.

Feelings against the Negro Seamen Acts ran particularly high in Massachusetts, where the laws were profoundly offensive to both commercial and abolitionist sentiment. In 1839 and again in 1842 the Massachusetts legislature passed resolutions protesting the imprisonment by other states of citizens of Massachusetts "without the allegation of the commission of any crime, and solely on account of [their] color." Such action was denounced as "a gross violation of the federal constitution, as well as the principles of rational liberty," and the governor was directed to take appropriate action, at public expense, to bring about the release of any citizen so imprisoned. Copies of the resolutions were officially transmitted to the governors of the several states.[18] The formal response of the Georgia legislature illustrates how far the southern position on "privileges and immunities" antedates its most famous expression in *Dred Scott:*

> Your Committee would have passed by these Resolutions, unnoticed, as the sickly effusions of a wild and reckless fanaticism, had they not pronounced [the Negro Seamen Act] a gross violation of the Federal Constitution.   .
>
> . . . No State has a legal or moral right to interfere with the domestic policy or internal regulations of a sister State. Georgia has never rebuked Massachusetts for fraternizing with negroes, nor held her up to the reprobation of the States of this Union, for her violations of the Charter of Confederacy, by proclaiming those citizens, who were not so at the time of the adoption of the Federal Constitution; thereby attempting to add to that sacred instrument, and thus violating the letter and spirit of the compact.
>
> If your Committee had no other lights to guide them, than those furnished by the Constitution, they would be at a loss to ascertain what clause is referred to by the Legislature of Massachusetts, as being violated by the law above alluded to; but we are constrained to suppose that this bold assertion is based upon that section which grants to the citizens of each State, all the privileges of citizens in the several States. . . . [T]he term citizen, as used in [the Constitution], can only refer to those who were embraced in its definition at the time of its adoption. . . .
>
> *Be it, therefore, Resolved,* That negroes, or persons of color, are not citizens, under the Constitution of the United States; and that Georgia will never recognize such citizenship.[19]

Massachusetts replied with further resolutions, in 1843 and 1844, authorizing the governor to appoint official agents in Charleston and New Orleans to bring lawsuits on behalf of Massachusetts citizens "imprisoned without the allegation of any crime," so that the legality of such imprisonment might be "tried and determined upon in the supreme court of the United States."[20] Action was delayed for a year and a half when it proved impossible, despite repeated attempts, to find any southern lawyer willing to act in that capacity. A distinguished Massachusetts lawyer, Samuel Hoar of Concord, was finally commissioned by the Commonwealth to serve as its consul in Charleston.[21] Hoar, then sixty-six years old, arrived at his post in late November 1844, accompanied by his daughter.

Evidently a man of considerable sang-froid, Hoar wrote at once to the governor of South Carolina to announce his mission; the next morning he attempted to call on the mayor of Charleston, seeking access to municipal records for the express purpose of preparing his lawsuits. The request precipitated further resolutions of the South Carolina legislature, in which the comity clause reappears as the central issue:

> *Resolved,* That the right to exclude from their territories, seditious persons, or others whose presence may be dangerous to their peace, is essential to every independent State.
>
> *Resolved,* That free negroes and persons of color are not citizens of the United States within the meaning of the Constitution, which confers upon the citizens of one State the privileges and immunities of citizens in the several States.
>
> *Resolved,* That the emissary sent by the State of Massachusetts to the State of South Carolina, with the avowed purpose of interfering with her institutions, and disturbing her peace, is to be regarded in the character he has assumed, and to be treated accordingly.
>
> *Resolved,* That his Excellency the Governor be requested to expel from our territory the said agent, after due notice to depart; and that the Legislature will sustain the Executive authority in any measures it may adopt for the purpose aforesaid.[22]

Hoar and his daughter left the city the next day, escorted to the Wilmington packet under the threat of mob violence. The commonwealth's envoy to New Orleans, Henry Hubbard, arrived there on January 1, 1845; met a reception similar to Hoar's; and left within the week.[23]

The requirements of the comity clause, and nothing else about the Constitution, lent urgency to a controversy that would otherwise have remained largely academic. The technical question was whether, in its various references to "citizens," the Constitution implied an unwritten and restrictive definition of national citizenship. The alternative interpretation—that a "citizen" for purposes of the Constitution was a citizen of one of the several states as defined by that state's laws—was particularly hard to resist in the context of article IV, which provided that "[t]he Citizens of each State" should be entitled to all privileges and immunities of "Citizens in the several States." The absence of a racial qualification to the comity clause meant that any free Negro claiming foreign-state citizenship had a substantial constitutional defense to prosecution for violation of state laws restricting his immigration or sojourn.²⁴ The assertion of this very plausible constitutional claim provoked, in response, the strained argument for a national citizenship to which blacks could never be admitted, because the plain language of the comity clause left no other means of escape.

The argument over the comity clause was not confined to the South. Before *Dred Scott*, the most elaborate attack on the possibility of Negro citizenship was advanced on behalf of the state of Connecticut, in defense of an 1834 statute that made it a crime to conduct a school at which nonresident Negro pupils received instruction. Counsel for the Quaker abolitionist Prudence Crandall, whose school in Canterbury, Connecticut, was the object of the law, argued that Connecticut had unconstitutionally denied to Miss Crandall's pupils, citizens of New York, the privileges and immunities of citizens of Connecticut. The trial court rejected this defense, holding that neither slaves, Indians, nor free Negroes were "citizens" within the meaning of the Constitution. The Connecticut Supreme Court of Errors reversed the conviction on technical grounds without reaching the constitutional question.²⁵

But in the deepening sectional crisis it was the South, not the North or West, that saw a race-neutral comity clause as a threat to essential liberties. Southern fear that free Negroes would incite the slaves to insurrection; southern fury at northern sermons on the states' constitutional obligations, delivered by the same people who advocated resistance to the fugitive slave clause; the South's increasingly aggressive defense of the peculiar institution as a positive good, a theory whose premises were violated by affording a citizen's privileges and immunities to even one black citizen of another state; all combined to make an issue of little practical significance one of burning sensitivity.

The intensity of southern feeling accounts in large part for the judicial phenomenon of *Dred Scott v. Sandford.*²⁶ The most notorious part of Chief Justice Taney's opinion for the Court—his demonstration that descendants of slaves were ineligible for citizenship within the terms of the Constitution—can only be understood as an attempt to correct the omission of the Continental Congress in neglecting to add the word "white" to the comity clause of the fourth article of confederation. The opinion itself makes this clear to anyone familiar with the dispute: Taney's twisted argument on the question of diversity jurisdiction reveals the true source of his agitation to be an obsession with privileges and immunities. Nothing else in the Constitution made Negro citizenship a threat.

There was no practical advantage to anyone in barring free Negroes from litigating in the federal courts: to deprive them of access to the diversity jurisdiction made them immune from it as well. There was no immediate likelihood that a black man would be elected president. Roswell Field, Dred Scott's counsel before the federal circuit court in St. Louis, persuaded himself that an affirmance of the "constitutional right of black men to sue in federal courts would probably make the Fugitive Slave Law 'of little value' to southern masters," arguing (as paraphrased by Fehrenbacher) that "an alleged fugitive might claim citizenship in the state where he was apprehended and secure a federal trial before a friendly jury. His right to do so, being derived straight from the Constitution, would presumably override the act of 1850 with its provisions for summary hearing and ex parte testimony."[27] It is not altogether clear, however, why recognition that the article III diversity jurisdiction extended to Negro *citizens* would materially have improved the situation of the fugitive *slave*, whose continued status as slave (not citizen) was guaranteed by the fugitive slave clause of article IV. The usual problem of a person accused (rightly or wrongly) of being a fugitive slave was not how to get into federal court but how to avoid it.

Taney's eagerness to address the question may be judged by how far out of his way he went to meet it. Federal jurisdiction to hear the suit by which Dred Scott, claiming to be a citizen of Missouri, sought to win his freedom from John Sanford,[28] a citizen of New York, was premised on diversity of citizenship: article III of the Constitution provides that the federal "judicial Power" shall extend to controversies "between Citizens of different States." Sanford's initial response to the proceedings in the federal circuit court had been to deny the existence of diversity jurisdiction, asserting that Dred Scott (as the descendant of a slave) could not be a "citizen" within the meaning of article III. The lower court denied the motion to dismiss: it held that Negro citizens of a state, whatever their status for other federal purposes, were at least to be counted among the "Citizens of different States" to whose lawsuits the federal judicial power was extended by article III of the Constitution. Having taken jurisdiction of the case, the court proceeded to find that Scott was Sanford's slave. The question was to be determined by Missouri law, and the Missouri courts had already made that decision in prior state-court proceedings.

In his determination to settle forever the question of Negro citizenship, Taney actually undercut the authority of the Court's more important holding on the great issue of the day. This was its discovery, employing an early form of "substantive due process," of a constitutional right to legal protection for slave property in the territories; with the consequence that the Missouri Compromise of 1820 had been unconstitutional. By insisting that the Court had no jurisdiction to hear the case, Taney invited his adversaries to claim that the controversial holding on slavery in the territories was sheer *obiter dictum*. His reasons for adhering to what might have seemed a self-defeating strategy become clear in the course of a strangely inverted argument, in which the need to exclude black litigants from the federal diversity jurisdiction was chiefly demonstrated by the horrors that would flow from their admission to the benefits of the comity clause.

The issue Taney was determined to address—whether free Negroes could be state "citizens" for purposes of article III—was not squarely presented by the facts in *Dred Scott;* and it was unnecessary to the decision for the same reason. Scott had already been adjudged a slave: the Missouri courts had so determined, and the Supreme Court was in the process of affirming Missouri's right to make that determination. A decision in *Dred Scott* that avoided unnecessary issues would thus have sidestepped the question of free Negro citizenship by observing that, in the view the Court took of the other issues in the case (primarily, the fact that Scott's status was properly determined by the law of Missouri), the question whether black citizens were included within article III could have no bearing on the outcome. A decision along just these lines, written by Justice Samuel Nelson, had originally been prepared as the opinion of the Court; and it was published unchanged as Nelson's concurring opinion.

Having thus reached out to discuss the availability of the diversity jurisdiction to those "Citizens of different States" who happened to be black, Taney framed the question with unnecessary breadth. Had he been genuinely concerned with the constitutional capacity of free Negroes to sue and be sued in the federal courts, we would expect Taney to have addressed head-on the precise holding of the decision under review: that whether or not Negro citizens of the several states were citizens of the United States in other respects, they were at any rate to be accounted "Citizens of . . . States" for purposes of article III. Taney undertook to demonstrate instead that the descendant of a slave could not be a "citizen" within the meaning of *any* provision of the Constitution. Ostensibly, Taney addressed the overall question of citizenship as a means of answering the specific question of article III diversity jurisdiction. In reality, he took an expansive view of a jurisdictional question he need not have addressed, as a means of settling old scores on the issue of privileges and immunities.

The federal diversity jurisdiction, in Taney's statement of the issue, was scarcely an afterthought to the real question he would answer in the negative:

> Can a negro, whose ancestors were imported into this country, and sold as slaves, become a member of the political community formed and brought into existence by the Constitution of the United States, and as such become entitled to all the rights, and privileges, and immunities, guarantied by that instrument to the citizen? One of which rights is the privilege of suing in a court of the United States in the cases specified in the Constitution.

The opinion was constructed accordingly, so that the jurisdictional issue might be resolved only in consequence of the disposition of a burning issue not before the Court:

> Does the Constitution of the United States act upon [the Negro] whenever he shall be made free under the laws of a State, and raised there to the rank of a citizen, and immediately clothe him with all the privileges of a citizen in every other State, and in its own courts?
>
> The court think the affirmative of these propositions cannot be maintained. And if it cannot, the plaintiff in error could not be a citizen of the State of Missouri, within the meaning of the Constitution of the United States, and, consequently, was not entitled to sue in its courts.[29]

Taney virtually acknowledged his objective when he attempted to resolve the question of Negro citizenship under article III by demonstrating its unthinkable consequences under article IV:

> [I]t cannot be believed that the large slaveholding States regarded them as included in the word citizens, or would have consented to a Constitution which might compel them to receive them in that character from another State. For if they were so received, and entitled to the privileges and immunities of citizens, it would exempt them from the operation of the special laws and from the police regulations which they considered to be necessary for their own safety. It would give to persons of the negro race, who were recognised as citizens in any one State of the Union, the right to enter every other State whenever they pleased, singly or in companies, without pass or passport, and without obstruction, to sojourn there as long as they pleased, to go where they pleased at every

hour of the day or night without molestation, unless they committed some violation of law for which a white man would be punished. . . .[30]

Taney's opinion on Negro citizenship is known today almost solely for its inaccurate remark that the black man, at the time of the framing of the Constitution, "had no rights which the white man was bound to respect."[31] In consequence, his baffling determination to read black Americans out of the Constitution tends to be seen as the product of an insane negrophobia. Taney's immediate political concern in the citizenship section of the opinion has become so remote to us as to be nearly invisible, but to his contemporaries it was perfectly obvious. Abraham Lincoln's "House Divided" speech, delivered at Springfield in 1858, included a summary of the *Dred Scott* decision that was entirely matter-of-fact:

> The *working* points of that machinery are:
>
> First, that no negro slave, imported as such from Africa, and no descendant of such slave can ever be a *citizen* of any State, in the sense of that term as used in the Constitution of the United States.
>
> This point is made in order to deprive the negro, in every possible event, of the benefit of this provision of the United States Constitution, which declares that—
>
> "The citizens of each State shall be entitled to all privileges and immunities of citizens in the several States."[32]

Taney was not coming to this question for the first time in *Dred Scott.* The Negro Seamen Acts, and the consequent imprisonment of West Indian sailors serving aboard British ships, had been for many years a source of friction in diplomatic relations between the United States and Britain.[33] As Andrew Jackson's attorney general in 1832, Taney had been asked for an opinion on the question, already much debated, whether enforcement of the acts violated the applicable treaty between the two nations. In a letter of some four thousand words, supplemented by another more than half that length, Taney dismissed Britain's objections on the basis of the treaty and proceeded to consider the objections that might one day be made on the basis of the privileges and immunities clause:

> The African race in the United States even when free, are every where a degraded class, and exercise no political influence. The privileges they are allowed to enjoy, are accorded to them as a matter of kindness and benevolence rather than of right. . . . They were never regarded as a constituent portion of the sovereignty of any state. But as a separate and degraded people to whom the sovereignty of each state might accord or

withhold such privileges as they deemed proper. They were not looked upon as citizens by the contracting parties who formed the Constitution. They were evidently not supposed to be included by the term *citizens.* And were not intended to be embraced in any of the provisions of that Constitution but those which point to them in terms not to be mistaken.[34]

These observations were as unnecessary to decide the question at hand—whether the actions of South Carolina violated the treaty obligations of the United States—as they were to the decision in *Dred Scott v. Sandford.*

A color-blind interpretation of the privileges and immunities clause was not even remotely at issue in *Dred Scott;* nor had it any bearing on the all-consuming constitutional issue of the 1850s, which was the question of slavery in the territories. Yet something in the idea was so threatening that Taney would seize the opportunity presented by the case to attempt to deny national citizenship to Negroes altogether. In 1778 the South had agreed, at least in theory, to accord a citizen's privileges and immunities to the rare black citizen of another state who might claim them. By 1857, the suggestion that the framers might have been willing to draw the line between slave and citizen, but not between black and white, had become so alarming to the South that the Supreme Court would attempt to rectify the omission.

The framers had compromised with slavery but not with racial discrimination: until the ratification of the Fifteenth Amendment, the language of the Constitution did not even acknowledge the existence of racial distinctions. The Constitution of 1787 not only accommodated the institution of slavery without naming it, but managed to describe a slavery having no necessary racial component, as if America were ancient Rome. Yet a color-blind Constitution imposed only marginal limitations on the freedom of the states, north and south, to treat their citizens differently on the basis of race, simply because the federal compact did not restrict the authority of the states in those areas of the law where racial discrimination is imposed or tolerated. The unusual provisions of article IV, section 2—requiring states to surrender fugitive slaves and to grant privileges and immunities—constituted the most notable intrusion of the original federal authority into what the Georgia legislature called a state's "domestic policy or internal regulations." That intrusion proved insupportable to both sections of the country.

The Constitution was color-blind from the outset; but so long as federal power was confined to the original federal concerns, the question of the

Constitution's tolerance for racial discrimination held but limited interest for anyone. When the federal compact was altered, and the reach of federal power into the states' domestic policy or internal regulations could no longer be questioned, the putative color blindness of the Constitution became incomparably more significant and correspondingly more difficult to uphold. It was relatively easy, after all, to maintain that the Constitution "knew nothing of white or black men" so long as the federal authority knew nothing—or almost nothing—of the sphere of government in which racial distinctions were typically drawn. The question, ironically enough, was whether the Constitution's pristine color blindness could survive the Reconstruction Amendments.

2 | The Lynn Petition

On New Year's Day, 1839, an "antislavery fair" was held at the town hall in Lynn, Massachusetts, under the auspices of the Lynn Women's Anti-Slavery Society.[1] Beneath a banner reading "Freedom and Truth! By These We Conquer," visitors found "an animated scene," enlivened by "varied exhibitions of ingenuity, taste, industry and energy"—handicrafts donated for sale by friends of the antislavery cause—and by "the interchange of earnest sympathies in view of past exertions and of heroic and holy determination for future ones. . . . From the aged fathers and mothers of the place, who honored the occasion with their presence and aid, to the active and beautiful youth and even to the glad children who lisped the inspiring mottoes hanging from the pine-boughs which overarched them, all were full of happiness and hope; for all were striving to give hope and happiness to the wretched and despairing."[2]

The fair succeeded in raising $575, of which $500 was speedily appropriated to support the *Liberator*, William Lloyd Garrison's antislavery weekly, just then under attack from rival factions within the abolitionist movement.[3] It was also the occasion, in all probability, on which Caroline Augusta Chase and her co-workers obtained the better part of the 785 signatures appearing on a petition that would shortly be presented to the Massachusetts legislature:

> To the Legislature of the State of Massachusetts, the undersigned ladies of Lynn, in the County of Essex, respectfully pray you immediately to repeal all laws in this State, which make any distinction among its inhabitants, on account of COLOR.[4]

The best known of the Massachusetts laws that in 1839 made any distinction between the races were the statutes prohibiting and invalidating marriages between a white person and "a negro, indian or mulatto."[5] In consequence, by the time the Lynn Petition (with similar petitions from women of Dorchester, Plymouth, and other towns) was formally disapproved by the Judiciary Committee of the Massachusetts House of Representatives,[6] the ladies of Lynn had become the object of public ridicule. Samuel Curtis and 192 other male citizens of Lynn petitioned the legislature, "as soon as convenient, [to] pass an act, granting a free and full privilege to the said Caroline Augusta Chase, and the seven hundred and eighty five other females of this town (excluding all those who are not of lawful age,) to marry, intermarry, or associate with any Negro, Indian, Hottentot, or any other being in human shape, at their will and pleasure."[7] The editor of the Boston *Morning Post*, like many of his colleagues, found the petition a ready subject for wit:

☞ Caroline Augusta Chase, and 735 [*sic*] other *ladies* in Lynn, have petitioned the Legislature for the privilege of marrying black husbands. This is rather a cut at the white Lynn beaux—or, perhaps some of these ladies despair of having a *white* offer, and so are willing to try *de colored race.*[8]

These and similar insults, no less than the occasional editorials supporting the petitioners, were duly reprinted in the *Liberator* (under caustic headings) by the irrepressible Garrison.[9]

Given that the laws of Massachusetts making a racial distinction were, in fact, essentially limited to the marriage prohibition,[10] a question naturally arose why the women's antislavery societies had framed their petitions in such comprehensive terms. The answer came to light when the Massachusetts House of Representatives, hearing allegations that some of the signatures on the petition "from S. P. Sanford and 210 other ladies of Dorchester" had been fraudulently obtained, appointed a special committee to look into the petition's origins. To the embarrassment of antislavery sympathizers, the committee's formal investigation revealed a variety of irregularities. Some of the signatures on the petition of the Dorchester Female Anti-Slavery Society had been placed there by the organizers without the consent of the persons named; some names appeared twice; some were names of young children. Examined under oath by a zealous committee, some of the Dorchester signers testified that they had joined a petition to repeal all laws making a distinction "on account of color" under the misapprehension—fostered by the fact that the petition was being circulated at all—that Negroes in Massachusetts suffered under a variety of discriminatory and oppressive laws. If, as they were now advised, the terms of such a petition in effect addressed only the marriage prohibition, its implications might appear indelicate; and some ladies begged leave to withdraw their names.[11]

The petitions on "distinctions of color" were invariably described in the Boston newspapers (including the *Liberator*) as if they were the spontaneous compositions of the female antislavery societies. They were in fact the uniform if somewhat accidental product of the nation's first experience with a phenomenon more familiar today: centrally directed, grass-roots, "single-issue" political mobilization. Each of the controversial petitions had been created by completing or transcribing a printed form recommended to the use of antislavery auxiliaries by the American Anti-Slavery Society.[12] Ironically, the Society's form of petition to state legislatures concerning "distinctions of color" produced the most interesting results in a state—Massachusetts—where its submission was essentially anomalous.

The standard historical account of the great "Petition Flood" of 1837–1840, with its dramatic focus on Congress, John Quincy Adams, and the "Pinckney gag," leaves the mistaken impression that the petition campaign orchestrated by the American Anti-Slavery Society was exclusively concerned with submitting memorials to Congress on the national antislavery issues of the day: the annexation of Texas, or the abolition of slavery in the District of Columbia. In fact, the Society's instructions for the gathering of petitions also proposed a number of petitions for circulation and submission to the legislatures of the free states: the most significant of these being the one brought to public notice by the ladies of Lynn.[13] While the federal petitions were naturally suited to nationwide use, it was more difficult to devise a standard petition directed at state laws that would prove equally effective when presented to the various state legislatures. A petition calling on states to repeal all laws making a distinction on the basis of color was clearly appropriate for, and had clearly been inspired by, the circumstances of those free states that subjected their black residents to express legal disabilities. The prime example was Ohio, whose laws in the 1830s denied Negroes the vote, hindered their immigration, prohibited them from testifying in court, and excluded their children altogether from the public schools.[14] Ohio's "black laws" were an early target of petitions circulated by the state's local antislavery societies;[15] while for the national organization they provided the standard example of iniquitous discrimination in the laws even of the free states.[16] When the American Anti-Slavery Society began to distribute blank petitions for the repeal of state laws making "distinctions of color," there can be no doubt that laws like Ohio's were what the authors of the brief text chiefly had in mind.

Presented to the legislature of a state like Ohio, where the existence of so many notoriously discriminatory laws made it natural to request their wholesale repeal, a petition for the repeal of "all laws in this State, which make any distinction among its inhabitants, on account of color" implied no more than the injustice of laws subjecting persons of one race to explicitly unequal treatment. In Massachusetts, by contrast, the only law obviously reached by the same description was a statute (the marriage law) that drew a racial distinction without imposing any outward inequality. An Ohio-style petition, presented to the Massachusetts legislature, was thus either a mistake or else the expression of a more radical proposition altogether: namely, that a law drawing any sort of a racial distinction (and regardless of equal treatment) was inherently improper. Unlike their more moderate sympathizers, the Garrisonians seized the opportunity to argue that a call to abolish distinctions of color from the laws of Massachusetts was not an inadvertence but a principled position. The ladies of Lynn had not been the first to petition for color-blind laws, but they were the first to justify such a demand.[17]

Thus while some ladies of Dorchester were testifying before the House investigating committee that they would never have submitted such a petition had they understood its implications, the Lynn Women's Anti-Slavery Society chose to reaffirm the principle of radical nondiscrimination that their petition, in context, had effectively enunciated. A resolution adopted by the Society's Board of Managers on March 30, 1839, underscored the conscious decision being made:

Resolved, That time and reflection have confirmed us in the belief, that all laws making a distinction on account of color, are unnecessary and unchristian, having a tendency to degrade a class of people entitled to the common and equal rights of citizens, who have been long and cruelly oppressed; and that petitions for the abolition of all such laws ought to be signed by all the women as well as men of this Commonwealth, who are actuated by principles of justice and humanity; and of course, we have never regretted that such petitions from this and other towns have been presented to our Legislature.

If the laws of Massachusetts made but few such distinctions, that was no reason for abolitionists to rest from their labors. On June 19, at the annual meeting of the Lynn society, it was accordingly "Resolved, That it is the duty of every Anti-Slavery Society to circulate petitions for the repeal of all laws making a distinction on account of color—therefore, having put our hands to the plough we press onward to the work with renewed faith that the seed strewn will yield a plenteous harvest."[18]

The seed strewn at Lynn was not ordinary abolitionist doctrine. Outside Garrison's Boston, most abolitionists concerned themselves with the civil status of free Negroes only as an afterthought; when they did so, the usual emphasis was on measures to elevate and improve the "free colored population," rather than the repeal of discriminatory northern laws.[19]

From the moral conviction that slavery must be eradicated it did not necessarily follow that the laws of free states must be devoid of racial distinctions. As the moderate abolitionists were at pains to emphasize, "immediate emancipation" did not even mean immediate civil equality. Thus James A. Thome, one of the Lane Seminary rebels and (to judge by his correspondence) the most energetic of the disciples sent forth from Oberlin in 1835 by Theodore Weld, described in a well-known letter his success in taming a lyceum audience in Akron, "rampant for discussion":

> First I was particularly careful to *disclaim* certain things which are confounded with abolitionism; such as social intercourse, amalgamation, etc. I further stated that we did not claim for the slave the right of voting, immediately, or eligibility to office. Also that we did not wish them *turned loose,* having the possession of unlicenced liberty; nor even to be governed by the same *code* of Laws which are *adapted* to intelligent citizens. That on the contrary we believed that it would be necessary to form a *special code* of Laws restricting them in their freedom, upon the same general principles that apply to foreigners, minors, etc.[20]

This, to be sure, was the moderate "New York doctrine" of "immediate emancipation, gradually accomplished."[21] But even Garrison himself, before his later refusal to concern himself with the practical steps by which emancipation would be accomplished, had expressed a view not substantially different:

> Immediate abolition does not mean that the slaves shall immediately exercise the right of suffrage, or be eligible to any office, or be emancipated from law, or be free from the benevolent restraints of guardianship. We contend for the immediate personal freedom of the slaves, . . . for their employment and reward as free laborers, . . . for their instruction and subsequent admission to all the trusts, offices, honors and emoluments of intelligent freemen.[22]

Strictly speaking, a theory of benevolent guardianship for the freedman implied no legal distinction between black and white, merely between the newly emancipated and the hereditary citizen. But the necessity of such disclaimers, evidenced by the defensive tone apparent in the words of both Thome and Garrison, must have discouraged most abolitionists from indulging controversial theories of civic equality so long as the main task before them remained to be accomplished.

There were a hundred arguments to be made against slavery before anyone would necessarily reach the idea—occupying, then as now, a relatively remote level of abstraction—that the law ought not to distinguish between persons on the basis of color. The argument from *equality* was, by contrast, ubiquitous: but as a century's experience of "separate but equal" would amply demonstrate, the principle of equality did not necessarily include as a correlative the principle of nondiscrimination. "Equality" was the foundation of American institutions; "equality," without more, proved the incompatibility of slavery with our republican precepts; by a natural extension, claims to equality of treatment, to "protection and equal laws," readily demonstrated the evil of laws that treated free Negroes less favorably than whites.[23] All this and more could be asserted without reaching the paradoxical proposition that the law, though treating all equally, might not properly take account of something so obvious as racial differences.

An exhaustive catalogue of antislavery arguments might nevertheless yield the antidiscrimination idea. Such a catalogue was published in 1838 by Charles Olcott, an Ohio lawyer and one of Theodore Weld's early converts: his *Two Lectures on the Subjects of Slavery and Abolition* constituted a compendium of abolitionist doctrine, "compiled for the special use of Anti-Slavery Lecturers and Debaters and intended for Public Reading."[24] Developing one of the commonest of themes—the injustice of laws protecting one class of persons but not another—Olcott suddenly took the argument a step further:

> If the least attempt is made to enslave a white person of any description, he or she can apply to the Law for redress, and have full and ample relief by due course of Law. . . . What abolitionists demand as naked justice is, that the benefit and protection of these just laws, be extended to all human beings alike, to the coloured as well as the white, the bond as well as the free man; and that all mankind be allowed the same legal rights and protection, without regard to colour or other physical peculiarities, as God originally gave them. . . . God has made but one law or rule of conduct for man; the latter has no right therefore, to make different laws for different men. God's law is without respect to colour or other physical peculiarities; man's laws ought not therefore to respect them.

A commonplace—that the law should be equal for all—here led to the novel idea that the law should abjure racial distinctions. The proposition could be stated in a way that blurred the distinction between the two ideas, as when Olcott asserted that the object of abolition was "to abrogate all unjust, unequal laws and customs whatever, and restore the supremacy of all just and equal laws within the jurisdiction, over all persons alike, without regard to colour or other physical peculiarities." But Olcott, the lawyer, had unmistakably discovered a congenial theme in the idea of color-blind laws as the key to abolition:

> The reason why so many people cannot see *how* slavery can be abolished, is for the want of reflecting how other crimes are abolished or abandoned. . . .
>
> In connexion with the law abolishing slavery, a short declaratory act should be passed, declaring the Common Law and all just and equal statute laws, to be in force over all persons within the jurisdiction, without any distinction. . . .
>
> Many have imagined, that the two races *cannot* live intermixed (not amalgamated) in society, on terms of legal equality. . . . Whether the two races, living together in the same society or country, *can* enjoy equal rights, primarily depends, as already remarked, on the equal operation of *equal Law.* Let the *Laws* be equal, and their *Rights* will be equal; and to render the laws equal, let them be made and administered, by all the citizens equally, without regard to color or other physical peculiarities.[25]

The concluding sentence announced one of the crucial themes of the color-blind argument: that the only sure guarantee of "equal laws" (the source, in turn, of "equal rights") is to prohibit racial classifications altogether. The Lynn Women's Anti-Slavery Society advanced the same contention when—as others were disavowing it—they chose to justify their submission of a "no distinctions" petition to the Massachusetts legislature.

Among the Garrisonians—a minority within the antislavery movement that could indulge the relative luxury of concern for such secondary issues as racial segregation—the antidiscrimination argument now evolved rapidly. The extent of that evolution, over a period of only ten years following the Lynn Petition, is readily visible in Charles Sumner's argument against the constitutionality of segregated public schools, delivered in 1849 on behalf of the plaintiff in *Roberts v. City of Boston.*[26] Although *Roberts* marked the first time the legality of racial segregation had ever been litigated, Sumner's argument was already so comprehensive that the argu-

ments of the next hundred years would not add significantly to the themes
he developed. And yet Sumner, for all his powers of eloquence, was not
known to his contemporaries as an original thinker. His mind, he himself
admitted, was "a cistern, not a fountain"; his strength as an orator, according to Horace Mann, "not originality . . . but skill in using."[27] The mature
argument of *Roberts* was the unique legacy of Garrisonian abolitionism,
which in embracing a series of civil rights causes over the preceding
decade had developed, by increments, the arguments against the legal
recognition of racial distinctions.[28]

The earliest of these campaigns had as its object the laws forbidding
interracial marriage. Traces of abolitionist agitation against "the marriage
law" appear in the earliest numbers of the *Liberator*,[29] and the campaign
would continue until its ultimate success in 1843.[30] The effort was unceas-
ing—"Let us make the repeal of that law which repeals the law of God,"
wrote Garrison in 1841, "the test question morally and politically for the
current year"[31]—but the argument advanced was rarely that of the Lynn
Petition. The law was much more easily attacked as unnecessary, unchristian, and, above all, unjust to the innocent offspring (whom it illegitimized)
of the occasional interracial marriage.[32] Still, the fullest exposition of the
case against the statute eventually reached the antidiscrimination argument.
In a committee report submitted to the Massachusetts House of Representatives in 1841, the Reverend George Bradburn, abolitionist member for
Nantucket, criticized the law as ineffectual, immoral (encouraging "vicious
connexions between the races"), and unjust (chiefly in its effects on descent
and distribution), before finally arguing that the law was "unequal" and
"of doubtful constitutionality." Its inequality, according to Bradburn, consisted "in denying to one portion of citizens the right, which is accorded
to others, of choosing whom they will marry, and in founding that denial
on mere diversities of complexion, or of race, when neither justice nor the
Constitution of either the State or the nation recognizes any distinction
between citizens on account of those diversities." The legislature had
unquestioned power to regulate marriages, Bradburn concluded, but such
regulations were to be made in accordance with "the equitable spirit of the
Constitution, which knows no distinction of races."[33]

Similarly, in the subsequent debate over segregated railway travel in
Massachusetts, the central theme of the abolitionist forces—the inequality
of treatment resulting from segregation in practice—was occasionally supplemented with a more radical argument that the legal recognition of racial
distinctions was incompatible with the organic law of the commonwealth.

Testifying in 1842 before a joint special committee of the Massachusetts legislature, to which various petitions protesting against the "Jim Crow car" had been referred, Wendell Phillips first asserted that railroad corporations which owed their existence to the laws of a state could not in their bylaws contravene its constitution. The railroads, accordingly, could not enforce regulations making a racial distinction:

> There are distinctions which the Commonwealth itself has no right to make—which it, therefore, entrusts to none of its inferior tribunals: and will you permit these rail-road corporations to assume a power greater than you may yourselves claim to exercise, and which the citizens would not for a moment have suffered from, had it not been for the creative and sustaining action of the Commonwealth's act of incorporation, the nature and scope of which these directors mistake and pervert?[34]

The subsequent report of the committee paraphrased Phillips's constitutional argument, asking "why should [Massachusetts] allow corporations a power she will not trust in her own courts? How shall the State be justified in allowing others to make differences in regard to her citizens, which she does not presume to make herself?"[35] The following session a Senate committee reported a bill prohibiting any railroad "by-law or regulation, which shall make any distinction, or give a preference to any one or more persons over others, on account of descent, sect, or color."[36] Massachusetts railroads thereupon desisted from the practice of segregation, and the proposed legislation was dropped.[37]

But it was the ensuing controversy over school segregation that most distinctly elicited the developing argument against racial classifications. Several Massachusetts cities having a significant black population maintained segregated public schools at the beginning of the 1840s. In the political climate that saw the repeal of the marriage law and the demise of the Jim Crow car, "caste" schools for black children naturally came under attack. The concerted movement for school desegregation enjoyed its first success in Nantucket in 1843, encouraging similar efforts in Salem and Boston.[38] The debate over separate schools in the latter cities would have a lasting influence on antidiscrimination doctrine.

In the fall of 1843, the School Committee of Salem undertook a special inquiry into the condition of the city's separate "Colored School." The committee, one of its members later reported, found that "the indifference of those who did attend was so marked, and farther, the hostility of those who did not attend, was so determined, and had such a semblance of right about it, that it could not be thought expedient, by those who had the matter in charge, to advise the continuance of it." In January 1844 the committee received a petition from forty-three colored citizens of Salem, setting forth in measured terms the reasons why the establishment of separate schools for colored children appeared to them inexpedient; and at a meeting in February, the committee voted to discontinue the separate school.[39]

Upon the initial establishment of the "Colored School," some ten years earlier, the School Committee had obtained formal assurances as to the legality of segregation from Salem's town solicitor, Leverett Saltonstall. Saltonstall had twice given his careful opinion that although Negro citizens were legally entitled to a strict equality of educational advantages, the mode in which their education was provided—specifically including, if deemed appropriate, the mandatory enrollment of colored children in separate schools—was a matter legally within the committee's discretion.[40] To bolster its position in the controversy surrounding the decision to discontinue the separate school, the committee now obtained contrary legal advice. Presumably at the initiative of its most distinguished member, Stephen Clarendon Phillips,[41] the committee secured an opinion asserting the unconstitutionality of separate schools from Richard Fletcher, an eminent Boston lawyer (and future justice of the Supreme Judicial Court) who had served with Phillips in Congress.[42] Fletcher's opinion, presented by Phillips on March 21, 1844, was adopted by the committee as the "explanation and vindication" of its earlier action and ordered placed on the record.[43]

Fletcher's Salem opinion begins at the usual starting point, asserting that "perfect equality is the vital principle of the [public school] system." Its initial thrust is by analogy: Fletcher argues that to single out "any particular class of white children," such as "the children of mechanics and laborers," and to "confine them to a separate school, distinct from the other classes," would be to deny them "a perfect equality with others, in the enjoyment of the free schools." This much of the argument is open to the inevitable rejoinder that a separate school might nevertheless be "equal," and the most interesting part of Fletcher's opinion is the passage in which this objection is anticipated:

But the question proposed to me, is, may the school committee of Salem, exclude the colored children from the free schools, and restrict them to a distinct school provided for them exclusively? After the view I have submitted, I can answer the question very briefly, by saying that neither the constitution nor the laws of this Commonwealth make any distinction between a colored person and a white person. . . . The children of colored parents are, therefore, entitled to the benefit of the free schools, equally with others. It may be said that the free school, provided exclusively for colored children, is equally advantageous to them. I think it would be easy to show that this is not the case. But suppose it were so, it would in no way affect the decision of the question. The colored children are lawfully entitled to the benefits of the free schools, and are not bound to accept an equivalent. Except in the case of taking property, for public use, no man can be compelled to relinquish what belongs to him, for an equivalent. Every one must have his own, unless he consents to relinquish it.[44]

In describing segregation as the compulsory relinquishment of a legal entitlement in exchange for an "equivalent," Fletcher suggested an original and intriguing answer to the latent logical problem of "separate but equal," avoiding any dispute over the "equality"—however measured—of the separate facilities. Even the perfect "equality" of a substitute will not afford equal treatment where some persons and not others are compelled to submit to an exchange.

Fletcher's opinion was later circulated on its own, in the form of a broadside;[45] but its greatest influence derived from the use made of Fletcher's arguments in the far more visible controversy over school segregation in Boston. Boston's primary and grammar schools had been formally segregated since the early nineteenth century, when separate schools were established "at the request of colored citizens, whose children could not attend the public schools, on account of the prejudice then existing against them."[46] Where the 1830s saw complaints about the low quality of the school facilities provided black pupils, the new militancy of the 1840s brought repeated challenges to the system of segregated education itself.[47] In 1840, and repeatedly throughout the decade, petitions were submitted to the Boston's primary and grammar school committees by Garrisonian abolitionists and Boston's more militant black citizens, asking that the separate schools be closed and that Negro pupils be admitted to the ordinary district schools nearest their homes. The petitions submitted in 1846 and 1849, though rejected like those that preceded them, gave rise to published majority and minority committee reports that constitute an early landmark in the public debate over the legality and policy of segregated schools. The petitioners' inability to obtain any change in the segregation policy of the school committees led to the legal challenge of the

Roberts case in 1849; the failure of the lawsuit produced renewed efforts to secure relief from the state legislature. There the fight against Boston's segregated schools was finally victorious in 1855.[48]

In the minority report submitted in August 1846 to Boston's Primary School Committee,[49] privately printed after the full committee decided that only the majority report should receive official publication, there appeared for the first time, in recognizable outline, what would become the standard legal argument for the color-blind Constitution. Like most legal inventions, the boldest form of the antisegregation position was the product of practical necessity. While the opponents of segregation naturally urged every available consideration against the institution of separate schools, arguments falling short of color blindness did not meet the case. The claim that black children had an equal right to primary school education was conceded; it was answered that Boston's separate primary schools for colored pupils were equal in all respects to those provided for white children. Arguments from policy, urging that segregated schools were inexpedient for a variety of reasons, were naturally contradicted; and it was observed that the legislature had entrusted the administration of the primary schools to the very committee that had determined separate schools to be in the best interest of the pupils of both races.

In short, if the legal issue was to turn on a question of fact (the equality of the separate schools) or a question of judgment (the sound discretion of the primary school committee), the opponents of segregation would lose. The recourse to which they were thus compelled by the logic of advocacy was to argue that the committee had exercised its discretion in a manner that was constitutionally forbidden. So firmly did Charles Sumner make the resulting argument his own that subsequent antidiscrimination tradition, turning to retrace its origins, has not generally looked beyond the masterly argument for the plaintiff in *Roberts v. City of Boston.* Yet the extraordinary fecundity with which Sumner was able to develop the antidiscrimination theme on that occasion is explained by the fact that he had the 1846 minority report open beside him as he wrote.[50]

The thirty-six-page pamphlet began with a formal report to the Primary School Committee, signed by the two dissenting members of the subcommittee to which the 1846 school petition had been referred: Edmund Jackson and Henry I. Bowditch. To this was appended a series of letters, apparently solicited by Jackson, "from highly respected and efficient members of the School Committees of Nantucket, New Bedford, Lowell and Salem," testifying to the benefits of the racially integrated school systems in those cities. The pamphlet concluded with some highly critical "Remarks on the Opinion of the City Solicitor," signed by the thirty-four-year-old Wendell Phillips. Peleg Chandler, later Sumner's adversary in *Roberts,* had furnished a legal opinion to the effect that the Boston School Committee had the statutory authority to assign students on the basis of race. Phillips, who had no official connection with the controversy, was identified in the minority report as "a member of the legal profession."[51]

Of the range of arguments reflected in the minority report, drawn from policy as well as principle, the broadest and most ambitious were asserted first. The starting point was the contention that American institutions, properly conceived, imposed a legal system in which racial distinctions were unknown and unknowable:

> It is the peculiar advantage of our republican system, that it confers civil equality and legal rights upon every citizen—that it knows no privileged class, and no degraded class—that it confers no distinction, and creates no difference, between rich and poor, learned and ignorant, white and black; but places all upon the same level, and considers them alike entitled to its protection and its benefits.

Classification along such lines was accordingly impermissible. Furthermore—and the report here inaugurated a line of argument running straight through Sumner to Justice Harlan's dissent in *Plessy v. Ferguson*—if one such impermissible classification were admitted, all must be:

> The question which first arises is; have the School Committee any right or reason to establish such schools, and separate the children of the community into classes, to decide that the children of the colored people shall go by themselves exclusively, or that the children of Irish parentage shall be excluded from all others and go by themselves—or the children of the poor in like manner? Shall any or all of these be selected, each from all, sorted out and confined to separate schools?
>
> If there is authority to do this in one instance, or to any one portion of the community who, in the exercise of our discretion or caprice, may be designated as a class, differing from others in some respect or circumstance, it seems clear, there is in all the cases supposed.

Implicit in the *reductio ad absurdum* is a challenge to the competence of legislative or administrative discretion to assess the propriety of certain classifications that we would call "suspect." Revisiting this theme in the context of constitutional litigation, both Sumner and Harlan would extend the proscription—where racial distinctions are concerned—to exclude judicial discretion as well.

After quoting at length from Richard Fletcher's Salem opinion on the fallacy of "equivalents" as a substitute for equality—the passage quoted being substantially the extract given above—the minority of the subcommittee offered its own summation of the constitutional issue:

> The whole argument may be stated thus. The colored man, as any other citizen, has the right to send his child to the nearest school, subject only to restrictions for good and lawful reasons. But his race or color is an unlawful and inhuman reason for restraining his right of choice; for our constitution and laws have everywhere repudiated all distinctions of citizens into classes, on this, or any other ground, and have pronounced all possible reasoning in support or justification of such distinctions insufficient and dangerous.[52]

"All possible reasoning" that may be advanced in support or justification of racial distinctions is not necessarily fallacious: it is rejected out of hand as "insufficient and dangerous," because the perils of racial discrimination demand the protection of a prophylactic rule. The dissenting members of the Primary School Committee had produced a reasoned argument to support the claim of the Lynn Petition.

The same conclusion, that the Massachusetts lawmaker or administrator was constitutionally deprived of the power to draw a racial distinction, was reiterated in the second section of the pamphlet, Wendell Phillips's reply to the opinion of the city solicitor. Peleg Chandler had concluded that the provision of "special schools for colored children, such schools being, in all respects, as good as those for white children," was an exercise of the committee's "lawful discretionary power" when, in the judgment of the committee, *"the best interests of such children will be promoted thereby."*[53] Phillips, in his rejoinder, did not bother to take issue with the committee's determination as to the children's best interests. Instead—developing the theme of his earlier testimony against the Jim Crow car—he insisted that the law of Massachusetts prohibited any "legal body" from employing a racial classification:

> The real question is simply this: "Have the Committee, in order to secure what they think the best interests of the children, the right to introduce into our schools distinctions utterly repugnant to the spirit and letter of our constitution and laws?" For certainly it will not be denied that in all the pages of the Massachusetts statutes there is no recognition

of race or color;—that our laws repudiate both, only submitting, from a necessity rather apparent than real, to the United States rule as to the militia. . . .

. . . The races which are so distinct as to require different training in the schools, cannot surely form a homogeneous basis for civil institutions, or allow of the same penal arrangements. England accordingly has one code for India, and another for Kent. Our laws on the contrary, negative all such distinctions; they practically assert that before the law, and in regard to such institutions as the law establishes, the differences of race, creed, complexion, and caste, melt away. . . . As members of a legal body, a School Committee, they should have eyes only for such distinctions among their fellow citizens as the *law* recognizes and points out. For the difference of age and sex, for regulations of health, &c., they find precedents; in acting upon these they stand within the margin of that discretion which the law allows. But when they open their eyes to varied complexion, to difference of race, to diversity of creed, to distinctions of caste, they will seek in vain through all our laws and institutions for any recognition of the spirit in which they act. They are attempting to foist into the legal arrangements of the land, a principle utterly repugnant to our Constitution. What the Sovereignty of the Constitution dared not attempt, the discretion of a School Committee accomplishes![54]

The contributions of the 1846 minority report to the legal case against school segregation were not limited to the argument for color blindness. Readers familiar with the arguments commonly advanced against school segregation during the 1950s and 1960s will recognize much of the modern argument—psychological and sociological as well as legal—here as well:

[The argument is made] that it is better for all, but more especially is it for the good of the colored children, that they should be educated by themselves. . . . This *surprising fact* is accounted for, if we understand aright, by the peculiarities of the colored race. Inferiority is by no means to be inferred from this arrangement, no sense of degradation is excited by it, but it is precisely the one of all others best adapted to promote their self-respect, advance their mental and moral development, and elevate their civilization! . . .

With such influences operating upon these [colored] schools, and to which they minister and tend greatly to perpetuate, what can be expected from them? The inevitable effect of such influences upon the energies and labors of the teachers, committee and children, must necessarily follow, and the want of heart and faith in the work, will enfeeble and paralize the school and all connected with it. . . .

The only security we can have for a healthy and efficient system of public instruction rests in the deep interest and vigilant care with which the more intelligent, watch over the welfare of the schools. This only will secure competent teachers, indefatigable exertion, and a high standard of excellence—and where the colored children are mingled up with the mass of their more favored fellows, they will partake of the advantages of this watchful oversight. Shut out and separated, they are sure to be neglected and to experience all the evils of an isolated and despised class.[55]

When it is seen how much of the twentieth-century argument against school segregation was anticipated by the 1846 minority report to the Primary School Committee, the question of its authorship assumes considerable interest. The contributions of two lawyers, Richard Fletcher and Wendell Phillips, are expressly identified; but the text of the report itself is not clearly attributed. Edmund Jackson and Henry Ingersoll Bowditch, the two committee members in whose names the report was submitted, were both Primary School Committee members of long standing and pillars of the Massachusetts Anti-Slavery Society.[56] That either of them could have been responsible for this strikingly original argument appears at first so improbable that one is tempted to attribute it to an anonymous hand, possibly that of Phillips.

Bowditch, by far the better known of the two men,[57] owes his reputation as an abolitionist to his role in the Latimer Case of 1842.[58] The available biographical materials (which in Bowditch's case are relatively extensive) contain no reference whatever to the 1846 minority report, to Bowditch's role as a member of the Primary School Committee, nor indeed to any stage of the controversy over the "caste schools" in the city of Boston. Edmund Jackson, who as a historical figure is almost invisible, seems at first an even less likely candidate. Like his older brother, Francis,[59] Edmund Jackson was a successful businessman and a generous supporter of abolitionist causes; he was fifty years old in 1846, the proprietor of a tallow chandlery situated on Long Wharf in Boston. Whereas Francis was a member of the Garrisonian inner circle, Edmund's name appears but rarely in antislavery annals, usually in connection with his material benefactions.[60] And while on at least two prior occasions Edmund Jackson had written brief essays for publication, neither betrayed any particular talent;[61] and no published work associated with his name is discoverable after 1846.

Had this middle-aged soap manufacturer, lacking a college education, suddenly produced even a part of the incandescent minority report on the caste schools, one would expect him to have been encouraged thereafter to give full rein to his evident gifts as an advocate.

The evidence for Edmund Jackson's authorship of the minority report is nonetheless conclusive. Wendell Phillips wrote to his friend Edmund Quincy (who was editing the *Liberator* during one of Garrison's absences abroad) to "bespeak one of your most pungent articles" on the recently published majority report, a copy of which he enclosed: "Don't say I ought to do it—nothing less than your pen could do justice to the rich absurdity of that Report. . . . Besides Edmund Jackson & I have said our say in the pamphlet reply . . . which the mean dogs of a Majority wd not print at public expense."[62] Quincy replied to Phillips that "in next week's paper" he would put in "sufficient extracts from Jackson's Minority Report to show what that is," while "the week after I think I shall put in Chandler's opinion & your Review of it, at length."[63]

In his editorial comment accompanying the publication of the minority report in the *Liberator,* Quincy praised it as a document "which for style, spirit and reasoning, would do honor to any mind in any community. It is certainly a credit to the common schools of New England, that they have sent forth a man capable of writing it. We earnestly hope that he will more frequently favor the Anti-Slavery presses with the clear and nervous productions of his pen."[64] This reference to the author of the minority report brought an appreciative acknowledgment from Phillips: "I cannot thank you too often for the very appropriate manner in which you notice Edmund Jackson. Occasion ought to be taken to bring him forward—Yours on the caste schools was capital—You'll have to set up a paper on your own account when Garrison returns—It will never do to let you slip your neck out when it so becomes the editorial collar."[65]

The following week, describing the caste schools controversy for the *National Anti-Slavery Standard* as the New York paper's semianonymous "Boston Correspondent," Quincy praised Jackson in terms that acknowledged his lack of celebrity:

> This [minority] Report is written with singular clearness, vigour and ability, and does the highest honour to its author Mr. Edmund Jackson. Mr. Jackson is a brother to Francis Jackson, a name so well known and beloved by Abolitionists everywhere. His anti-slavery is of the most

thorough and uncompromising character, having been learned in a good school, during a residence of some years in Charleston, S.C. and improved by extensive travel in the slave States. Though he has had no advantages of education besides those afforded by the common schools and that "best of educations," as Gibbon calls it, which a man gives himself, there are few technically "educated men" who equal him, not only in completeness and arrangement of matter, but in terseness and elegance of style. I hope you will endeavour to induce him to become one of your regular contributors.[66]

Edmund Jackson was never brought forward; nor, despite Quincy's public encouragement, did he devote himself to the antislavery presses. Francis Jackson's death in 1861 was marked by generous tributes at a public ceremony; Edmund died in 1875 virtually unnoticed. Apart from Quincy's kind words in the *Liberator* and the *Standard,* the most visible acknowledgment he had received for his remarkable contribution came from an incongruous source. The 1852 edition of *The Rich Men of Massachusetts,* a racy little booklet purporting to identify the wealthiest citizens of the commonwealth and the size of their reputed fortunes, with brief appreciations of their characters, included this entry:

Jackson, Edmund   *$100,000*
   Soap and candle manufacturer. Inherited some of his property; a man highly esteemed by the Garrisonian Abolitionists, and one of their soundest writers. A very plain and benevolent man.[67]

The color-blind Constitution that Sumner and Harlan later brought to wider public notice was discovered in Boston through an oddly assorted collaboration. Edmund Jackson, a middle-aged merchant, produced a denunciation of segregated schools that provided much of Sumner's famous argument in *Roberts* while it anticipated contentions about educational policy that would be argued to judges a century thereafter. The ladies of Lynn had earlier made a vital point, both theoretical and practical, about the constitutional means of achieving a rigorous legal equality between the races. Their petition of 1839 showed precisely how that end might be accomplished by any legislature not afraid of the consequences. Events have since shown that there is, in fact, no other way to do it.

3 | Sumner and Shaw

In the mid-nineteenth century, at a time when the nation's major civil rights problem was still Negro slavery, black and white activists instituted a twentieth-century lawsuit demanding that the system of segregated public schools in the city of Boston be declared unconstitutional. Sarah C. Roberts, then four years old, had been refused admission in April 1847, "on the sole ground of color," to the primary school nearest her home; she was directed to apply instead to one of the two primary schools maintained exclusively for black children. After a similar rejection a year later, Sarah (through her father, Benjamin F. Roberts) brought suit against the city under a Massachusetts statute providing that anyone unlawfully excluded from public school instruction might recover damages from the municipality.[1] The legal arguments against separate schools, recently elaborated by Richard Fletcher, Edmund Jackson, and Wendell Phillips, were now to be tested in the courts. The ensuing debate over the lawfulness of segregation between Charles Sumner, attorney for the plaintiff, and Chief Justice Lemuel Shaw, author of the opinion for the Supreme Judicial Court, is more closely reasoned and more eloquently expressed than anything that lawyers and judges (Justice Harlan excepted) would again write on the subject; and it would prove to have defined, for a century and more thereafter, the constitutional arguments on either side of the question.

Two decades before the ratification of the Fourteenth Amendment, Sumner's great argument in *Roberts v. City of Boston* addressed the central problem still facing the advocate who seeks to locate a principle of non-discrimination in American constitutional law.[2] The constitution of Massachusetts, as Sumner argued with Shaw's acquiescence, guaranteed "equality before the law"; it said nothing about racial discrimination. Sumner's adversaries conceded his client's right to a perfect legal equality, but argued that equality was respected when identical benefits were provided separately to white and black citizens. The problem was to find a theory by which the constitutional materials at hand—a command of equality—might be made to yield a rule of nondiscrimination. The problem has been the same ever since.

The argument retains its pertinence because the equal protection clause of the Fourteenth Amendment would require nothing of the states that Sumner and Shaw did not already regard, in 1849, as part of the constitutional law of the commonwealth, and because Sumner elected not to contest the objective "equality" of the facilities provided at the school to which Sarah Roberts was relegated. While there is ample evidence that the separate "colored schools" were markedly inferior to Boston's primary and grammar schools for white pupils,[3] Sumner's argument avoided any reference to the fact. The omission was intentional and strategic. Sumner's concern was not with equal treatment but—in the spirit of the Lynn Petition—with racial discrimination per se: "Can any discrimination, on account of color or race, be made, under the Constitution and Laws of Massachusetts, among the children entitled to the benefit of our public schools?"[4] As counsel for the plaintiff in history's first school segregation case, Sumner took up the argument at a point that civil rights advocates would not reach again for more than a century, until they finally dared to concede the objective equality of segregated school facilities so as to test the bare fact of the racial distinction. As a result he went to the heart of the matter.

The first task facing Sumner, who did not have the Fourteenth Amendment to work with, was to discover constitutional ground on which to place the argument against segregation. Taking as his starting point the statement of the Massachusetts Declaration of Rights that "All men are born free and equal," Sumner devoted the first section of his argument to the history of equality as a political ideal, trying to show that the equality of birth recognized by American institutions implied a principle of "equality before the law," and indeed "a complete civil and political equality" without regard to race. This proposition, for which Sumner was unable to cite any judicial authority, was by no means self-evident. The Massachusetts Declaration, contemporary with the Declaration of Independence, employed the same vagueness of expression on the subject of equality. Whatever it meant to the citizens of Massachusetts in 1780 to be "born free and equal," it did not then mean an entitlement to equality of civil and political privileges. (To take an obvious example, the "men" who were born free and equal evidently included women, yet women were not entitled to vote in Massachusetts in 1780; nor were men who did not satisfy a property qualification.)

Sumner's explication of "equality" relied heavily on the French constitutions of 1791 and 1793. These documents offered the great advantage of referring, not merely to an abstract equality of birth, but to a more concrete equality of rights and (in Sumner's favorite phrase) to a principle of *equality before the law*. The later expressions might be read, Sumner urged, as a guide to the interpretation of the earlier ones: "Though [the Declaration of Independence and the Massachusetts Constitution] preceded, in point of time, the ampler declarations of France, they may, if necessary, be construed in the light of the latter. It is evident that they aim to declare substantially the same things."[5] Whether or not he was persuaded by Sumner's historical demonstration, Chief Justice Shaw—as will be seen—was perfectly willing to accept "equality before the law" as the test for the legality of segregation.

This derivation of "equality before the law" from "All men are born free and equal" occupied the first section of Sumner's argument. Sections II and III set forth a brief demonstration that the school law of Massachusetts, statutory and decisional, contained no express authorization of racial discrimination. In Section IV, arguing that the practical inconvenience to Sarah Roberts of traveling the extra distance to the "colored school" constituted a violation of equality,[6] Sumner raised a point which as an advocate he no doubt felt obliged to make: the fact that Sarah had to walk past other schools to reach hers, while white children attended the schools nearest their homes, was an element of unequal treatment that (unlike the quality of school facilities) the Primary School Committee could not dispute. But the contention actually tended to undercut Sumner's more ambitious arguments against racial discrimination. An argument based on inconvenience to Sarah, like an argument asserting the inequality of segregated facilities, necessarily implied that by curing the inconvenience or inequality of segregation, the school committee might also cure its illegality. (Such was the logical trap the U.S. Supreme Court would later construct for itself, in twenty-five years of equality-based desegregation decisions leading up to the School Segregation Cases of 1954.) The broader objections to discrimination asserted in subsequent sections of Sumner's argument would not have been satisfied by the establishment of a "colored school," offering identical or even superior facilities, immediately adjacent to every white primary school in Boston.

Inspired by the abolitionist vocabulary in which separate schools for Negroes were habitually referred to as "caste schools," Sumner next argued that a system of segregated schools "is in the nature of *Caste*," and as such a violation of equality. The discussion, somewhat literal-minded, proceeded with quotations from a dozen eminent divines as authority for "the unchristian character of Caste, as it appears in India, where it has been most studied and discussed."[7] But in asserting that racial segregation automatically "constitutes the relation of Caste," and that "[w]here Caste is, there cannot be Equality," Sumner advanced a significant argument that others would take a long time to rediscover. If we can agree that a caste society is bad, then segregation is to be condemned without inquiring into the equality of the segregated facilities or the harm (by stigma or otherwise) to class members.

Section VI, the core of Sumner's argument, contained a number of distinct themes. The policy of segregation, Sumner knew, would be defended on the basis of the school committee's discretionary powers of administration. Sumner argued first that discretion could not go so far as to "ingraft upon the schools a principle of inequality, unknown to the Constitution," or to "brand a whole race with the stigma of inferiority," or to "nullify a sacred and dear-bought principle of Human Rights." But each of these contentions begged the question. His next tack, introducing what would become one of the most familiar arguments in the law of racial discrimination, was to contend that a racial classification of schoolchildren could not be "legally reasonable" and that it was therefore, by the common law, inoperative and void. To demonstrate the unreasonableness of the regulation, Sumner pointed out that (so far as the laws of Massachusetts were concerned) a black citizen might occupy every other position in the hierarchy of the public school system, from the governorship of the commonwealth on down "to the humblest usher in the humblest primary school," yet be denied admission as a pupil. "It is when we reach the last stage of all, the children themselves, that the beautiful character of the system is changed to the deformity of Caste; as, in the picture of the ancient poet, what was a lovely woman above terminated in a vile, unsightly fish below."[8]

But the ultimate futility of the "reasonableness" argument was already apparent in Sumner's fuller statement of it:

> It is clear that the Committee may classify scholars, according to their age and sex; for the obvious reasons that these distinctions are inoffensive, and especially recognized as *legal* in the law relating to schools. . . . They may also classify scholars according to their moral and intellectual qualifications, because such a power is necessary to the government of

the schools. But the Committee cannot assume . . . that an *entire race* possess certain moral or intellectual qualities, which shall render it proper to place them all in a class by themselves. Such an exercise of the discretion with which the Committee are intrusted, must be unreasonable, and therefore illegal.[9]

The same argument as to the unreasonableness of a racial classification may be found, without significant change, in briefs submitted by desegregation plaintiffs a century afterward. By a strictly legal standard the argument is inherently a weak one: it affords no means, other than an appeal to the political and moral sense of judges, by which to separate those distinctions that are inoffensive and useful from those that are arbitrary and invidious. The claim that school segregation is "legally unreasonable" could no more succeed in 1849 than it could fail today, because the argument in either case is essentially political.

The principal difficulty attending the equality-based argument against segregated schools, for Sumner as for later advocates, was the rejoinder that came to be known by the shorthand expression "separate but equal":

But it is said that the Committee, in thus classifying the children, have not violated any principle of Equality, inasmuch as they have provided a school with competent instructors for the colored children, where they have equal advantages of instruction with those enjoyed by the white children.[10]

To this critical contention Sumner offered three distinct answers. The first approach, distinctly unpersuasive, argued on the basis of a strained reading of the Massachusetts school statutes that the school for colored children "has no legal existence, and, therefore cannot be a legal equivalent."[11] The second went much further:

[I]n point of fact, [the separate school] is not an equivalent. We have already seen that it is the occasion of inconveniences to the colored children and their parents . . . besides inflicting upon them the stigma of Caste. Still further, and this consideration cannot be neglected, the matters taught in the two schools may be precisely the same; but a school, exclusively devoted to one class, must differ essentially, in its spirit and character, from that public school known to the law, where all classes meet together in equality. It is a mockery to call it an equivalent.[12]

When the Supreme Court, 101 years later, held that a separate law school for black students would not afford education "substantially equal" to that available at the University of Texas Law School, its reasoning was essentially that of the passage just quoted.[13]

Sumner's third response to the argument from "equivalents" is even more suggestive:

> But there is yet another answer. Admitting that it is an equivalent, still the colored children cannot be compelled to take it. . . . They have an equal right with white children to the general public schools. . . . The Jews in Rome are confined to a particular district, called the Ghetto. In Frankfort they are confined to a separate quarter, known as the Jewish quarter. It is possible that the accommodations allotted to them are as good as they would be able to occupy, if left free to choose throughout Rome and Frankfort; but this compulsory segregation from the mass of citizens is itself an *inequality* which we condemn with our whole souls. It is a vestige of ancient intolerance directed against a despised people. It is of the same character with the separate schools in Boston.[14]

The great interest of this passage lies in the ease with which it avoids the logical impasse of "separate but equal." If the conferring of equal benefits will satisfy the requirement of legal equality, then—so long as equality is the constitutional standard—hypothetically identical (though segregated) facilities should be constitutionally permissible. The Supreme Court would eventually escape from this result only by refusing to find that segregated facilities could ever be "equal"; but that solution was not only arbitrary, it left unanswered the question of whether there was anything wrong with segregation in and of itself. Sumner's view of the case allowed him to begin his answer by admitting, for the sake of argument, the objective equivalence of the segregated facilities. This elementary step was one the Supreme Court, in the entire course of its decisions on racial segregation, never once dared to take. The simple analogy proposed by Sumner, rejoining his argument on the basis of caste, reminds us that the real problem of segregation is not about unequal facilities but about the drawing of class distinctions on racial lines.

Sumner's refutation of what he called "the doctrine of equivalents, as a substitute for equality" was followed by the familiar *reductio ad absurdum,* introduced by Edmund Jackson in the 1846 minority report and taken up again by Justice Harlan in *Plessy v. Ferguson.* If the school committee had the power to make a distinction on the basis of race, why might it not establish separate schools for Irish and Germans, for Catholics and Protestants, for Presbyterians and Baptists? "Let it not be said that there is little danger that any Committee will exercise their discretion to this extent," Sumner declared. "They must not be entrusted with the power. In this is the only safety worthy of a free people."[15]

The answer Sumner anticipated is the one that would be given by Justice Henry Billings Brown for the majority in *Plessy v. Ferguson:* that the political power to draw racial distinctions is unobjectionable so long as it is reasonably exercised. Sumner's answer, in which he would be joined by Harlan, is that racial classifications are so dangerous that they cannot safely be left to legislative discretion nor, by extension, to a standard of "reasonableness" enforced after the fact by judges. The alternative, assuring "the only safety worthy of a free people," is that the legislature be denied altogether the power to employ race as a means of classification. The contention that racial classifications are so peculiarly invidious as to require a per se constitutional proscription remains the core of the argument for the color-blind Constitution.

Sumner concluded his constitutional argument with a reference to Chief Justice Shaw's opinion in a landmark abolition case, *Commonwealth v. Aves,* in which Shaw had held that the Massachusetts constitution of 1780 abolished slavery in the commonwealth by virtue of the very language now relied on by Sumner: the statement in the first article that "All men are born free and equal."[16] If this language prohibited slavery, likewise it must prohibit racial segregation, since "[t]he same words which are potent to destroy slavery, must be equally potent against any institution founded on inequality or *caste.*"[17] Sumner's graceful reference to Shaw's famous decision depended for its logic on an implicit identification of racially discriminatory laws with "badges and incidents of slavery," thereby prefiguring one of the major themes of Justice Harlan's dissenting opinion in the *Civil Rights Cases.*[18] The idea recurred in Sumner's peroration: "You have already banished slavery from this Commonwealth. I call upon you now to obliterate the last of its footprints, and to banish the last of the hateful spirits in its train, that can be reached by this Court."[19]

In his treatment of "matters not strictly belonging to the juridical aspect of the case, and yet of importance to its clear comprehension," Sumner drew on Edmund Jackson's 1846 minority report to frame a defense of the benefits of racially integrated schools that would become common currency more than a century later. Sumner's explanation of the harm to black children from segregated schools might be a paraphrase of the "psychological" portion of Chief Justice Warren's opinion in *Brown v. Board of Education:*

Who can say, that [segregation] does not injure the blacks? . . . Shut out by a still lingering prejudice from many social advantages, a despised class, they feel this proscription from the Public Schools as a particular brand. Beyond this, it deprives them of those healthful animating influences which would come from a participation in the studies of their white brethren. It adds to their discouragements. It widens their separation from the rest of the community, and postpones the great day of reconciliation which is sure to come.[20]

Sumner, bolder than Warren on this point, argued that segregation injured the white children as well.[21] And in deprecating the effect of segregation on the school system as a whole, Sumner's argument anticipated the rationale of racial balance in the post-*Brown* school busing era:

The law contemplates not only that they shall all be taught, but that they shall be taught *all together*. They are not only to receive equal quantities of knowledge, but all are to receive it in the same way. . . . The school is the little world in which the child is trained for the larger world of life. . . . And since, according to our institutions, all classes meet, without distinction of color, in the performance of civil duties, so should they all meet, without distinction of color, in the school, beginning there those relations of equality which our Constitution and laws promise to all.[22]

Sumner's more practical arguments for school desegregation—closely paraphrased from Edmund Jackson—are equally modern in spirit. Integrated schools will ensure superior facilities for children who are otherwise disadvantaged, because they will "draw upon the whole school the attention which is too apt to be given only to the favored few, and thus secure to the poor their portion of the fruitful sunshine." By promoting mutual acquaintance between the races, they will "remove antipathies, promote mutual adaptation and conciliation, and establish relations of reciprocal regard."[23]

Three days after the argument, a brief item in that week's *Liberator* gave it prophetic notice:

Mr. Sumner's argument was a most luminous and profound one, and we hope to see it in print. Had the question been one of temporary local interest, his manner of treating it would have ensured it a permanent value; but the same point, either in this shape or some similar one, will be long [a] matter of debate in this and other States, and the comprehensive view of Mr. Sumner will long be a treasure-house for other laborers to draw from.[24]

Sumner's argument was that and more; but Chief Justice Shaw's opinion for a unanimous court,[25] dismissing the suit by Sarah Roberts, has proved even more influential. Correctly identified as the source of the "'separate but equal' doctrine," the opinion quite unfairly shares the reactionary reputation that attaches to the majority opinion in *Plessy v. Ferguson. Roberts* was an innovative decision, answering new questions with an analysis that, in its broader implications, remains equally good law today. The unacceptability of that analysis as applied to the issue of racial segregation derives, not from any flaw in Shaw's reasoning, but from the inadequacy of "equal protection" as a standard for resolving the question.

The *Roberts* opinion is essentially forward-looking. The necessary condition of its subsequent influence was Shaw's willingness to follow Sumner in an extremely broad reading of the first article of the Massachusetts Declaration of Rights. If Shaw had not been prepared to agree that the words "All men are born free and equal" constituted a command of "equality before the law," the ratification of the Fourteenth Amendment would have left *Roberts* a dead letter. "Separate but equal"—neither the phrase nor anything like it appears in *Roberts*—was merely one of the lessons that subsequent generations would derive from two broader rules taught by Shaw's opinion. Whereas Sumner had made the novel assertion that racial distinctions formed a special and impermissible category of government discretion, Shaw determined to treat them like other instances of government classification: to be held valid where reasonable. While the requirements of "reasonableness" in this context have since been transfigured, the essential legitimacy of reasonable racial classifications—a premise the U.S. Supreme Court has yet to repudiate—is one of the rules traceable to Shaw's opinion in *Roberts.* Even more significantly, Shaw's acceptance of Sumner's premise of legal equality led him to anticipate, and to solve in advance, the conundrum created by the requirement that the government provide "equal protection of the laws" to persons it must inevitably treat differently.

All of this was done in an opinion of great simplicity. Shaw first noted the relevant facts, not challenged by the plaintiff: that the Primary School Committee had determined, "apparently upon great deliberation," that "the continuance of separate schools for colored children . . . [was] best adapted to promote the instruction of that class of the population"; and that the segregated school to which the plaintiff had access was "as well conducted in all respects, and as well fitted, in point of capacity and qualification of the instructors, to advance the education of children under seven years old, as the other primary schools."[26] Shaw's reference to the school board's policy determination led him directly to his major premise. "It will be considered," he wrote, "that this is a question of power, or of the legal authority of the committee intrusted by the city with this department of public instruction; because, if they have the legal authority, the expediency of exercising it in any particular way is exclusively with them."[27] With these words Shaw effectively adopted Sumner's statement of the question presented.[28] Both men saw as the central issue, not the expediency of segregated schools, but whether a constitutional rule deprived the committee of its ordinary authority—which manifestly extended to the classification of pupils—when the classification in question rested on a racial distinction.

Sumner's central contention was that the principle of equality before the law put racial discrimination beyond the reach of government power. Shaw replied that equality and discrimination—the government's decision to treat different people differently—were not incompatible:

> The great principle, advanced by the learned and eloquent advocate of the plaintiff, is, that by the constitution and laws of Massachusetts, all persons without distinction of age or sex, birth or color, origin or condition, are equal before the law. This, as a broad general principle, such as ought to appear in a declaration of rights, is perfectly sound; it is not only expressed in terms, but pervades and animates the whole spirit of our constitution of free government. But, when this great principle comes to be applied to the actual and various conditions of persons in society, it will not warrant the assertion, that men and women are legally clothed with the same civil and political powers, and that children and adults are legally to have the same functions and be subject to the same treatment; but only that the rights of all, as they are settled and regulated by law, are equally entitled to the paternal consideration and protection of the law, for their maintenance and security. What those rights are, to which individuals, in the infinite variety of circumstances by which they are surrounded in society, are entitled, must depend on laws adapted to their respective relations and conditions.[29]

Shaw's language in this much-quoted passage is liable to misinterpretation. We are accustomed to use the term *legal rights* to describe claims

that all persons do assert on equal terms, and Shaw's reference to individuals' "rights" as something "adapted to their respective relations and
conditions" can therefore come as a surprise.[30] It is apparent from the
context, however, that in speaking of "rights" Shaw is describing the
consequences of government decisions with respect to the individual and
those similarly situated: the "right" to attend school, or to practice law, or
to pay income tax at one rate rather than another. Shaw's analysis, recast
in modern terms, makes a readily acceptable account of the working of
the equal protection clause. When Shaw says that the rights of individuals
differently situated "must depend on laws adapted to their respective
relations and conditions," he is saying that government must classify in
order to legislate. When he says that "the rights of all, as they are settled
and regulated by law, are equally entitled to the paternal consideration and
protection of the law," he is saying, among other things, that the classifications by which the individual's rights are "settled and regulated" must
be reasonable ones. If we have difficulty in understanding what Shaw is
talking about—the problem of reconciling the principle of legal "equality"
with the political fact of unequal treatment—it is because modern constitutional theory has so thoroughly incorporated Shaw's solution that we no
longer recognize the problem.

By a simple reference to the different legal rights of children and adults,
or men and women, Shaw effectively refuted the suggestion that classification is incompatible with legal equality, at least as that term must be
understood in organized society. (One example that was obvious in 1850,
the distinctions between men and women in "civil and political powers,"
has become an anachronism; but the logic of the argument is unaffected.)
It was equally easy to show that classification was essential to the duties
of the school authorities. The school committee, wrote Shaw, was invested
by the statute with "a plenary authority . . . to arrange, classify, and
distribute pupils, in such a manner as they think best adapted to their
general proficiency and welfare." Thus the committee could establish
separate schools for the very young, or for male and female pupils, or for
children requiring special training; and the statute, far from restricting such
"distribution and classification," virtually required it for the proper effec-
tuation of the legislative purpose.[31]

Sumner had argued that regulations must be reasonable. Shaw found
that this requirement presented no difficulty:

> In the absence of special legislation on this subject, the law has vested
> the power in the committee to regulate the system of distribution and

classification; and when this power is reasonably exercised, without being abused or perverted by colorable pretences, the decision of the committee must be deemed conclusive. The committee, apparently upon great deliberation, have come to the conclusion, that the good of both classes of schools will be best promoted, by maintaining the separate primary schools for colored and for white children, and we can perceive no ground to doubt, that this is the honest result of their experience and judgment.

Questions as to the expediency of segregation, such as the idea that it fostered racial prejudice, were naturally debatable, but in the absence of some direction or limitation by constitution or statute their determination was properly left to the sound discretion of the committee:

> Whether this distinction and prejudice, existing in the opinion and feelings of the community, would not be as effectually fostered by compelling colored and white children to associate together in the same schools, may well be doubted; at all events, it is a fair and proper question for the committee to consider and decide upon, having in view the best interests of both classes of children placed under their superintendence, and we cannot say, that their decision upon it is not founded on just grounds of reason and experience, and in the results of a discriminating and honest judgment.[32]

If Sarah Roberts had challenged some form of discrimination still generally regarded as noninvidious—for instance, the committee's decision to teach children aged four to seven in separate schools—Shaw's opinion might be admired today, as it was in the nineteenth century, as a lucid introduction to the theory of equal protection.[33] Its only flaw, by present-day constitutional standards, is its failure to anticipate our political conviction that the racial classification at issue in *Roberts* is not a reasonable one. Our difference with Shaw on that point is paramount, but it is not a difference of legal principle.

If a school committee finds it expedient to separate primary and grammar school pupils, and in so doing can still afford to both groups "equality before the law," why may it not do the same with white and black children? There are numerous answers to this question: in one form or another, Sumner offered them all. But the strongest answers for legal purposes—those that do not depend on factual assertions not susceptible of legal proof—are not reached by forcing the meaning of the word *equality*. They depend instead on a premise that there is something uniquely bad about racial classification and that this form of discrimination, unlike the others and with or without measurable "equality," is inconsistent with American ideals.

So Sumner had urged; but his arguments to this effect took him beyond the point to which a strictly legal reasoning can compel others to follow. The difficulty lay, not with Sumner's powers of argument or the accuracy of his judgment, but with "equality" as a starting point for the legal argument. Its necessary consequences, as opposed to its expansive possibilities, are theoretically compatible with racial segregation: the interpretation that allowed a rule of "separate but equal" was politically but not logically deficient. Sumner tried to derive a rule of nondiscrimination from the principle of equality, not because "equality" was the ideal starting point but because "equality" was all he had to work with in the constitution of Massachusetts.

The attempt had now been made; and it had been demonstrated, to anyone who read Sumner's argument and Shaw's opinion, that a constitutional guarantee of equal treatment was insufficient as a legal weapon to overturn racial segregation. If Sarah Roberts was to win her lawsuit on constitutional grounds, the rule that was needed was not "equality" but nondiscrimination. The framers of the Fourteenth Amendment, who at one point considered writing nondiscrimination into the constitutional text, chose to abandon it in favor of "equal protection." Defining the new federal guarantee of civil rights against infringement by the states, they would leave the claims of black citizens precisely where Shaw had left them under the Massachusetts constitution.

The Reconstruction Amendments of Wendell Phillips

Late in 1863 the abolitionists recognized, belatedly and with some misgivings, that the way to extend and secure the crowning achievement of emancipation was by the unaccustomed means of a constitutional amendment. The euphoria with which they initially greeted the Emancipation Proclamation on January 1, 1863, had given way to a general feeling that the Proclamation did too little, and did that much for the wrong reasons.[1] Many found it intolerable that emancipation, when it finally came, should leave anyone in slavery; yet by the terms of Lincoln's order, carefully justified "as a fit and necessary war measure," slavery in the border states and in specified counties of Louisiana and Virginia was "for the present, left precisely as if this proclamation were not issued."[2]

In the initial phase of the ensuing campaign for "universal emancipation," abolitionists proposed to remedy these shortcomings of the presidential order by a simple act of Congress. The "mammoth petition" on which the newly formed Women's National Loyal League (organized by Elizabeth Cady Stanton and Susan B. Anthony) announced that it would "concentrate all its efforts" prayed Congress to "pass, at the earliest practicable day, an act emancipating all persons of African descent held to involuntary service or labor in the United States."[3] The League's petition received the enthusiastic endorsement of the American Anti-Slavery Society, which took the view that the appropriate disposition of "that remnant of the slave institution which was exempted by the Proclamation" was a "decree" to be passed by the next Congress—to accomplish which, the Society believed, "the constitutional powers of the Federal Government are now ample."[4] Throughout 1863 the idea of a constitutional amendment prohibiting slavery was mentioned in the editorial columns of the *National Anti-Slavery Standard*—the official organ of the Society, and at this time a fair index of middle-of-the-road abolitionist opinion—only in observing that such an amendment was both unnecessary and unlikely to be enacted.[5]

The idea of an emancipation amendment can be dated in one sense to the Fourth of July 1863, when Union victories at Gettysburg and Vicksburg foretold the war's ultimate outcome. If the war was going to be won by the North, it was easier to agree that the southern states were, as they claimed, out of the Union; readmission might accordingly take place under a Constitution different from the one the confederate states had left behind. Abolitionists, however, many of whom had been accustomed to regard the Constitution as a proslavery document, were slow to realize that the time had come when the tragic failure of 1787 might at last be corrected. The first idea of an antislavery amendment is traceable, not to those New Englanders who denounced the Constitution as "a covenant with death and an agreement with hell,"[6] but to radicals from a border state, held for the Union by military force, whose own experience of federal authority was necessarily more immediate.

On July 1, 1863, the extraordinary State Convention that served as a provisional government in wartime Missouri ordained the gradual abolition of slavery in that state beginning in 1870.[7] The compromise decision to defer emancipation for seven years represented a setback for Missouri's radicals—called the "Charcoals," to emphasize the "blackness" of their Republicanism—who had urged that emancipation be immediate. Over the summer the Charcoals regrouped, organizing a convention of "Radical Emancipationalists" at Jefferson City on September 1. Renewing the demand for immediate emancipation in Missouri, the delegates also proposed a constitutional formula to prohibit slavery in the rest of the nation: they urged "our Legislature and Senators and Representatives in Congress to use their utmost endeavors to have our National Constitution amended so as to prohibit Slavery forever in States now free or hereafter applying for admission into the Union."[8]

A delegation of Missouri radicals thereupon traveled to Washington to address the president on their political grievances; Lincoln received them politely but repeated that his own policy favored gradual, rather than immediate, emancipation in Missouri.[9] Proceeding to New York, the Charcoals were welcomed on October 2 with a mass meeting at the Cooper Institute. While the speeches at the rally were preoccupied with the struggles between Radicals and Copperheads under military occupation in Missouri, one of the delegates adverted in his closing remarks to the proposed amendment. "But if the Constitution of the United States recognized slavery—though he did not believe it did—he wanted it amended, so that the provision should be stamped plainly and surely in it before this fight is over, that the American territory shall not hereafter contain a slave. (Tremendous applause.)"[10] Thus was the Missouri idea carried eastward.

A more visible call for an antislavery amendment now came from Wendell Phillips. Addressing a Boston lyceum audience in mid-November on the subject of Reconstruction, Phillips declared, "I would have Congress *now* initiate measures for an amendment of the Constitution to this effect:—Slavery shall henceforth have no place in any State within this Union. When this is done, let the States come back as soon as they please."[11] Once it was made, the merits of the proposal seemed obvious to many. At the December 4 meeting of its triumphal "Third Decade," or thirtieth anniversary celebration, the American Anti-Slavery Society unanimously adopted a resolution and memorial calling on Congress "so to amend the Constitution that slavery shall be forever prohibited within the limits of the United States."[12] On December 14, in the second week of the new Thirty-eighth Congress, Representatives James M. Ashley of Ohio and James F. Wilson of Iowa introduced separate measures proposing the constitutional prohibition of slavery.[13]

Some friends of abolition, accustomed to regard the Constitution with abhorrence, were only reluctantly persuaded that it was worth amending. Elizabeth Cady Stanton deplored "the bad policy" of a petition to amend the Constitution, believing that "[t]he petition for universal emancipation covers all these specific abuses"; while the old radical Gerrit Smith felt that it would be "time enough to amend the Constitution after we shall have ended the Rebellion," and that "now is not the time either to improve the Constitution or to be solicitous to save it." Despite such doubts, the petitions being circulated by the abolitionist forces were eventually revised to seek universal emancipation by constitutional amendment as well as by statute.[14]

It was in late December 1863 that the idea of an antislavery amendment received what stands in retrospect as its definitive public introduction. The occasion was a speech by Wendell Phillips on President Lincoln's plan of reconstruction, given before a group of Republicans at New York's Cooper Institute. A milestone in the history of the Thirteenth Amendment, the speech of December 22, 1863, is even more significant to the history of the color-blind Constitution. Phillips proposed to resolve the status of America's black population by means of two constitutional amendments: one prohibiting slavery, the other prohibiting the states from drawing legal distinctions on racial lines. His unparalleled suggestion was that the U.S. Constitution be made color-blind by means of an amendment saying so in so many words. Phillips's speech marked the beginning of a campaign that would last some two and a half years before it ground to a halt in the Thirty-ninth Congress: the first and last concerted attempt to achieve the legal prohibition of racial classifications by constitutional amendment. That the attempt was ever made has been virtually forgotten. Once the Constitution had been amended to include instead the protean guarantee of "equal protection of the laws," the color-blind argument necessarily assumed the form of a claim that "equal protection" excluded racial distinctions.

The Cooper Institute address attracted wide notice. With the beginning of the war and his dramatic decision to support it, Wendell Phillips had become a figure of political consequence. After a lifetime spent on the margin of public affairs he was suddenly one of the most influential political speakers in the country, the charismatic leader of the radical wing of the party of the administration.[15] In December 1863, moreover, the prospect of a speech by Phillips on the subject of the president's plan of reconstruction carried the promise of political fireworks. In his annual message to Congress on December 8, Lincoln had responded to abolitionist fears of a possible revocation of the Emancipation Proclamation with an express pledge that "while I remain in my present position I shall not attempt to retract or modify the emancipation proclamation." The message contained, in addition, a gentle endorsement of further emancipation by act of Congress. But the effect of these welcome assurances was undercut by the striking qualifications appearing in the text of a proposed loyalty oath set forth in the "Proclamation of Amnesty and Reconstruction" which accompanied the president's message. According to Lincoln's proposal, former rebels would be required to swear to

> abide by and faithfully support all acts of Congress passed during the existing rebellion with reference to slaves, so long and so far as not repealed, modified or held void by Congress, or by decision of the Supreme Court; [and] in like manner, abide by and faithfully support all proclamations of the President made during the existing rebellion having reference to slaves, so long and so far as not modified or declared void by decision of the Supreme Court.

This looked to the abolitionists as if Lincoln was virtually inviting a Supreme Court determination that emancipation by presidential proclamation was unconstitutional. The president's remarks about the appropriate civil status of the freedman were equally dismaying:

> And I do further proclaim, declare, and make known that any provision which may be adopted by such [reconstructed] State government in

relation to the freed people of such State, which shall recognize and declare their permanent freedom, provide for their education, and which may yet be consistent, as a temporary arrangement, with their present condition as a laboring, landless, and homeless class, will not be objected to by the national Executive.[16]

Former slave states, in other words, would not be disqualified for readmission to the Union should they choose to qualify the freedom of the former slaves by some form of mandatory "apprenticeship."[17] There was a time when abolitionists, Garrison included, had spoken favorably of temporary apprenticeship as a means of smoothing the transition from slavery to freedom; but to Phillips and his followers, it was inconceivable at this juncture that the rights of the freedman should be entrusted to the guardianship of his former masters. On both critical points—the irrevocability of emancipation, and the need to ensure that emancipation brought an unqualified freedom—Phillips's speech of December 22 proposed a radical alternative to the president's plan.

On the issue of universal emancipation, Phillips supplied in forceful terms the reasons for seeking a constitutional amendment rather than an act of Congress. President Lincoln himself, said Phillips, did not know the meaning of the Emancipation Proclamation. Nobody could be sure of its meaning or validity until the measure, justified under the war power, had been passed on by the Supreme Court:

> In other words, the proclamation of the 1st of January, 1863, is to be filtered through the secession heart of a man [Taney] whose body is in Baltimore, but whose soul, if he has one, is in Richmond (applause). . . . It has to pass the ordeal of a set of Judges the majority of whom are Southerners and the servants of Southerners, and who reached their places by pandering to the Slave Power. . . . Now, God help the negro if he hangs on Roger B. Taney for his liberty! . . . Leave the Supreme Court all the power it claims. But call into exercise the reserved sovereignty of the nation, and provide a safeguard which is, constitutionally, beyond the reach of that Court, as far as anything can be in our system. . . . As Commander-in-Chief, [the president] has *freed slaves*. I ask the *Nation* to *abolish slavery*. As Commander-in-Chief, he has done an act which the Supreme Court may reverse, and may set aside in part or wholly. Of the Nation I claim an amendment of the Constitution which that Court is sworn to obey, and in such plain terms as they cannot misconstrue. . . .
>
> Now, what I should ask of Mr. Lincoln in this behalf is, an amendment of the Constitution, which his advice to Congress would secure in sixty

days. Submit to the States an amendment of the Constitution which shall say, "Hereafter, there shall be neither slavery nor involuntary servitude in any State of this Union" (cheers).[18]

Protesting that presidential emancipation "frees the slave but ignores the negro," Phillips next attacked Lincoln's apparent willingness to allow the former slaveholding states to experiment with apprenticeship arrangements. The history of such schemes in connection with the abolition of slavery in the West Indies demonstrated "that all the trouble attending emancipation . . . came from the attempt of the planters to recreate by tricky legislation that slavery which England had abolished." England had "given her blacks, technically free, into the keeping of slaveholders turned into landowners, which is just what Lincoln proposes to do." And while Britain retained a power of veto over colonial laws, the southern states, once readmitted to the Union, would be free of federal control in regulating their former slaves. Rather than attempt to anticipate the specific forms of discriminatory legislation that might then be attempted, Phillips proposed for the federal Constitution the radical solution worked out by the Garrisonians for the Commonwealth of Massachusetts:

> The nation owes the negro, after such a war, in which he has nobly joined, not technical freedom, but substantial protection in all his rights. It should never admit State sovereignty between it and the negro, until both by constitutional guarantees and by natural laws it has insured him full, real liberty. I would have an amendment of the Constitution providing that "no State shall make any distinction among its citizens on account of race and color."[19]

The conjunction of the two propositions at the origin of each, and the prophetic arguments advanced by Phillips as to the necessity of the second guarantee to secure the work of the first, merit some consideration in the long-standing debate over the original understanding of the scope of the Thirteenth Amendment. A substantial tradition of interpretation takes the view that the authors of an amendment prohibiting slavery, influenced by the constitutional arguments of the abolitionists, intended by that prohibition to effect an affirmative guarantee of rights inhering in the condition of freedom.[20] Section 2 of the Thirteenth Amendment (authorizing Congress "to enforce this article by appropriate legislation") becomes, in this view, a broad grant of legislative power to secure civil rights, unhampered by any "state action" requirement; with the consequence that the traditional "state action" limitation on the Fourteenth Amendment guarantees becomes (whether right or wrong) substantially beside the point.[21]

Two distinguished modern adherents argue that "[i]n considering links between the Thirteenth and Fourteenth Amendments, it is desirable also to keep in mind the admonition that persons who enacted the Thirteenth in early 1865 and who ratified it later that year did not know that *a* Fourteenth (much less *the* Fourteenth) was to be needed."[22] But Wendell Phillips had been telling them precisely that since December 1863.

Had Phillips argued at this point merely that the former slave required the protection of the ballot, he would still have asserted a position well in advance of most of his fellow abolitionists. Among the movement's leading figures, only Phillips and Frederick Douglass were advocating Negro suffrage by December 1863.[23] But even the great issue of suffrage—not to be resolved until the end of the decade, with the ratification of the Fifteenth Amendment—was here grandly disposed of merely as a necessary consequence of Phillips's proposal to establish, once and for all, the unconstitutionality of legal classification on racial lines. As a leader of the civil rights battles of the 1840s in which the antidiscrimination principle had first evolved, Wendell Phillips was one of the few people in the country to whom this extraordinary solution could have occurred. The leap of radical generalization was the method of the Lynn Women's Anti-Slavery Society, which had proposed in 1839 to deal with the one instance of discrimination immediately in view (a Massachusetts law prohibiting interracial marriage) by repealing all Massachusetts statutes drawing a racial distinction.

Phillips intended his proposal literally. Earlier in 1863, responding to a speech by Theodore Tilton on the future of the Negro, Phillips had observed that he thought race "of secondary importance"; that "colorphobia"—racial prejudice—would soon disappear in the face of legislative determination; and that the black man's civil rights would be effectively secured as soon as he was given the ballot. "Give the negro a vote in his hand, and there is not a politician . . . who would not do him honor. As to this matter of race, friend Tilton, the politician would not know one from the other." Phillips concluded with the hope that abolitionists might soon rejoice "that there is nothing in the heart of the American which recognizes the distinction of races."[24] Before an even more sympathetic audience, at the abolitionists' annual Fourth of July picnic in Framingham, Phillips expressed the wish that racial distinctions might be physically obliterated:

> Amalgamation! Remember this, the youngest of you: that on the 4th day of July, 1863, you heard a man say, that in the light of all history, in virtue of every page he ever read, he was an amalgamationist, to the

utmost extent (applause). I have no hope for the future . . . but in that sublime mingling of races, which is God's own method of civilizing and elevating the world (loud applause). Not that amalgamation of licentiousness, born of slavery—the ruin of both races—but that gradual and harmonizing union, in honorable marriage, which has mingled all other races, and from which springs the present phase of European and Northern civilization.[25]

Ordinary political opinion, including much of Republican opinion, now took Phillips at his word. It found his proposal for a color-blind Constitution extravagant to the point of absurdity. The *New York Times* reminded its northern readers that Phillips was proposing an intolerable interference with their own laws as well:

He would not content himself with compelling every State to make an end of Slavery forthwith, but would also force them to clear their statute books of every distinction between the black man and the white. If Maine law doesn't allow black men upon juries, the Federal arm must force it; if Massachusetts law don't allow them to muster indiscriminately into the militia, the Federal arm must force it. So, too, must the Federal arm force New-York to abolish all of her property limitations upon the elective franchise possessed by black men; Ohio to strike down every bar against the election of black men to any and all offices; Illinois to abrogate her statutes against black immigration into her borders; . . . Maryland to expunge every law forbidding amalgamation by marriage; and Georgia, and Mississippi, and Alabama, and Louisiana to remit their entire civil control to the black majority now within their limits. In other words, every State, loyal and disloyal, is to be deprived of all power to regulate its own most vital concerns.[26]

Two years later, when proposals for Wendell Phillips's fourteenth amendment were finally voted down in the Joint Committee on Reconstruction of the Thirty-ninth Congress, it is doubtful that the arguments against them (not recorded in the committee's journal) added significantly to this common editorial wisdom.

For a year and a half following his speech at the Cooper Institute, well into the summer of 1865, Phillips's proposal for an antidiscrimination amendment remained at the center of his public statements on reconstruction and the rights of the ex-slave. In January 1864, at the annual meeting of the Massachusetts Anti-Slavery Society, Phillips proposed and obtained a resolution calling upon Congress to "take measures to amend the Constitution, so as to provide that there shall be no slavery in any State of the

Union, and no law in any State making any distinction on account of race."[27] The idea recurred in both speeches and writings throughout the spring.[28] Phillips attracted a notable supporter in Robert Dale Owen, son of the English socialist, whose own varied career (spent mostly in America) saw him by turns a free-thinker, a Democratic congressman from Indiana, and an essayist and reformer in a variety of causes. Plainly inspired by Phillips, Owen suggested that slavery and racial discrimination be prohibited by a single amendment:

> We cannot expect, in a democratic republic, to maintain domestic tranquillity, if we deprive millions of freemen of their rights as such.
>
> Public opinion may not, at the present time, have reached this conviction, but it is fast approaching it. Three-fourths of the States might not to-day, but ere long they will, pass some such amendment to the Constitution as this:—
>
> "Slavery shall not be permitted, and no discrimination shall be made, as to the civil or political rights of persons, because of color."[29]

Returning to the lecture platform after the presidential election campaign of 1864, Phillips reverted to the theme of an antidiscrimination amendment: his speeches now evoked "a government color-blind."[30] In January 1865, as it had the year before, the annual meeting of the Massachusetts Anti-Slavery Society voted in favor of resolutions offered by Phillips declaring the necessity of both antislavery and antidiscrimination amendments.[31] An optimistic editorial in the *Standard* declared that "[a]n amendment to the Constitution forbidding any State to make distinctions among its inhabitants because of their color is now infinitely more likely than the one forbidding slavery appeared a short year ago."[32]

An inevitable casualty of abolition was the abolitionist movement. At the meeting of the Massachusetts Anti-Slavery Society in January 1863, just after the Emancipation Proclamation, William Lloyd Garrison had already begun to speak of the time when the work of abolitionists would be completed: he regretted that it was not yet, but he implied that it would come no later than universal emancipation.[33] To Garrisonians more radical than Garrison—a faction that came to be led by Phillips—it was obvious that formal emancipation would not secure adequate protection to the former slave; they saw the struggle to obtain civil rights for the freedman as the necessary continuation of the abolitionist task. Political differences exacerbated the tension between the camps, as Garrison supported Lincoln's renomination and was slow to see the wisdom of immediate

Negro suffrage. In 1865, with a constitutional amendment abolishing slavery finally in view, the breach rapidly widened.

Open warfare was barely avoided in January, at an acrimonious meeting of the Massachusetts Anti-Slavery Society. Garrison's resolution that the Society be dissolved upon ratification of the Thirteenth Amendment was tabled, while Phillips's color-blind resolution was adopted. Garrison made it clear that in May, at the annual meeting of the American Anti-Slavery Society, he would offer resolutions encompassing the Society's dissolution; and that on the failure of his resolutions, he himself would resign from the Society he had helped to found, and whose presidency he had held for twenty-two years. Phillips and his followers were equally determined that the nation's preeminent organization devoted to the welfare of the Negro should not abandon its work at the moment of crisis. The two positions could no longer be reconciled. At the close of a sanguinary meeting, Phillips inherited the *National Anti-Slavery Standard* and what was left of the American Society from Garrison and his followers, accepting the presidency that Garrison had declined.[34] In his inaugural address as the Society's president, Phillips defined the continuing battle (and justified by implication the break with Garrison) by reference to his color-blind amendment. "I shall never relax my advocacy of the question of race represented in the negro," said Phillips, "till I see inscribed in the Constitution of the United States this amendment: 'No State shall make any distinction in civil privileges among persons born on her soil of parents permanently resident there, on account of race, color, or descent.' (Loud applause.)"[35]

On July 22, in its ninth week under the effective editorial control of Wendell Phillips,[36] the *Standard* inserted a prominent legend at the head of its principal editorial column:

PROPOSED AMENDMENT
OF THE UNITED STATES CONSTITUTION.

NO STATE SHALL MAKE ANY DISTINCTION IN CIVIL RIGHTS AND PRIVILEGES AMONG THE NATURALIZED CITIZENS OF THE UNITED STATES RESIDING WITHIN ITS LIMITS, OR AMONG PERSONS BORN ON ITS SOIL OF PARENTS PERMANENTLY RESIDENT THERE, ON ACCOUNT OF RACE, COLOR, OR DESCENT.[37]

The identical legend appeared in the *Standard* every week for nine months, before its disappearance under circumstances to be noted presently.

The proposed amendment's temporary elevation to the masthead of the

Standard, attesting to its reception as abolitionist dogma, marked the high point of the campaign to fix a rule of nondiscrimination in the constitutional text. Phillips himself now turned his attention elsewhere. In the summer of 1865, with ratification of the Thirteenth Amendment proceeding through the states, abolitionist interest in further constitutional amendments was eclipsed by the pressing necessity of organizing Republican opposition to reconstruction policies of President Andrew Johnson. The all-encompassing strategic issue was whether the temporary political leverage afforded by Reconstruction might be used to force the southern states to grant their former slaves the protection of the ballot.[38] Unlike the color-blind amendment, the "inexorable demand" of *"No Reconstruction without Negro Suffrage,"*[39] announced in the first number of the *Standard* under Phillips's control, seemed for a time an attainable goal. A suffrage-based Reconstruction policy found favor initially with a number of moderate as well as radical Republican leaders, though their views would change as the extent of northern opposition became apparent.[40] By early 1866, when antidiscrimination amendments in the terms he had proposed had been introduced in Congress and were being debated in the Joint Committee on Reconstruction, Phillips was seemingly too much engaged in the day-to-day battle between president and Congress to attend to his vision of "a government color-blind." The *Standard,* meanwhile, offered no support for the color-blind position in the Thirty-ninth Congress beyond the weekly publication of the "Proposed Amendment" motto.

Even that outward sign of Phillips's commitment was suddenly withdrawn when it had to yield—as circumstantial evidence suggests—to the emerging politics of Reconstruction. The "Proposed Amendment" appeared in the *Standard* as usual on March 31, 1866; a week later it was removed, without editorial acknowledgment. The explanation is presumably to be found in the controversy over the pending civil rights bill, the most important section of which secured to all persons in every state "the same right . . . to make and enforce contracts, to sue, be parties, and give evidence, to inherit, purchase, lease, sell, hold, and convey real and personal property, and to full and equal benefit of all laws and proceedings for the security of person and property, as is enjoyed by white citizens."[41] On March 27, President Johnson had delivered to the Senate his veto of the bill on the grounds, *inter alia,* of its unconstitutionality.[42] The constitutional objection, already voiced in Congress by the Democrats and some conservative Republicans, was that the Thirteenth Amendment (which authorized "appropriate legislation" to "enforce" the abolition of slavery) gave Congress no authority to legislate with regard to those matters, traditionally the concern of the states, that the civil rights bill proposed to regulate.

The veto was Johnson's declaration of war with the Republican Congress over the direction of Reconstruction. The challenge was immediately accepted, as the Senate (on April 6) and the House (on April 9) voted to pass the civil rights bill over the president's veto. With the issue thus joined between president and Congress, on constitutional grounds among others, it was essential that a vision of the ideal not be allowed to comfort the enemies of radical Reconstruction. Phillips's standing proposal for a color-blind amendment, reprinted week after week, could be read to imply indirect support for the president's constitutional argument: namely, that the discriminatory state laws addressed by the civil rights bill, falling well short of "involuntary servitude," could not be prohibited by an ordinary act of Congress. In the present controversy, therefore, the less said about the proposed amendment the better.

Of the two amendments proposed by Wendell Phillips in December 1863, the first had finally been ratified by the states; but the "bright dream" of the second now seemed to have vanished, as Thaddeus Stevens shortly said of it, "like the baseless fabric of a vision." The Fourteenth Amendment that shortly emerged from Congress was, Stevens conceded, an "imperfect proposition" omitting "many better things."[43] Phillips had long since determined to judge the amendment by a single standard: whether it contained a practical guarantee of Negro suffrage as a minimum condition of reconstruction. When the Fourteenth Amendment failed to do so, Phillips denounced it as "a fatal & total surrender," "an infamous breach of the national pledges to negroes . . . a party trick designed only for electioneering purposes."[44] Phillips and the *Standard* campaigned vigorously to defeat the amendment, calling it "unjust to the negro and disgraceful to the nation"; "a flagrant, cruel cheat"; "fundamentally wrong," "unworthy of ratification," and "a mean and cowardly abandonment of the negro." Phillips appeared before a joint committee of the Massachusetts legislature to urge a vote against ratification.[45]

In Phillips's later speeches on racial questions, the idea of a color-blind constitutional amendment received only infrequent mention.[46] His more characteristic emphasis was on the need to extend military reconstruction as long as possible: "to hold the South quiet while the seeds of Republicanism get planted." Phillips advocated constitutional amendments guaranteeing universal suffrage and the establishment of common schools at state expense. "To these measures we must educate the public mind. These are the soil in which the seeds of good government and equal rights can alone be trusted."[47] The end of the decade saw a newly pragmatic Phillips chide the Senate radicals who, in attempting to extend the scope of the proposed Fifteenth Amendment to prohibit the denial of suffrage on grounds in addition to race, were jeopardizing the passage of any suffrage amendment at all by the lame-duck Fortieth Congress.[48] An amendment restricted to race, Phillips advised, covered "all the ground that the people are ready to occupy"; it had "all the chance that exists for any form of Amendment being ratified"; and the attempt to extend it to other forms of discrimination betrayed "a total forgetfulness of the commonest political prudence." Phillips urged the Republican senators to resume some part of their habitual caution: "For the first time in our lives we beseech them to be a little more *politicians*—and a little less *reformers*."[49] According to the Massachusetts radical George Boutwell, Phillips's editorial in the *Standard* secured passage of the Fifteenth Amendment in the Senate, where his "name and opinion settled the controversy."[50] In 1867 Phillips had reminded the American Anti-Slavery Society that "[t]he first thing to consult in arranging statesmanship is the ideal, then afterward if you cannot reach it be content with the possible; but always shape for yourself the ideal—the perfect. Remember when you sell out to sell out for as much as you can get."[51]

Phillips the politician no longer urged the adoption of a color-blind constitutional amendment; but when he consulted the ideal, the perfect, Phillips still saw a government color-blind. When he addressed the New England Anti-Slavery Convention in May 1867 on the politics of Reconstruction, it was the antidiscrimination principle—rather than universal suffrage or education—that Phillips described as the ultimate goal of the old antislavery movement:

> we should devote ourselves singly and exclusively to securing . . . the absolute certainty, so far as national organization admits it, that the question of color, the issue of race, the idea of any distinction between men on account of their blood, shall be hereafter forever excluded from American politics. (Applause.) . . . It is not for us to say whether suffrage shall be universal, whether it shall be founded on property or education . . . ; but it is our duty . . . to say that no civil, no social, no political right shall in any instance, in any part of the nation, be dependent on race; especially that the negro race shall not be excluded from any right on account of their blood. . . . When once the nation is absolutely, irrevocably pledged to the principle that there shall be no recognition of race by the United States or by State law, then the work of the great anti-slavery movement which commenced in 1831, is accomplished.[52]

Before a nonabolitionist lyceum audience the following winter he appealed to the same idea: "God has chained this generation to the one great duty of eliminating from American politics the idea of *race*. Whenever an American magistrate . . . is color-blind, unable to distinguish white from black—when that day comes, the duty of this generation is done and sealed, and this epoch is closed. (Applause.)"[53] In May 1869, with the politician's version of the Fifteenth Amendment before the country, Phillips the reformer could still urge the annual meeting of the American Anti-Slavery Society to contemplate "the strong, living heart that makes the nation, its growing wealth, the mind that takes up the problems of the age . . . all these forces moving in one direction, and writing on the national banner, as clearly as a great natural force can ever write it, 'This is a nation that does not know black from white.' (Applause.) That is my hope."[54]

When a constitutional provision does not readily yield a desired meaning, it is tempting to suppose that its authors did not foresee our present circumstance and that, had they done so, they might have written it differently. Wendell Phillips makes it appreciably more difficult to take such a view of any of the Reconstruction Amendments, because he understood at the time the consequences of the choices being made and explained them in language that his contemporaries understood as well as we do. More accurately than anyone else, Phillips understood the problem of securing equality before the law to persons of different races; his proposal for a fourteenth amendment would have placed the legal issue as far as possible beyond dispute. A rigorous equality before the law, Phillips recognized, can be enforced only by a rule of nondiscrimination; and nondiscrimination can be secured only by requiring it in terms. His conclusions have been amply borne out by the constitutional law of racial discrimination over the ensuing 125 years.

Phillips had drawn these conclusions, in advance of any constitutional amendment, from observing the legal fight against Jim Crow laws in Massachusetts. Massachusetts Negroes in the 1840s were free citizens enjoying an acknowledged right to equality. The fact that they still suffered from discrimination made it clear that neither a prohibition of slavery nor a guarantee of equality was adequate constitutional protection. Phillips saw this and explained it; his counsels were rejected; and things turned out as he said they would. Wendell Phillips's fourteenth amendment was rejected, not because his campaign went unheard, but because the Republicans who amended the Constitution understood Phillips's proposals and preferred John Bingham's, the consequences of which were considerably less clear.

In the opening days of the Thirty-ninth Congress, the men who would shortly be drafting the Fourteenth Amendment were presented with a choice that would define the scope of America's constitutional revolution. Culminating the campaign begun by Wendell Phillips two years earlier, an idea of breathtaking radicalism—that racial equality be secured by prohibiting government from distinguishing between black and white—was formally placed before the House on the second day of the session. On December 5, 1865, Thaddeus Stevens introduced a resolution to amend the Constitution in substantially the terms Phillips had recommended:

> *Resolved by the Senate and House of Representatives in Congress assembled,* That the following amendment to the Constitution of the United States shall be proposed, and when ratified by the Legislatures of three fourths of the States shall be valid to all intents and purposes as part of the Constitution of the United States:
> ARTICLE XIII. All national and State laws shall be equally applicable to every citizen, and no discrimination shall be made on account of race and color.[1]

The following day brought a counterproposal:

> Mr. BINGHAM also introduced a joint resolution to amend the Constitution of the United States so as to empower Congress to pass all necessary and proper laws to secure to all persons in every State of the Union equal protection in their rights [of] life, liberty, and property. . . .[2]

The adoption of John Bingham's proposal, as subsequently modified, would permit both the agenda of modern constitutional law and the nation's present-day political form. "Privileges and immunities," "due process," and "equal protection" opened the way to a transformation of the federal system, a shift in the Constitution's center of gravity, beyond the imagination of the most extreme radicals in 1866. What made these developments possible, ironically, was the decision of the Republicans in the Thirty-ninth Congress to reject what in 1866 was the truly radical program.

Political objectives shared by all Republicans in December 1865, from the radicals to the conservatives, provided the immediate inspiration for these contrasting proposals. Laws depriving one race of ordinary civil rights, exemplified by the "Black Codes" enacted that year in some southern states, must be prohibited;[3] and the reconstructed South could not be allowed additional seats in Congress on account of its new black citizens if it denied them the vote. As remedies for these particular instances of racial discrimination, the choice between the Stevens and the Bingham proposals was unusually clear. The radical answer (previously elaborated by Wendell Phillips) was to prohibit racial distinctions altogether; the moderate response would allow those distinctions consistent with "equal protection." The genuine radicals thus proposed to solve the question of representation by imposing impartial suffrage as part of a general abolition of racial distinctions; the moderates were left free to argue that impartial suffrage was not a necessary condition of equality. The radical proposal obviously meant Negro suffrage and an end to laws requiring segregation; it might even have forbidden laws restricting interracial marriage. Much of Republican opinion did not favor any of these consequences, and as a platform for the 1866 elections they would have been nothing short of disastrous. The greatest single attraction of Bingham's alternative was that its consequences were comparatively uncertain. As William Nelson has observed, "Americans of 1866, like Americans of today, could all agree upon the rightfulness of equality only because they did not agree on its meaning."[4]

The choice of the moderate over the radical formula for a constitutional guarantee of civil rights is consistent with the picture of the Thirty-ninth Congress drawn by modern historians, showing a Republican majority dominated, not by radicals, but by a coalition of moderates and conservatives to whose measures the radicals could oppose at most a power of veto.[5] The Republicans' determination to institute national protection for individual rights was qualified by their unwillingness to abandon a constitutional view in which the regulation of civil society was the proper concern of state, not federal, government.[6] In their attitudes toward race, their views of the relative capacities of blacks and whites, Republicans may have differed little from Democrats.[7] The recharacterization of the

Republican consensus as "moderate" rather than "radical" has not affected the continuing debate over the "original understanding" of the Fourteenth Amendment: the genuinely difficult problem of determining the nature and scope of the guarantee of individual rights that the Thirty-ninth Congress and the ratifying state legislatures thought they were adding to the Constitution.[8] But the materials of this familiar controversy have traditionally been limited to those that illuminate the various aspects of the moderate position; while the points at which a moderate proposal stood in opposition to a truly radical one have received curiously little emphasis. The interesting fact that Congress in 1866 considered and rejected a series of proposals that would have made the Constitution explicitly color-blind has been, in consequence, largely forgotten.

The essential distinction between radical and moderate proposals for the federal protection of civil rights lay between a rule of nondiscrimination on the one hand and a guarantee of equality on the other. The choice between the two alternatives recurs in one form or another, directly or indirectly, in the debate over each of the major civil rights issues of the session (with the exception of the bill expanding the powers of the Freedmen's Bureau). Nondiscrimination was rejected in the successive contexts of Negro suffrage and the basis of representation; the civil rights bill; the proposed "Bingham Amendment"; and the Fourteenth Amendment itself. In each instance, Congress indicated that it preferred the more malleable notions of equality and "equal protection" to an unyielding rule of nondiscrimination. By the time it produced a Fourteenth Amendment that countenanced racial discrimination in the franchise even as it guaranteed "the equal protection of the laws," the Thirty-ninth Congress had effectively demonstrated the great political advantage of Bingham's pleasant phrases, which was that they need not mean anything in particular.

The ill-defined promise of "equal protection" and "privileges and immunities" has had political consequences incomparably greater than could have been produced by a constitutional prohibition of racial discrimination. Its Republican sponsors doubtless intended, as Alexander Bickel argued in what remains the single most influential commentary on the subject, that its future effect be left to some extent to future determination.[9] Yet unless we are to attribute to its framers "an undisclosed, conspiratorial purpose" (a view of the matter that Bickel rightly rejected), the evidence shows that an open-ended promise of equality was added to the Constitution because to its moderate proponents it meant less, not more, than the rule of nondiscrimination that was the rejected radical alternative.

The Basis of Representation

In the spring and summer of 1865, as they laid their plans for the convening of the Thirty-ninth Congress, the initial goal of the Republicans was to insist on Negro suffrage as a minimum condition of the southern states' readmission to the Union. By the time Congress met in December, however, it was clear that a suffrage amendment was not politically feasible.[10] Only five states, all in New England (Maine, Massachusetts, New Hampshire, Rhode Island, and Vermont), extended the franchise impartially to black and white citizens.[11] In the fall elections of 1865, voters in Connecticut, Minnesota, and Wisconsin had rejected referendum proposals to permit Negro suffrage in their own states.[12] The persistent unpopularity of impartial suffrage (demonstrated by repeated referenda both before and after congressional passage of the Fourteenth Amendment)[13] made its inclusion in a Republican platform out of the question.

At the opening of Congress, the debate over suffrage took a more practical turn. Whatever their views on the possibility or the desirability of giving the ballot to the ex-slave, all Republicans agreed on the need to do something about the "basis of representation." Unless the Constitution were amended, the abolition of slavery would increase by two-thirds the number of House seats previously allocated to the southern states in respect of their black population; and each additional seat in the House meant an additional seat in the electoral college.[14] To Republicans it was intolerable that the former slave power should enjoy, as the result of the war and emancipation, an accession of influence beyond its already formidable power in the antebellum Congress. The direction of southern political influence would presumably change if the new black citizens, henceforth entitled to representation as "free persons" rather than "other persons," were also permitted to vote; but Republicans whose own states rejected Negro suffrage could see that the freedmen were unlikely to vote in the South for the foreseeable future. The political dilemma was more easily addressed by a change in the basis of federal representation (even though this required a constitutional amendment) than by a quixotic attempt to impose Negro suffrage.

Having reached this preliminary conclusion, the Republican leadership initially favored an amendment to the Constitution making voters, rather than population, the basis of representation.[15] Further examination revealed, however, that such a rule would bring about reapportionment in favor of the West at the expense of the Northeast. Westward migration had left states such as Massachusetts with a relatively high female population; other northeastern states such as New York had a large population of immigrants not yet naturalized. As neither women nor aliens were voters, these states would lose representation under the "voter basis"; without their support the measure had no chance. The ingenious solution, first proposed by Representative James G. Blaine of Maine, was to retain population as the basis of representation but to exclude from the calculation the entire black population of any state in which adult black males were not permitted to vote.[16]

The Blaine Amendment was a particularly callous triumph of expediency over principle. Because the black population of the northern states (most of which denied or restricted Negro suffrage) was not large enough to make a difference in the apportionment, the Republicans could propose, in effect, to exclude all of the nation's black people (rather than just two-fifths of them) from the basis of representation. Because the whole idea of the Blaine Amendment (as opposed to the "voter basis") was that other classes of nonvoters, notably women, should continue to be represented, it was impossible to frame the new proposal in terms that did not countenance denial of the franchise on the basis of race. The Blaine Amendment would thus have placed in the Constitution what the framers had managed to avoid in 1787: an explicit recognition of racial differences, and an express acknowledgment that race might be made the basis of distinctions in political rights.

This question of principle, which eventually caused the defeat of the Blaine Amendment in the Senate at the hands of Charles Sumner, divided the Republican members of the Joint Committee on Reconstruction.[17] At a meeting of the committee on January 12, 1866, after a straw vote showed the Republicans divided between the "voter basis" and the Blaine proposal, the question was referred to an all-Republican subcommittee whose membership included both Stevens and Bingham, as well as William Pitt Fessenden of Maine, chairman of the committee on behalf of the Senate. The contrasting proposals of Stevens and Bingham for a constitutional amendment to guarantee civil rights—substantially identical with those they had introduced in the House a month earlier—were referred to the same subcommittee, to be considered in conjunction with the basis of representation.[18]

The subcommittee's report was presented to the full committee on January 20; and in this document the critical relationship between the issues of representation and civil rights became clear. Three constitutional amendments were proposed for consideration, the first two in the alternative:

Article A.

Representatives and direct taxes shall be apportioned among the several States within this Union, according to the respective numbers of citizens of the United States in each State; and all provisions in the Constitution or laws of any State, whereby any distinction is made in political or civil rights or privileges, on account of race, creed or color, shall be inoperative and void.

Or the following:

Article B.

Representatives and direct taxes shall be apportioned among the several States which may be included within this Union, according to their respective numbers, counting the whole number of citizens of the United States in each State; provided that, whenever the elective franchise shall be denied or abridged in any State on account of race, creed or color, all persons of such race, creed or color, shall be excluded from the basis of representation.

Article C.

Congress shall have power to make all laws necessary and proper to secure to all citizens of the United States, in every State, the same political rights and privileges; and to all persons in every State equal protection in the enjoyment of life, liberty and property.[19]

"Article A" is recognizably Stevens's attempt to ground a civil rights amendment on the principle of nondiscrimination. It makes no change in the basis of representation, because it imposes impartial suffrage as one consequence of a general color blindness. "Article B" is the Blaine Amendment. "Article C" is one version of Bingham's civil rights amendment, momentarily expanded (by comparison with earlier and subsequent formulations) to enable Congress to legislate on the question of suffrage at some future date.

Following a discussion that the committee's journal does not record, Stevens was persuaded was to abandon his own proposition. On Stevens's motion, the Joint Committee voted eleven to three (one absent) to take Article B rather than Article A as the starting point for its work on a constitutional amendment.[20] The Blaine Amendment was reported out separately by the committee: Stevens introduced the resolution and led the debate in the House. But on January 31, as he closed the debate and called for a vote, Stevens made clear his personal preference for another approach:

> I had another proposition, which I hope may again be brought forward. It is this:
>> All national and State laws shall be equally applicable to every citizen, and no discrimination shall be made on account of race or color.
>
> There is the genuine proposition; that is the one I love; that is the one which I hope, before we separate, we shall have educated ourselves up to the idea of adopting, and that we shall have educated our people up to the point of ratifying. But it would not be wise to entangle the present proposition [the Blaine Amendment] with that one. The one might drag down the other; and although I have not obtained what I want, I am content to take what, after comparing ideas with others, I believe we can carry through the States; and I believe we can carry this proposition.[21]

Those with whom Stevens had compared ideas certainly included Fessenden. A week later, when Fessenden replied in the Senate to the first of Sumner's attacks on the Blaine Amendment,[22] his remarks doubtless reflected the discussions that had taken place as the Joint Committee debated the merits of Article A versus Article B. Why not propose a simple amendment, Fessenden asked Sumner,

> doing away at once with all distinctions on account of race or color in all the States of this Union so far as regards civil and political rights, privileges, and immunities? That would go to the root of the matter. . . . [A]lthough I can see difficulties that would arise from it, yet trusting to time to soften them, and being desirous, if I can, to put into the Constitution a principle that commends itself to the consideration of every enlightened mind at once, I would prefer something of that sort. . . . But the argument that addressed itself to the committee was, what can we accomplish? What can pass? If we report a provision of this kind is there the slightest probability that it will be adopted by the States and become a part of the Constitution of the United States? It is perfectly evident that there could be no hope of that description.[23]

Democrats in the House had attacked the Blaine Amendment for its indirection. Fessenden made this a virtue, protesting that "the great excellence of [the amendment]—and I think it is an excellence—is, that it accomplishes indirectly what we may not have the power to accomplish directly. If we cannot put into the Constitution, owing to existing prejudices and existing institutions, an entire exclusion of all class distinctions, the next question is, can we accomplish that work in any other way?"[24] The salve to Republican consciences was that the prospect of increased representation would eventually induce the southern states to permit their black citizens to vote. Nothing in the amendment, of course, would have operated directly or indirectly to effect "an entire exclusion of all class distinctions." That objective had been left in the committee room with Article A.

At the conclusion of Senate debate on the Blaine Amendment, March 7 and 9, Sumner renewed his attack in violent language. The proposal of the Joint Committee, "the most utterly reprehensible and unpardonable" ever brought into Congress, was merely "a device to crystallize into organic law the disfranchisement of a race," defying "the sovereign rule of the Constitution, which knows no distinction of color." "Adopt this proposition," Sumner informed his Republican colleagues,

> and you will be little better than the foul Harpies who defiled the feast that was spread. The Constitution is the feast spread for our country, and you are now hurrying to drop into its text a political obscenity, and to spread on its page a disgusting ordure,
> > "Defiling all you find,
> And parting leave a loathsome stench behind."
> If I use plain language it is because the occasion requires it.[25]

Sumner can scarcely have hoped to gain adherents with such expressions, and he was duly rebuked by Fessenden.[26] A color-blind joint resolution proposed by Sumner as a substitute for the Blaine Amendment was defeated by a vote of thirty-nine to eight (three absent).[27] A companion measure offered by Richard Yates of Illinois was defeated by the same margin.[28] Two more last-ditch Sumner amendments—one prohibiting the denial of suffrage on account of race, the other providing that any race denied the vote should be exempt from taxation—were summarily voted down in the minutes before the final vote.[29] Even so, Sumner's unlikely coalition of extreme radicals, conservative Republicans, and Democrats— "the united forces of self-righteous Republicans and unrighteous copperheads," according to Stevens[30]—succeeded in denying the Blaine Amendment the necessary two-thirds majority in the Senate, and the proposal was defeated.[31]

In the view of practical men like Fessenden and Stevens, the only result of Sumner's narrow-minded opposition was to deprive the country of a stronger measure and leave it to make do with a weaker one: Stevens complained that the Blaine Amendment had been "slaughtered by a puerile and pedantic criticism."[32] In the end, section 2 of the Fourteenth Amendment (passed by the Senate without comment from Sumner but with his vote) was devised to do the same political work as the Blaine Amendment, but with a mechanism so much less effective that it has never been put to use.[33] Supporters of Negro suffrage like Wendell Phillips rightly considered section 2 no less an abandonment of the freedman than the Blaine Amendment would have been. Even so, Sumner's intractability helped to preserve for the Reconstruction Amendments an important part of their range of available meaning. On its face, the language of section 2 acknowledged no more than the undisputed power of the states to regulate the franchise. By contrast, the Blaine Amendment would necessarily have acknowledged the states' power to deny the franchise on the basis of race. It would be appreciably more difficult to argue for a color-blind interpretation of Bingham's equal protection clause if the Congress that adopted it had also added to the Constitution a provision to be applicable "whenever the elective franchise shall be denied or abridged in any State on account of race." If a rule of color blindness is one of those we may legitimately choose to see today in the language of the Fourteenth Amendment,[34] that possibility exists in no small measure as a result of Charles Sumner's intransigence.

The Civil Rights Bill

It was the demonstrable consensus of the Thirty-ninth Congress that section 1 of the Fourteenth Amendment "constitutionalized" the Civil Rights Act of 1866.[35] This meant either that the amendment protected the principles of the Act from repeal by a simple majority of the next Democratic Congress (the view of the Republican leadership), or that it attempted to confer constitutional authority after the fact for what had been an unconstitutional enactment (the view of the Democrats), or both (the view of John Bingham). Because congressional debate on the Fourteenth Amendment itself virtually ignored its all-important first section, except to identify it with the principles of the Civil Rights Act, the debates on the civil rights bill earlier in the session have been minutely examined for evidence as to the "original understanding" of the effect of the constitutional amendment. For present purposes it will be sufficient to recall the single most notable incident in the legislative history of the Civil Rights Act of 1866: the amendment of the civil rights bill in the House, at the instance of John Bingham, to delete from the original proposal its broad antidiscrimination provision.

As introduced in the Senate on January 29 by Lyman Trumbull of Illinois, chairman of the Senate Judiciary Committee, the first section of the bill provided:

> *That there shall be no discrimination in civil rights or immunities among the inhabitants of any State or Territory of the United States on account of race, color, or previous condition of slavery;* but the inhabitants of every race and color, without regard to any previous condition of slavery or involuntary servitude, except as a punishment for crime whereof the party shall have been duly convicted, shall have the same right to make and enforce contracts, to sue, be parties, and give evidence, to inherit, purchase, lease, sell, hold, and convey real and personal property, and to full and equal benefit of all laws and proceedings for the security of person and property, and shall be subject to like punishment, pains, and penalties, and to none other, any law, statute, ordinance, regulation, or custom to the contrary notwithstanding.[36]

Debate in both houses over this section of the bill centered on two issues: the authority of Congress to enact it, and the meaning of the phrase "civil rights or immunities." On the latter question, the position of the Republican leadership was that "civil rights and immunities" included only those rights that were specifically enumerated in the remainder of the paragraph, and that they assuredly did not include suffrage, said to be a "political" rather than a "civil" right.[37] The enumerated rights were thought to require federal protection because precisely those incidents of citizenship—the right to contract and to hold property, the freedom from special and unequal punishments—were denied to freedmen by the Black Codes adopted in 1865 in certain of the former slave states.[38]

Senate Democrats expressed alarm at the potential reach of a prohibition of discrimination in "civil rights or immunities." Willard Saulsbury of Delaware argued, quite plausibly to modern ears, that the term *civil rights* "in its most comprehensive signification includes every species of right that man can enjoy other than those the foundation of which rests exclusively in nature and in the law of nature." While Trumbull was no doubt sincere—Saulsbury conceded—in asserting that by "civil rights" he meant only the right to make contracts, to sue, and so forth, "the question is not what he means, but what the courts will say the law means."[39] Reverdy

Johnson of Maryland argued, over Trumbull's protestations, that the bill would invalidate state laws prohibiting interracial marriage, adding that "whether I am wrong or not . . . I suppose all the Senate will admit that the error is not so gross a one that the courts may not fall into it."[40] Republicans treated these warnings as a partisan attempt to discredit a measure whose plain meaning was unexceptionable, and the bill passed the Senate easily on a straight party vote.[41]

Bingham's intervention made the difference in the House. The early stages of the House debate on the civil rights bill paralleled the debate in the Senate: the Republican leadership reassured members that only the enumerated civil rights would be guaranteed, while the Democrats warned that the breadth of the term *civil rights* was potentially limitless.[42] On March 8 Bingham moved to recommit the bill with instructions to strike the clause prohibiting discrimination in civil rights or immunities.[43] In a speech on March 9 (the day the Senate voted down the Blaine Amendment), Bingham explained his opposition to the antidiscrimination provision. In view of Bingham's tireless efforts on the Joint Committee, ultimately successful, to avoid recourse to antidiscrimination language as the foundation of section 1 of the Fourteenth Amendment, his remarks on this occasion are of considerable significance.

Bingham agreed with the Democrats that Congress lacked authority to enact a federal guarantee of civil rights. For this reason, he explained, he would vote against the bill in any event; yet he urged his colleagues that by striking the antidiscrimination clause they might "take from the bill its oppressive and I might say its unjust provisions." For Bingham, the scope of "civil rights" was virtually unlimited:

> What are civil rights? . . . I respectfully submit . . . that by all authority the term "civil rights" as used in this bill does include and embrace every right that pertains to the citizen as such . . . every right that pertains to the citizen under the Constitution, laws, and Government of this country. . . . If this be so, are not political rights all embraced in the term "civil rights," and must it not of necessity be so interpreted?

The bill would therefore interfere with the domestic institutions of nearly every state.

> If civil rights has this extent, what, then, is proposed by the provision of the first section? Simply to strike down by congressional enactment every State constitution which makes a discrimination on account of race or color in any of the civil rights of the citizen. I might say here, without

the least fear of contradiction, that there is scarcely a State in this Union which does not, by its constitution or by its statute laws, make some discrimination on account of race or color between citizens of the United States in respect of civil rights. . . .

By the constitution of my own State neither the right of the elective franchise nor the franchise of office can be conferred upon any citizen of the United States save upon a white citizen of the United States. What do you propose to do by this bill? You propose to make it a misdemeanor, punishable upon conviction by fine and imprisonment in the penitentiary, for the Governor of Ohio to obey the requirements of the constitution of the State. . . .[44]

The extent of Bingham's commitment to civil rights for the Negro is controversial, and the significance of this speech has been much debated.[45] But if one idea emerges clearly, it is that Bingham did not favor federal interference with every state constitution or statute making "some discrimination on account of race or color between citizens of the United States in respect of civil rights." Subsequent passages of the speech express Bingham's readiness to use constitutional means to protect from discrimination those rights enumerated in the civil rights bill; he expands this list at one point to include the right to hold public office.[46] But Bingham makes no favorable reference even to Negro suffrage, let alone to the abolition of all forms of legal discrimination. From the first days of the session Bingham had been offering plausible alternatives to the blanket rule of nondiscrimination favored by men like Phillips and Stevens; and in his remarks on the civil rights bill Bingham plainly implied, if he did not state, that an unqualified rule of nondiscrimination would constitute an excessive and inappropriate guarantee of civil rights for the Negro.

Bingham's motion to recommit was defeated, as the Democrats (who wished to leave the bill as oppressive as possible) voted solidly with the Republican leadership.[47] But his arguments told. When the civil rights bill was reported back on March 13, the Judiciary Committee proposed to strike the antidiscrimination clause as Bingham had suggested. James Wilson of Iowa, the committee chairman, explained that while he did not himself think the change would make any material difference, "some gentlemen were apprehensive that the words we propose to strike out might give warrant for a latitudinarian construction not intended."[48]

The Republicans in the House were astute enough to recognize, after Bingham joined the Democrats in pointing it out, that the courts' interpretation of "civil rights and immunities" would not ultimately be restricted by Trumbull's enumeration, and that—with rare exceptions—the constitutions and laws of their own states imposed distinctions on racial lines that a federal rule of "no discrimination" might very well upset. By deleting the antidiscrimination clause, the Thirty-ninth Congress did what it could to ensure that the Civil Rights Act of 1866 would be what the Republican leadership had represented: a measure directed primarily at the Black Codes, and a civil rights act for the southern states only. As such it could readily be passed (over President Johnson's veto) by a Congress in which the South was not represented.

When the issue was joined, an unqualified rule of nondiscrimination mustered no measurable support in the Thirty-ninth Congress. Bingham's striking success in procuring the amendment of a bill he continued to oppose[49] paralleled his accomplishments in the Joint Committee, where he had already prevailed over Stevens's antidiscrimination proposals and would shortly succeed in excluding "no discrimination" from the text of the Fourteenth Amendment.

The Bingham Amendment

Bingham's position throughout the House debate on the civil rights bill was that federal protection of civil rights should be effected by means of a constitutional amendment. One such amendment, drafted by Bingham for the Joint Committee, had already been debated and effectively rejected in the House:

> Article—. The Congress shall have power to make all laws which shall be necessary and proper to secure to the citizens of each State all privileges and immunities of citizens in the several States, and to all persons in the several States equal protection in the rights of life, liberty, and property.[50]

Debate on this proposal was largely taken up with members' concerns about the new and expansive authority the amendment would confer upon Congress.[51] From a modern perspective, the most striking feature of Bingham's proposal is that it left the legal protection of black citizens entirely to the possibility of future congressional action. The amendment of its own force would not have eliminated a single racial classification. Its immediate effect on the laws of the states—unlike the antidiscrimination amendments Stevens had proposed—would thus have been nil. Bingham's amendment would merely have authorized Congress to pass laws eliminating those discriminations of which it disapproved, without disturbing those that were expedient and beneficial.

It was only in the last minutes of a three-day debate that anyone pointed out how little the amendment would actually do for civil rights. Giles Hotchkiss, Republican of New York, rose to explain why he would vote against the proposal. While freedom from class discrimination should be a constitutional right, he argued, the Bingham Amendment "proposes to leave it to the caprice of Congress":

> Mr. Speaker, I make these remarks because I do not wish to be placed in the wrong upon this question. I think the gentleman from Ohio [Mr. BINGHAM] is not sufficiently radical in his views on this subject. I think he is a conservative. [Laughter.] I do not make the remark in any offensive sense. But I want him to go to the root of this matter. . . . Why not provide by an amendment to the Constitution that no State shall discriminate against any class of its citizens[?][52]

Hotchkiss, of course, had not been party to the deliberations of the Joint Committee in which "equal protection," rather than nondiscrimination, had been chosen as the basis on which civil rights should be protected.

One further exchange from the House debate on the Bingham Amendment is worth noticing. Robert Hale of New York, criticizing the reach of authority conferred by the amendment, argued that it would enable Congress to override "all State legislation . . . affecting the individual citizen." Thaddeus Stevens interrupted:

> Does the gentleman mean to say that, under this provision, Congress could interfere in any case where the legislation of a State was equal, impartial to all? Or is it not simply to provide that, where any State makes a distinction in the same law between different classes of individuals, Congress shall have power to correct such discrimination and inequality? Does this proposition mean anything more than that?[53]

Stevens's attention is here so firmly fixed on what he understands to be the object of the amendment—a grant of power to Congress to legislate against the Black Codes—that he fails to see that the reach of the proposed language is actually very different. Hale offers an example: state laws restricting the property rights of married women would, by the Bingham

Amendment, become liable to displacement by federal enactment. But Stevens still has not seen the point:

> Mr. STEVENS. If I do not interrupt the gentleman I will say a word. When a distinction is made between two married people or two *femmes sole,* then it is unequal legislation; but where all of the same class are dealt with in the same way there is no pretense of inequality.
>
> Mr. HALE. The gentleman will pardon me; his argument seems to me to be more specious than sound. The language of the section under consideration gives to *all persons* equal protection. Now, if that means you shall extend to one married woman the same protection you extend to another, and not the same you extend to unmarried women or men, then by parity of reasoning it will be sufficient if you extend to one negro the same rights you do to another, but not those you extend to a white man.[54]

This brief exchange, which reveals more about the real significance of "equal protection" than the entire debate on the Fourteenth Amendment in the Thirty-ninth Congress, illuminates the antagonism between "equal protection" and nondiscrimination as a basis for protecting civil rights. It also illustrates, in Stevens's mistake, how easy it was even for those members most interested in the subject to underestimate the significance of the choice between the two principles. Either would accomplish the objective immediately in view, which was the elimination of the Black Codes. Men like Stevens thought it was so obvious which "inequalities" they were aiming at that (as Hale deftly demonstrated) they momentarily lost sight of the fact that the entire legal system is necessarily a fabric of inequalities and discriminations, of categories and classifications.

The antidiscrimination principle would forbid discrimination on account of race, not discrimination in general: its application is self-defining and limits government discretion. Bingham's "equal protection" was profoundly different at this key point, for reasons that are implicit in Hale's argument. "Equal protection," if it is not to destroy altogether the possibility of government, can mean only "equal treatment for those who should be treated equally." Its application requires another theory to determine which classifications are appropriate. By themselves, however, the words *equal protection* tell us little or nothing about a theory of classification. And even supposing "equality" can be readily ascertained, the problem of classification—implicit in almost every act of government—comprehends the whole difficulty of government itself. Bingham's easy formula, in short, commands the application of a rule without standards; it is accordingly, as Hale perceived, a grant of plenary authority. If Congress is authorized to legislate for "equal protection," Congress is necessarily authorized to classify; if Congress may classify, Congress may govern. If such authority extends to measures for the protection of "life, liberty, and property," its minimum scope, as Hale accurately stated, includes "all State legislation . . . affecting the individual citizen." In the Bingham Amendment, Hale saw a threat that any aspect of such legislation might thereafter be "overridden, . . . repealed or abolished, and the law of Congress established instead."[55] The change that was made when the Bingham Amendment later reappeared as section 1 of the Fourteenth Amendment (from "Congress shall have power" to "No State shall") made the Supreme Court, rather than Congress, the principal instrument of Hale's prophecy.

Few members saw as lucidly as Hale the implications of "equal protection"; Bingham himself manifestly did not. With respect to the immediate significance of an "equal protection" rather than a "no discrimination" standard, however, Bingham was surely not mistaken. Either approach would dispose of the Black Codes. But whereas "no discrimination" would "simply . . . strike down . . . every State constitution which makes a discrimination on account of race or color," the Bingham Amendment left it to Congress to determine which forms of discrimination were consistent with "equal protection" and which were not. Bingham's preference— shared by the Thirty-ninth Congress and by most of our government authorities, most of the time since—was to retain the discretion to discriminate by race as appropriate.

The Fourteenth Amendment

By mid-April 1866 the Joint Committee was under increasing pressure to be seen to be doing something about Reconstruction. So far, the committee had reported two constitutional amendments (Blaine's on the basis of representation, Bingham's on civil rights), neither of which had found favor with Congress. Returning to the task, the committee was evidently prepared to turn to outsiders for suggestions. On April 16, meeting for the first time since March 5, the committee invited William Stewart (a Sumnerite radical from Nevada) to address it in support of an antidiscrimination constitutional amendment he had just introduced in the Senate.[56] Stewart's proposal was not favorably received.[57] But on April 21, when Stevens presented a proposed amendment "not of his own framing, but which he should support,"[58] the Joint Committee appeared to have found a compromise it could work with.

The new draft had been proposed to Stevens by Robert Dale Owen, one of the earliest advocates of Wendell Phillips's antidiscrimination amendment.[59] It ran as follows:

Article—

Section 1. No discrimination shall be made by any state, nor by the United States, as to the civil rights of persons because of race, color, or previous condition of servitude.

Sec. 2. From and after the fourth day of July, in the year one thousand eight hundred and seventy-six, no discrimination shall be made by any state, nor by the United States, as to the enjoyment by classes of persons of the right of suffrage, because of race, color, or previous condition of servitude.

Sec. 3. Until the fourth day of July, one thousand eight hundred and seventy-six, no class of persons, as to the right of any of whom to suffrage discrimination shall be made by any state, because of race, color, or previous condition of servitude, shall be included in the basis of representation.

Sec. 4. Debts incurred in aid of insurrection or of war against the Union, and claims of compensation for loss of involuntary service or labor, shall not be paid by any state nor by the United States.

Sec. 5. Congress shall have power to enforce by appropriate legislation, the provisions of this article.[60]

The proposal was an astute compromise. To make antidiscrimination palatable, Owen proposed to delay for ten years the imposition of Negro suffrage. Prevailing Republican sentiment conceded that the freedman would scarcely be qualified to vote before he had received some education;[61] and apart from the question of qualifications, the Joint Committee had reached the conclusion that immediate suffrage was not politically feasible. Under Owen's plan, the nation would celebrate the centennial of the Declaration of Independence under a color-blind Constitution. In the meantime, the political influence of the South would be restrained by a temporary version of the Blaine Amendment.[62]

The committee proceeded to consider the Owen proposal section by section. Bingham immediately proposed to amend the first section by adding the following: "nor shall any state deny to any person within its jurisdiction the equal protection of the laws, nor take private property for public use without just compensation." Bingham's amendment was defeated in a bipartisan vote, whereupon section 1 as proposed by Owen was adopted by a vote of ten to two (three absent).[63] The second, third, and fourth sections were successively adopted. Bingham then moved to insert a new section 5 before the enforcement provision, in which there appeared for the first time the language now included in section 1 of the Fourteenth Amendment:

> Sec. 5. No state shall make or enforce any law which shall abridge the privileges or immunities of citizens of the United States; nor shall any state deprive any person of life, liberty or property without due process of law, nor deny to any person within its jurisdiction the equal protection of the laws.

The most significant sentence of the most significant constitutional amendment in American history had apparently been drafted by Bingham in the course of the meeting, while discussion droned on about sections 2, 3, and 4 of the Owen proposal. Bingham's new section was adopted, the vote being precisely the same as on section 1.[64]

The committee's actions thus far are already puzzling. Why, after refusing to let Bingham add "equal protection" to Owen's first section, should it vote a few hours later to add not just "equal protection" but also "privileges and immunities" and "due process"? Why, for that matter, did Bingham first try to link "equal protection" with a state "takings clause" before eventually hitting on the winning combination? But the committee's baffling reversals were only beginning. When it next took up the Owen proposal, on April 25, George Williams of Oregon (a conservative Republican senator) moved to *strike* section 5—the section just added, on Bingham's motion, at the previous meeting. The motion carried by a vote of seven to five (three absent), and the committee voted to report the amendment as modified.[65] Bingham then moved that the committee report his section as a separate constitutional amendment; the motion was soundly defeated.[66] For whatever reasons, Bingham and "equal protection" had now suffered a decisive rejection: the amendment that the committee was about to report was Owen's antidiscrimination proposal in its original form. At this critical moment, Williams moved to reconsider the vote to report the amendment. Fessenden, who was suffering from varioloid (a mild form of smallpox), had missed all the meetings at which the proposal had been discussed, and on reflection the committee thought it might reflect a lack of courtesy to make its most important report in the absence of its chairman.[67] The motion to reconsider was carried, and the committee adjourned to await Fessenden's return.[68]

When the committee reconvened on April 28 with Fessenden presiding, it completely overhauled the draft amendment that three days earlier it had voted to report. Section 2, conferring prospective Negro suffrage, was deleted on Stevens's motion. Section 3 (the ten-year Blaine Amendment) was replaced by a provision reducing the basis of representation in proportion to the number of adult males denied the vote: this became the second section of the proposal and, eventually, section 2 of the Fourteenth Amendment. The committee proceeded to tinker with Owen's section 4, the language repudiating Confederate debt; after lengthy discussion it added a new section 3 disfranchising, for the congressional and presidential elections of 1866 and 1868, "all persons who voluntarily adhered to the late insurrection."[69] Finally, Bingham moved to strike out Owen's section 1 ("no discrimination") and to replace it with his own "equal protection" provision: the language that had earlier been adopted, and then deleted, as section 5. Bingham's motion was carried, ending the last chance that an explicit statement of the antidiscrimination principle might be added to the Constitution.[70]

What had happened between April 25 and April 28 to bring about this extraordinary reversal? Stevens's explanation as quoted by Owen—who saw his proposal emerge from the Joint Committee in nearly unrecognizable form—is the only testimony by a committee member:

Our action on your amendment had, it seems, got noised abroad. In the course of last week the members from New York, from Illinois, and from your State too, Owen,—from Indiana,—held, each separately, a caucus to consider whether equality of suffrage, present or prospective, ought to form a part of the republican programme for the coming canvass. They were afraid, so some of them told me, that if there was "a nigger in the wood-pile" at all (that was the phrase), it would be used against them as an electioneering handle, and some of them—hang their cowardice!—might lose their elections. By inconsiderable majorities each of these caucuses decided that negro suffrage, in any shape, ought to be excluded from the platform; and they communicated these decisions to us. Our committee hadn't backbone enough to maintain its ground. Yesterday the vote on your plan was reconsidered, your amendment was laid on the table, and in the course of the next three hours we contrived to patch together—well, what you've read this morning.[71]

Although Stevens was less than candid about his own role in the committee's change of course, his account has about it the ring of truth. On April 26 the *New York Times* had already reported a division within the committee between the supporters of Negro suffrage and those who were "willing to throw the question overboard."[72] State delegations were convening, as Stevens reported, and the work of the committee was widely assessed in light of its probable impact on the fall elections.[73] Of the various amendments made by the committee on April 28, the tendency of all those whose import is clear is in the direction of political expediency and partisan advantage. In speculating as to the significance of the day's final amendment—the mystifying reinsertion of Bingham's language in place of Owen's section 1—we may conjecture that similar motives inspired the Republican votes.[74]

It is not, finally, very difficult to imagine the thrust of Bingham's remarks when he moved the deletion of "no discrimination." The consensus of the Republican members was that nothing in the committee's proposal should hold out the prospect of Negro suffrage, immediate or prospective. That being the case, what was Congress likely to make of "no discrimination in civil rights"? This was the very language that Bingham, in early March, had persuaded the House to strike from the civil rights bill. Members were concerned, as the earlier debate had made clear, that the term *civil rights* either included suffrage or might, through some "latitudinarian interpretation," be held to do so. Bingham himself had urged the House on March 9 that political rights were "all embraced in the term 'civil rights.'"[75] Of course, Bingham might be wrong: no one could know for certain what "civil rights" might include. But what Republican wanted to hear his Democratic opponent, during the fall campaign that was fast approaching, explain the proposed constitutional amendment by quoting Representative Bingham on the meaning of "civil rights"?

At the opening of the session, both Stevens and Bingham had proposed constitutional amendments affording a federal guarantee of what Sumner liked to call equality before the law. As a matter of legal workmanship, Stevens's nondiscrimination formula (devised for him by Wendell Phillips) was incomparably superior, displaying at the same time the greater economy of means and the certainty of greater effectiveness. A prohibition of federal and state laws that discriminate on account of race or color was readily understandable, its violation easily recognized. Without using the word "equality," it contained, in its promise of nondiscriminatory treatment, the most substantial guarantee of legal equality the law can enforce. Its simple, comprehensive prohibition would have resolved in favor of the Negro every issue of civil rights and legal equality still visible after the abolition of slavery. It was the uncompromising effectiveness of the formula that made it politically unacceptable. In its place Bingham proposed an unwieldy guarantee of affirmative rights, the source and scope of which were alike unknowable. The absence of any clear meaning to Bingham's guarantee meant that its enforcement, in an unsympathetic climate, would narrow to the vanishing point. And although it added to the Constitution in so many words a promise of equal treatment, a guarantee of "equal protection," unlike the rule of nondiscrimination, had no content of its own; it could impose no constitutional limitation independent of the social and political values of judges.

For Bingham and others, a constitutional amendment guaranteeing the natural rights of citizens against infringement by the states (however such rights were identified) may conceivably have been the paramount object. The Republican consensus as a whole—the votes that carried the Fourteenth Amendment in the Thirty-ninth Congress—chose Bingham's formula as the lesser of two evils. Requiring a constitutional provision that would make Black Codes impossible, Republicans embarked on the perilous course of protecting undefined rights against state infringement, despite their fundamental disinclination to disturb the federal structure, because the straightforward alternative had consequences that were clear but unacceptable. The effective way to secure the equality of the races before the law was to impose a rule of nondiscrimination. Contemplating the consequences of such a rule in 1866, Republicans decided that what they wanted after all was only a selective and partial equality before the law. The way to achieve this, they discovered, was to guarantee "equality," leaving it to others to determine what "equality" might entail.

6 | The Judicial Assessment

When the Fourteenth Amendment emerged from the Thirty-ninth Congress without the explicit antidiscrimination provision that Phillips and Stevens had favored, the task facing proponents of a color-blind Constitution was to explain that a prohibition of racial classifications was nevertheless implicit in the document. Writing to Chief Justice Salmon P. Chase in January 1867, the New York lawyer and reformer John Jay (grandson of the first chief justice) urged that the Thirteenth Amendment might still be made to yield the rule of nondiscrimination that Congress had failed to include in the Fourteenth:

> The decision which I most wish to see pronounced by your Court is that the adoption of the Amendment abolishing Slavery destroyed the only exception recognized by the Constitution to the great principle of the Declaration of Independence, and that from the date of the adoption of the Amendment all persons black and white stand upon an equal footing; that all state legislation establishing or recognizing elass distinctions of elas race or color are void. This is a proposition easy to be understood, & I think capable of easy demonstration. It would give us a broad National policy on which to reconstruct the Union . . . [and would] clear our path of various troublesome questions that make our progress difficult.[1]

In January 1875, protesting the failure of the pending civil rights bill to require integrated public schools, Phillips appealed to an unwritten color-blind amendment: "If the war settled anything it settled this: that neither Law nor Constitution here can *recognize race* in any way, or in any circumstances."[2] This was not the conclusion of the courts. During the thirty years that separated the drafting of the Fourteenth Amendment from Justice Harlan's opinion in *Plessy v. Ferguson,* state and lower federal courts were repeatedly called upon to determine whether the amendment embodied a rule of nondiscrimination; quite naturally, from a lawyer's point of view, they found that it did not. There were isolated exceptions to this judicial consensus, but it would be exaggerating their importance to see in the cases a real division of opinion.

The testing question was the legality of state-imposed racial segregation. Beginning with *Roberts* in 1849, and continuing through more than a century of litigation thereafter, segregation was the issue that called forth the color-blind contention because segregation—viewed in the abstract, as courts chose to view it—was the issue on which a rule of equality and a rule of nondiscrimination no longer yielded the same result. Following the ratification of the Fourteenth Amendment in 1868, the few northern states that still provided public schools for white children only (making no provision for blacks or other minorities) amended their school statutes to substitute "separate but equal" provisions;[3] southern laws providing that black and white citizens be separately taxed to support separate (and consequently unequal) school systems were at least occasionally held unconstitutional.[4] This much followed from "equal protection" without great difficulty. But as Sumner had already discovered, the further contention that "equal protection" forbade the government to teach black and white children separately proved very difficult to establish. The framers of the Fourteenth Amendment had declined to write the antidiscrimination principle into the Constitution, and the first generation of judges to construe the amendment declined to read what had not been written.

The Supreme Court decisions ultimately present no exception to the rule. Although the question whether the Reconstruction Amendments prohibited segregation did not come before the Court until *Plessy* in 1896, earlier decisions had already established the majority's disinclination to allow any broader meaning to the amendments than their language plainly required.[5] The critical decision in the *Slaughter-House Cases* denied even that much meaning to the "privileges or immunities" clause of the Fourteenth Amendment.[6] The Supreme Court cases of the period nevertheless proved a source of encouragement for subsequent generations of civil rights plaintiffs, who could disregard the almost uniformly negative thrust of the decisions while emphasizing some positive things that had been said along the way. Isolated statements held out the possibility of a different judicial development, one by which the antidiscrimination principle might eventually be discovered within the generality of Bingham's "equal protection." From the 1880s to the 1950s, the antidiscrimination passages from the opinions in the *Slaughter-House Cases* and *Strauder v. West Virginia*[7] were so frequently cited by opponents of segregation that it was their expansive statements, and not their narrower holdings, for which these landmark cases seemed sometimes to stand.

The *Slaughter-House Cases* arose from a contest between rival factions of New Orleans politicians over the spoils to be extracted from the privilege of operating the municipal abattoirs.[8] The complaining parties asserted, among other things, that a corrupt legislature's award of a monopoly to their competitors denied them privileges or immunities guaranteed by the Fourteenth Amendment against abridgment by the states. A narrow majority of the Supreme Court declined, for the time being, the invitation to elaborate and enforce against the states an open-ended list of "privileges or immunities" attaching to national citizenship. Explaining this abrupt refusal, Justice Samuel Miller referred to the history of the amendments and their evident purpose. His language on this occasion, the first time the Reconstruction Amendments had ever been construed by the Court, could be quoted thereafter to justify an expansive reading of their provisions whenever the rights of black citizens might be at issue:

> [I]n the light of this recapitulation of events, almost too recent to be called history, but which are familiar to us all; and on the most casual examination of the language of these amendments, no one can fail to be impressed with the one pervading purpose found in them all, lying at the foundation of each, and without which none of them would have been even suggested; we mean the freedom of the slave race, the security and firm establishment of that freedom, and the protection of the newly-made freeman and citizen from the oppressions of those who had formerly exercised unlimited dominion over him.

The Court, he continued, would respect the language of the amendments as well as their spirit, and thus would not deny the protection of rights "which properly and necessarily fall within the protection of these articles . . . though the party interested may not be of African descent."

> But what we do say, and what we wish to be understood is, that in any fair and just construction of any section or phrase of these amendments, it is necessary to look to the purpose which we have said was the pervading spirit of them all, the evil which they were designed to remedy, and the process of continued addition to the Constitution, until that purpose was supposed to be accomplished, as far as constitutional law can accomplish it.[9]

In context, the reference to the "pervading spirit" of the amendments was intended to be restrictive. Quoted countless times thereafter by civil rights plaintiffs, Justice Miller's remarks were taken as summing up (with the authority of the Court) an affirmative and expansive reading of the Fourteenth Amendment, one in which the "process of continued addition to the Constitution" should be honored by a judicial interpretation that reflected its "pervading spirit" as a means to racial justice. The words came to represent an alternative view of the Fourteenth Amendment that the Supreme Court, having once enunciated it, might still reclaim when it chose.[10]

The following term, in *Railroad Co. v. Brown*,[11] the Court gave an unusually expansive reading to a civil rights statute, going out of its way to find a command of nondiscrimination in words whose necessary meaning was something narrower. Catharine Brown, a black woman traveling from Alexandria to Washington, refused to leave her seat in a railroad car reserved for white passengers, whereupon she was ejected "by force and with insult."[12] She sought damages from the railroad in tort. In most jurisdictions at this time, a railroad was permitted to enforce "reasonable regulations" segregating its white and black passengers, so long as the separate accommodations were equal in comfort and convenience.[13] The particularity of *Railroad Co. v. Brown* was that the federal charter under which the defendant operated had been amended in 1863 (at the instance of Charles Sumner) to provide that "no person shall be excluded from the cars on account of color."[14]

The case caused a considerable stir. Mrs. Brown was an employee of the Senate, in charge of its ladies' rest room. A Senate committee investigated the possibility of revoking the railroad's charter, and threatened to do so if a satisfactory judgment were not forthcoming in Mrs. Brown's lawsuit.[15] Mrs. Brown was awarded damages of $1,500 in the District of Columbia courts. On appeal to the Supreme Court, the railroad argued *inter alia* that it was in compliance with the charter provision because it had never excluded anyone from its cars on account of color, merely directed them to separate accommodations.

Justice David Davis, for a unanimous Court, characterized the railroad's argument as follows:

> This is an ingenious attempt to evade a compliance with the obvious meaning of the requirement. . . . There was no occasion in legislating for a railroad corporation to annex a condition to a grant of power, that

the company should allow colored persons to ride in its cars. This right had never been refused. . . . It was the discrimination in the use of the cars on account of color, where slavery obtained, which was the subject of discussion at the time, and not the fact that the colored race could not ride in the cars at all. Congress, in the belief that this discrimination was unjust, acted. It told this company . . . that this discrimination must cease, and the colored and white race, in the use of the cars, be placed on an equality.[16]

The liberal statutory interpretation engaged in by Justice Davis, finding the "obvious meaning" of the provision to be a prohibition of segregation, is the more interesting because that meaning was something less than obvious. If he in fact meant to provide that "no person shall be segregated," it was curiously inept draftsmanship on Sumner's part to write that "no person shall be excluded." The statutory basis of the suit in which Sumner had represented Sarah Roberts in challenging (unsuccessfully) her assignment to a segregated school in Boston was a Massachusetts statute of 1845 providing a remedy in damages for anyone "unlawfully excluded" from a public school. The brief Senate debate on the provision (there is no indication that the Court or the litigants considered it) likewise supported the railroad's position:

> Mr. SUMNER. Now I move an amendment to come in immediately after the amendment last adopted:
> *And provided also,* That no person shall be excluded from the cars on account of color.
> I have only to say that a statement was made the other day in the House of Representatives which certainly was a new illustration, as it seemed to me, of the barbarism left here from slavery: that an aged colored person had been excluded from the cars and dropped in the snow and mud. . . . That such an incident as that could occur here in Washington seems to me discreditable; and I think that Congress, in laying down regulations and rules for this railroad, ought to interfere. I am sorry there should be any occasion for it. . . .
> Mr. HOWE. I should like to ask the Senator from Massachusetts, as a question of law, whether if this railroad company, being common carriers, should drop any person or refuse to carry any person who offered them their fare, they would not be liable, as the law now stands, without any express enactment?
> Mr. SUMNER. If you ask me the question as a lawyer, I should say they would be liable; but I believe the experience is that that liability is

not recognized here; and the Senator knows very well that wherever slavery is in question, human rights are constantly disregarded—those principles of law which he recognizes are constantly set aside; and therefore it becomes the duty of Congress to interfere, and specially declare them.[17]

Equally interesting is the readiness with which Justice Davis implies, in the passage previously quoted, that the mere separation of the races is inconsistent with their being "placed on an equality." In *Railroad Co. v. Brown,* the "equality" of the separate facilities was hypothetically perfect: the defendant's trains consisted of two identical cars, assigned alternately to the two races depending on the direction of travel.[18] On those facts, the flat refusal to consider a "separate but equal" justification, the blunt reference to segregated facilities as an "unjust" discrimination, and the matter-of-fact link between nondiscrimination and "equality" are strongly suggestive of the steps in a chain of reasoning by which equal protection might eventually have been brought to yield a constitutional rule of nondiscrimination. Subsequent decisions of the Court merely ignored these anomalous implications.

The Court's most frequently quoted nineteenth-century statements about the antidiscrimination implications of the Fourteenth Amendment are contained in *Strauder v. West Virginia,*[19] the first of a trio of cases on racial discrimination in jury selection decided March 1, 1880, in opinions by Justice William Strong of Pennsylvania.[20] *Strauder* presented the question whether the trial of a black criminal defendant before a jury from which blacks were excluded by state law would deny him rights guaranteed by the Fourteenth Amendment. In the course of holding that such discrimination was constitutionally prohibited, Justice Strong revisited the historical context and purport of the Reconstruction Amendments. After recapitulating the analogous discussion in the *Slaughter-House Cases,* quoting for emphasis Justice Miller's reference to "the one pervading purpose" found in all the amendments, Justice Strong offered his own construction in even more generous terms:

If this is the spirit and meaning of the [fourteenth] amendment, whether it means more or not, it is to be construed liberally, to carry out the purposes of its framers. It ordains that no State shall make or enforce any laws which shall abridge the privileges or immunities of citizens of the United States (evidently referring to the newly-made citizens, who, being citizens of the United States, are declared to be also citizens of the State in which they reside). It ordains that no State shall deprive any person of life, liberty, or property, without due process of law, or deny to any person within its jurisdiction the equal protection of the laws. What is this but declaring that the law in the States shall be the same for the black as for the white; that all persons, whether colored or white, shall stand equal before the laws of the States, and, in regard to the colored race, for whose protection the amendment was primarily designed, that no discrimination shall be made against them by law because of their color? The words of the amendment, it is true, are prohibitory, but they contain a necessary implication of a positive immunity, or right, most valuable to the colored race,—the right to exemption from unfriendly legislation against them distinctly as colored,—exemption from legal discriminations, implying inferiority in civil society, lessening the security of their enjoyment of the rights which others enjoy, and discriminations which are steps towards reducing them to the condition of a subject race.[21]

Strong's paraphrase of Bingham's formulas offered a rhetorical bridge by which a different Court, in a different history, might have passed from the *Slaughter-House Cases* to Harlan's opinion in *Plessy*. When he asked, "What is this but declaring that the law in the States shall be the same for the black as for the white," Strong—on the facts of *Strauder*—was merely condemning a state law that put the black under an express disability to which the white was not subject. But the words had great expansive power, and it was tempting to read them to mean something close to what Phillips and Stevens had urged, that states be denied the power to classify by race.

As an indication of the Court's direction on civil rights for the Negro, this generous language would prove misleading. In 1883, when it nullified the operation within the states of the public accommodations provisions of the Civil Rights Act of 1875, the Court was visibly losing patience with a subject it already found tiresome. "When a man has emerged from slavery," complained Justice Bradley, "and by the aid of beneficent legislation has shaken off the inseparable concomitants of that state, there must be some stage in the progress of his elevation when he takes the rank of a mere citizen, and ceases to be the special favorite of the laws, and when his rights as a citizen, or a man, are to be protected in the ordinary modes by which other men's rights are protected."[22] By 1896, when the Court finally considered the permissibility under the Fourteenth Amendment of legally imposed racial segregation, its expansive remarks about the civil rights objectives of the Reconstruction Amendments belonged to another era. The question, moreover, had long since been resolved in the state and lower federal courts.

As suits challenging segregated schools began to assert federal constitutional claims in addition to arguments based on state statutes or constitutions, the nearly unanimous judicial response was that the recent constitutional amendments made no difference to the existing law of segregation—laid down by Chief Justice Lemuel Shaw's 1850 opinion in *Roberts v. City of Boston*—because what the Constitution commanded was not the abolition of racial distinctions, merely equality of treatment. This common theme was announced in an early and influential decision by the Supreme Court of Ohio:

> At most, the 14th amendment only affords to colored citizens an additional guaranty of equality of rights to that already secured by the constitution of the State.
>
> The question, therefore . . . is the same that has . . . been heretofore determined in this State [in Van Camp v. Board of Education of Logan, 9 Ohio St. 406 (1859)], that a classification of the youth of the State for school purposes, upon any basis which does not exclude either class from equal school advantages, is no infringement of the equal rights of citizens secured by the constitution of the State.
>
> We have seen that the law, in the case before us, works no substantial inequality of school privileges. . . . Equality of rights does not involve the necessity of educating white and colored persons in the same school, any more than it does that of educating children of both sexes in the same school, or that different grades of scholars must be kept in the same school. . . . There is, then, no ground upon which the plaintiff can claim that his rights under the fourteenth amendment have been infringed.[23]

Another frequent theme of the school cases reflected the observation that Congress itself continued to support segregated schools in the District of Columbia.[24] The implications of this fact were developed by the Supreme Court of Indiana in another widely cited opinion:

> The action of Congress, at the same session at which the fourteenth amendment was proposed to the states, and at a session subsequent to the date of its ratification, is worthy of consideration as evincing the concurrent and after-matured conviction of that body that there was nothing whatever in the amendment which prevented Congress from separating the white and colored races . . . and that such separation was highly proper and conducive to the well-being of the races, and calcu-

lated to secure the peace, harmony, and welfare of the public; and if no obligation was expected to be or was imposed upon Congress by the amendment, to place the two races and colors in the same school, with what show of reason can it be pretended that it has such a compelling power upon the sovereign and independent states forming the Federal Union?[25]

The rhetorical flourish was bad constitutional law (because the Fourteenth Amendment limited state action, not federal), but the point about District of Columbia schools was a telling one. Its obvious implications would only have been confirmed by the minute study of the *Congressional Globe* that no one, at the time, saw any need to undertake. The men who wrote and voted for the Fourteenth Amendment did not thereby intend to prohibit school segregation, as the judges who heard these cases—who had lived through the Thirty-ninth Congress, and who shared the prejudices of their contemporaries—were well aware.[26] The overwhelming majority of judges who ruled on the constitutionality of school segregation followed the Ohio and Indiana courts in their reasoning and their result.[27]

A related line of cases, dealing with the right of railroads and steamship companies to enforce regulations segregating their passengers by race, turned primarily on common-law doctrines about the duties of carriers; but the usual answer was largely indistinguishable from the evolving rule of constitutional law regarding segregated public schools. Passengers paying the same fare had a right to equal accommodations; but equal accommodations did not require common facilities, and carriers were entitled to enforce "reasonable regulations" by which passengers of different races were carried separately.[28] Where, notwithstanding the absence of state action, the argument was advanced that segregation in transportation violated rights guaranteed by the Fourteenth Amendment, the unsurprising answer was that it did not.[29] The closeness of the related doctrines in the school and railroad cases reinforced the confidence of judges in the correctness of both. Contemporary commentators treated the school and transportation questions in parallel and regarded them as essentially settled.[30]

These literal-minded, lawyerly conclusions are uncongenial; they have long since been discredited in the sense that they have proved profoundly inadequate. But they were faithful, rather than the contrary, to the cautious objectives of the authors of the Fourteenth Amendment, the men who substituted "equal protection" for "no discrimination." According to the words they adopted, the Constitution might be color-blind when the country chose; it need be so no sooner. Advocates who tried to find the antidiscrimination principle in the Reconstruction Amendments could only repeat, with less eloquence, the arguments that Sumner had built on the guarantee of equality in the Massachusetts constitution; and those arguments had been answered before the Fourteenth Amendment was written. The few reported cases antedating *Plessy* in which the antidiscrimination principle received any sympathetic consideration added little to what had already been said.

The most widely cited of the nineteenth-century cases holding school segregation to be unlawful, *Clark v. Board of Directors,*[31] did not even reach the federal constitutional question. The 1868 decision of the Iowa Supreme Court considered a challenge to the legal authority of the Muscatine school board to operate a separate school for black children. Justice Chester Cole prefaced his opinion for the court with an observation sufficient to decide the case. "In view of the principle of equal rights to all, upon which our government is founded," he wrote, "it would seem necessary, in order to justify a denial of such equality of right to any one, that some express sovereign authority for such denial should be shown." Because uncontroverted pleadings described the "colored school" as being equal in all respects to the schools provided for white children, the premise thus introduced—that mere separateness constituted a denial of "equality of right"—effectively decided the issue before the court.

The same premise would plainly have sufficed to establish the antidiscrimination character of the Fourteenth Amendment, at least to the extent of prohibiting racial segregation. But the Fourteenth Amendment, then in the final months of ratification, was nowhere mentioned in the opinion; nor was the illegality of the school board's action ultimately identified with the denial of "equality of right" to which Justice Cole referred at the outset. Instead the holding was made to turn exclusively on the issue of the school board's statutory authority, based on an interpretation of successive versions of the Iowa school statutes. Laws providing expressly for the separate education of "colored youths" had been succeeded in Iowa by laws referring to "the instruction of youth" generally, without mention of racial distinctions. From a juxtaposition of these statutes, read in light of "the tendency of our institutions" and "the spirit of our laws," the court concluded that Iowa school boards lacked statutory authority to discriminate between students on the basis of race.[32]

By its holding as well as its language the decision in *Clark* was a distinctly liberal one, but the court's chosen ground of decision was such that the case offered subsequent civil rights advocates little more than moral support. Some state courts followed Iowa in holding segregated schools to be illegal; but their decisions, with rare exceptions, were based exclusively on state-law grounds.[33] Indeed, the most frequent ground of decision among the nineteenth-century cases that may be counted against school segregation was merely the interpretation, usually straightforward, of a state statute forbidding the practice.[34] As a result, those state court cases that did strike down segregated schools provided no counterpoise to the weight of adverse decisions on the constitutional issue.[35]

Five years after *Clark*, the Iowa Supreme Court produced an even more widely noticed antidiscrimination decision, this time in the area of transportation. Although the court on this occasion did not hesitate to extend its discussion to matters of federal law, its undiminished liberal views gained no standing as precedent. The opinion in *Coger v. North West. Union Packet Co.*[36] was written by Joseph Beck, one of the judges who had decided *Clark*, now presiding as chief justice. The plaintiff, a schoolteacher "partly of African descent," had been refused stateroom accommodations and dining room meals on the defendant's river steamer in the course of a voyage from Keokuk, Iowa, to Quincy, Illinois. Obtaining a meal ticket through the intermediary of another passenger, she took a seat in the dining saloon; when requested by the captain "to leave the table and take her meal on the guards or in the pantry," she refused and was forcibly ejected. Justice Beck's opinion includes an appreciative but two-edged description of the scene:

> She resisted so that considerable violence was necessary to drag her out of the cabin, and, in the struggle, the covering of the table was torn off and dishes broken, and the officer received a slight injury. The defendant's witnesses testify that she used abusive, threatening and coarse language during and after the struggle, but this [the plaintiff] denies. Certain it is, however, that by her spirited resistance and her defiant words, as well as by her pertinacity in demanding the recognition of her rights and in vindicating them, she has exhibited evidence of the Anglo-Saxon blood that flows in her veins. While we may consider that the evidence, as to her words and conduct, does not tend to establish that female delicacy and timidity so much praised, yet it does show an energy and firmness in defense of her rights not altogether unworthy of admiration.[37]

The case concerned the common law of the duties of carriers, not statutory or constitutional questions, but Beck drew his opinion with a broad brush. The plaintiff's counsel first challenged the reasonableness of the defendant's regulations as applied to their client, arguing "that, as white blood predominates in her veins, she is, in law, to be regarded as belonging to the white race, and is not, therefore, subject to rules or restrictions that may be imposed upon negroes." Happily, Beck would have none of this. "We do not propose to pursue the inquiry to which we are thus directed by plaintiff's counsel," he declared, adding that in the opinion of the Iowa court, "the doctrines and authorities involved in the argument are obsolete, and have no longer existence and authority, anywhere within the jurisdiction of the federal constitution, and most certainly not in Iowa. The ground upon which we base this conclusion will be discovered, in the progress of this opinion, to be the absolute equality of all men." These hints at color blindness were confirmed in a subsequent paragraph:

> The doctrines of natural law and of christianity forbid that rights be denied on the ground of race or color; and this principle has become incorporated into the paramount law of the Union. It has been recognized by this court in a decision wherein it is held that the directors of a public school could not forbid a colored child to attend a school of white children simply on the ground of negro parentage, although the directors provided competent instruction for her at a school composed exclusively of colored children.[38]

The reference is to *Clark v. Board of Directors,* thus cited in retrospect as support for a constitutional holding that the earlier case had actually avoided. The decision in *Clark,* Beck continued, "is planted on the broad and just ground of the equality of all men before the law," a principle "announced and secured" by the declaration of the Iowa constitution that "All men are, by nature, free and equal."[39]

Here Beck turned to situate his opinion on federal constitutional grounds, noting that "the doctrine of equality and its application to the rights of the plaintiff, as presented in the record before us, depend, for support, not alone upon the constitution of this State and adjudications of this court. They are recognized and secured by the recent constitutional amendments and legislation of the United States." After quoting and paraphrasing the initial sections of the Fourteenth Amendment and the Civil Rights Act of 1866, Beck offered an interpretation of their joint thrust that is one of the most liberal ever pronounced:

> Under [section 1 of the Civil Rights Act], equality in rights is secured to the negro. The language is comprehensive and includes the right to property and all rights growing out of contracts. It includes within its

broad terms every right arising in the affairs of life. . . . The colored man is guaranteed equality and equal protection of the laws with his white neighbor. These are the rights secured to him as a citizen of the United States . . . and constitute his privileges, which are secured by the constitutional amendment above considered. The peculiar privilege of the colored man intended to be guarantied by these constitutional and statutory provisions, is equality with the white man in all affairs of life, over which there may be legislation, or of which the courts may take cognizance.[40]

This, though an extraordinary reading of "privileges or immunities," was arguably more faithful to the original understanding than the restrictive explanation promulgated some months earlier by Justice Miller in the *Slaughter-House Cases.* Combining an expansive reading of the right to make and enforce contracts guaranteed by the Civil Rights Act of 1866—Beck anticipated such modern decisions as *Runyon v. McCrary*[41] in suggesting that the right included legal protection against another party's discriminatory refusal to contract—with the assumption that the constitutional rule of "equal protection" was intended to embody the principles of the Civil Rights Act, Beck's syllogism produced a constitutional civil rights formula that would have circumvented once and for all the "state action" problem, forbidding racial discrimination in both public and private legal relations.

Coger was frequently cited on the issue of segregation in transportation, but its constitutional authority was slight. The enthusiastic reasoning of the opinion was easily criticized by anyone who did not share Beck's commitment to racial equality. In order to decide the case, the Iowa court had only to decide that the defendant's rule of segregation constituted an unreasonable regulation; so that what Beck had to say about the Civil Rights Act and the Fourteenth Amendment was certainly not necessary, and arguably not relevant, to the decision of the case. Another reason for the limited influence of *Coger* lay in its facts, which made it amply clear that the accommodations offered to the plaintiff were neither equal, nor claimed to be equal, to those offered white passengers. Because the common law required, in theory, that segregated passenger facilities be equal in comfort and convenience, Justice Beck's repeated references to the unequal accommodations provided in *Coger* made the case all too easy to distinguish.[42]

Of the handful of liberal state court decisions on school segregation in this period, the most interesting for a number of reasons is the Kansas case, *Board of Education v. Tinnon* (1881).[43] The trial court judge in *Tinnon* published an opinion that appears to have been the first (and was very nearly the only) nineteenth-century judicial holding that the Fourteenth Amendment barred segregated schools. (The Kansas Supreme Court, though it affirmed the decision, was careful to rest its judgment on other grounds.) Meanwhile, the circumstances of the Kansas litigation remind us that the isolated nineteenth-century decisions on school segregation addressed a problem far removed from its customary twentieth-century context. It will be interesting, therefore, to interrupt our review of the cases for a closer look at events in Ottawa.

The public schools in Ottawa, Kansas, were desegregated in 1876 in circumstances reminiscent of the school segregation fight in Boston thirty years before. Room 3 of the Central School Building was being used at the time for a "colored school." This meant that black pupils of all grades were taught in that one room, by a black teacher, Mr. B. B. Wade, instead of being assigned to the several grades in the other rooms of the building. In September 1876 the Ottawa Board of Education received a petition "from John Hogan and six others asking for the removal of Mr. Wade and the appointment of another teacher for the public school," whereupon "Wm McElroy and Elijah Tinnin [*sic*] on leave addressed the Board relative to said petition." As earlier in Boston, a militant faction of black parents was opposed to separate education, while others preferred to have their children taught in a separate classroom or at any rate by a black teacher. A week later, at a special meeting of the board called "to consider the matter of the colored school,"

> Mr. Benson from the Committee on Teachers reported: That said Committee had inquired into the complaints mentioned in said petition. That a large majority of the colored people were in favor of Mr. Wade, but that several parents insisted on having their children placed in the various grades, whether Mr. Wade was retained or not. Also that Mr. McElroy had served a written notice on the principal with reference to the matter. That the Com. had caused Mr. Wade to be examined by the Ex'g Com, resulting in his obtaining a 2d grade cert.

The reference to Wade's appearance before the Examining Committee implied that the school board had not previously bothered to ascertain his qualifications for teaching; certification by the Examining Committee being an unvarying precondition of employment for white teachers.[44]

The superintendent of schools, William Wheeler, then advised the board "that Mr. Hogan—colored—and others had on the opening of the school to-day demanded admission for their children into the proper grades of the public school, and that he had deferred action until the orders of the Board could be issued." The board's deliberations resulted in the appointment of a special committee "to confer with Mr. Wade and procure his resignation upon the best possible terms in their discretion." The special committee reported the next evening that it had obtained Wade's resignation "upon payment of one month's wages $40"; whereupon the board voted "that the Colored School lately taught by Mr. Wade be discontinued, and the pupils in attendance there be assigned to the various rooms in the graded school, according to their qualifications under direction of the principal. And a new grade established in Room No. 3."[45]

Such, seemingly, had been the simple course of desegregation in Ottawa. But less than four years later, in May 1880, the school board's Committee on Buildings and Grounds recommended

> that the colored children in rooms Nos. 1, 2, 3, 4, 5 & 6 be placed in the frame school house and a teacher of their own color be employed to instruct them, and that they be advanced into rooms Nos. 7, 8, 9, 10, 11 & 12 as fast as they make suitable proficiency and in the same manner as the whites. This in our judgment will remedy the evil complained of and at the same time furnish the colored children in the primary departments better advantages than they can possibly have under the present management.

After a brief postponement "to find out from other cities how they arranged as to their colored children," the board adopted the recommendation.[46] At the opening of school the following September, the more militant black parents refused to enroll their children in the reconstituted "colored school" and joined forces to challenge the board's action in court.[47] Elijah Tinnon, who had addressed the school board on the subject of the desegregation petition in 1876, brought suit on behalf of his son Leslie to compel Leslie's admission to the "graded school."

What had happened between 1876 and 1880 to reopen the segregation issue in Ottawa? A significant cause, in all likelihood, was the "Exodus of 1879," an extraordinary rural migration that briefly drew the attention of the nation to the plight of displaced southern plantation workers at the close of Reconstruction. Banished from the plantations of the lower Mississippi, or else refusing to remain there in conditions of peonage, thousands of southern blacks crowded the riverboats in search of free homesteads thought to be awaiting them in Kansas.[48] During a single month in the first wave of the Exodus, from mid-March to mid-April 1879, some six thousand "Exodusters" disembarked at St. Louis en route to Kansas City. By the end of the year, one report from Topeka estimated the number of Exodusters in Kansas at between fifteen and twenty thousand, adding that only a fifth of them had been able to buy land.[49] The Exodus resumed briefly in the spring of 1880; a contemporary report placed the total number of immigrants to Kansas in the two seasons of the Exodus at forty thousand, "nearly all field-hands, and exceedingly ignorant."[50]

Finding no land in Kansas, many of these migrants continued north or west; others eventually returned south. Of the families who remained, those who could not establish themselves in farming tended to settle in the cities and larger towns of eastern Kansas. Their influx prompted a movement to segregate the schools in several communities where the children of earlier Negro immigrants—more prosperous than the Exodusters, and arriving more gradually—had previously been taught side by side with white pupils. The return to segregation would have been most bitterly resented by people like Elijah Tinnon, participants in an earlier wave of black migration to Kansas,[51] who thought the battle against segregated schools had already been fought and won.

Ottawa was a small but rapidly growing city, less than sixty miles by rail from the Kansas City gateway. The number of Exodusters who sojourned in Ottawa, however briefly, must have been relatively large.[52] Even if relatively few of the migrants sent their children to the Ottawa schools, the addition of these highly visible newcomers, especially poor and especially backward, will have strengthened the hand of those whites who preferred that black schoolchildren be formally segregated. The primary classrooms of the Central School Building were seriously overcrowded, and there are indications that the Negro children were already being taught separately within their integrated classrooms.[53] A small but noticeable increase in their numbers may well have hardened feelings against them to the point that in May 1880, "the evil complained of" (as the committee report obliquely put it) seemed to the board to require the remedy of separate schools.

On January 18, 1881, Judge N. T. Stephens of the Franklin County District Court issued an order directing Superintendent Wheeler to admit Leslie Tinnon to the regular public school, on the ground that the Fourteenth Amendment deprived both the Kansas legislature and the local school board of the power to authorize or maintain a separate school for black pupils. The Kansas judge evidently preferred the higher, constitutional ground of decision: he began his opinion by rejecting the more cautious approach to the segregation problem, seen earlier in the Iowa school case, which consisted in finding that the applicable school laws conferred no authority on the local board to maintain separate schools. On the contrary, Judge Stephens announced that the Board of Education's "plenary power" over the free schools in the city of Ottawa conferred "a power broad enough to authorize the action of the School Board complained of in this case, and were there no other questions to be considered the case might be here dismissed."[54]

Stephens moreover rejected the suggestion, apparently made by Tinnon's counsel, that black children should be afforded "the benefits to be obtained from social intercourse and example set by those brought up in a more refined manner." No one had the right, he declared, "even for the great purpose of public education, to thrust his own vulgarity upon and compel its association with people of better manners; and children virtuously brought up ought to have the right of exemption from contaminating influences, let them come from whatever source they may." Still, in Stephens's view, the Fourteenth Amendment left the school board no choice in the matter. Stephens quoted expansive civil rights language from the *Slaughter-House Cases* and the famous nondiscrimination passage from *Strauder;* he cited *Railroad Co. v. Brown,* pertinently, to show that "separate but equal" segregation had been held to constitute "discrimination on account of color" and, in itself, a denial of equality. The action of the Ottawa school board, Stephens concluded, was

> a rule plainly discriminating against the relator on account of his race or color, pointing out himself and others of his class, by reason of their color, as not being eligible to school privileges with white children.
>
> It is no answer to the proposition to say that white children are excluded from the African school room. It is evident as to the purpose of the rule. Under the construction the Supreme Court of the United States has put upon the 14th amendment of the constitution it is evident to every mind that the Legislature of the State of Kansas had no power to confer authority upon the School Board of the city of Ottawa to make the order complained of. The rule itself is a violation of the rights conferred by the 14th amendment, and is inoperative and void.[55]

On the school board's appeal to the Kansas Supreme Court, the constitutional arguments were rehearsed at length by counsel on either side. The higher court affirmed the trial court's order but declined to adopt its reasoning. Justice Daniel M. Valentine began his opinion by observing that, in light of the Fourteenth Amendment, the constitutionality of segregated schools might be doubted; to reinforce this suggestion he quoted at length the nondiscrimination paragraph from *Strauder.* But having thus adverted to the possibility of a color-blind Constitution. Valentine stopped short, observing only that "The question whether the legislatures of states have the power to pass laws making distinctions between white and colored citizens, and the extent of such power, if it exists, is a question which can finally be determined only by the supreme court of the United States; and hence we pass this question, and proceed to the next, over which we have more complete jurisdiction."[56] Reexamining the Kansas school statutes in light of the "tendency of the times," which was "to abolish all distinctions on account of race, or color, or previous condition of servitude, and to make all persons absolutely equal before the law," Justice Valentine reached a conclusion opposite to that of Judge Stephens. Kansas law, he found, failed to confer on local school boards the authority to segregate pupils on the basis of race.[57] Justice David Brewer, who would be appointed in 1889 to the U.S. Supreme Court, filed a vigorous dissent. Attacking Valentine's construction of the relevant Kansas statutes, Brewer noted in passing that he "dissent[ed] entirely from the suggestion that under the fourteenth amendment of the federal constitution, the state has no power to provide for separate schools for white and colored children."[58]

Justice Brewer might have been surprised to learn the result of the judgment he so strenuously resisted, as might those historians who have assumed (on the basis of *Board of Education v. Tinnon*) that Kansas schools were judicially desegregated in 1881. Such an outcome had certainly been anticipated: earlier that year, the Ottawa school board had taken the precaution of reappointing its black teacher, Mr. M. O. Ricketts, only "upon the condition that the Sup. Court of the state does not prohibit a separate school in the case now pending." By the time the Supreme Court judgment was handed down, however, the board's lawyers had evidently explained that the consequences of an adverse ruling need not be so drastic. Although two courts had now held that Ottawa's separate school was illegal, the judicial order issued to the board merely commanded it to admit Leslie Tinnon to his proper grade in the Central School Building. This much the board undoubtedly did. The board may also have agreed to admit any other Negro pupil whose parents insisted, while encouraging the majority to continue to attend the "colored school"—offering, in this case, an early example of the kind of "freedom of choice" school desegregation held to be illegal around 1960. No word of such calculations appears in the school board minutes. What is clear, however, is that school segregation in Ottawa continued for some years, very nearly as if nothing had happened.

The decision of the Kansas Supreme Court in *Board of Education v. Tinnon* was announced in mid-September 1881.[59] On October 3 Superintendent Wheeler reported to the Ottawa school board that "the colored school is crowded with numbers; as is also the High School." M. O. Ricketts, the black teacher provisionally appointed the previous spring, walked off the job at the end of October; his official letter of resignation stated no reasons. If Ricketts thought he would thereby precipitate the abandonment of the "colored school," he was mistaken: Mr. J. W. Johnson was promptly hired to replace him. Toward the end of the school year the board commissioned a special visiting committee—composed of "a suitable number of ladies and gentlemen capable of judging in such matters"—to examine and report on the overall state of the Ottawa schools, including "the efficiency of the teachers." When the committee's report was submitted in June, its veiled but pointed criticisms brought about the swift resignation of longtime superintendent William Wheeler. (The "great need of the schools," the visitors believed, was "some such supervision as will stimulate both teachers and pupils.") The committee selected only one teacher for special mention: "Of course in schools graded or ungraded the best teacher has the best school. Without wishing to discriminate between teachers the Com. desire to mention with special commendation the teacher of the colored school. He is accurate and thorough, stimulates his pupils to do their best and is peculiarly adapted to his school." The board received the report, thanked the committee for its labors, and "on motion voted to continue the colored school for the ensuing year."[60]

Continued again a year later, Ottawa's segregated school remained in operation through the 1883–84 school year with no hint of judicial interference. Finally, on September 22, 1884, "[t]he matter of discontinuing the colored school coming up for consideration it was on motion voted to discontinue the same, and the Com. on [Teachers and Salaries] were instructed to confer with Mr. Johnson and see if he would voluntarily resign his position as teacher." When the board reconvened that same evening, the committee reported that Johnson "was not prepared to give an answer, and asked for more time to consider the matter, and that he thought he should have at least $200." On motion it was then voted "that Mr. Sheldon for the Bd. be authorized to receive the resignation of Mr. Johnson and to settle with him in an amount not to exceed $100."[61]

In Ottawa, Kansas, the "colored school" was thus finally discontinued—
not in obedience to a judicial order, but when the local school board
managed to come to terms with its one black teacher, Mr. J. W. Johnson,
about a settlement of his employment contract. In countless northern and
western communities where schools were once legally segregated, factors
such as the changing school population, the economics of teachers' sala-
ries, and the political composition of the school board were naturally more
significant in bringing about the end of segregation than were the distant
abstractions of the Fourteenth Amendment—so far, at least, as the latter
depended on judicial interpretation and enforcement.

The trial court opinion in the Ottawa case is, in fact, one of only two
discoverable nineteenth-century decisions actually holding that the Fourteenth Amendment prohibited segregated schools. *Commonwealth ex rel.
Allen v. Davis,*[62] decided shortly thereafter in June 1881, considered the
legality of segregated schools in Meadville, Pennsylvania. The opinion in
Allen was the idiosyncratic production of one Pearson Church, presiding
judge of the Court of Common Pleas of Crawford County and a former
president of the Meadville school board.[63] So unrestrained were Judge
Church's constitutional views that his legal conclusions are finally less
interesting than those of Judge Stephens. Drawing on the *Slaughter-House
Cases* and *Strauder* for a liberal reading of the Reconstruction Amendments, and on Sumner's argument in *Roberts* for his antidiscrimination
theory, Church had no difficulty in finding that an 1854 Pennsylvania
statute authorizing segregated schools was repugnant to the Fourteenth
Amendment and void. He then indicated that he was ready to find it void
under the Thirteenth Amendment as well, as creating a "badge of servitude," besides being an evasion of "the spirit or policy" of both the
Fifteenth Amendment and the Civil Rights Act of 1875. The authority of
the decision would not have been great under any circumstances: Church
cited no precedents on the issue of segregation and ignored entirely the
Gordian knot of "separate but equal." As it happened, the life of the opinion
was cut short even before it was published, when Pennsylvania adopted a
new statute prohibiting school segregation.[64] *Commonwealth ex rel. Allen
v. Davis* was not cited in subsequent decisions and does not appear to have
been widely known.

The *Tinnon* and *Allen* decisions, though historically noteworthy, are
untypical in the extreme. A more characteristic example of the color-blind
theme prior to *Plessy* appears in a leading New York case, but in a
dissenting opinion. New York's consolidated school laws of 1864—confirming existing law and practice—authorized local school authorities

"when they shall deem it expedient" to establish "separate schools for the instruction of children and youth of African descent."[65] (The provision was reenacted in 1894 before its eventual repeal in 1900.)[66] The validity of the law was repeatedly upheld by the New York courts, in a series of cases that challenged segregated schools in Buffalo, Albany, Brooklyn, and Queens.[67] The most influential treatment of the constitutional argument appeared in the 1883 decision by the Court of Appeals in *People ex rel. King v. Gallagher,* rejecting a suit brought on behalf of "a colored female about twelve years of age, residing in public school district No. 5, of the city of Brooklyn, [who] would be entitled to attend that school but for the regulations of its board of education."[68] The dissenting opinion, by Judge George Franklin Danforth, can be placed in the tradition that links Sumner's argument in *Roberts* with Harlan's in *Plessy;* at one or two points it may well have contributed to the latter. At the same time, a comparison of the dissenting and majority opinions helps to show why the pro-segregation majority had the best of the constitutional argument in 1883.

The strongest arguments against Brooklyn's segregated schools were not constitutional but statutory. The civil rights act passed by New York's Republican legislature in 1873 provided that no citizen should be "excluded," by reason of race or color, from "the full and equal enjoyment" of the public schools.[69] Because New York's laws already provided that the common schools "shall be free to all persons over five and under twenty-one years of age residing in the district,"[70] a plausible reading of the prohibition of "exclusion" in the 1873 act was that it prohibited the segregated schools that the 1864 school statutes expressly permitted. The court's Democratic majority, however, refused to find that the 1873 civil rights act had displaced the express authorization of school segregation contained in the earlier laws.

Counsel for the plaintiff placed primary reliance on the view that school segregation was prohibited by the Fourteenth Amendment. Judge Danforth indirectly acknowledged the difficulty of this contention: "[Plaintiff] brings her case within the spirit, the intention and the meaning of the fourteenth amendment of the Constitution of the United States," he wrote, "as she does also within the letter of [the civil rights act of 1873]." Preferring not to rest his opinion on constitutional grounds, Danforth referred to the Fourteenth Amendment primarily for confirmation of his reading of the New York statute:

In *Ex parte Virginia* and *Strauder v. West Virginia* it is in substance said that one great purpose of the then recent amendments to the Constitution was to remove the colored race from a condition of inferiority and servitude into perfect equality of civil rights with all other persons within the jurisdiction of the States; that they were intended to take away all possibility of oppression by law because of race or color, and amounted to a declaration that the law should be the same for the black as for the white. Our own statute is more specific, but both were designed to release that race from any disability or restraint to which the other was not subjected, and make their rights and responsibilities the same.[71]

Danforth was careful to refute any inference that the challenge to segregated schools depended on the inequality of the facilities provided. Recounting the facts of *Railroad Co. v. Brown* and emphasizing the perfect equality of the segregated railroad cars considered in that case, Danforth (like Judge Stephens in Kansas) employed the decision as Supreme Court authority supporting his central proposition: that segregation, regardless of the equality of the facilities, was an "exclusion" condemned by the New York statute. "In one case, as in the other, is discrimination on account of color. The fatal defect is in the fact of discrimination and its cause." A subsequent passage of the opinion recalled Sumner's argument and anticipated Harlan's:

If the respondent is right, then with equal plausibility it might be said that the city of Brooklyn could provide parks, streets and sidewalks exclusively for persons of color . . . denying them access to other streets, parks, sidewalks and seats. It would not answer in either case to say all these things are equal or even better in degree than those. This would still be discrimination against the race, and so with the school, the main business of which is to prepare a youth for his future duties as a citizen in his various relations towards the State, the performance of obligations due to other citizens, and possibly even forbearance and conduct toward opposing races.

"Separate but equal" was brushed aside in a single sentence that anticipated Harlan's answer to the same argument in *Plessy v. Ferguson.* "[A]ny regulation," Danforth wrote, "by which the black is kept in a state of separation is in fact one of exclusion and reflects the sentiment by which the white [is] assumed to be the superior race, a discrimination against which the law is now directly aimed."[72]

The truth of these assertions is easier to see now than it was when Danforth made them. The more conventionally telling arguments, at the time, fell to the apologists of "separate but equal." The majority opinion in *People ex rel. King v. Gallagher,* by Chief Judge William Ruger, failed to explain why New York's 1873 civil rights act referred to schools at all if not to prohibit racial segregation. But on the constitutional question—which he accordingly emphasized, just as Danforth downplayed it—Judge Ruger's arguments were straightforward, concrete, and easy to understand. It is finally not surprising that most judges found them more persuasive.

Judge Ruger was brutally contemptuous of the antidiscrimination claim, which he characterized by saying that the plaintiff "complains, not but that she is receiving the highest educational advantages that the city is capable of giving her, but that she is not receiving those facilities at the precise place which would be the most gratifying to her feelings."[73] He adopted the flagrant dishonesty, later indulged by the Supreme Court majority in *Plessy,* of pretending that segregation carried no stigma: "We cannot see why the establishment of separate institutions for the education and benefit of different races should be held any more to imply the inferiority of one race than that of the other."[74] These are debater's points, inspired by racial prejudice. But when he emphasized the problem of finding in the general words of the Fourteenth Amendment a prohibition of racial classifications, but not of classifications generally, Ruger identified a genuine intellectual difficulty:

> The claim which is now made, that any distinction made by law and founded upon difference of race or color is prohibited by the Constitution, leads to startling results and is not believed to be well-founded. . . . [The language of the Fourteenth Amendment] embraces and is addressed to all classes alike, and if susceptible of the construction attempted to be placed upon it, must inhibit any enactment by the State which classifies the citizens . . . .
>
> . . . If the argument should be followed out to its legitimate conclusion, it would also forbid all classification of the pupils in public schools founded upon distinctions of sex, nationality or race, and which, it must be conceded, are essential to the most advantageous administration of educational facilities in such schools. Seeing the force of these contentions the appellant concedes that discrimination may be exercised by the school authorities with respect to age, sex, intellectual acquirements and territorial location, but he claims that this cannot, under the Constitution, be extended to distinctions founded upon difference in color or race. We think the concession fatal to his argument.[75]

It was to avoid this objection that Phillips and Stevens had proposed an amendment forbidding the states to distinguish between citizens *on the basis of race.*

To find a prohibition of racial distinctions in Bingham's language, Danforth had to appeal to the amendment's "spirit, intention and meaning." Ruger was in the position, incomparably more advantageous, of being able to insist on its literal wording: "Equality and not identity of privileges and rights is what is guaranteed to the citizen."[76] He could buttress this simpler reading of the constitutional language with evidence as to legislative intent—in Congress's uninterrupted support for segregated schools in the District of Columbia—that was both readily understandable and difficult to refute.[77] Reviewing the authorities, Ruger could assert truthfully that "[the] cases show quite a uniform current of authority in favor of that interpretation of the constitutional amendment which we have given to it." Cases holding segregation illegal were not to the contrary because, as he noted, they "arose under statutes which either expressly forbid or did not authorize the school authorities to separate the races and assign them to different places for instruction."[78] Ruger, in short, enjoyed the easier argument about the plain meaning of the constitutional language, the difficulties attendant upon his opponent's construction, the evidence as to legislative intent, and the state of the authorities. To counter this panoply of orthodox legal reasoning, Danforth could only assert that "the spirit, the intention and the meaning" of the Fourteenth Amendment prohibited something that its language did not.

Before judges who assumed they should interpret the Fourteenth Amendment according to the plain meaning of its words and their best understanding of the intent of its framers, the argument that the amendment forbade school segregation was already a difficult one to make; to contend that it prohibited racial classifications altogether would have seemed merely quixotic. The language adopted by the Thirty-ninth Congress is capable of bearing a color-blind interpretation, but not of imposing one: words that would have left judges no choice in the matter were what the framers had considered and rejected. By 1954, when the Supreme Court finally held that school segregation violated the Fourteenth Amendment, it had long since decided that the original understanding of the amendment's framers need not be the outer limit of its meaning thereafter. But the judges who decided segregation cases in the thirty years following the drafting of the amendment did so in advance of the history that shapes our understanding of the question. They saw no reason, and assuredly felt no inclination, to extend the amendment's meaning to encompass a prohibition that its authors had apparently not intended and that its words would not easily support.

The assessment they made under the circumstances was above all else unsurprising. With the abolition of slavery, as Russel Nye has suggested, "[t]he Negro was no longer a problem in morality, but a problem in politics."[79] The political problem was one in which, following the close of Reconstruction, very few white Americans took any sympathetic interest. The argument that guarantees of legal equality should be read to prohibit racial distinctions in what were considered "social" contexts appeared fanciful and untoward to the majority of judges, who assumed, with most of their fellow citizens, that the black race was inherently and significantly inferior to the white. Far from challenging these racist assumptions, the advances of modern science during the last third of the nineteenth century appeared to be placing them on ever securer and more objective foundations.[80] If the scientific racism of the late nineteenth century had still been regarded as good social science in 1954, the School Segregation Cases would have been decided the other way. The nineteenth-century judicial consensus as to the reasonableness, by constitutional standards, of laws requiring segregation is neither more nor less than we should expect to find.

The pivotal importance of *Plessy v. Ferguson*[1] to the history of the color-blind Constitution has been recognized only in part. In a decision that attracted little attention when it was announced in May 1896,[2] the Supreme Court held that Louisiana's "separate car law," requiring railroads in that state (other than streetcar lines) to provide "equal but separate accommodations for the white and colored races,"[3] violated no right guaranteed by the Thirteenth or Fourteenth Amendment. The Court's businesslike announcement that nothing in the Constitution prevented the states from imposing reasonable measures of racial ordering inspired, in the celebrated dissenting opinion of John Marshall Harlan, a statement of the antidiscrimination principle that remained its lodestar. To the arguments inherited from Charles Sumner, Harlan added not only new rhetorical force but also a new and complementary legal analysis that avoided the familiar stalemate over "separate but equal" by denying the authority of the courts to police the reasonableness of legislative classifications. The opinion for the seven-man majority[4] by Justice Henry Billings Brown was at least as significant as Harlan's dissent, because it announced for the first time the Court's considered opinion about the ordinary meaning of "equal protection" as applied to the legislative use of racial classifications. The majority opinion in *Plessy* makes a comfortable target, and it is routinely vilified.[5] But in its broad holding as opposed to its particular application, *Plessy* has never been overruled, even by implication. On the contrary, it announced what has remained ever since the stated view of a majority of the Supreme Court as to the constitutionality of laws that classify by race.

The relation between "equal protection" and racially discriminatory statutes was problematical from the outset. Although southern laws abridging the civil rights of black persons were the evil against which the first section of the Fourteenth Amendment was primarily directed, the language adopted said nothing about race. So far as Bingham's words revealed, a racial classification stood on the same constitutional footing as every other classification the law might impose. A prohibition of some classifications and not others was the only possible meaning of "equal protection"; but the words added to the Constitution gave little indication of where the line should be drawn.

In practice, the nineteenth-century Supreme Court readily accorded special constitutional significance to a limited class of racial classifications—those that created an explicit legal inequality—while denying that the equal protection clause had any particular concern with racial classifications in general. When Justice Miller, in the *Slaughter-House Cases,* made his famous mistaken prophecy about the future application of the equal protection clause—"We doubt very much whether any action of a State not directed by way of discrimination against the negroes as a class, or on account of their race, will ever be held to come within the purview of this provision. It is so clearly a provision for that race and that emergency, that a strong case would be necessary for its application to any other"[6]—it is likely that he had in mind the most obvious form of racial discrimination by state action, laws subjecting black citizens to an explicit legal disability or expressly denying to the black what was given to the white.[7]

Thaddeus Stevens, in the course of debate, had explained the function of the equal protection clause in precisely those terms:

> This amendment . . . allows Congress to correct the unjust legislation of the States, so far that the law which operates upon one man shall operate *equally* upon all. Whatever law punishes a white man for a crime shall punish the black man precisely in the same way and to the same degree. . . . Whatever law allows the white man to testify in court shall allow the man of color to do the same. These are great advantages over their present codes. Now different degrees of punishment are inflicted, not on account of the magnitude of the crime, but according to the color of the skin. Now color disqualifies a man from testifying in courts. . . . I need not enumerate these partial and oppressive laws. Unless the Constitution should restrain them those States will all, I fear, keep up this discrimination, and crush to death the hated freedmen. Some answer, "Your civil rights bill secures the same things." That is partly true, but a law is repealable by a majority.[8]

The Court's unhesitating identification of "equal protection" with some limited degree of *racial* equality was made in deference to this legislative history, not to the constitutional text. The "equal protection of the laws" was promised to "any person," but laws denying ordinary civil rights to women were not unconstitutional.[9]

Laws that created an express inequality between the races, exemplified by the southern Black Codes, were the one indisputable instance of what the equal protection clause was intended to eradicate; and the Court never hesitated to give it that much effect. When a rare surviving example of explicit legal inequality reached the Supreme Court from a border state— West Virginia's law prohibiting blacks from serving as jurors—the Court had no difficulty in finding that "equal protection," despite the generality of the language, was aimed especially at racial distinctions:

> We do not say that within the limits from which it is not excluded by the amendment a State may not prescribe the qualifications of its jurors, and in so doing make discriminations. It may confine the selection to males, to freeholders, to citizens, to persons within certain ages, or to persons having educational qualifications. We do not believe the Fourteenth Amendment was ever intended to prohibit this. Looking at its history, it is clear it had no such purpose. Its aim was against discrimination because of race or color. . . . We are not now called upon to affirm or deny that it had other purposes.[10]

This primary meaning of the equal protection clause was never repudiated, but its direct application was to a class of cases that by 1880 had virtually ceased to exist.[11] Government action that by its terms afforded explicitly unequal treatment based on a racial classification did not reappear before the Supreme Court until the next century, under the very different circumstances that gave rise to *Hirabayashi v. United States*[12] and *Fullilove v. Klutznick.*[13] Laws requiring separation of the races created no legal inequality in the *Slaughter-House* and *Strauder* sense. They were accordingly tested only by a secondary meaning of "equal protection," one in which racial classifications were accorded no special status.

Given the words of the equal protection clause and their expansive possibilities, the meaning of "equal protection" could not long be confined to problems of racial discrimination.[14] Its broader application, devised by Chief Justice Shaw even before the Fourteenth Amendment was written, derived from the requirement of equal protection a constitutional command that legislative classifications be reasonably drawn. If the true meaning of "equal protection" was that all classifications had to be reasonable ones, then laws treating people differently on the basis of race were appropriately judged by a standard to which all laws were uniformly subject. The broader, secondary meaning of the equal protection clause thus tended implicitly to refute the premise of *Slaughter-House* and *Strauder,* the idea that racially discriminatory laws presented a special constitutional problem.

The color-blind contention in what might be called its absolute form, illustrated by Wendell Phillips's claim that "neither Law nor Constitution here can *recognize race* in any way," was implicitly rejected early on. In *Pace v. Alabama,*[15] the Court unanimously upheld a conviction under a statute that punished adultery or fornication more severely when the parties to the crime were of different races. Justice Stephen J. Field's brief opinion observed merely that the statute created no inequality, since persons of all races were subjected to the same penalties for the same offenses.[16] While the decision in *Pace* necessarily implied that a legislature was not prohibited from taking account of racial differences in the framing of police measures—a holding inconsistent with a rule of absolute color blindness—it did not foreclose a more favorable decision on the more important issues of racial segregation. Despite *Strauder* and *Pace,* the Supreme Court had not yet addressed the issue on which the prima facie legality of segregation would be decided: the constitutionality of laws that treat the races differently without creating an explicit legal inequality.

The fact that the Court had not yet addressed the issue did not mean that the outcome was in doubt. By the time the constitutionality of racial segregation finally came before the Supreme Court, two decades of decisions in the lower courts had broadly established that equality did not mean identity; that the *Roberts* framework of reasonable classification provided the key to the problem; and that a law imposing racial segregation was not inherently unreasonable. In retrospect, *Plessy*'s principal contribution to constitutional doctrine was to restate the premises underlying the earlier cases at a useful level of generalization. Counsel for Homer Plessy had advanced the argument, inherited from Sumner and Danforth and strongly urged in Harlan's dissent, that if the Constitution were read to permit segregated transportation it would necessarily permit more extensive and even absurd forms of racial discrimination. Justice Brown responded with serenity:

> [I]t is also suggested by the learned counsel for the plaintiff in error that the same argument that will justify the state legislature in requiring railways to provide separate accommodations for the two races will also

authorize them to require separate cars to be provided for people whose hair is of a certain color, or who are aliens, or who belong to certain nationalities, or to enact laws requiring colored people to walk upon one side of the street, and white people upon the other, or requiring white men's houses to be painted white, and colored men's black, or their vehicles or business signs to be of different colors, upon the theory that one side of the street is as good as the other, or that a house or vehicle of one color is as good as one of another color. The reply to all this is that every exercise of the police power must be reasonable, and extend only to such laws as are enacted in good faith for the promotion for [*sic*] the public good, and not for the annoyance or oppression of a particular class.[17]

This is not a thoughtful response, but its implications go deep. If we limit ourselves to logically distinct solutions, there were only three answers to the puzzle of determining the relationship between "equal protection" and laws making a racial classification. At a minimum, the Fourteenth Amendment prohibited the Black Codes and any other laws subjecting colored persons to an explicit legal inequality. If it meant only this, then statutes that drew a racial distinction but did not in terms abridge the legal rights of a racial class were subject to no constitutional limitation at all. At the other extreme was the radical view, adopted in Harlan's dissenting opinion, that the equal protection clause prohibited racial classifications altogether. In the wide middle ground between the two extremes lay moderation, common sense, and a more generous role for the judiciary.

The primary meaning of the equal protection clause, established by *Strauder*—its prohibition of laws creating an explicit legal inequality on racial lines—was not at issue in *Plessy* and was not questioned by the decision. The argument was confined to the secondary meaning of the clause: the guarantee of reasonable classifications, the command that like be treated alike, that was logically implicit in a promise of "equal protection." In the *Roberts* opinion by which he first explicated this consequence of legal "equality," Chief Justice Shaw had treated a racial classification on the same footing as any other, to be judged by a uniform standard of reasonableness. For opponents of segregation, at the time of the *Roberts* litigation and for a hundred years thereafter, reasonableness was inadequate protection: judges might agree with legislators (as they did in *Roberts* and in *Plessy*) that a segregation law was a reasonable disposition.

The broader question for decision in *Plessy* was then whether, in its secondary as well as its primary meaning, the equal protection clause (though it said nothing about race) imposed a different constitutional standard, more stringent than "reasonableness," for racial classifications generally. The only logically distinct alternative was that proposed in Justice Harlan's dissenting opinion: that legal distinctions on the basis of race be altogether prohibited. The broad holding of *Plessy* is its rejection of Harlan's alternative in favor of Shaw's. Racial classifications, announced Justice Brown, are like every other sort of classification, and those racial classifications will be constitutional that a majority of the Supreme Court considers to be "reasonable." That rule of constitutional law, and no other, will explain every Supreme Court decision in the area of racial discrimination from 1896 to the present. The true holding of *Plessy* is not "separate but equal" but the Supreme Court's refusal to deny to the state the option of treating citizens differently according to race. The whole development of the question since 1896 has been merely the ebb and flow of the Court's idea of what constitutes reasonable discrimination.

Surprisingly soon after *Plessy,* the Supreme Court would begin to decide segregation cases in a manner clearly indicating that racial classifications were constitutionally disfavored. Subsequent decisions gave rise to the modern taxonomy of equal protection, in which racial classifications are typically stated by courts and commentators to be "suspect," subject to the Court's "strict" or "rigorous" scrutiny. Yet the evolution by which the Supreme Court came to find racial classifications less often "reasonable," or else "reasonable" when employed for different purposes from those of the nineteenth century, is fully consistent with Shaw's original proposition. "Reasonable" inevitably means "reasonable under the circumstances": the idea necessarily incorporates a weighing of costs and benefits and a comparison of means and ends, as well as a judgment about the desirability of the ends.[18] Justice Harlan advanced a flat prohibition as the only alternative to a rule permitting reasonable racial classifications, because no rule short of a flat prohibition will remove the issue from the discretion of judges to approve or disapprove policy.

Plessy embodies both our constitutional law of racial discrimination and its antithesis, crystallized in Justice Harlan's dissent; and the legacy of the case is the choice it presents us. With Justice Harlan's dissenting opinion, the color-blind Constitution became one of the available meanings of the Fourteenth Amendment; that it "has never been adopted by [the Supreme] Court as the proper meaning of the Equal Protection Clause"[19] has not detracted from its standing as the alternative against which the more prosaic meanings adopted by the Court are inescapably measured. Harlan's luminous opinion gave lasting form to an idea that might not otherwise have survived him.

He did so, not least, by giving it a name. Wendell Phillips had demanded in 1864 that the federal government "ignore the difference between white and black, be blind to color."[20] Theodore Tilton, editor of the religious weekly *The Independent,* wrote at the same period in praise of impartial suffrage: "Give the ballot to the negro on the same terms as to the white man. Why not? Is justice blind, as poets say? Then let her see no distinction of color."[21] Harlan, in all likelihood, took the figure from the brief submitted by Albion W. Tourgée, the former carpetbagger, best-selling novelist, and newspaper columnist who served as Homer Plessy's lead counsel.[22] "Justice is pictured blind," wrote Tourgée, "and her daughter, the Law, ought at least to be color-blind."[23] This rather lame suggestion was transfigured by Harlan's more vigorous prose: "Our Constitution is color-blind, and neither knows nor tolerates classes among citizens."[24] The legal argument underlying this moral appeal was likewise Harlan's alone.

Plessy marked the intersection of the careers of the two white men most prominently associated with the cause of Negro rights in the last decade of the nineteenth century. Harlan's reputation as a friend of the black man was established at a stroke in 1883, with his dissenting opinion in the *Civil Rights Cases.*[25] Tourgée, the principal adviser to the New Orleans Citizens' Committee to Test the Constitutionality of the Separate Car Law,[26] was not only a novelist but an immensely prolific journalist and lecturer. His weekly column in the Chicago *Inter Ocean,* "A Bystander's Notes," was a forum for the tireless advocacy of racial equality at a time when the expression of such views by white Americans was virtually unheard of.[27] Shortly after the appearance of a column in which Tourgée attacked the new Texas and Louisiana Jim Crow laws as "legislation especially designed to degrade and oppress [the Negro]," the New Orleans committee sought his aid in mounting a legal challenge to the Louisiana statute.[28]

As a civil rights advocate, Tourgée was concerned with the obvious forms of inequality that were the lot of the southern Negro: his arguments for the ballot, for education, against lynch law, never implicated a prohibition of racial classifications. The "Bystander's" one deprecating reference to a full-fledged rule of color blindness (an idea he attributed to "the old abolitionists") appears in an explanation of why the Republican party had turned aside from what Tourgée regarded as its historic commitment to freedmen's education and political rights. First, Tourgée suggested, the "leaders and shapers of party policy" had been willing a colored man should fight for the Union, but to think of making provision for his education and self-support stirred the fear of ridicule, which is the very strongest sentiment in the mind of the average Northern man. . . . Side by side with this in its tendency was the curious dread of the old abolitionists of any legislation respecting color or race. They must needs avoid that at all hazard of uncertainty and insufficiency. The struggle for the expurgation of "white" as a restrictive term in our law had given them a strange horror of "colored" as an enabling description.[29]

As an explanation of Republican Reconstruction policy this is purely fanciful. As a historically based criticism of color blindness by a supporter of affirmative action (which for his time Tourgée assuredly was), the words may seem strikingly apt.

Not surprisingly, then, Tourgée's Supreme Court brief for Homer Plessy contained no substantial argument for a constitutional command of non-discrimination as the grounds on which segregation should be ruled illegal. The brief is a disappointing performance overall: a jumble of preconceived notions, quarrelsome and repetitive, that is never molded into an argument of coherent force.[30] Still, its most telling passages—they convey, in addition, a fair notion of Tourgée's style as an essayist—will be seen to have influenced both the majority and dissenting opinions later delivered by the Court:

[A] discrimination intended to humiliate or degrade one race in order to promote the pride of ascendency in another, is not made a "police regulation" by insisting that the one will not be entirely happy unless the other is shut out of their presence. Haman was troubled with the same sort of unhappiness because he saw Mordecai the Jew sitting at the Kings gate. He wanted a "police regulation" to prevent his being contaminated by the sight. He did not set out the real cause of his zeal for the public welfare: neither does this statute. He wanted to "down" the Jew: this act is intended to "keep the negro in his place." The exemption of nurses shows that the real evil lies not in the color of the skin but in the relation the colored person sustains to the white. If he is a dependent it may be endured: if he is not, his presence is insufferable. . . .

. . . Suppose a member of this court, nay, suppose every member of it, by some mysterious dispensation of providence should wake to-morrow with a black skin and curly hair . . . and in traveling through that portion of the country where the "Jim Crow Car" abounds, should be ordered into it by the conductor. . . .

What humiliation, what rage would then fill the judicial mind! How would the resources of language not be taxed in objurgation! Why would this sentiment prevail in your minds? Simply because you would then feel and know that such assortment of the citizens on the line of race was a discrimination intended to humiliate and degrade the former subject and dependent class—an attempt to perpetuate the caste distinctions on which slavery rested—a statute in the words of the Court "tending to reduce the colored people of the country to the condition of a subject race."[31]

Justice Brown's answer to this argument is the one passage of his opinion that probably merits the contempt with which it is usually received:

We consider the underlying fallacy of the plaintiff's argument to consist in the assumption that the enforced separation of the two races stamps the colored race with a badge of inferiority. If this be so, it is not by reason of anything found in the act, but solely because the colored race chooses to put that construction upon it.[32]

Harlan's rejoinder distilled in a few words the whole force of Tourgée's discursive analogies: state legislation "conceived in hostility to, and enacted for the purpose of humiliating citizens of the United States of a particular race" must be "hostile to both the spirit and letter of the Constitution of the United States."[33] This is a better explanation of the illegality of racial segregation than has yet appeared in any opinion for a majority of the Supreme Court. It is not, of course, an argument for a color-blind Constitution. Racially discriminatory legislation may be neither conceived in hostility to, nor enacted for the purpose of humiliating, citizens of the United States of a particular race. Alternatively, Jim Crow laws might be rejected on the ground that they impose an unreasonable classification, without implying any broader rule of antidiscrimination. Harlan consciously went further: he developed an argument for a color-blind Constitution because he was unwilling to rely on judges to distinguish a good racial classification from a bad one.

The passages of the opinion that set forth this part of the argument are so much less familiar than its rhetorical heights that Harlan's stated rationale for the color-blind Constitution has gone largely unnoticed. It depends, not on any extraordinary sympathy for the plight of the black man—Harlan's remarks about the continued superiority of the white race are the preferred citation of his latter-day detractors[34]—but on a relatively humdrum point about judicial restraint in the construction of statutes. Rehearsing the *reductio ad absurdum* inherited from Sumner, Danforth, and Tourgée—whites on one side of the street, blacks on the other—Harlan addressed the heart of the majority position:

> The answer given at the argument to these questions was that regulations of the kind they suggest would be unreasonable, and could not, therefore, stand before the law. Is it meant that the determination of questions of legislative power depends upon the inquiry whether the statute whose validity is questioned is, in the judgment of the courts, a reasonable one, taking all the circumstances into consideration? A statute may be unreasonable merely because a sound public policy forbade its enactment. But I do not understand that the courts have anything to do with the policy or expediency of legislation.

Because any inquiry into reasonableness, policy, or expediency is foreclosed by a proper understanding of the judicial role, the courts may decline to give effect to a statute only when the enactment is outside the legislative power altogether:

> There is a dangerous tendency in these latter days to enlarge the functions of the courts, by means of judicial interference with the will of the people as expressed by the legislature. . . . [T]he intent of the legislature is to be respected, if the particular statute in question is valid, although the courts, looking at the public interests, may conceive the statute to be both unreasonable and impolitic. If the power exists to enact a statute, that ends the matter so far as the courts are concerned. The adjudged cases in which statutes have been held to be void, because unreasonable, are those in which the means employed by the legislature were not at all germane to the end to which the legislature was competent.[35]

Harlan avoided saying that the reasonableness of a statute was *never* material to its validity. In his opinion for the Court in *Mugler v. Kansas*,[36] upholding that state's prohibition law, Harlan himself had endorsed the notion that a classification bearing no rational relation to the accomplishment of the legislative purpose would be unconstitutional, presumably as a violation of equal protection. This much judicial comparison of legislative means and ends is required by the equal protection clause, if the latter is to be allowed its secondary meaning; but as Harlan insisted, it is readily distinguishable from the power to pass on the policy or expediency of every police regulation. The means/ends test of "reasonableness" that Harlan accepted might invalidate an occasional instance of disguised racial discrimination (as in *Yick Wo v. Hopkins*),[37] but it was powerless against laws enforcing the separation of the races, where means and ends are so close as to be nearly indistinguishable. Harlan therefore set out to show that both the means and ends of racial segregation lay entirely beyond the power of the legislature.

Harlan's discussion of the limited judicial competence is followed by the most famous lines of the opinion:

> But in the view of the Constitution, in the eye of the law, there is in this country no superior, dominant, ruling class of citizens. There is no caste here. Our Constitution is color-blind, and neither knows nor tolerates classes among citizens. . . . The law regards man as man, and takes no account of his surroundings or of his color when his civil rights as guaranteed by the supreme law of the land are involved. It is, therefore, to be regretted that this high tribunal, the final expositor of the fundamental law of the land, has reached the conclusion that it is competent for a State to regulate the enjoyment by citizens of their civil rights solely on the basis of race.[38]

The argument seems to rest on a syllogism whose central, actuating term has not been explicitly stated. (1) If it is competent for the legislature to regulate by race, judicial review will be powerless to prohibit invidious and unreasonable racial distinctions, because (with a narrow exception not applicable to this class of cases) the judiciary has no authority to consider the policy or expediency of enactments. (2) But the history and the future of this nation imperatively require that a statute such as the Louisiana separate car law be unconstitutional. (3) The meaning of the Constitution must therefore be that classification by race, regardless of its reasonableness in a particular instance, is beyond the legislative competence.

The remainder of the opinion consists largely of Harlan's defense of his unstated central premise. When he argues that "the judgment this day rendered will, in time, prove to be quite as pernicious as the decision made by this tribunal in the *Dred Scott case*," and that it will "not only stimulate aggressions . . . upon the admitted rights of colored citizens, but will encourage the belief that it is possible, by means of state enactments, to defeat the beneficent purposes which the people of the United States had in view when they adopted the recent amendments to the Constitution," Harlan's essential appeal is neither to the amendments' language nor to their legislative history but to an appreciation of the nation's political needs:

The destinies of the two races, in this country, are indissolubly linked together, and the interests of both require that the common government of all shall not permit the seeds of race hate to be planted under the sanction of law. What can more certainly arouse race hate, what more certainly create and perpetuate a feeling of distrust between these races, than state enactments, which, in fact, proceed on the ground that colored citizens are so inferior and degraded that they cannot be allowed to sit in public coaches occupied by white citizens? That, as all will admit, is the real meaning of such legislation as was enacted in Louisiana.[39]

By ordinary rules of constitutional interpretation this was reasoning backward, reading a meaning into the text on the ground that it was politically necessary. Such reasoning could not and did not command the agreement of contemporaries who lacked Harlan's breathtaking prescience about the American problem of race and our continuing political inability to deal with it. To most Americans today—looking backward rather than forward at the near-century that separates us from *Plessy*—the idea that the Constitution *must somehow* prohibit legally imposed racial segregation, whatever the interpretive means by which we reach that conclusion, seems as obvious as it did to Harlan. For a modern observer, therefore, the crucial and controversial point about Harlan's color-blind syllogism is not its unstated central premise, long since validated by experience, but the rather old-fashioned contention about the separation of the legislative and judicial functions with which it begins. Few people today would attempt to limit the role of judges with the observation that the courts have no proper concern with policy; yet the modern argument for the color-blind Constitution turns to a considerable extent on a point that is at least analogous to Harlan's. If we ought to refuse to let judges distinguish the reasonable from the unreasonable racial classification it is largely because history, *Plessy* included, shows that the courts are not to be trusted on the subject and that we would be better off with a per se prohibition. If on the other hand, when all is said and done, we are willing or even relieved to let judges decide these matters, then Harlan's syllogism falls, and much of the argument for a color-blind Constitution falls with it.

The color-blind Constitution is a profoundly radical notion, and the sheer improbability that any nineteenth-century Supreme Court justice could have proposed it—let alone a former slaveholder, who at an earlier stage of his career had denounced the Emancipation Proclamation and the Thirteenth Amendment[40]—naturally leads one to ask whether Justice Harlan really meant what he said. Revisionist critics have argued that there is less to Harlan's *Plessy* dissent than meets the eye;[41] and the suggestion that "even Harlan" saw nothing unconstitutional about segregated public schools, based on his opinion (three years after *Plessy*) in *Cumming v. Richmond County Board of Education*,[42] has attracted the support of distinguished historians.[43] Harlan never reiterated his arguments for the color blindness of the Constitution, and in his surviving papers there is no direct evidence of his mature views on the legality of segregated public schools. That said, the burden rests heavily with those who would argue that Harlan did not intend or fully understand the implications of his color-blind rhetoric. All the available evidence is consistent with the assumption that Harlan in *Plessy* meant precisely what he said. The *Cumming* opinion, properly understood, is not to the contrary.

The hostility toward the judicial evaluation of policy that led Harlan to propose a per se prohibition of racial classifications, when he might have contented himself with a demonstration that Louisiana's separate car law constituted a denial of equal treatment, is easy to discount in an era when we are all legal realists. Taken seriously, as Harlan took it, it makes a strong argument against a rule that racial classifications are unconstitutional only when they are unreasonable. Harlan's strictures against "judicial legislation" began with his earliest dissenting opinion.[44] The claim that courts have no business judging the policy of legislation represented through most of the nineteenth century the purest judicial orthodoxy;[45] the theme was a standby of Harlan's, recurring in many of his most significant opinions.[46] Harlan's demand that courts renounce any role in assessing policy may have been shortsighted and even self-deceiving,[47] but that is no reason to think he would have tried to avoid its more obvious consequences.

So long as we are satisfied that Harlan would not have admitted that a court might properly distinguish, on the basis of policy, between a law requiring separate railroad cars and a law requiring separate schools, then we may even assume for the sake of argument that Harlan in 1896 personally favored segregated schools—consistent with his stated views as a political candidate twenty-five years earlier[48]—without calling into question the sincerity of his preference for a per se rule of nondiscrimination. If the courts are forbidden to judge policy and expediency, we must allow both forms of segregation, or neither; and between those alternatives Harlan's choice seems clear. A color-blind Constitution requires us to forgo the racial classifications we might approve as well as those we deplore, but this Harlan had not denied.

Leaving aside the logical constraints of his color-blind rationale, there is still no evidence that Harlan, while a member of the Supreme Court, would have defended the constitutionality of school segregation. Harlan's famous dissenting opinion in the *Civil Rights Cases*, written in 1883, included passages that implicitly rejected any law requiring separate schools:

> But I hold that since slavery . . . was the moving or principal cause of [the thirteenth] amendment, and since that institution rested wholly upon the inferiority, as a race, of those held in bondage, their freedom necessarily involved immunity from, and protection against, all discrimination against them, because of their race, in respect of such civil rights as belong to freemen of other races.

Other judges at this time could readily have explained why a segregated school was not "discrimination against them, because of their race, in respect of . . . civil rights." The arguments are familiar, but it is impossible to imagine them in Harlan's mouth.

> But what was secured to colored citizens of the United States . . . by the national grant to them of State citizenship? With what rights, privileges, or immunities did this grant invest them? There is one, if there be no other—exemption from race discrimination in respect of any civil right belonging to citizens of the white race in the same State.[49]

The words leave no room for segregated schools, unless we can conceive of an argument that public transportation, hotel accommodations, and theater admissions—the transactions addressed by the Civil Rights Act of 1875—involved "civil rights" while public education did not.

The only basis, finally, for doubting Harlan's commitment to a rule of color blindness lies in the notion that his *Cumming* opinion shows that he "saw nothing unconstitutional in segregated public schools."[50] But this view of the case condemns Harlan for declining to state an opinion on a question not before the Court. Public schools in Richmond County, Georgia (including the city of Augusta), were segregated, and the facilities afforded black pupils were manifestly inferior. When the Ware High School, established for Negro students in 1880, was discontinued in July 1897, one aspect of this unequal treatment consisted in the fact that public funds went to support two high schools open to white students, while no state-suppported high school was provided for blacks.[51] A group of black parents, angered by the school board's decision to close the Ware school, brought suit to challenge this inequality of treatment, alleging a denial of equal protection. A decision by the trial court in their favor was overturned by the Georgia Supreme Court.[52] In a unanimous decision written by Justice Harlan, the U.S. Supreme Court agreed that the plaintiffs had demonstrated no violation of their constitutional rights.[53]

The foregoing version of *Cumming,* accurate so far as it goes, suggests why the case has been thought to reveal a complacency about school segregation on the part of John Marshall Harlan. The contrary view depends on lawyers' distinctions that nonlawyers may find tedious but that are not particularly arcane. The constitutionality of school segregation was not addressed in Harlan's opinion because the issue had not been raised by the plaintiffs, whose claim was rather that the Fourteenth Amendment—as construed in *Plessy*—entitled them to an equality of segregated facilities.[54] A passage in Harlan's opinion is the only evidence we have that the issue of segregation was ever addressed at all:

> It was said at the argument that the vice in the common school system of Georgia was the requirement that the white and colored children of the State be educated in separate schools. But we need not consider that question in this case. No such issue was made in the pleadings. Indeed, the plaintiffs distinctly state that they have no objection to the tax in question so far as levied for the support of primary, intermediate and grammar schools, in the management of which the rule as to the separation of races is enforced. We must dispose of the case as it is presented by the record.[55]

No modern judicial opinion would refer to "the rule as to the separation of races" without adding words of censure, but Harlan's failure to do so will not support any inference about his views on the subject. Had he voiced any doubts about the legality of that rule, Harlan would no longer have been writing the opinion of the Court; had he persisted to the point of dissent, the majority opinion would in all likelihood have included a plain statement endorsing the propriety of separate but equal schools. As it was, Harlan secured the authority of the Court for an opinion which stated that the constitutionality of school segregation need not be considered, thereby implying—notwithstanding the emanations of *Plessy*—that it had not yet been decided.[56]

Even when it is recognized that the constitutionality of school segregation was not before the Court in *Cumming,* Harlan has been accused of betraying a lack of sympathy with the plight of black litigants seeking to assert their right to a minimum of equal treatment. Harlan indeed found that the plaintiffs had failed to show a violation of their constitutional rights, noting that "the education of the people in schools maintained by state taxation is a matter belonging to the respective States, and any interference on the part of Federal authority with the management of such schools cannot be justified except in the case of a clear and unmistakable disregard of rights secured by the supreme law of the land."[57] One commentator has suggested that this holding raises "serious questions about Justice Harlan's devotion to civil rights."[58] Another finds Harlan's opinion "particularly obtuse in failing to acknowledge that any racial inequality existed at all."[59]

But unless Harlan is to be blamed for his determination to "dispose of this case as it is presented by the record," these accusations are misdirected. To begin with, the existence or nonexistence of a "public high school" for a given class of students did not have the practical significance it would today. Secondary education in Richmond County was predominantly private, and all high schools, public as well as private, charged tuition at comparable rates. The school board had never established a system of public high schools in Richmond County; rather, it operated or subsidized a small number of schools on an ad hoc basis. After the board discontinued the Ware High School, attended by sixty black students, public support for secondary education was limited to the operation of one high school for white girls in Augusta and a subsidy for one private academy for white students in a rural part of the county. White boys of high-school age in Augusta attended the private Richmond Academy, which received no subsidy. Black students in Augusta could attend three other high schools, supported by the Methodist Episcopal, Baptist, and Presbyterian educational missions.[60] All these schools had been founded subsequent to the establishment of Ware High School; all appear to have attracted substantially larger numbers of students and to have enjoyed greater financial resources than did the public high school in the last year of its operation. The school board contended that its operation of a high school for white girls was proper, since no other high school was available to them; that the subsidy for the rural academy was anomalous, but that to discontinue it now would do more harm than good; and that (in view of the denominational high schools available to black students) the money previously spent on the Ware school would be better used to expand the admittedly inadequate primary school facilities available for colored children.[61]

In fact, *so far as secondary education in Richmond County was con-*

cerned, plaintiffs had not made out a prima facie case of unequal treatment. The equal protection clause was never thought to guarantee a per capita identity of benefits to blacks and to whites; yet beyond this implicit premise there was little substance to the plaintiffs' claim. If the entitlement at issue was access to a high school supported by public funds, black children in Augusta stood on exactly the same footing as white boys in Augusta: no such school was provided. Yet the parents of a white boy who might have preferred to send him to a publicly funded high school could not have established a denial of equal protection merely by showing that such a school was available to their neighbors' daughter. Rather than "a system which flatly denied to blacks a service which it offered to whites,"[62] the school system disclosed by the record on appeal was one that offered a service to some whites while denying it to other whites and to blacks, in an exercise of discretion that was not unreasonable on its face if the propriety of racial segregation was not contested. The vice of the arrangement, as Harlan implied, was not that a subvention was given to some schools and not others—for this much discrimination attends the granting of nearly every public benefit—but that access to the favored schools was limited by race. The argument thus came full circle to the contention the plaintiffs had disclaimed.

It is easy to overlook these difficulties with the plaintiffs' case because the overall inequality of school facilities in Richmond County was indeed obvious. It was implicit even in the school board's justification for closing Ware High School, which was that the money would be better spent on primary schools for colored children who would otherwise not be admitted to school at all. An elementary school system that accommodated all whites while it denied admission to some blacks should have been vulnerable to a "separate but equal" challenge, but that was not the grounds of suit in *Cumming:* on the contrary, plaintiffs went out of their way to disclaim any objection to Richmond County's separate and unequal "primary, intermediate and grammar schools system."[63] *Cumming* presented for decision neither the issue of segregation nor a well-founded challenge to unequal treatment on racial lines, and it is a mistake to judge Harlan's opinion as if the case were what later generations of civil rights lawyers would have made it.

Harlan might not, in the end, have agreed with Phillips and Sumner that all racial classifications are inherently and necessarily invidious; but the question was not presented to him in those terms. The Constitution must be color-blind, according to Harlan, because the nation would be better served by forbidding the use of racial classifications altogether, rather than by permitting their use under judicial supervision. The latter proposition was the reasonable alternative, favored by Justice Brown's tranquil majority opinion. Harlan's famous dissent in *Plessy* is customarily praised as a glowing affirmation of human rights, but its darkly skeptical premise is that American society is incapable of benign self-government on the fatal issue of race. Brown's opinion for the majority, though unpalatable for its racist assumptions, embodies an optimistic political response: the confidence that on the issue of race as on any other, American government (subject to the vigilant oversight of judges) can ameliorate our social condition by choosing good measures over bad ones. Harlan's pessimism held sway in liberal opinion so long as the only racial classifications in view were those that made up the structure of southern segregation; but the broad premise underlying present-day affirmative action (in political as well as constitutional terms) is the optimism of Justice Brown.

In the familiar view of *Plessy v. Ferguson* as a "national decision against equality,"[1] Justice Brown's opinion is seen as inaugurating a dark age in the American law of civil rights: more than fifty years in which the power of courts and Constitution to vindicate the most basic guarantees of equal treatment was rarely more than negligible. The period is one in which the American legal system failed the cause of racial justice. But to attribute that failure to the constraints of legal doctrine—let alone to the doctrine of *Plessy v. Ferguson* itself—generously overestimates the importance of lawyers' reasoning. The real history of the judicial role in ending racial segregation, from the earliest twentieth-century cases to *Brown v. Board of Education* and beyond, is less a story of evolving constitutional doctrine than a story of evolving judicial power. As concerns the doctrine, moreover, the notorious decision in *Plessy* marked an end rather than a beginning.

Faced with the challenge to reconcile racial classifications with the guarantee of "equal protection," *Plessy* endorsed a theoretical solution that had been worked out half a century earlier by Chief Justice Lemuel Shaw and applied in the interim by scores of lesser judges. Its central idea was that "equal protection," of necessity, guaranteed not the absence of legal distinctions but like treatment to those situated alike in a system of reasonable classifications. Employed to justify racial segregation, as it was in both *Roberts* and *Plessy*, this reasoning carried with it two apparent implications: not only that racial classifications were to be judged by the same standard of "reasonableness" as any other classifications, but also that racial classification for the purpose of segregation was not unreasonable where equal treatment was provided. In so holding, Brown's 1896 opinion in *Plessy* accurately restated the American law of racial discrimination that had developed in the wake of Shaw's 1850 opinion in *Roberts*. Yet while

Plessy would stand as a leading case for half a century in the state and lower federal courts, no case subsequently arising in the U.S. Supreme Court was ever decided on its authority. On the contrary, the real authority of *Plessy*—its vitality as a source of reasoning for the determination of future cases—appears to have been exhausted as soon as the opinion was announced.

Plessy was the first Supreme Court decision to uphold the legality of racial segregation against a direct challenge based on the Reconstruction Amendments, and it was very nearly the last. The single exception was the *Berea College* decision of 1908, in which the Court's formalistic and artificial reasoning showed plainly enough that it was already uncomfortable with the result being reached. Having implied in *Plessy* that segregation laws were not unconstitutional so long as the separate facilities were "equal," and further—on the facts of the case—that the required "equality" would not be found to be destroyed by the mere fact of separateness, the Supreme Court never once found separate facilities to be "equal" when the equality of segregated facilities was challenged thereafter. "Separate but equal" described factual circumstances that had frequently been observed by nineteenth-century judges but that the Supreme Court, after *Plessy,* would never encounter again.

This is not to say that the illegality of racial segregation was promptly established. In the first decades after *Plessy,* as Benno Schmidt has properly noted, the Court's "sympathy for the rights of black people did not go so far as to embrace any broad willingness to strike at Jim Crow whenever the opportunity was presented."[2] *Cumming* was an instance of this judicial restraint, as was *South Covington & Cincinnati Street Ry. v. Kentucky,* a 1920 case in which the Court voted six to three to uphold Kentucky's separate coach law against a very plausible claim that, as applied to the operations of the plaintiff, it constituted an unlawful interference with interstate commerce.[3] Chief Justice William Howard Taft's 1927 opinion in *Gong Lum v. Rice*[4] leaves no doubt that he, at least, considered school segregation to be permissible under the Fourteenth Amendment, assuming an equality of facilities; and an unequivocal holding to that effect may well have been avoided only because the challenge raised by the petitioners, Mississippi citizens of Chinese ancestry, was not to the institution of segregated schools (which they unreservedly approved) but to their own classification by the state as "colored" rather than "white." It is nevertheless a striking and somewhat unexpected fact that—within the narrow but significant confines of Supreme Court adjudication—"separate but equal," the supposed rule of *Plessy v. Ferguson,* ceased almost as soon as it was announced to be a doctrine by which segregation might justified, becoming instead the doctrine in the name of which segregation would consistently be held illegal.

The Supreme Court's twentieth-century decisions on legally imposed racial segregation cannot be adequately explained without attributing to the Court the conviction that racial distinctions imposed by law, with or without ostensible "equality," were the particular though unacknowledged object of the Fourteenth Amendment's prohibitory language. The difference between *McCabe v. Atchison, T. & S.F. Ry.* in 1914 (overturning an Oklahoma statute requiring segregated facilities for railroad travel) and *Brown v. Board of Education* in 1954 lies less in the constitutional principle being vindicated than in the magnitude of the contrary dispositions the Court was prepared to challenge. Considering them in retrospect, it would not occur to anyone to account for this line of decisions as an application of what was popularly taken to be the rule of *Plessy:* a rule, that is, that the Fourteenth Amendment *permitted* segregation, provided only that segregated facilities be "equal." Such, however, was the explanation on which the Court usually insisted, pointing in case after case to some measurable inequality of the separate facilities as it struck down segregation in one context after another.

These decisions were announced in opinions that consistently misrepresented, by understating, the scope of the constitutional rule actually being applied. A choice of tactics dictated by necessity had far-reaching effects. Given the need to resolve every segregation case by a finding of unequal treatment, without calling into question the legality of racial segregation per se, the long road to desegregation had to be covered one laborious step at a time. This built-in brake on the progress of judicially ordered desegregation may have been politically desirable. But the Court's reluctance to acknowledge the existence of broader grounds for questioning the constitutionality of government-sponsored racial discrimination stifled the development of constitutional theory on a vital question that the framers of the Fourteenth Amendment had left unresolved. Each successive decision holding segregation unlawful on the narrow ground preferred by the Court, that segregation resulted in unequal treatment, carried the renewed implication that segregation per se posed no constitutional problem. Meanwhile the only intelligible basis of the decisions—the fact that racial classifications were increasingly, perhaps categorically, disfavored—left no explicit trace in the Court's opinions.

The atrophy that beset the *Plessy* rationale is already evident in the Court's manner of deciding *Berea College v. Kentucky* in 1908.[5] A Kentucky statute, specifically directed at the famous private college, made it a crime for "any person, corporation or association of persons" to "maintain or operate any college, school or institution where persons of the white and negro races are both received as pupils for instruction."[6] Kentucky's highest court upheld the validity of the act against the college's constitutional challenge; the U.S. Supreme Court affirmed the decision. But whereas the Kentucky court had enthusiastically endorsed the state's vital interest in the separation of the races as justification for the reasonableness of the racial classification—the relevant consideration under *Plessy,* and the question naturally presented by the facts of the case—the Supreme Court managed to avoid the real issue altogether. Its affirmance (in an opinion by Justice David Brewer, for a majority of seven) was based instead on the narrow grounds, formalistic and tautological, of a state's authority to define the powers of its domestic corporations. Because Berea College (being a corporation) was entirely a creature of law, it could have no existence at all except as state law might permit; the legislature could therefore limit its powers and activities as it saw fit.[7] Disposition of the *Berea College* case in this manner was palpably artificial, as Justice Harlan pointed out in dissent.[8] In its eagerness to avoid the constitutional issue presented by the case, the Court simply ignored parallel provisions of the Kentucky law that had nothing to do with corporations—making it a crime both to teach at an integrated school and to attend one as a student. The Court's willingness to resort to this transparent and undignified evasion suggests that a majority of its members found the straightforward alternative—to defend the constitutionality of the measure, as had the Kentucky court, in terms of its reasonableness—even more distasteful.

In 1914, returning to the context of segregated railway travel, the Court for the first time (and by a bare majority) employed the implicit corollary of *Plessy*—the requirement that separate facilities be "equal"—to suggest that a segregation law was invalid. *McCabe v. Atchison, T. & S.F. Ry.*[9] considered a "separate coach law" enacted by the new state of Oklahoma. The law required railroads to provide "separate coaches or compartments, for the accommodation of the white and negro races," specifying that they "be equal in all points of comfort and convenience." Another section of the act provided that it should not be construed to prevent railway companies "from hauling sleeping cars, dining or chair cars attached to their trains to be used exclusively by either white or negro passengers, separately but not jointly."[10] Such facilities, in other words, might be provided for white passengers only. Few Negro passengers required Pullman, dining, or parlor car accommodations; railroads could not economically provide these facilities in duplicate and preferred not to divide their cars by the "good and substantial wooden partition" otherwise required by the Oklahoma law.

The fact that the Supreme Court said anything at all about the constitutionality of racial segregation in *McCabe* was the result of a judicial tour de force by the author of the opinion, Charles Evans Hughes. A progressive Republican governor of New York for two terms before his appointment to the Court in 1910, Hughes seems to have regarded the authority of *Plessy*, still a relatively recent decision, as the burdensome legacy of an earlier era. He now took the first step toward dismantling it. Seeking to enjoin compliance with the Oklahoma statute before it went into effect, the plaintiffs in *McCabe* had brought their suit prematurely, upon allegations judged (in a day of more formal pleading) "too vague and indefinite" to warrant the relief requested. Their action had been dismissed on this basis in the lower federal courts; the Supreme Court unanimously affirmed the dismissal on the same procedural grounds. But the opinion of the circuit court had gone on to discuss the constitutionality of the Oklahoma statute, finding not only that its "separate but equal" provisions were fully authorized by *Plessy* but that the provision on sleeping and dining cars was likewise admissible:

> This provision in itself makes no more discrimination against one race than the other. The Legislature having in mind doubtless, what we judicially know, that the ability of the two races to indulge in luxuries, comforts and conveniences was so dissimilar that sleeping and dining cars which would be well patronized by one race might be very little if at all by the other, legislated accordingly, and made a provision by which carriers might supply them for the exclusive use of either race as circumstances might dictate.
>
> It may be conceded that the general principle of equality of service . . . must be observed by all carriers. . . . Equality of service, however, does not necessarily mean identity of service; and manifestly this rule does not require permanent provision for equal service, irrespective of the demand for it.[11]

If a segregation ordinance was unobjectionable per se, in the evident spirit of *Plessy*, this conclusion was at least plausible. But if segregation was allowed only on sufferance, and if a rigorous equality of segregated facilities was to be exacted as the constitutional price of segregation, then Oklahoma's proviso on sleeping cars and the lower court's finding of constitutionality were dangerously retrograde. Justice Hughes persuaded four of his colleagues to join an opinion, technically unnecessary, in which he sharply repudiated the circuit court on this point before affirming the dismissal of the case on the inadequacy of the pleadings.[12]

The court of appeals had stressed the importance of "practical considerations" in determining what constituted "equality of service to the two races in Oklahoma." Practical considerations of this order would have sufficed to establish the reasonableness of Oklahoma's regulatory scheme, had the necessary classifications been drawn along other than racial lines. Justice Oliver Wendell Holmes, who was not prepared to concede that the racial character of the regulation made any difference, would have affirmed the circuit court decision had he reached the merits of the case. Holmes's view of the matter may be inferred from a note addressed to him by Hughes, replying to a memorandum that has not been preserved:

Washington, D.C., Nov. 29 1914

Dear Judge,

I return herewith your memorandum in No. 15—*McCabe v. Atchison etc Rwy Co.*—I cannot construe the statute as requiring the carriers to give equal, though separate, accommodations so far as sleeping cars, dining cars and chair cars are concerned. All agree—both parties and the Attorney General—that such cars may be provided exclusively for whites—that a black man must sit up all night just because he is black, unless there are enough blacks to make a "black sleeping-car" pay.

I don't see that it is a case calling for "logical exactness" in enforcing equal rights, but rather it seems to me it is a bald, wholly unjustified, discrimination against a passenger solely on account of race.

Faithfully,

Charles E. Hughes

To Mr. Justice Holmes[13]

Comparison of this note with Hughes's opinion in *McCabe* makes it clear what Holmes's objection had been. Hughes was determined to hold a racially discriminatory law to a stricter constitutional test than that applicable to other sorts of regulations. In the face of *Plessy*, which implied the contrary, his weapon was to insist on the "'logical exactness' in enforcing equal rights" deprecated by Holmes's letter. "This argument with respect to volume of traffic," wrote Hughes,

> seems to us to be without merit. It makes the constitutional right depend on the number of persons who may be discriminated against, whereas the essence of the constitutional right is that it is a personal one. Whether or not particular facilities shall be provided may doubtless be conditioned upon there being a reasonable demand therefor, but, if facilities are provided, substantial equality of treatment of persons traveling under like conditions cannot be refused. It is the individual who is entitled to the equal protection of the laws, and if he is denied by a common carrier, acting in the matter under the authority of a state law, a facility or convenience in the course of his journey which under substantially the same circumstances is furnished to another traveler, he may properly complain that his constitutional privilege has been invaded.[14]

The conclusion now seems so obvious that its true point of interest—the fact that it does not follow from Hughes's acknowledged premises—probably needs some demonstration. The opinion is written within a legal regime, established by *Plessy*, in which Jim Crow laws were supposedly unobjectionable per se. Hughes was careful to say nothing to the contrary. Yet his conclusion makes sense only if laws imposing segregation are in fact disfavored. How else could an "argument with respect to volume of traffic" possibly be "without merit," when the issue is the reasonableness of a regulation specifying services to be provided by common carriers? The tendentious character of the argument in *McCabe* is easier to see if we test it against some other form of railroad regulation. Suppose that Oklahoma had authorized railroads to discontinue service altogether at any station where annual passenger traffic failed to exceed a certain level. In Waynoka (where service has now been suspended), the relatively few citizens who wish to travel would not be heard to argue that the volume of traffic was beside the point, nor to demand equality of treatment with the more favored residents of Ponca City on the ground that "it is the individual who is entitled to the equal protection of the laws." The comparison is ludicrous, but that is because we do not judge classification by race and classification by town by the same constitutional standard. Hughes applied to the racial classification before him in *McCabe* the "heightened scrutiny" (in modern parlance) that *Plessy* had implied was unnecessary.

Hughes's insistence on the "personal" nature of the constitutional right to equal protection was a brilliant tactical stroke that would be influential in later decisions. Although the protections of the Fourteenth Amendment extend literally to "any person," they are inevitably given effect, most of the time, by measuring how the law treats groups of persons similarly situated. An idiosyncratic difference from the traits of a group in which one is reasonably classified does not normally permit a complaint on equal protection grounds. The contention that "it is the individual who is entitled to the equal protection of the laws" was employed in *McCabe,* as later in *Shelley v. Kraemer,*[15] not as a reliable guide to the logic of "equal protection" but as a means of rendering the test more difficult to meet. Similarly, when he insisted that black and white travelers sought first-class accommodations "under substantially the same circumstances," Hughes announced in effect that the requirement of "substantial equality of treatment" would be aggressively employed to invalidate legal distinctions between black and white citizens—to the point of disregarding differences in circumstance that, in another context, might well be thought to justify differences in treatment.

Read closely, *McCabe* necessarily implied that laws requiring segregation were constitutionally disfavored. If so, then the antidiscrimination content of the Fourteenth Amendment included something more than those minimum elements that the Court had previously acknowledged: the prohibition of state statutes that expressly established one law for white and another for black *(Strauder),* or that were applied "with an evil eye and an unequal hand" to oppress a racial group *(Yick Wo v. Hopkins),* or that drew racial distinctions not reasonably justifiable as an exercise of legislative discretion *(Plessy).* To some greater but unspecified degree, the antidiscrimination principle was already part of our constitutional law by 1914—although Hughes's bare liberal majority thought it wiser not to acknowledge the fact.

Three years later, in the more celebrated case of *Buchanan v. Warley,*[16] the Court not only relied on the antidiscrimination principle to reach its result but openly acknowledged it as the principal basis of the decision. The dramatic context of the case was the rapid spread of legally imposed residential segregation, an American apartheid, that began in Baltimore in 1910 and was quickly adopted by a number of southern and border-state cities.[17] The municipal ordinances by which segregation was to be achieved generally forbade the occupancy by a person of one race, white or black, of residential property located on a city block predominantly occupied by persons of the other race. Such an ordinance, containing typical provisions, was enacted in Louisville in 1914; the Louisville chapter of the National

Association for the Advancement of Colored People was formed to challenge the ordinance in court. *Buchanan v. Warley* was the collusive suit arranged for that purpose.[18]

A unanimous Supreme Court held Louisville's segregation ordinance unconstitutional. Because the law applied to white and black residents with scrupulous evenhandedness, its invalidation could not readily be made to turn, *McCabe* fashion, on a denial of equal treatment. Justice William Day's opinion for the Court met the issue head on, resting the decision on the antidiscrimination themes of pre-*Plessy* Fourteenth Amendment jurisprudence. Both the result and its rationale were plainly inconsistent with *Plessy* in its commonly accepted meaning.

The usual explanation for how it came about that the Supreme Court should vote unanimously to strike down a segregation ordinance in 1917—a time when the Court is presumed to have been indifferent to racial discrimination—is that *Buchanan* is essentially a decision in defense of property rights. Such a view is difficult to maintain on the basis of Justice Day's opinion. Its cursory references to property rights are no more than was logically necessary, given that the case had been intentionally structured to present a constitutional challenge in property-rights terms. *Buchanan v. Warley* was a suit for specific performance of a contract for the sale of real estate in a neighborhood reserved by the ordinance for white residents. The purchaser, a Negro, refused to perform under the contract, asserting as his defense a contractual clause that purported to excuse him from the obligation to purchase should he be prohibited by law from residing on the property. The white seller responded that the Louisville ordinance triggering the contractual condition was unenforceable and void, being an unconstitutional interference with his right to dispose of the property in question. Day refers to "the property rights of the plaintiff in error" chiefly to refute the argument that the case should have been dismissed for lack of standing.[19] The fact that the Court was prepared to entertain this transparently manufactured lawsuit demonstrates the importance it attached to a prompt ruling on the constitutionality of the new segregation laws.

The dominant theme of the opinion in *Buchanan* is not the one the NAACP had so carefully invited—the constitutionally protected rights of the white property owner—but simple antidiscrimination. After noting that the police power, broad as it is, is nevertheless subject to constitutional limitations, the opinion moves immediately into the antidiscrimination litany that no Supreme Court majority had evoked since *Strauder:* the

Reconstruction Amendments; the *Slaughter-House Cases* as the great expositor of the amendments' central purpose; *Strauder* itself, with its famous antidiscrimination passages quoted at length; *Ex parte Virginia;* and the 1866 and 1870 Civil Rights Acts for good measure.[20] Offered a variety of grounds on which to invalidate the segregation ordinance, the Court elected to base its decision on the theory that the racial discrimination effected by the enactment was impermissible under the guarantees of the Fourteenth Amendment.

Despite the evident tension between the authorities evoked to strike down the Louisville ordinance and the authority of *Plessy,* the latter case was merely distinguished as inapplicable to the problem of housing segregation. Without inviting a challenge to established precedents, the Court in *Buchanan* announced that the precedents would not be extended:

> As we have seen, this court has held laws valid which separated the races on the basis of equal accommodations in public conveyances, and courts of high authority have held enactments lawful which provide for separation in the public schools of white and colored pupils where equal privileges are given. But in view of the rights secured by the Fourteenth Amendment to the Federal Constitution such legislation must have its limitations, and cannot be sustained where the exercise of authority exceeds the restraints of the Constitution. We think these limitations are exceeded in laws and ordinances of the character now before us.[21]

In one sense, the Court in *Buchanan* was merely applying a more fundamental rule of *Plessy:* that the constitutional limitations to the legislature's use of racial classifications would be determined by the judges' sense of what was reasonable. But by refusing to apply the logic of segregated transportation to segregated housing the Court drew an important line. Above all else, *Plessy* had been understood as holding that laws designed to separate the races were subject to no intrinsic constitutional objection. In view of the way the Court chose to explain it, the decision in *Buchanan v. Warley* was no less than a repudiation of what most people took to be the rule of the earlier case.

Those who find it incongruous in its historical setting have tended to dismiss the decision in *Buchanan* as an aberration. Taken instead at face value, however, *Buchanan* implies that *Plessy* was the aberration. Justice Day's opinion announced in plain language that the Court would not thereafter expand the existing exceptions to a constitutional rule of nondiscrimination that it traced directly to the Reconstruction Amendments.

None of this altered in the slightest the reality that black citizens were everywhere the victims of unequal treatment. Another three or four decades would pass before the federal courts assumed a role in the vindication of civil rights that would begin to fulfill present-day expectations. But the decision in *Buchanan v. Warley* suggests that the slow course of judicially ordered desegregation thereafter is to be explained chiefly by political considerations, not by the evolution of legal arguments. *Buchanan* contains more antidiscrimination theory than *Brown v. Board of Education,* and more than enough to explain the unconstitutionality of segregated schools—had the Supreme Court been persuaded, in 1917, both that school segregation was undesirable and that the country would allow judges to decide the question.

Charles Evans Hughes, who had demonstrated in *McCabe* how "separate but equal" could be employed as a weapon against segregation, returned to the Supreme Court as chief justice in 1930. The same year saw the origins of the NAACP/Garland Fund project to attack segregation in education by systematic litigation directed at the inequality of segregated facilities.[22] When the results of the NAACP campaign first reached the Supreme Court in *Missouri ex rel. Gaines v. Canada,*[23] a case involving the exclusion of a black applicant from the law school at the University of Missouri, Hughes assigned to himself the writing of the critical opinion.

As presented to the Court, Missouri's system of segregated higher education provided facilities for black students that in a different context— if segregation, that is, were not inherently objectionable—might well have been found to constitute substantially equal treatment. Students who wished to pursue a course of study not offered at all-black Lincoln University were invited to apply to Lincoln's board of curators for a tuition grant to support such study at the university of any adjacent state. Petitioner Lloyd Gaines wished to study law, and Lincoln University had no law school. Rather than apply for out-of-state tuition, Gaines applied for admission to the law school of the University of Missouri; rejected, he brought suit alleging a denial of equal protection. The number of black residents of Missouri who in 1938 desired to study law and were qualified to do so was undoubtedly very small, and no one, Gaines included, had yet applied to study law at Lincoln. The state of Missouri claimed that it would organize a law school at Lincoln as soon as any prospective student asked it to do so, urging that in the meantime the availability of out-of-state tuition made a reasonable substitute.

Seven members of the Court now agreed that Missouri's discriminatory statute constituted a denial of equal protection. (A bitter dissent by James McReynolds and Pierce Butler, the two survivors of the conservative "Four Horsemen" who led the Court's resistance to the New Deal, merely underscored the thoroughness with which the old views had been left behind.) The opinion by Chief Justice Hughes followed the lines laid down in *McCabe. Gaines* nevertheless represented a significant advance over the earlier case because Missouri's statute, by comparison with Oklahoma's treatment of black railroad passengers, came much closer to affording equal treatment to prospective black law students. While Hughes quoted his own statement that "[i]t is the individual who is entitled to the equal protection of the laws," that formula was less clearly dispositive of Missouri's position than it had been of Oklahoma's: Missouri stood ready to accommodate Lloyd Gaines even though he constituted a class of one. Hughes felt constrained to add a further requirement, unexplained and not self-evident, that "[m]anifestly, the obligation of the State to give the protection of equal laws can be performed only where its laws operate, that is, within its own jurisdiction." The unabashedly ad hoc nature of this contention made the real message of the opinion even plainer.

Counsel for Lloyd Gaines, trying to show that some practical inequality resulted from Missouri's arrangements, urged that an out-of-state law school provided imperfect training for a future Missouri practitioner. Hughes declined this invitation because he intended to place the decision further out of reach:

> We think that these matters are beside the point. The basic consideration is not as to what sort of opportunities other States provide, or whether they are as good as those in Missouri, but as to what opportunities Missouri itself furnishes to white students and denies to negroes solely upon the ground of color. The admissibility of laws separating the races in the enjoyment of privileges afforded by the State rests wholly upon the equality of the privileges which the laws give to the separated groups within the State. . . . The white resident is afforded legal education within the State; the negro resident having the same qualifications is refused it there and must go outside the State to obtain it. That is a denial of the equality of legal right to the enjoyment of the privilege which the State has set up, and the provision for the payment of tuition fees in another State does not remove the discrimination.[24]

The announcement that may be read between these lines is the same that appeared in *McCabe*. It gained force with each repetition, as applied to facts that came progressively closer to establishing an outward "equality." The Court would henceforth employ the supposed doctrine of "separate but equal" only to strike down racially discriminatory arrangements, not to justify them. When Hughes wrote, in the passage just quoted, that "[t]he *admissibility* of laws separating the races . . . rests wholly upon the equality of the privileges which the laws give to the separated groups within the State," the implication—visible in retrospect—was that laws imposing segregation went against the constitutional grain; that their admissibility depended entirely on the anomalous authority of *Plessy;* and that they would henceforth be upheld only if they could satisfy the strictest test of "equality" the Court could devise. The possibility that the Court would ever again find "equality" in segregated facilities was by this time wholly illusory.

Hindsight helps us to read between the lines in *Gaines* because the constitutional rule of nondiscrimination intimated by Hughes, whatever its precise definition, scope, or rationale, was the law that the Court would now consistently apply on its continued course to the decision in *Brown.* Never acknowledged, the rule of nondiscrimination applied in the twentieth-century segregation cases was naturally never defined. In none of the cases up to and including *Brown* did the Court acknowledge that it was vindicating any principle beyond a mechanical test of equal treatment: the intervening cases on segregation simply reiterated *Gaines* on ever-closer facts. As a fitting conclusion to this logical sequence, the Court finally managed to stop measuring the equality of segregated educational facilities by declaring them all "inherently unequal." The resolution was arbitrary, but then the search for "equality" had been essentially a pretext.

It was in the extraordinary circumstances of the Japanese Relocation Cases that the Court directly addressed the legality of racial discrimination for the first time since *Plessy.* In *Hirabayashi v. United States*[25] and *Korematsu v. United States,*[26] the Supreme Court upheld the constitutionality of military curfew and exclusion orders, issued in the aftermath of Pearl Harbor, that led to the wartime internment of American citizens of Japanese ancestry. Some of the justices, painfully uncomfortable with the result that was required, as they then felt, by the exigencies of wartime, sought to anchor the law against the pull of the decisions they were announcing by stating what they believed to be the constitutional status of racial discrimination.

It is a historic and fateful irony that the only opinion on behalf of a majority of the Supreme Court to give explicit support to a color-blind reading of the Constitution was delivered in a case in which the Court found the classification before it to fall within an exception to the rule. Had the justices not been moved to establish a counterpoise to the result in the Japanese Relocation Cases, the Court's clearest affirmations of the principle of nondiscrimination would never have been written. It is true, too, that these decisions confirming the existence of an antidiscrimination principle constitute the most notable failure to protect citizens against racial discrimination in the modern history of the Court. None of these ironies, however, gives reason to doubt the sincerity of the language of the opinions. On the contrary, the Japanese Relocation Cases provide in certain respects a uniquely revealing context in which to assess the Court's evolving views on the legality of racial discrimination per se. For once, the problem of discrimination was detached from its familiar surroundings, arising in a context in which "separate but equal" would not frame the question presented. The issue could not be finessed by concentrating on equality of treatment; nor did the authority of *Plessy* stand in the way of the Court's addressing the question directly.

Chief Justice Harlan Fiske Stone's opinion in *Hirabayashi* contained one sentence that seemed for a time to put the authority of the unanimous Court behind Harlan's color blindness: "Distinctions between citizens solely because of their ancestry are by their very nature odious to a free people whose institutions are founded upon the doctrine of equality." Nor did the holding of the case detract significantly from the reach of the principle that was apparently being announced:

> The adoption by Government, in the crisis of war and of threatened invasion, of measures for the public safety, based upon the recognition of facts and circumstances which indicate that a group of one national extraction may menace that safety more than others, is not wholly beyond the limits of the Constitution and is not to be condemned merely because in other and in most circumstances racial distinctions are irrelevant.[27]

There is, realistically, no constitutional guarantee that is not subject to qualification if a majority of the Court conceives that the country faces imminent peril. If racial distinctions are "irrelevant" and therefore inadmissible in all but such extreme circumstances as "the crisis of war and of threatened invasion," the Constitution may fairly be described as color-blind.

The Justices wrote as if *Plessy* did not exist, or as if the authority of that case were understood to be an empty relic. Justice Frank Murphy's concurring opinion in *Hirabayashi* contained the following curious passage:

> Distinctions based on color and ancestry are utterly inconsistent with our traditions and ideals. . . . We cannot close our eyes to the fact that for centuries the Old World has been torn by racial and religious conflicts and has suffered the worst kind of anguish because of inequality of treatment for different groups. There was one law for one and a different law for another. Nothing is written more firmly into our law than the compact of the Plymouth voyagers to have just and equal laws.[28]

Whether the irony was conscious or unconscious, the implication for the Court's peacetime agenda was the same. Dissenting in *Korematsu,* Justice Murphy would declare that "Racial discrimination in any form and in any degree has no justifiable part whatever in our democratic way of life."[29] Although this statement was not made with the authority of the Court, it was a fair paraphrase of what the Court had said about distinctions that are "by their very nature odious."

This forthright manner of stating the issue was dangerous, because it could commit the Court to moving more quickly on ordinary segregation than might otherwise seem prudent. The more flexible formula with which Justice Hugo Black began his opinion for the majority in *Korematsu* reasserted the Court's discretion in the matter: "It should be noted, to begin with, that all legal restrictions which curtail the civil rights of a single racial group are immediately suspect. That is not to say that all such restrictions are unconstitutional. It is to say that courts must subject them to the most rigid scrutiny."[30] Consistent with the one surviving principle of *Plessy,* the Court might still judge racial classifications by a "rule of reason": the results in the Japanese Relocation Cases form one example of its operation. In every other respect, the authority of *Plessy* was again repudiated. By its statements that racial distinctions were "odious," that they were "subject to the most rigid scrutiny," the Court indirectly acknowledged that its views of the constitutionality of racial discrimination had been radically altered since the last time it had explicitly addressed the subject. The acknowledgment was made at a time when *Plessy* might be momentarily disregarded; and the problem of what to do with a precedent that the Court was no longer disposed to follow, yet hesitated to overrule, could therefore be deferred a while longer.

By the time the Court returned to the subject of racial discrimination, in postwar cases involving segregation in graduate education and railroad dining cars,[31] civil rights lawyers could point to recent Supreme Court authority supporting a more radical approach to the issue: the idea that the real vice of segregated institutions was not the inequality of facilities but the underlying racial discrimination itself. Besides the statements to be found in the Japanese Relocation Cases, there was Justice Robert Jackson's widely repeated epigram in *Edwards v. California,* arguing against the denial of equal protection to the indigent: "The mere state of being without funds is a neutral fact—constitutionally an irrelevance, like race, creed or color." A constitutional "irrelevance," for Justice Jackson, was "neither a source of rights nor a basis for denying them."[32] Justice Wiley Rutledge could be quoted, straining the context of his remarks only slightly, for the view that a racial classification was a "forbidden discrimination" and "a wholly arbitrary exercise of power."[33] For the purposes of advocacy, the constitutional argument against segregation might henceforth be made on two levels. Racial classifications were impermissible to begin with; and in any event, the particular segregated facilities in suit were "unequal." The choice of means was necessarily left to the Court.

Thus it was that civil rights plaintiffs came once again to argue to the Supreme Court that the Constitution was color-blind, approximately half a century after Justice Harlan had last done so. In his brief for Ada Sipuel, denied admission to the law school of the University of Oklahoma while the state set about establishing a separate law school for black students, Thurgood Marshall stated the antidiscrimination position in unmistakable terms:

> Classifications and distinctions based on race or color have no moral or legal validity in our society. They are contrary to our constitution and laws, and this Court has struck down statutes, ordinances or official policies seeking to establish such classifications.[34]

Once revived by Marshall and his colleagues, the color-blind argument was promptly seconded from other quarters. Preparing the appeal in *Sweatt v. Painter,*[35] in which the Court would consider the adequacy of a makeshift law school hastily established at Texas State University for Negroes, the civil rights forces decided to divide the broad lines of argument between them. While the NAACP Legal Defense Fund directed its arguments primarily to refuting the state's claim of equal treatment, a group of law professors pressed the more radical antidiscrimination argument as *amicus curiae.*[36] The professors' briefs, submitted in the name of the ad hoc Committee of Law Teachers Against Segregation in Education, embodied the liberal academic opinion of the generation that worked for and later celebrated *Brown*. Introduced by lengthy quotation of the obligatory passages from Harlan's dissent in *Plessy*, the constitutional position asserted was carefully stated and uncompromisingly color-blind:

> Laws which give equal protection are those which make no *discrimination* because of race in the sense that they make no *distinction* because of race. As soon as laws make a right or a responsibility dependent solely on race, they violate the 14th Amendment. Reasonable classifications may be made, but one basis of classification is completely precluded; for the Equal Protection clause makes racial classifications unreasonable per se. . . .
>
> . . . We contend that the Equal Protection clause forbids distinctions because of race, and that state-enforced segregation is therefore unconstitutional because it makes such a distinction.[37]

A few months later, the Office of the Solicitor General lent the authority of the United States to the color-blind contention. The brief for the United States in *Henderson v. United States*,[38] a challenge to the segregated dining cars operated (with the approval of the Interstate Commerce Commission) by the Southern Railway, referred to "the basic constitutional doctrine which condemns racial discriminations having the sanction of law or the support of an agency of government." The brief went on to quote the "color-blind" sentence from *Plessy* before stating flatly: "Racial discriminations effected by action of the Federal Government, or any agency thereof, are prohibited by the due process clause of the Fifth Amendment." The solicitor general was not as theoretically rigorous as the law professors: references on succeeding pages to "the right to equal treatment" and to the Negro's right "to be free from governmentally-enforced discrimination against him" qualified the government's position with a more familiar argument based on inequality of treatment.[39] But color-blind language in a brief for the United States marked a turning point.

The facts of *McLaurin v. Oklahoma State Regents*, one of the trio of segregation cases decided in June 1950,[40] pushed the Supreme Court closer than ever to ruling on the constitutionality of segregation per se. Following a judicial determination that George McLaurin could not be constitutionally excluded from the graduate school of the University of Oklahoma (there being no other state institution where he could pursue a doctoral degree in education), the legislature amended its segregation statutes to provide that when black students were necessarily admitted to white institutions, the program of instruction should at least be provided "upon a segregated basis." By the time the case reached the Supreme Court, this meant in practice that McLaurin was required to sit by himself in a specified row in the classroom and at specified tables in the library and the cafeteria.

Because the inequality of treatment in *McLaurin* was so nearly intangible, the constitutional objections to this petty and vestigial form of segregation were most readily stated as a broad challenge to government-sponsored racial distinctions. Preparing their jurisdictional statement in early 1949, attorneys for the Legal Defense Fund (led by Thurgood Marshall, Robert L. Carter, and Constance Baker Motley) summarized the antidiscrimination position that could be supported by an optimistic view of the past decade's decisions:

The United States Constitution Prohibits Government Classifications Based on Race or Ancestry

In recent cases the Supreme Court has held on many occasions under a variety of circumstances that racial criteria are irrational, irrelevant, odious to our way of life and specifically proscribed under the Fourteenth Amendment. Whether this proscription against racial classifications be found in the constitutional concept of equal protection or is included within the meaning of due process, the result is the same. The only apparent limitation on this doctrine appears to be that of a national emergency such as the danger of espionage and sabotage in time of war which might control the decision of the Court.[41]

A reevaluation of familiar authorities, the lawyers argued, would reveal that a prohibition of racial classifications was already implicit in the decisions. Noting correctly that "[t]he rationale of the *Plessy* case as to the classification of Negroes" could not be squared with the antidiscrimination principle that underlay *Buchanan v. Warley,* the authors continued:

More recent decisions of the Supreme Court . . . have made it clear that the basis for the decision in the *Plessy* case that the Fourteenth Amendment "could not have been intended to abolish distinctions based upon color" is no longer valid. . . .

The recent cases, standing as they do for the principle that racial classification by government is unconstitutional because "(d)istinctions between citizens solely because of their ancestry are by their nature odious to a free people," have completely repudiated the doctrine of *Plessy* v. *Ferguson* that the Fourteenth Amendment "could not have been intended to abolish distinctions based upon color."[42]

The Court's opinions in *Sweatt, McLaurin,* and *Henderson,* announced together on June 5, 1950, formed its last pronouncement on segregation prior to *Brown.* Striking down segregation in each case, the Court pointedly declined to rest its decisions on the antidiscrimination grounds that now existed. *Sweatt* and *McLaurin* were decided by finding inequality on the authority of *Gaines.* In *Henderson,* the Court held merely that the dining car arrangements of the Southern Railway violated the requirement of equal accommodations imposed by the Interstate Commerce Act. The narrowness of the chosen grounds of decision was emphasized and defended by Chief Justice Fred Vinson, writing for the Court in *Sweatt v. Painter:* "Broader issues have been urged for our consideration, but we adhere to the principle of deciding constitutional questions only in the context of the particular case before the Court. We have frequently reiterated that this Court will decide constitutional questions only when necessary to the disposition of the case at hand, and that such decisions will be drawn as narrowly as possible."[43]

Urgent political considerations, and not the platitudes invoked by Chief Justice Vinson, counseled disposition of the "1950 Trilogy" on the narrowest possible grounds. As the justices were acutely aware, to decide *Sweatt, McLaurin,* and *Henderson* on the broad grounds urged by the plaintiffs would be effectively to decide all the remaining issues of racial classification as well: segregated public education at all levels; segregation of other public facilities; even the laws against interracial marriage.[44] There can have been little doubt in 1950 about the ultimate outcome; but the sequence of steps by which it would be reached, and the propitious moment for taking each, remained difficult and perilous choices. Ordinary political prudence dictated that the Court retain the utmost freedom to choose its means and its moment.

Beginning early in the half-century after *Plessy,* the consensus of the Supreme Court about the extent to which the Fourteenth Amendment permitted racial classifications underwent a profound shift. Two extraordinary constraints, however, prevented the normal expression of this change of views in the published opinions of the Court. One was the ostensible authority of *Plessy* itself, a decision too visible to be easily repudiated, although it quickly lost any attraction as a controlling precedent. The other was the Court's political judgment that the way to challenge segregation was by narrow, cautious increments. Because the Court's growing hostility to racial distinctions carried unmistakable implications for controversial future decisions, the Court in its opinions elected to dissemble its constitutional views.

The ingenious contribution of Charles Evans Hughes, first sketched in *McCabe* and then reinforced in *Gaines,* was a judicial method by which a rule of "separate but equal" might be turned against itself, and the legal shield of segregation made the chief weapon against it. But the device involved the Court in a fundamental duplicity that repeated use made increasingly difficult to renounce. Every new decision striking down segregation on the artificially narrow grounds of unequal treatment constituted additional and more recent authority for the proposition that segregation affording equal treatment was both constitutionally unobjectionable and (by implication) possible. At the same time, the Court's unwillingness to voice its evolving hostility to racial classifications, relying instead in case after case on findings of unequal treatment, left the antidiscrimination theme of Fourteenth Amendment interpretation relatively impoverished. One consequence is that when the Court was finally prepared to declare that "racial segregation as such" was unconstitutional, it found itself incapable of explaining why.

Hopeful that the long-awaited decision in the School Segregation Cases[1] might be the occasion on which the Court finally announced that the Constitution forbade racial classifications, sympathetic observers watched so intently that many saw what they had come to expect. On the Sunday after the decision was handed down, in May 1954, the *New York Times* put it into historical perspective:

> It is forty-three years since John Marshall Harlan passed from this earth. Now the words he used in his lonely dissent in an 8-to-1 decision in the case of Plessy v. Ferguson in 1896 have become in effect by last Monday's unanimous decision of the Supreme Court a part of the law of the land.
> Justice Harlan said: "Our Constitution is color-blind and neither knows nor tolerates classes among citizens. . . ."
> Last Monday's case dealt solely with segregation in the schools, but there was not one word in Chief Justice Warren's opinion that was inconsistent with the earlier views of Justice Harlan. This is an instance in which the voice crying in the wilderness finally becomes the expression of a people's will and in which justice overtakes and thrusts aside a timorous expediency.[2]

The reader who turns to the opinion in *Brown* expecting the vindication, or even an acknowledgment, of Justice Harlan's lonely dissent will in fact find nothing of the sort. The Court's willingness to confront school segregation in 1954 was an act of courage and a wager at the highest stakes, setting the Court's political authority substantially at risk. The eventual outcome was a monumental triumph for the nation, for the Constitution, and not least for the Court, whose political role underwent a historic transformation as a result of this great case. But the greatness of the case is not to be found in the opinion. History does not always rise to the occasion; and the most important Supreme Court decision of the twentieth century, one that marked a turning point in the institutional role of the Court and in the life of the nation, was announced in an opinion that was historically and legally jejune.

That this was Chief Justice Earl Warren's intention was almost expressly acknowledged, and from a political standpoint it is entirely comprehensible. It was not clear, until the attempt had succeeded, that the southern states could be brought to obey a judicial mandate to desegregate their schools. No explanation of the decision could disguise the fact that it would be, as Justice Robert Jackson had put it, "making new law for a new day";[3] the Court's authority to do so was certain to be fiercely attacked. The immediate task confronting the chief justice in preparing the opinion was not to write history or constitutional law but to obtain the broadest possible consensus on the Court while offering the smallest possible target to its adversaries. Ideally, in Alexander Bickel's sly suggestion, the decision was one that "should not mean / But be."[4] The chief justice informed his colleagues that his drafts of the opinions in *Brown* and *Bolling v. Sharpe* (the companion case from the District of Columbia) had been prepared "on the theory that [they] should be short, readable by the lay public, non-rhetorical, unemotional and, above all, non-accusatory."[5] To these ends, the stated rationale of the momentous decision was narrowed to the vanishing point.

The claims of history were disposed of first. In its order the previous term, assigning the consolidated segregation cases for reargument, the Court had plainly intimated that the views of those who framed and ratified the Fourteenth Amendment were pertinent to deciding whether the amendment prohibited segregated schools:

> In their briefs and on oral argument counsel are requested to discuss particularly the following questions insofar as they are relevant to the respective cases:
>
> 1. What evidence is there that the Congress which submitted and the State legislatures and conventions which ratified the Fourteenth Amendment contemplated or did not contemplate, understood or did not understand, that it would abolish segregation in public schools?
>
> 2. If neither the Congress in submitting nor the States in ratifying the Fourteenth Amendment understood that compliance with it would require the immediate abolition of segregation in public schools, was it nevertheless the understanding of the framers of the Amendment

(a) that future Congresses might, in the exercise of their power under section 5 of the Amendment, abolish such segregation, or

(b) that it would be within the judicial power, in light of future conditions, to construe the Amendment as abolishing such segregation of its own force?[6]

The questions had been propounded at the instigation of Justice Felix Frankfurter, largely for purposes of delay;[7] although few lawyers, prior to the decision in *Brown,* would have doubted their relevance. The Court's questions produced a major effort of historical research, both by the parties and by Alexander Bickel as Frankfurter's clerk, and the Court now had its answers.[8] To the first question, asking whether the amendment was originally understood to prohibit school segregation of its own force, the clear answer was "no." To question 2(b) of the order, asking whether it had been understood at the time that future courts might so construe the amendment, the most optimistic conclusion could be only "perhaps." Although such answers did not foreclose the issue, they did not assist in reaching the desired result; and the issues to which the Court had earlier directed the parties' particular attention were now unceremoniously brushed aside. The original understanding of the effect of the Fourteenth Amendment on segregated schools—a complicated and troubling problem if the question was a legitimate one at all—was dealt with by describing the evidence as "inconclusive." The very relevance of history to the issues before the Court was dismissed with the observation that "we cannot turn the clock back to 1868 when the Amendment was adopted."[9] The Court was prepared to announce new law for a new day but not to justify its doing so.

It remained to explain the decision. The straightforward approach, urged in the briefs of the antisegregation forces, would have been to declare the unconstitutionality of segregation itself, without regard to equality of treatment in separate facilities. The alternative, pressed notably in a brief for the United States as *amicus curiae* in the first round of argument in 1952,[10] was to decide the School Segregation Cases the way *Gaines, Sipuel, Sweatt,* and *McLaurin* had been decided: by refusing to find the necessary "equality" in segregated schools. The first choice meant overruling *Plessy v. Ferguson;* the second meant finding for the plaintiffs virtually on the authority of *Plessy,* insisting as always on the "equal" side of "separate but equal" but without calling the doctrine into question.

The latter course appeared the more prudent, but the opinion written in consequence is not an edifying one. Considering the decision in its historical context, it is impossible to resist the conclusion that the Court in 1954 accepted the basic contention of the lawyers opposed to segregation: that the unconstitutionality of segregated schools was independent of anything that might be said about their measurable equality or inequality. But to acknowledge that conviction meant disavowing *Plessy.* The will of the Court was that segregated schools be henceforth illegal, without further inquiry into "equality"; the function of the opinion was to reach that result without acknowledging that "separate but equal" had long since lost its authority as a defense of segregation before the U.S. Supreme Court. The long-standing limitation of "equality" as a weapon in the legal battle against segregation—the fact that it could have no application to segregated schools whose equality or inequality had not been judicially established—was now circumvented in the famous conclusion that, because of their adverse psychological impact, "[s]eparate educational facilities are inherently unequal."[11]

The decision in *Brown* thus turned on the "social science" portion of the opinion: the psychological findings of the Kansas trial court, supported by the Supreme Court's famous "social science footnote," to the effect that legally imposed segregation retards the educational and mental development of black children.[12] That the unconstitutionality of school segregation should be explained on this basis was, for a number of reasons, profoundly unsatisfactory. Taken at face value, the opinion necessarily implied that there was nothing wrong with racial segregation in and of itself: "separate but equal" facilities, were they only attainable, would be as constitutional as ever. The constitutionality of racial segregation was left hostage, moreover, to modern authority in the social sciences. Should subsequent, more modern authority question the sociological wisdom of 1954—as has in fact occurred—the authority of the constitutional rule, were its basis really as described in the opinion, would be to that extent diminished.[13]

The chief justice's appeal to psychological findings as a basis of constitutional law in this area had a close but distasteful precedent. When Albion Tourgée, representing Homer Plessy, urged that black citizens were stigmatized by Louisiana's separate car law, Justice Henry Billings Brown replied that if "the enforced separation of the two races stamps the colored race with a badge of inferiority" it was "not by reason of anything found in the act, but solely because the colored race chooses to put that construction on it." Should a statute "in precisely similar terms" be reenacted by a Louisiana legislature in which "the colored race" was once again dominant, "the white race," Brown imagined, "would not acquiesce in this assumption." Nor, for the matter, was Brown prepared to accept the proposition "that social prejudices may be overcome by legislation."[14] If the opinions of Justice Brown and Chief Justice Warren are set side by side for comparison, their most pronounced point of divergence lies in their respective assumptions about the psychology of race relations—assumptions that neither justice was in a position to validate. But if the legality of racial segregation properly depends on the current state of psychological opinion, expert or homespun, then it is probably an error to regard it as a constitutional question at all.

Finally, and most critically, the acknowledged reasoning of *Brown* was unsatisfactory because it was false to the historic legal conclusions to which the Supreme Court in 1954 had evidently come. The ostensible, "psychological" justification for the decision in *Brown* is singularly unconvincing: rather than an explication of the Court's reasoning, it was a carefully chosen, essentially artificial explanation of a result reached on fundamentally different grounds. The Supreme Court had finally come to grips with the enduring moral and political problem of the nation at a moment when most Americans were prepared to hear that racial segregation imposed by law was morally and politically wrong. That this conviction moved the Court to its decision—and not, as the opinion would have it, a hasty conclusion that segregated schools could never be "equal" in psychological effect—is clear from the available evidence as to the Court's deliberations;[15] it is clearer still from the legal context in which the case was decided and the tendency of the preceding decisions. The opinion written to mark this watershed in the nation's history was designed not to illuminate but to disguise the road being traveled.[16]

Whether the political acceptability of the decision in the School Segregation Cases was actually enhanced by the pretense that the Court was deciding them within the bounds of "separate but equal," it is impossible to say even in retrospect. There are reasons to doubt it. Those hostile to the decision were not deceived about its implications, and those who welcomed it tended to see in the opinion what the Court had been careful to omit. Meanwhile the Court lost the opportunity, in the context of the most important civil rights case it would ever decide, to explore a vital question left unanswered in 1866: the terms of the Fourteenth Amendment's command with respect to laws making a distinction between citizens on the basis of color. On this crucial point, *Brown* was a blank slate on which the Court and its commentators might thereafter write a changing constitutional law, supplying the missing rationale in consequence of what later cases appeared to require.

The Court's failure to explain the segregation decision in more forthright terms was not the result of any deficiency in the argument. The briefs and arguments in the School Segregation Cases crystallized the legal position of the civil rights movement for the period when its avowed legal objective was a color-blind Constitution. Taken together, they represent the high-water mark of the attempt to persuade the Court to adopt Justice Harlan's view of the Fourteenth Amendment. Although the two rounds of argument and the multiplicity of cases allowed the nation's leading civil rights lawyers[17] to assert alternative grounds on which segregated schools should be held illegal, the thrust of their joint position was plainly toward the per se illegality of racial distinctions. Within the range of arguments proposed by the briefs, the *narrow* alternative most frequently argued—that in the context of education, race was an unreasonable and hence impermissible basis of classification—was itself significantly broader than the "inequality" rationale acknowledged in the Court's opinion.[18] The *broad* alternative—that racial discrimination was impermissible per se—was prominently represented in the initial round of briefing in 1952 and constituted the leading contention of the consolidated brief on reargument filed by the antisegregation forces in November 1953.

The Brief for Appellants submitted in September 1952 in the Kansas case, *Brown v. Board of Education of Topeka,* began its summary of argument in unqualifiedly color-blind terms: "The Fourteenth Amendment precludes a state from imposing distinctions or classifications based upon race or color alone." The premise was developed in Point I of the brief—the district court's findings as to psychological impact being relegated to Point II—with an argument tending to show that racial classifications were unreasonable per se:

> When the distinctions imposed [upon selected groups of citizens] are based upon race and color alone, the state's action is patently the epitome of that arbitrariness and capriciousness constitutionally impermissive [*sic*] under our system of government. . . . A racial criterion is a constitutional irrelevance . . . and is not saved from condemnation even though dictated by a sincere desire to avoid the possibility of violence or race friction. . . . Only because it was a war measure designed to cope with a grave national emergency was the federal government permitted to level restrictions against persons of enemy descent. . . . This action, "odious" . . . and "suspect" . . . even in times of national peril, must cease as soon as that peril is past. . . .
>
> Since 1940, in an unbroken line of decisions, this Court has clearly enunciated the doctrine that the state may not validly impose distinctions

and restrictions among its citizens based upon race or color alone in each field of governmental activity where [the] question has been raised. . . .[19]

In the South Carolina case, *Briggs v. Elliott,* successive briefs stated the color-blind position even more plainly. The Jurisdictional Statement argued that classifications "based solely on race or color" were not only "arbitrary and unreasonable" but were "the very kind the equal protection clause was specifically designed to prohibit"; that "the citizen's right to have his rights, obligations, and duties to the state determined without regard to his race or color is a fundamental right essential to our democratic society"; in sum, that "the Fourteenth Amendment has stripped the state of power to make race and color the basis for governmental action."[20] The Brief for Appellants in the same case relied on standard equal protection doctrine to argue that racial classifications were impermissible:

A state legislative classification violates the equal protection clause of the Fourteenth Amendment either if it is based upon nonexistent differences or if the differences are not reasonably related to a proper legislative objective. Classifications based on race or color can never satisfy either requirement and consequently are the epitome of arbitrariness in legislation.[21]

Finally, the Reply Brief argued for the color-blind Constitution through an appeal to history, referring to

the historic fact that the Fourteenth Amendment represents an effort permanently to debar the states from imposing disadvantages upon individuals because of their race or ancestry. In contemporary recognition of this constitutional purpose opinions of this Court have more than once indicated that our civilization has advanced to the point where all governmentally imposed race distinctions are so odious that a state, bound to afford equal protection of the laws, must not impose them.[22]

The Jurisdictional Statement in the Virginia case, *Davis v. County School Board of Prince Edward County,* emphasized the boldness of the chosen ground of argument:

Indeed, we take the unqualified position that the Fourteenth Amendment has totally stripped the state of power to make race and color the basis for governmental action. . . . While an exception may be made with respect to the federal government in a grave national emergency, . . . no state can show any such overriding necessity which would warrant sustaining state action founded upon these constitutionally irrelevant and arbitrary considerations. . . . For this reason alone, we submit, the state separate school laws in this case must fall.[23]

The companion case from the District of Columbia, *Bolling v. Sharpe*, had been framed from the outset to constitute an inescapable challenge to the legality of segregation per se: counsel for the plaintiffs, James M. Nabrit, Jr., intentionally omitted from his pleadings any allegation of the inequality of the plainly unequal schools that the District provided for black children.[24] The argument of Nabrit's Supreme Court brief was similarly unqualified:

> *One of the constitutional guarantees, which petitioners may not lawfully be deprived of the benefit of, is that as citizens no distinctions be made between them and other citizens because of race or color alone.*[25]

Finally, the Legal Defense Fund's consolidated brief on reargument (filed in late 1953) pointedly reaffirmed the antidiscrimination theme of the previous term's briefs. The Summary of Argument stated as its first point that "Distinctions drawn by state authorities on the basis of color or race violate the Fourteenth Amendment." The fuller argument of the brief began with the statement that "This Court in a long line of decisions has made it plain that the Fourteenth Amendment prohibits a state from making racial distinctions in the exercise of governmental power." Pursuing the discussion, the lawyers referred to "judicial recognition that race is an irrational basis for governmental action under our Constitution," to "the constitutional prohibition against Congressional action grounded upon color except in so far as it may have temporary justification to meet an overwhelming national emergency," and to "abhorrence of race as a premise for governmental action," all as justification for "this Court's basic premise that, as a matter of law, race is not an allowable basis of differentiation in governmental action."[26]

The color-blind position would not have been argued so consistently and so prominently if the Legal Defense Fund attorneys had felt that such a resolution of the segregation issue was out of reach. In a theoretical sense it probably was not. A majority of the justices in 1954 might well have been persuaded that racial classifications were presumptively impermissible, had their sense of the Court's political position permitted them to entertain the proposition. What seems clear in retrospect, by contrast, is that no amount of argument could have induced the Court to decide the School Segregation Cases on the basis that the Constitution was color-blind, or on any other basis that implied a resolution of issues of racial discrimination not yet before it. The considerations that had counseled a narrow disposition of the "1950 Trilogy" applied with redoubled force to the situation confronting the Court four years later, when no one could predict with certainty that a desegregation mandate, whatever its terms, would prove to be enforceable.

The unwelcome implications of a broad rationale for desegregation—though unwelcome only in that the Court did not wish to acknowledge them in 1954—included every other form of legally imposed segregation; these the Court would deal with presently, but piecemeal and by unadorned fiat. A color-blind rationale would further have raised the Gorgon's head of miscegenation. The extent to which the Court feared the latter issue, as potentially undermining its authority in the more important desegregation agenda, was demonstrated by its humiliating refusal to hear the appeal in *Naim v. Naim*—a Virginia case that arose, most inopportunely, in the term immediately following *Brown II*.

Mr. and Mrs. Naim (one of whom was white, the other of Chinese ancestry) were residents of Virginia; they traveled to North Carolina to be married in 1952, returning to live as husband and wife in Norfolk. Following the breakdown of the relationship Mrs. Naim sued her husband for an annulment, alleging the invalidity of their marriage under Virginia's miscegenation statutes. The decree was granted. Mr. Naim appealed, arguing that Virginia's laws prohibiting interracial marriage violated his rights under the Fourteenth Amendment. Applying a nearly unanimous line of authorities, which included the 1883 Supreme Court decision in *Pace v. Alabama,* Virginia's Supreme Court of Appeals upheld the constitutionality of the state's miscegenation laws and affirmed the decree.[27]

Mr. Naim's appeal to the U.S. Supreme Court came up for consideration in the fall of 1955, only months after the School Segregation Cases had been remanded to the district courts for further proceedings "with all deliberate speed." The Court was determined not to hear the case. In a memorandum to the Supreme Court conference, Justice Frankfurter warned that "to throw a decision of this Court other than validating this legislation into the vortex of the present disquietude would . . . seriously, I believe very seriously, embarrass the carrying-out of the Court's decree of last May." The result was an order remanding *Naim* to the Virginia courts on the pretext that the record in the case was inadequate to raise the constitutional issue. Virginia's Supreme Court of Appeals promptly affirmed its earlier decision, declaring (and pointedly demonstrating) that the constitutional issue was clearly presented on the record. A renewed appeal to the Supreme Court was simply dismissed.[28]

The *Naim v. Naim* episode makes it easy to imagine the nature of

Frankfurter's warnings—if any were needed—against adopting a rationale for the decision in the School Segregation Cases that carried implications for future cases. The same episode reveals, ironically enough, how closely the unannounced law of the Fourteenth Amendment already approached a rule of color blindness. *Naim v. Naim* was an embarrassment only because it was out of the question, in 1955, that the Court *uphold* the constitutionality of a law prohibiting interracial marriage. Yet the constitutional objection to such a law could not readily be described as a violation of equal treatment; nor was it easily demonstrable from the constricted rationale of *Brown.* The natural objection to a "marriage law," as the Lynn Women's Anti-Slavery Society had perceived in 1839, was to the racial classification itself. The contention that a "marriage law" is *unconstitutional* (as opposed to the argument that it is bad policy) leads very quickly, as the Garrisonians discovered, to the contention that racial classifications are inherently improper. The fact that the Supreme Court was unwilling to discuss *Naim v. Naim* suggests how close it was in 1955 to accepting the Garrisonian proposition.

Whether a more candid explanation of the result in the School Segregation Cases would really have had the consequences the Court went so far to avoid is naturally another question; and had the Court in 1954 and 1955 declared the Constitution to be color-blind while mandating its enforcement "with all deliberate speed," the immediate political consequences might not have been significantly different.[29] The Court's actions, as opposed to its words, quickly demonstrated to anyone who was watching that it had reached conclusions about racial segregation far surpassing what was acknowledged in *Brown.* A week after announcing the decisions in the School Segregation Cases, the Court summarily vacated a lower court decision finding no constitutional violation in the refusal of a private theater company to admit black patrons to operatic performances at a leased municipal amphitheater, remanding the case "for consideration in the light of [*Brown*] and conditions that now prevail."[30] In the rapid series of memorandum decisions by which the Court now attacked segregation in the remaining areas where it was still legally imposed—on public beaches, in municipal parks and recreational facilities, in intrastate transportation—the Court abandoned the outworn pretense that the Fourteenth Amendment commanded only equal treatment, but substituted nothing in its place. In each instance, the Court struck down the challenged practice without any explanation at all.[31] After enough cases had been decided in this manner that the country might be expected to have got the message, the Court bluntly declared the legality of segregation to be "foreclosed as a litigable issue."[32]

The difficulty for analysis was that the stated rationale of *Brown*, the Court's final word on the legality of racial segregation, did not explain what was unconstitutional about "separate but equal" tennis courts or bathhouses. Following its consistent practice ever since *Gaines*, the Court had explained the school segregation decision in an opinion that misrepresented the true scope of the conclusions it had reached. When the Court then turned to dispose of segregation in other areas, the opinion in its leading case would not serve as authority. Each of the disingenuous "separate but equal" decisions had made it more difficult to offer principled reasons for the next one, and the addition of *Brown* to the list made the task harder still.

The memorandum decisions appeared to illuminate, in retrospect, the rationale of the School Segregation Cases. If segregated golf courses and city buses were illegal on the authority of *Brown*, then the holding of *Brown* was necessarily broader than that acknowledged in the opinion. The real basis of the decision, it now transpired, must have been the conclusion that "a State may not constitutionally require segregation of public facilities."[33] But what was the reasoning behind that conclusion? Perhaps the Court's idea was that racial segregation in any context constituted a denial of equal protection, for reasons adumbrated by Sumner's argument about caste; perhaps it was that no form of state legislation "conceived in hostility to, and enacted for the purpose of humiliating citizens of the United States of a particular race"[34] could ever be constitutional; perhaps, inspired by *Strauder* and *Hirabayashi* as well as by the other passages of Justice Harlan's famous opinion, the Court had come to the conclusion that the Fourteenth Amendment prohibited the government in most circumstances from classifying citizens on the basis of race. So long as the target was state-imposed segregation, the choice between broader and narrower rationales made no practical difference. When these same distinctions became all-important, as the country wondered about the legality of racial discrimination favoring formerly disfavored groups, those who looked for guidance to the Supreme Court's segregation decisions would find an intellectual void.

Addressing themselves directly (as few contemporary observers seem to have done)[35] to the question of what constitutional rule the Court was actually applying, Albert Blaustein and Clarence Ferguson concluded in 1957 that "What the Supreme Court did on May 17, 1954, was to adopt a constitutional standard . . . [declaring] that all classification by race is unconstitutional *per se*. . . ."[36] In support of their conclusion, the authors pointed to (1) a brief reference in *Brown* to the early, antidiscrimination interpretation of the Fourteenth Amendment;[37] (2) selected language from the Japanese Relocation Cases and other antidiscrimination dicta of the 1940s, such as Justice Jackson's statement that race is "constitutionally an irrelevance"; (3) the fact that the implementation opinion in the School Segregation Cases was so worded as to condemn "discrimination" rather than "segregation" in education; and (4) the way in which the authority of *Brown* had subsequently been used to strike down racial segregation outside the field of public education. It followed that *Brown* was more than the "judicial erosion" of *Plessy,* it was "an affirmative statement of a contrary principle of law"; and that Justice Harlan's dissenting opinion, stating that our Constitution is color-blind, "had become the unanimous view of the nine men of 1954."[38]

At this remove the evidence is unpersuasive, and the authors' reading of the significance of *Brown* has long since been overtaken by events. About its meaning in 1957, however, they may well have been correct. Precisely because it was never disclosed, the rationale of the segregation decisions was uniquely malleable; and the Court's subsequent disavowal of the color-blind reading of *Brown* does not foreclose the possibility that segregation decisions of the 1950s might have been justified at the time in terms of a rule of color blindness, had the Court been obliged to explain what it was doing. The answer that would be given today, making the constitutionality of a racial classification turn on the Court's assessment of its usefulness in furthering important governmental objectives, would have been unthinkable in the 1950s. The issues that would shortly cause the color-blind ideal to be abandoned by its proponents lay invisible in the future.

The post-*Brown* segregation cases of the 1950s did not oblige judges to decide whether or to what extent the Constitution was color-blind, since the pragmatic assumption that all separate facilities were now presumptively "unequal" was a sufficient guide to correct decision. Racial classifications in which inequality was harder to discern would require a more radical rule of antidiscrimination: this was the aspect of *Naim v. Naim* that made the Court's reaction to it so revealing. Before the end of the decade, a case presenting a reasonably close analogy to the miscegenation problem was the occasion for the first judicial statement of the per se illegality of racial classification.

In *Dorsey v. State Athletic Commission,*[39] a three-judge district court considered a constitutional challenge brought by a black professional prizefighter to a rule of the Louisiana Athletic Commission prohibiting the licensing of any boxing match between black and white fighters or of any boxing exhibition in which black and white fighters appeared on the same card, and a Louisiana statute that (among other provisions) made it a misdemeanor to sponsor, arrange, or participate in "any dancing, social functions, entertainments, athletic training, games, sports or contests . . . in which the participants or contestants are members of the white and negro races."[40] The discrimination effected by the rule and the statute could not comfortably be addressed on the authority of the earlier segregation decisions, all of which involved the maintenance of segregated public facilities. Nor was there any obvious inequality of treatment. On their face, the challenged laws treated black and white prizefighters precisely alike, in that what was denied to one race was denied to the other.

Equality of treatment is not enough if the Fourteenth Amendment forbids racial classifications. In his opinion for the district court, Judge John Minor Wisdom of the Fifth Circuit adopted the conclusion of Blaustein and Ferguson: not just that race was an impermissible classification, but that the Supreme Court *had so held* on May 17, 1954. The prohibition of interracial prizefights was unconstitutional, wrote Judge Wisdom, because

> [i]n the School Segregation Cases . . . the Supreme Court held that classification based on race is inherently discriminatory and violative of the Equal Protection Clause of the Fourteenth Amendment.[41]

If it is useful to identify a brief period during which our Constitution was effectively color-blind, that period may be dated from the Supreme Court's affirmance of *Dorsey,* by memorandum decision without citation of authorities, on May 25, 1959.[42]

10 | The Road Not Taken

For a brief period in the early 1960s, some members of the Supreme Court appeared to regard the color blindness of the Constitution as a settled thing. An opinion by Justice Tom Clark in 1963 explained the unconstitutionality of the "minority transfer rule" in southern school districts with the blanket observation that "racial classifications are 'obviously irrelevant and invidious,'" citing as analogies the full range of cases—from the modern segregation decisions all the way back to *Strauder v. West Virginia*—in which racial classifications had been held invalid.[1] A dissenting opinion by Justice Potter Stewart, also in 1963, referred to *Brown v. Board of Education* as having established the per se impermissibility of classification on racial lines: "A segregated school system . . . is invalid simply because our Constitution presupposes that men are created equal, and that therefore racial differences cannot provide a valid basis for government action."[2] Justice Arthur Goldberg, in a concurring opinion the following term, stressed the Court's obligation to "do justice to a Constitution which is color blind."[3] But statements of this kind suddenly disappeared from the opinions of the justices. Their absence was the more striking because the Court was being pointedly asked to announce that government might not constitutionally take account of racial distinctions, and because some of the antidiscrimination decisions that followed were difficult to explain on any other principled basis.

In the 1964 case of *Anderson v. Martin*[4] the Court struck down a Louisiana statute requiring that nomination and ballot papers specify the race of candidates for office. Why such a requirement should be unconstitutional is an interesting question. The statute had of course been drawn to apply without distinction to candidates of all races; and the complaining parties—black candidates for election to the school board of East Baton Rouge Parish—could never have demonstrated, by the ordinary standards of judicial proof, that it operated in a discriminatory fashion against them.[5] The statute did not deny equal treatment; nor did it subject any person to distinctive treatment because of his race. The state of Louisiana, meanwhile, was fostering an informed electorate by providing an identification that some voters presumably considered as significant to their choice as the other information commonly printed on the ballot, the candidates' names and political affiliation.

That such a statute is politically offensive is not difficult to see. To find it unconstitutional as well—for reasons independent of the disapprobation of judges—implied a Constitution profoundly color-blind, to the point that the government was not only forbidden to treat one citizen differently from another because of his race (this much *a fortiori*), but was moreover forbidden to suggest, directly or indirectly, that racial distinctions could be relevant to the citizen's own choices in matters of public importance. Such was the basis on which the unconstitutionality of the statute was argued by the dissenting member of the three-judge district court and by the civil rights forces on appeal. The Supreme Court, significantly, chose to rest its decision on other grounds.

The district court had found the statute constitutional. Judge John Minor Wisdom, dissenting, emphasized that the vice of the Louisiana statute was something absolute, in no way dependent on inequality of treatment or disparity of impact. Drawing an analogy to the earlier segregation cases he recast them in the same light, presenting a view of segregation in which "inequality" was irrelevant:

> When courts have struck down statutes and ordinances requiring separate seating arrangements in buses, separate restrooms, and separate restaurants in state-owned or operated airports and bus terminals, it was not because the evidence showed that negroes were restricted to uncomfortable seats in buses, dirty restrooms, and poor food. It was because they sat in buses behind a sign marked "colored," entered restrooms under the sign "colored," and could be served food only in restaurants for "colored." It is the stamp of classification by race that makes the classification invidious. . . .
>
> Considering the extent of media of information today, it is highly unlikely that any voters will be confused by lack of racial identification of candidates on the ballot. Considering the number of parishes having a large Negro population, it is entirely likely that a racial stamp will help as much as it will hinder Negro candidates for public office in Louisiana. The vice in the law is not dependent on injury to Negroes. The vice in

the law is the State's placing its power and prestige behind a policy of racial classification inconsistent with the elective processes. Justice Harlan put his finger on it many years ago when he said that the "Constitution is color-blind." If there is one area above all others where the Constitution is color-blind, it is the area of state action with respect to the ballot and the voting booth.[6]

Representing the complainants on appeal, the NAACP Legal Defense Fund placed its primary reliance on the contention that racial classifications, being "presumptively invidious," were constitutionally prohibited. "Contrary to the equal protection clause of the Fourteenth Amendment, this statute on its face classifies persons according to race. . . . But"—the brief then quoted from Wisdom's dissenting opinion—"'In the eyes of the Constitution a man is a man. He is not a white man, he is not an Indian, he is not a negro.'" After quoting with approval the "color-blind" passage from Justice Harlan's dissent in *Plessy*, the Brief for Appellants continued as follows:

> Racial differences do exist, and acknowledgment of these differences, even by the State, can occasionally serve some useful purpose. The national census, by taking note of race, contributes information of considerable value to social research. The constitutional ban on racially discriminatory state action could not be enforced if courts were truly blind to racial groupings. In such cases the notation of racial differences is unlikely to be objectionable to any person or group, and in any event, it has some reasonable relation to the achievement of a legitimate governmental object.[7]

The lawyers for the NAACP Legal Defense Fund filed their principal brief in *Anderson v. Martin* on August 26, 1963, two days before Martin Luther King, Jr., speaking at the march on Washington, evoked the day when his children might "live in a nation where they will not be judged by the color of their skin but by the content of their character." The conjunction helps to date an era. At this climactic moment in the history of the civil rights movement, the formal contention of its preeminent legal strategists was that state action to classify citizens by race, let alone treat them differently, was presumptively unconstitutional. The standard advanced was Harlan's color-blind Constitution, and the color-blind figure was so seriously intended that the authors of the brief—Jack Greenberg and James M. Nabrit III—thought it advisable to indicate their conception of the proper limits to its literal application. It would be difficult to contend for a broader rule of color blindness, inasmuch as the two qualifications they conceded are probably the minimum required to save the idea from logical absurdity.

How many members of the Supreme Court might have subscribed to the color-blind view of *Anderson v. Martin* it is impossible to say. What is clear is that the justices declined to commit themselves to any doctrine so uncompromising. An opinion by Justice Clark announced merely that "the compulsory designation by Louisiana of the race of the candidate on the ballot operates as a discrimination against appellants and is therefore violative of the Fourteenth Amendment's Equal Protection Clause."[8] Clark's ipse dixit made an interesting case into a routine one and avoided the need for explanation.

The uninformative opinion in *Anderson v. Martin* marked an important turning point. The instances of racial discrimination previously struck down by the Court had all been segregation laws, the unconstitutionality of which might be consistently attributed to the inequalities they created, objective or "inherent." The racial classification at issue in *Anderson v. Martin* defied such analysis. The obvious recourse, in the view of men like John Minor Wisdom and the Legal Defense Fund attorneys, was to ground the decision on the antidiscrimination principle: the flat prohibition of racial classifications that many observers thought or hoped had been the unacknowledged basis of *Brown.* Instead, the Court's first civil rights case not involving "equality" was decided by an approach to racial classifications that was essentially ad hoc. Perceiving a bad law enacted for a bad purpose the Court declared it unconstitutional, without explaining in what way it denied to any person the equal protection of the laws.

In *Hamm v. Virginia State Board of Elections,*[9] also decided in 1964, the Court appeared to accept the argument that racial classification was normally impermissible (subject to an exception for statistical purposes) despite the absence of discriminatory treatment or even discernible consequences; but the decision was a memorandum affirmance stating no rationale. The case involved challenges to Virginia statutes requiring variously that voter registration records and tax rolls be maintained separately for black and white citizens, and that divorce decrees recite the race of husband and wife. The district court had overturned the requirements of segregated lists of voters and taxpayers but held that a reference to race in divorce decrees was permissible, in view of its potential statistical value.

Leaving aside the matter of the divorce decrees—which both courts chose to regard, rightly or wrongly, as analogous to the use of race by the national census—the case was interesting precisely because the discrimination at issue was seemingly both pointless and harmless. No assertion was made that Virginia's maintenance of separate lists of voters and taxpayers was directly or indirectly connected with inequality of treatment, or indeed that the requirement of segregated bookkeeping had any consequences whatever beyond the existence of the practice itself. The district court found it "axiomatic that no State can directly dictate or casually promote a distinction in the treatment of persons solely on the basis of their color,"[10] but here there was no distinction in treatment in the ordinary sense of the words. What was condemned in *Hamm*, as in *Anderson v. Martin*, was not a "distinction in treatment" but unnecessary race consciousness on the part of the government. A constitutional rule that would justify such a holding must, it seemed, be close to the color blindness for which the Legal Defense Fund had argued in *Anderson*.

The most natural occasion on which to announce the color blindness of the Constitution might have been the long-awaited decision in which the Court finally held, as it was bound to do, that states might not prohibit marriage between persons of different races.[11] By late 1964, when *McLaughlin v. Florida*[12] addressed the cognate issue of a statute punishing the habitual cohabitation of any man and woman not of the same race, there was reason to anticipate that the constitutional rule found to be dispositive of the case might be the blanket impermissibility of racial classifications. *Anderson v. Martin* and *Hamm v. Virginia State Board*, decided earlier in the year, both seemed to point in that direction. Challenging the constitutionality of the statute, the NAACP Legal Defense Fund made the obligatory points that the legislation was "unreasonable" and that it attempted "to require separation of the races by imposing criminal penalties" (a characterization permitting an analogy to the segregation cases), but the heart of its argument was the broader proposition that followed: "In short, 'race is constitutionally an irrelevance,' and '. . . discriminations based on race alone are obviously irrelevant and invidious.' In the words of the first Justice Harlan, the Constitution is 'color blind.'"[13]

Approached from this theoretical high ground, the Court's opinion in *McLaughlin* is a tedious anticlimax. Only Justice Stewart, joined by Justice William O. Douglas, was prepared to decide the case on antidiscrimination grounds:

> There might be limited room under the Equal Protection Clause for a civil law requiring the keeping of racially segregated public records for statistical or other valid public purposes. But we deal here with a criminal law which imposes criminal punishment. And I think it is simply not possible for a state law to be valid under our Constitution which makes

the criminality of an act depend upon the race of the actor. Discrimination of that kind is invidious *per se*.[14]

The Court's future direction was more accurately indicated by Justice Byron White's principal opinion. Declining to rule that any discrimination was illegal per se, even in the context of criminal law, Justice White employed instead a mechanical means-and-ends analysis by which racial discrimination would be found unconstitutional wherever it effected a classification not "reasonable in light of its purpose." Thus the state of Florida, to which Justice White attributed the purpose of suppressing promiscuous behavior in general, could not (he found) reasonably treat interracial promiscuity differently from the ordinary kind.[15]

This way of dealing with the question was plainly artificial. The purpose of a statutory scheme that prohibits interracial marriage, and treats certain offenses (adultery, fornication, cohabitation) more harshly when the actors are of different races, is to deter and punish interracial sexual relations. The question is not whether the legislation employs a "reasonable classification" in terms of means and ends—in a candid assessment of legislative purpose, the classification is not only reasonable but indispensable—but whether the Constitution allows the legislature to pursue its race-conscious objective. A simple statement that it did not would seem to have been well within the Court's reach at the time.

Ten years after *Brown v. Board of Education,* the Supreme Court was still not prepared to acknowledge the principle of nondiscrimination, derived from the Fourteenth Amendment, that was the straightforward explanation of its decisions in racial cases. Some of the reasons were by this time familiar. Candid disposition of Florida's cohabitation statute would effectively have foreclosed the miscegenation question; and even in 1964 that issue may have been one the Court still wished to defer. Again, *McLaughlin* (like *Brown*) was decided in the face of substantial contrary authority: in this instance, the Court's 1883 decision in the closely analogous case of *Pace v. Alabama.* Justice White's approach allowed him to assert (quite incorrectly) that he was pursuing a line of equal protection analysis that *Pace v. Alabama* had neglected to take into account.[16]

Tactical considerations of this sort, however, do not adequately explain the Court's continued reticence.[17] More significant reasons may perhaps be found in institutional concerns. In the twenty-five years since its decision in *Missouri ex rel. Gaines v. Canada,* and even more obviously in the ten years since *Brown,* the Court had established that it could rule on the constitutionality of racial classifications without disclosing its reasoning.

To state a rule—for instance, that racial classifications were presumptively impermissible—could only diminish the justices' freedom to decide future cases when and how they wished. Urged (for the last time) to state such a rule in *McLaughlin*, the Court moved instead toward its modern posture in racial cases, in which it would frankly review and pass upon the policy of the legislative objective and the appropriateness to that end of the legislative means.

When the Court finally addressed the question of interracial marriage in *Loving v. Virginia*,[18] the justices held unanimously that the Commonwealth of Virginia had no power to regulate marriages on the basis of race. But the antidiscrimination rule announced in *Loving* is not the one that had seemed so close at hand in *McLaughlin*. During the two and a half years that separated the decisions, the restrictions on judicial freedom of action threatened by an acknowledged rule of color blindness—once a largely theoretical problem—had assumed specific and unwelcome form. By the time *Loving* was decided, in June 1967, federal judges in the still-segregated South were fighting massive resistance with massive desegregation. Civil rights lawyers who read the opinions being written in the Fifth Circuit school cases could not fail to perceive the conflict between the emerging law of school desegregation and a constitutional prohibition of racial classifications. For the first time since the 1940s, in a case involving comparable issues, the Legal Defense Fund briefs in *Loving* omitted any reference to the inherently invidious nature of racial classifications or to race as a constitutional "irrelevance."

Chief Justice Earl Warren's opinion in *Loving* included stronger antidiscrimination language than any Supreme Court opinion since *Hirabayashi*, but his statements were repeatedly qualified to exclude any inference that the Court was applying a per se rule. Rebutting the traditional contention (from *Pace v. Alabama*) that the "equal application" of Virginia's miscegenation statutes was enough to satisfy constitutional requirements, Warren appealed directly to "the Fourteenth Amendment's proscription of all invidious racial discriminations." Yet the same paragraph seemed to qualify any absolute proscription by referring to "the very heavy burden of justification which the Fourteenth Amendment has traditionally required of state statutes drawn according to race." Warren's ringing statement that "[t]he clear and central purpose of the Fourteenth Amendment was to eliminate all official state sources of invidious racial discrimination in the States" was followed by a significantly more modest gloss:

> At the very least, the Equal Protection Clause demands that racial classifications, especially suspect in criminal statutes, be subjected to the "most rigid scrutiny," *Korematsu* v. *United States,* 323 U.S. 214, 216 (1944), and, if they are ever to be upheld, they must be shown to be necessary to the accomplishment of some permissible state objective, independent of the racial discrimination which it was the object of the Fourteenth Amendment to eliminate.[19]

So stated, the constitutional rule imposes no effective constraint on the Court's judgment as to which forms of racial classification are reasonable and appropriate.

The formal constitutional analysis of racial classifications in the post-segregation era draws its elements from what was said in *Loving*. Racial classifications are subjected to judicial "scrutiny" that is "rigid" or at least "strict," to determine whether they are "necessary" or at least appropriate means to a "permissible state objective," preferably a "compelling" one. They are, in short, disfavored; and a racial classification will not be held constitutional unless a majority of the Court is persuaded that it is being used appropriately for a good purpose. Judicial oversight in these terms is the use made by the modern Court of the Fourteenth Amendment's anti-discrimination principle.

In the course of its prolonged attack on the legal structure of segregation, the Supreme Court had consistently elected to rely on the literal terms of the equal protection clause rather than on the rule of nondiscrimination it had been found to contain. The meaning of the latter, in consequence, never required precise explication. But the racial classifications that survived segregation were subject to constitutional limitation, if at all, only by virtue of an unwritten rule of nondiscrimination that it was now necessary to define. From *Sweatt v. Painter* to *McLaughlin v. Florida,* civil rights advocates urged the Court to define that constitutional rule to be one of color blindness. But by 1967, if not before, the Court had concluded that it would be unwise to accept the restrictions that a color-blind Constitution would place on its power to pick and choose among racial classifications. In place of a rule of color blindness, *Loving* announced a pledge of the Court's assiduous oversight of the politics of race.

In 1954 and 1955, the Supreme Court's strategic decision was that a constitutional command to desegregate the nation's schools need not be complied with immediately. Ten years later, when the federal government finally decided that compliance was overdue, the governing notion of what constituted "desegregation" had undergone significant change. The Court's eventual acceptance of the revised goals for desegregation—developed in the interim by education theorists, civil rights lawyers, and southern federal judges—obliged it to repudiate the color-blind implications of a quarter-century of decisions.

On May 31, 1955, the Supreme Court remanded *Brown v. Board of Education of Topeka* and the other School Segregation Cases with instructions to the several district courts to "take such proceedings and enter such orders and decrees consistent with this opinion as are necessary and proper to admit to public schools on a racially nondiscriminatory basis with all deliberate speed the parties to these cases."[20] The first trial court decree pursuant to the *Brown II* mandate was announced six weeks later in the South Carolina case, *Briggs v. Elliott.* The district court took pains to explain its understanding of what the Supreme Court had ordered:

> [I]t is important that we point out exactly what the Supreme Court has decided and what it has not decided in this case. . . . It has not decided that the states must mix persons of different races in the schools or must require them to attend schools or must deprive them of the right of choosing the schools they attend. What it has decided, and all that it has decided, is that a state may not deny to any person on account of race the right to attend any school that it maintains. . . . The Constitution, in other words, does not require integration. It merely forbids discrimination.[21]

There can be little doubt that such was indeed the meaning, at the time of their announcement, of the Supreme Court's decision in the School Segregation Cases. The paraphrase in *Briggs v. Elliott* was not a hostile, artificially narrow construction of the desegregation mandate by unreconstructed southerners; it was an appeal for calm by judges whose readiness to follow *Brown* even in its unstated implications had already been demonstrated.[22] The correctness of their assessment is borne out by the language of *Brown II* itself. The Supreme Court's desegregation mandate, practically the only hint of the Court's contemporary conception of how desegregation might practically be achieved, refers to the "revision of school districts and attendance areas into compact units to achieve a system of determining admission to the public schools on a nonracial basis."[23]

A mandate forbidding discrimination, rather than one commanding integration, was moreover what the Court had previously signaled was at stake in the School Segregation Cases and what the proponents of desegregation had asserted was constitutionally required. Propounding the questions for reargument at the 1953 term, the Court had framed the issue as to remedy in these terms:

> 4. Assuming it is decided that segregation in public schools violates the Fourteenth Amendment
>> (a) would a decree necessarily follow providing that, within the limits set by normal geographic school districting, Negro children should forthwith be admitted to the schools of their choice, or
>> (b) may this Court, in the exercise of its equity powers, permit an effective gradual adjustment to be brought about from existing segregated systems to a system not based on color distinctions?[24]

This statement of the issue echoed the discussion that had taken place at the first Supreme Court argument in the South Carolina case, *Briggs v. Elliott:*

> MR. JUSTICE FRANKFURTER: It would be more important information in my mind to have you spell out in concrete what would happen if this Court reverses and the case goes back to the district court for the entry of a decree.
>
> MR. MARSHALL: I think, sir, that the decree would be entered which would enjoin the school officials from, one, enforcing the statute; two, from segregating on the basis of race or color. Then I think whatever district lines they draw, if it can be shown that those lines are drawn on the basis of race or color, then I think they would violate the injunction. If the lines are drawn on a natural basis, without regard to race or color, then I think that nobody would have any complaint.[25]

As late as 1959, Professor Jack Greenberg—whose authority in civil rights matters was enhanced by his position as one of the senior attorneys for the NAACP Legal Defense Fund—concluded: "If . . . there were complete freedom of choice, or geographical zoning, or any other nonracial standard, and all Negroes still ended up in certain schools, there would seem to be no constitutional objection."[26]

"Desegregation" took its original meaning from its context: the battle against state laws requiring the separation of the races. Racially integrated schools would be an incidental consequence, under certain circumstances, of ceasing to assign pupils by race. The further contention that integrated education would constitute a positive good (at least for the black pupils) had been latent in antidiscrimination arguments running back to Edmund

Jackson, but it did not become a commonly articulated part of civil rights claims until the early 1960s. Its emergence can be traced with the help of Jack Greenberg's 1959 study, in which he noted that "[t]he real, pressing racial problem in Northern education is becoming what must be called *'de facto'* segregation" and reviewed the arguments in favor of what he then called "affirmative integration."[27] The arguments were of recent date. Greenberg's citations indicate that they reached the level of newspaper commentary only in 1957, although he identifies as "the most fully articulated legal exposition of this position" a brief submitted in 1954 by the attorney general of New Jersey in a state administrative proceeding.[28] But the evolution of attitudes toward "affirmative integration" had not yet, in 1959, produced an assertion that the benefits of integrated schools were a constitutional right:

> While [opponents of de facto segregation] have not gone far in implementing their espousals, we must recognize the relative newness of the proposition and the political and administrative problems it sometimes poses. Besides, unlike officially enforced segregation which is concededly subject to courtroom attack, there has so far been no clearly recognized way of achieving affirmative integration other than by persuading, through ordinary political means, officers of government.[29]

Two independent, mutually reinforcing developments now converged in the judicial and political process by which "desegregation" came to mean "integration." The first was the rapid development of the argument that the benefits of racially integrated education might be claimed as an affirmative constitutional right. The second was the gradual discovery, by the federal judges charged with its enforcement, that "desegregation" even in its original meaning could scarcely be achieved unless recalcitrant school boards were ordered to assign pupils on the basis of race.

In the early 1960s, the view that predominantly black schools were intrinsically harmful to black pupils—regardless of the factors determining the schools' racial composition—came to be widely held among educators, particularly in more liberal jurisdictions. State boards of education and education commissioners in New York, California, New Jersey, and Massachusetts adopted policy statements and regulations declaring that "racial imbalance" in public schools was damaging to the self-confidence and motivation of Negro children, thereby denying them equality of educational opportunity.[30] *Brown v. Board of Education* could now be cited—ignoring the fact that the 1954 decision considered segregation imposed by law—as authority for the unqualified proposition that "a segregated Negro school, whether in the North or in the South, is inherently unequal to its white counterpart." The supporting arguments—that to educate Negroes apart from whites was "to brand them as inferior"; that the Negro school was, in fact, incorrigibly inferior to its white counterpart; that Negro children "suffer from lack of exposure to the middle class culture found in white but not in Negro schools"—might all have been paraphrased from Edmund Jackson's committee report of 1846.[31]

On this view of the effects of de facto segregation, the argument for its unconstitutionality was easily stated. By 1965, civil rights advocates had identified two lines of attack by which municipalities might be required to correct racial imbalance in the public schools when the nonjudicial officers of government were not persuaded "through ordinary political means." The first contention, eventually adopted by the Supreme Court as its rationale for northern desegregation, asserted that the government might be held responsible for the combination of housing patterns and school districting that produced the isolation of racial minorities in a neighborhood school system. The second asserted that racial imbalance, however caused, infringed an affirmative constitutional right to equal educational opportunity.[32]

This second line of argument, bolder in conception and more sweeping in its application, was the basis of several decisions by northern judges prepared to find a constitutional remedy for de facto segregation in the early 1960s.[33] Its immediate impact was greater in the South, where for ten years district judges had been struggling to define the indicia of a "plan of desegregation" meeting constitutional standards. In the mid-1960s, the idea that there might be an affirmative constitutional entitlement to integrated education reinforced a practical conclusion to which many southern judges had come by an entirely different route: that the only effective weapon against informal methods of purposeful segregation (and against the lingering effects of segregation previously imposed by law) was to order that white and black children attend school together. Where these two ideas intersected, the distinction between "desegregation" and "integration" was no longer perceptible.

The record of school desegregation since 1955 had been a history of the South's successive attempts to discover the means of literal compliance with *Brown II* producing the smallest degree of racial integration. "Pupil placement laws" that initially replaced the old system of racial assignment provided that every student should be individually assigned to a school, on the basis of specified criteria other than race. Alabama's pupil placement law, which served as a model for other southern states, directed that assignment be made on the basis of such factors as the availability of classroom and transportation facilities, "the suitability of established curricula," and "the adequacy of a pupil's academic preparation," while taking into account as well "the possibility or threat of friction or disorder among pupils or others" and "the possibility of breaches of the peace or ill will or economic retaliation within the community."[34] Not surprisingly, the initial assignment of schoolchildren under the pupil placement laws invariably followed racial lines. In 1958 a federal district court held Alabama's pupil placement law constitutional "on its face," and the Supreme Court affirmed without opinion.[35] By the early 1960s, however, the use of pupil placement laws to perpetuate segregated schools had been found unconstitutional by the lower federal courts.[36]

Formal compliance now moved through the gradations of "freedom of choice." The baldest proposition—that a plan of "desegregation" might consist in a free choice between integrated schools and schools open only to a single race—was promptly rejected in several cases.[37] The "minority transfer rule," a modification of geographic zoning permitting any student assigned to a school in which he was a member of a racial minority to transfer to one in which his race was in the majority, plainly tended to perpetuate a system of segregated schools; this form of "freedom of choice" was held unconstitutional by the Supreme Court in 1963.[38] Desegregation plans offering a more plausible freedom of choice between "formerly white" and "formerly Negro" schools, as well as plans to achieve desegregation by an unqualified right of transfer, were initially approved by the courts.[39] Doubts arose, however, as it became apparent that the exercise of "freedom of choice" might be substantially inhibited in practice by a variety of factors, and that the "freedom of choice" conferred on pupils and parents was usually a choice between what were still "white schools" and "Negro schools" in everything but legal designation.

The southern objective—desegregation with a minimum of integration—was constitutionally permissible only in the abstract. Following a history of legally enforced segregation, ostensibly nondiscriminatory methods of pupil assignment (such as "freedom of choice") were often the means of maintaining an intentionally segregated system.[40] After ten years of southern foot-dragging, courts and federal officials came to insist on desegregation decrees that could not be evaded. Practical limits to the framing of such decrees, and to determining when "choice" was being freely exercised, meant that the extent of desegregation would inevitably be measured by the percentage of black and white children attending school together. Both the meaning of "desegregation" and the nature of the constitutional right being vindicated were inevitably changed in the process.

The catalyst of this redefinition was the belated decision of the federal government, apart from the judiciary, to concern itself with southern schools. Title VI of the Civil Rights Act of 1964 prohibited racial discrimination in federally funded programs; direct aid to elementary and secondary schools became economically important (and a significant instrument of federal persuasion) as a result of further legislation in 1965.[41] To be eligible to receive federal funds, a southern school district now had to persuade the Department of Health, Education and Welfare that it had ceased all prohibited discrimination.[42] "Guidelines" for determining the adequacy of a desegregation plan for this purpose were promulgated by HEW's Office of Education in April 1965 and again in April 1966. The importance of the HEW guidelines far transcended the allocation of federal funds for education, because they were promptly adopted by judges hearing desegregation cases as a guide to the constitutional standards for desegregation under *Brown.* With the later ratification of this conclusion by the Supreme Court, the Office of Education had effectively made constitutional law.

A comparison of the two sets of HEW guidelines marks the point at which "desegregation" was redefined. The 1965 guidelines were still consistent with the view that desegregation would occur when race was obliterated as a factor in pupil assignment, without regard to the degree of racial integration achieved thereby. Thus a desegregation plan based on geographic zoning would be acceptable where district lines followed "natural boundaries or perimeters of compact areas surrounding particular schools." With regard to the vexed area of "freedom of choice," the 1965 guidelines required that school districts provide adequate notice and adequate opportunity, annually, to make the permitted election; and that an initial school assignment, or any subsequent assignment when no choice had been indicated, be made on a nonracial basis. The fall of 1967 was set as the target date by which desegregation in this form was to be extended to all grades of a school system; every school system was expected to make at least "a substantial good faith start" in 1965–66.[43]

HEW's 1965 guidelines were indirectly but severely criticized in an influential report by the U.S. Commission on Civil Rights, published in February 1966.[44] Investigations by the staff of the commission in the fall of 1965 revealed that "freedom of choice," by far the most popular method of desegregation, produced virtually no measurable results: white pupils never chose to attend schools that were "formerly Negro," and black pupils only rarely chose to attend schools that were "formerly white." Although the report acknowledged a variety of factors contributing to the disinclination of black students and parents to exercise their legal right to integrated schooling, its most compelling passages were its accounts of brutal harassment of the rare black students who chose to "integrate" white schools, and of violent methods of intimidation by which others were dissuaded from doing so.

The report's most fundamental and significant criticism of the existing guidelines was implicit in its central methodological assumption. For the authors of the report, the success or failure of desegregation policy could be measured by a single statistic: "the number of Negro children actually attending school with white children in the Deep South." The implication was spelled out in the report's major policy recommendation: "The Office of Education should revise its standards governing free choice plans in light of experience accumulated thus far. The purpose of such revision should be to ensure that free choice plans are adequate to disestablish dual, racially segregated school systems and to achieve substantial integration within such systems."[45]

The Office of Education responded swiftly. Under its 1966 guidelines, issued two months later, a desegregation plan meeting the requirements of Title VI was effectively redefined as one resulting in integration (though the word was carefully avoided). Geographic attendance zones, albeit "non-racial," might not be drawn so as "to perpetuate or promote segregation, or to limit desegregation or maintain what is essentially a dual school structure." Transfers between geographic zones might be permitted, or even required, if the transferred student moved "from a school where students of his race are a majority to any other school, within the system, where students of his race are a minority." A "free choice plan" would gain approval only where it actually resulted in integrated schools:

(d) The single most substantial indication as to whether a free choice plan is actually working to eliminate the dual school structure is the extent to which Negro or other minority group students have in fact transferred from segregated schools. Thus, when substantial desegregation actually occurs under a free choice plan, there is strong evidence that the plan is operating effectively and fairly, and is currently acceptable as a means of meeting legal requirements.

The test of "substantial desegregation" would be the percentage of minority group students "transferred from segregated schools," the acceptable minimum for the 1966–67 school year lying somewhere between 12 and 18 percent.[46]

The emerging theory of a constitutional right to integrated schooling; the frustration experienced by the southern federal judges in seeking the elusive standards by which to enforce nondiscrimination; the tactical alliance with the federal executive branch, which decisively favored integration as the remedy for segregation—all now converged in a judicial opinion that, more than any other single decision, placed the color-blind Constitution out of reach of the generation that followed. Its author was John Minor Wisdom, whose opinions only a few years earlier in *Dorsey v. State Athletic Commission* and *Anderson v. Martin* had made him the first federal judge in the country to announce a constitutional rule of color blindness as a consequence of *Brown.* In *United States v. Jefferson County Board of Education,*[47] announced in December 1966, Judge Wisdom rewrote the Supreme Court's 1955 desegregation mandate to make it require that black and white pupils attend school together. The sacrifice of the color-blind vision was a necessary consequence.

Imperative necessities—of a workable standard for desegregation, of equal educational opportunity for black schoolchildren—demanded a different desegregation mandate from that announced in 1955. The central method of Judge Wisdom's opinion in *Jefferson County* was simply to assert that what he judged to be the necessary rule had been the rule all along:

> The United States Constitution, as construed in *Brown,* requires public school systems to integrate students, faculties, facilities, and activities. If *Brown I* left any doubt as to the affirmative duty of states to furnish a fully integrated education to Negroes as a class, *Brown II* resolved that doubt. A state with a dual attendance system, one for whites and one for Negroes, must "effectuate a transition to a [unitary] racially nondiscriminatory school system." . . .
> *The only school desegregation plan that meets constitutional standards is one that works.*[48]

The addition of the bracketed word "unitary," Judge Wisdom's own gloss on the meaning of "nondiscriminatory," made this nearly a misquotation. In the political and judicial context of 1966, Judge Wisdom was obliged to repudiate the familiar, historically accurate conception of the

Brown mandate: that it did not require integration but merely forbade discrimination. Pages and pages of the lengthy opinion in *Jefferson County* were devoted to attacking that idea, disparaging it as the dictum of the South Carolina district court in *Briggs v. Elliott* and denying that it had any basis in the Supreme Court decisions.[49] Wisdom went further than this, devoting a footnote more than a page long to "the supposed difference between 'desegregation' and 'integration,'" in which he argued that the two ideas were one and the same and cited "the vernacular," the federal bureaucracy, and a number of federal courts for the proposition that the words could and should be used interchangeably.[50] These passages of the opinion were an overt attempt to rewrite legal history, and the most conspicuous fact about them is their ultimate success.[51]

The aphorism that followed, declaring that a constitutional desegregation plan was "one that works," had even greater influence on subsequent judicial thinking about desegregation. Bypassing any need to discuss "integration" or the extent to which it might be constitutionally required, the insistence on a plan that "works" implicitly answered the question of what "desegregation" was supposed to accomplish. A plan that "works" is a plan producing measurable results, and no one had devised a means of measuring the results of desegregation except by counting the number of black children attending "white" schools.

Judge Wisdom gave the 1966 guidelines the fullest possible judicial endorsement, holding not only that they were a valid interpretation of Title VI of the Civil Rights Act (though this was doubtful),[52] but that they were "required by the Constitution" and might be regarded as "a restatement of the judicial standards applicable to disestablishing de jure segregation in the public schools." The conclusion that integration was constitutionally required was reinforced, for Wisdom, by an appreciation of the underlying wrong to be remedied. Wisdom condemned de facto segregation—racial imbalance, however caused—as a source of psychological harm, destructive of educational opportunity. Pupils at "schools identified as Negro" were attending "by definition, inherently unequal schools and wearing the badge of slavery separation displays." Whether or not *Brown* stood for an affirmative constitutional right to integrated education, it imposed "[a]t the very least . . . a duty to integrate in the sense that integration is an educational goal to be given a high, high priority . . . in the proper administration of a system beset with de facto segregated schools."[53]

In the immediate context of southern desegregation the message was clear: "The position we take in these consolidated cases is that *the only adequate redress for a previously overt system-wide policy of segregation directed against Negroes as a collective entity is a system-wide policy of integration.*"[54] A policy whose avowed end is racial integration rather than nondiscriminatory assignment can no longer be squared with a color-blind Constitution. The argument against de facto segregation already recognized as much: a year earlier, Judge J. Skelly Wright had written slightingly of the "beguiling . . . cliché" of color blindness, urging that the Constitution, "while in some respects color-blind," was "not insensitive to inequality."[55] Judge Wisdom, whose opinions only recently had heralded the realization of the color-blind Constitution, did not linger over it now:

> The Constitution is both color blind and color conscious. To avoid conflict with the equal protection clause, a classification that denies a benefit, causes harm, or imposes a burden must not be based on race. In that sense, the Constitution is color blind. But the Constitution is color conscious to prevent discrimination being perpetuated and to undo the effects of past discrimination. The criterion is the relevancy of color to a legitimate governmental purpose.[56]

This attempt to explain how the Constitution might be partly color-blind was hasty and unsuccessful. As the nation would learn, classifications intended "to undo the effects of past discrimination" might also deny benefits, cause harm, and impose burdens based on race. "Relevancy of color to a legitimate governmental purpose" was the legal standard of *Plessy.* Judge Wisdom, its former champion, now saw a rule of color blindness as an obstacle to the performance of his most urgent duties; and with *United States v. Jefferson County* he banished it from contemporary constitutional law.

The opinion in *Jefferson County* identifies not only the moment at which the color-blind ideal was jettisoned by its former proponents but also the theory by which this abandonment of principle was rationalized. This was the proposition that race-conscious measures might properly be employed "to prevent discrimination being perpetuated and to undo the effects of past discrimination." If color-conscious measures are authorized to eliminate the effects of past discrimination, and if those effects are defined—as they seemed to be in *Jefferson County*—to include an unequal allocation of social resources resulting from the present-day application of race-neutral standards, then color-conscious government action is broadly authorized in the interest of compensatory justice to racial groups.

11 | Benign Racial Sorting

With the passage of the Civil Rights Act of 1964 and the Voting Rights Act of 1965, the civil rights movement celebrated the formal achievement of its historic objectives: a legal regime from which racial classifications had been largely expunged, and under which the most salient forms of private discrimination (in public accommodations and employment) were finally prohibited. The meaning of the word *discrimination,* in 1964, was not yet ambiguous. As explained by Hubert Humphrey during the Senate debate on the civil rights bill, it meant "a distinction in treatment given to different individuals because of their different race." A prohibition of discrimination against individuals necessarily barred "preferential treatment for any particular group." The ordinary understanding of "discrimination," moreover, was such that a violation of the legal prohibition "would seem already to require intent."[1]

Liberals believed in 1964 that the Constitution imposed a rule of color blindness on government; and a color-blind standard, for most civil rights advocates, was the obvious choice to govern those areas of private conduct addressed by the new legislation.[2] Not only was the right of the individual to nondiscriminatory treatment central to the traditional ideology of civil rights, but—by stressing the protection it afforded to all individuals, white as well as black—such a rule provided the natural ground of compromise necessary to obtain passage of the civil rights bill in the Senate. The argument for compensatory racial preferences, though rigorously excluded from the orthodox civil rights agenda, was already being formulated by 1964; conservative southerners were doubtless more alive to its possibilities than were other members of the Senate. In the whole of the congressional debate over the Civil Rights Act of 1964, no theme is more prominent than the exasperated insistence of the bill's supporters, in answer to repeated southern fears, that a law prohibiting discrimination must necessarily prohibit preferential treatment. Had the Senate been left in any doubt on this point, the Civil Rights Act of 1964 would not have been passed.[3]

The color-blind consensus, so long in forming, was abandoned with surprising rapidity. By the end of the first Nixon administration, a significant part of the "civil rights" being enforced by the federal government could be described more plainly as a system of compensatory preferences for racial and ethnic groups. The transformation was accomplished without resummoning the great national convention on civil rights that produced the 1964 act after eighty-three days of Senate debate. It was brought about instead by judges and administrators, who gave effect to a profound and sudden change in the views of liberal policymakers regarding the utility of race-specific government action. It is ironic but understandable, in retrospect, that this revolution took place just when Charles Sumner's vision of "equality before the law" had finally become the law of the land.

The dramatic struggle to overturn the vestiges of legal inequality, reaching its climax in the fight against southern segregation in the late 1950s and early 1960s, had absorbed everyone's attention; so that only with victory was it apparent how little would actually change. The problem was that residents of Harlem and Watts already enjoyed equality before the law. Writing in February 1965, civil rights strategist Bayard Rustin suggested that the successful attack on the "imposing but hollow structure" of Jim Crow by the "classical" civil rights movement had involved "institutions which are relatively peripheral both to the American socio-economic order and to the fundamental conditions of life of the Negro people." These conditions were well known to anyone who paid attention:

> More Negroes are unemployed today than in 1954, and the unemployment gap between the races is wider. The median income of Negroes has dropped from 57 per cent to 54 per cent of that of whites. . . . More Negroes attend *de facto* segregated schools today than when the Supreme Court handed down its famous decision. . . . And behind this is the continuing growth of racial slums, spreading over our central cities and trapping Negro youth in a milieu which, whatever its legal definition, sows an unimaginable demoralization. . . .
>
> These are the facts of life which generate frustration in the Negro community and challenge the civil rights movement. At issue, after all, is not *civil rights*, strictly speaking, but social and economic conditions.

The civil rights movement, Rustin noted, was undergoing an evolution "calling its very name into question." It would henceforth be concerned "not merely with removing the barriers to full *opportunity* but with achieving the fact of *equality.*"[4]

The movement to obtain legal recognition of *civil rights,* strictly speaking, had in fact just come to an end. Its successful conclusion revealed something that the movement's long prominence had ultimately obscured: that the demand for civil rights, for equality before the law, was only one part of a broader and even longer struggle to ameliorate the condition of black people in American society. The effort to redress in some measure this deeper inequality antedated, in the moral arguments of the abolitionists, any recognizable claim for civil rights. It has survived the civil rights movement by one generation already, and it will remain at the center of American politics for the foreseeable future.

Writing at the same time as Bayard Rustin, the anonymous author of a government report (not originally intended for publication) reached similar conclusions. The United States, he declared, was "approaching a new crisis in race relations." In the decade that followed *Brown,* "the demand of Negro Americans for full recognition of their civil rights" had finally been met. A new period was beginning:

> In this new period the expectations of the Negro Americans will go beyond civil rights. Being Americans, they will now expect that in the near future equal opportunities for them as a group will produce roughly equal results, as compared with other groups. This is not going to happen. Nor will it happen for generations to come unless a new and special effort is made.
>
> There are two reasons. First, the racist virus in the American blood stream still afflicts us: Negroes will encounter serious personal prejudice for at least another generation. Second, three centuries of sometimes unimaginable mistreatment have taken their toll on the Negro people. The harsh fact is that as a group, at the present time, in terms of ability to win out in the competitions of American life, they are not equal to most of those groups with which they will be competing.[5]

The author of the report was Daniel Patrick Moynihan, then assistant secretary of labor. Quoting a recent observation by sociologist Nathan Glazer that "[t]he demand for economic equality is now not the demand for equal opportunities for the equally qualified: it is now the demand for equality of economic results,"[6] Moynihan stressed the fact of this transformation and spelled out its political implications:

> The ideal of equality does not ordain that all persons end up, as well as start out equal. . . . But the evolution of American politics, with the

distinct persistence of ethnic and religious groups, has added a profoundly significant new dimension to that egalitarian ideal. It is increasingly demanded that the distribution of success and failure within one
group be roughly comparable to that within other groups. It is not enough
that all individuals start out on even terms, if the members of one group
almost invariably end up well to the fore, and those of another far to the
rear. This is what ethnic politics are all about in America, and in the
main the Negro American demands are being put forth in this now
traditional and established framework. . . .

The principal challenge of the next phase of the Negro revolution is
to make certain that equality of results will now follow. If we do not,
there will be no social peace in the United States for generations.

Moynihan's next point was equally prophetic. "There is considerable
evidence," he wrote, "that the Negro community is in fact dividing between
a stable middle-class group that is steadily growing stronger and more
successful, and an increasingly disorganized and disadvantaged lower-
class group." A failure to recognize the distinction would carry related
dangers:

> First, the emergence and increasing visibility of a Negro middle-class
> may beguile the nation into supposing that the circumstances of the
> remainder of the Negro community are equally prosperous, whereas just
> the opposite is true at present, and is likely to continue so.
> Second, the lumping of all Negroes together in one statistical mea-
> surement very probably conceals the extent of the disorganization among
> the lower-class group.[7]

The well-known and controversial hypothesis of the Moynihan Report
was that the deteriorating circumstances of the lower-class black population—the worsening competitive inequality that would drive the wedge
between "equal opportunities for the equally qualified" and equality of
results for Negroes as a group—could be traced to the instability of family
structure in the urban ghetto. The focus on the ghetto family, with its
self-perpetuating pattern of broken homes, female-headed families, and
illegitimate births, was a staple of American sociology;[8] but in the unaccustomed context of an argument about racial policy, reported in newspapers rather than scholarly journals, it struck a nerve. The political furor
that engulfed the Moynihan Report entirely overshadowed its implicit
policy recommendations, and it placed further inquiry into black cultural
disadvantage virtually off-limits for the generation of sociologists that
followed.[9] Twenty-five years later, the reverberations of that old contro-

versy still obscure the extraordinary interest of the document as political prophecy and historical landmark.

The political premises and the implicit policy prescription of the Moynihan Report epitomized the thinking of traditional liberalism on the subject of black equality, just as the clamorous rejection of the report presaged the coming of a new order. At a critical moment—the close of what Rustin called the "classical" civil rights movement—Moynihan observed that blacks as a group, judged by color-blind standards, would not achieve the equality of results that would henceforth be demanded. His implicit recommendation for policy was that they be assisted to achieve higher performance, measured by unchanged standards. A closer equality of results, counting by groups, was to be brought about by increasing the Negro's "ability to win out in the competitions of American life"—not by changing the terms of the contest, but by helping to form a stronger competitor. This could be done, Moynihan suggested, only by strengthening the institution of the Negro family, which he saw as "the fundamental source of the weakness of the Negro community at the present time." Measures to strengthen families were not spelled out, but the implication was clear that the stable, two-parent family would not become the norm for the black lower class without a dramatic, sustained increase in levels of employment for black males. The report's implicit prescription was for massive government intervention to this end. The proposal thus hinted at within the Labor Department was the one Bayard Rustin had made openly:

> I fail to see how the movement can be victorious in the absence of radical programs for full employment, abolition of slums, the reconstruction of our educational system. . . . Adding up the cost of such programs, we can only conclude that we are talking about a refashioning of our political economy. . . . [A] multi-billion dollar federal public-works program . . . is required to reabsorb unskilled and semi-skilled workers into the labor market—and this must be done if Negro workers in these categories are to be employed. "Preferential treatment" cannot help them.[10]

Revised for public consumption by Moynihan and presidential aide Richard N. Goodwin, the Moynihan Report formed the basis of President Johnson's celebrated Howard University commencement speech of June 4, 1965. This was the occasion on which Johnson made the memorable declaration: "You do not take a person who, for years, has been hobbled by chains and liberate him, bring him up to the starting line of a race and then say, 'you are free to compete with all the others,' and still justly believe that you have been completely fair." Revered as a founding text of affirmative action by many of those who disparage its source, the speech actually presented, in veiled terms, the same uncompromising analysis as the report. What was needed, in the words of the address, was "not just legal equity but human ability," ability that was "stretched or stunted by the family you live with, and the neighborhood you live in, by the school you go to and the poverty or richness of your surroundings." Human ability was to be fostered at its source, above all by combatting "the breakdown of the Negro family structure": the prescription was jobs, housing, and "[w]elfare and social programs better designed to hold families together."[11]

The underlying assumptions of Moynihan's proposals, as of Rustin's, mark them indelibly as the product of an era that in 1965 was coming to an abrupt end. These assumptions included, notably, the idea that individual ability or competitiveness was properly measured by a single standard; so that a genuine "equality of results" could be obtained only by increasing the "human ability" of a disadvantaged group, not by altering outcomes directly. The process would necessarily be time-consuming: the traditional prescription assumed the availability of time. An equally critical assumption was that massive public resources could be devoted to redress the competitive imbalance between racial groups. Commenting favorably on the Howard University speech, a *New York Times* editorial observed that "[t]he cures for the social afflictions that hold the Negro in thrall lie in public and private programs that make the present War on poverty and all its related undertakings for expanded education, urban renewal and improved welfare services seem incredibly puny."[12]

In 1965 it still went without saying that any such remedial programs would be race-neutral in their operation. Not only was this (for most liberals) the vital legal point that had just been gained, but the traditional welfare and employment strategies advocated by Rustin and Moynihan would have been politically inconceivable in any race-specific formulation. It should be noted, finally, that the concern for "equality of results" expressed in 1965 was explicitly focused on the disadvantaged members of the disadvantaged class: the black ghetto poor.

Events conjoined in the summer of 1965 to mark a watershed in the struggle for racial equality, and when the divide had been crossed each of these assumptions would quickly appear outdated. When the Moynihan controversy was at its height, the background of recent events included not only the enactment of the Voting Rights Act and the Howard University address, but also the start of the Vietnam buildup, the commitment of American ground troops to combat, and the riot in Watts. The vehemence with which the Moynihan Report was condemned, particularly on the political left, suggests the suddenness with which the familiar liberal assumptions about the preconditions of racial equality were perceived as erroneous. There was no time; there would be no money. From this pessimistic perspective, any explanation of unequal results in terms of unequal abilities became an apology for continued inequality and a contemptible exercise in "blaming the victim."

Riots in hundreds of cities in the summers of 1966 and 1967, culminating in the epidemic of violence that followed the assassination of Martin Luther King, Jr., in April 1968, convinced policymakers at every level that something extraordinary had to be done to improve the lot of black Americans. The common wisdom was distilled by the report of the Kerner Commission, appointed to investigate the causes of the 1967 riots:

> [T]he development of a small but steadily increasing Negro middle class while the greater part of the Negro population is stagnating economically is creating a growing gap between Negro haves and have-nots.
>
> This gap, as well as the awareness of its existence by those left behind, undoubtedly adds to the feelings of desperation and anger which breed civil disorders. Low-income Negroes realize that segregation and lack of job opportunities have made it possible for only a small proportion of all Negroes to escape poverty and the summer disorders are at least in part a protest against being left behind and left out. . . .
>
> What the American economy of the late 19th and early 20th century was able to do to help the European immigrants escape from poverty is now largely impossible. New methods of escape must be found for the majority of today's poor.[13]

Although the "new methods of escape" recommended by the commission still echoed the employment and welfare strategies of Rustin and Moynihan, the architects of post-1968 racial policy never commanded even a fraction of the resources whose availability such proposals presupposed. This penury of means assured that the programs actually undertaken would be largely limited to the policies of racial preference.

The older prescription for equality of results was discredited in the eyes of the policymaking elite, not because its liberal ideals had become any less attractive, but because they now seemed unattainable. Proclaiming the need to achieve "equality of results," Moynihan's assumption in 1965 was still that the nation could help the black lower class attain the preconditions of such equality: equality of competitive skills, of "human ability." By 1968 the idea that the nation would agree to pay the price in dollars was probably less plausible than ever; but what seemed clear in any event, after the riots, was that it would take too long. "The vital element of time," the Kerner Commission suggested, was simply not available. In the face of a sudden and universal conviction that the whole process would cost too much and take too long, it was inevitable that equality of results would come to be sought by different means. The obvious alternative was to address the results directly, rather than the preconditions; though the "equality of results" that could be achieved in this manner would necessarily be something different. Expenditure was minimized, because the really expensive part of the traditional prescription—substantial government intervention to alter the lives of the truly disadvantaged—was being abandoned.

Racial policy in the aftermath of the riots was made in the absence of a popular mandate, sometimes (as in the case of school busing) in the face of the popular will, by courts and federal agencies rather than the national legislature. Judges and administrators can effect only those policies they have the means to carry out: normally, those that require neither the levying of taxes nor other forms of political affirmation. The consequences of this fundamental limitation have been profound for American policy on racial matters since 1968. While the Kerner Commission proposed a broad range of programs requiring massive public expenditure—for education, housing, job creation, and welfare reform—those "new methods" that were most decisively given effect were the relative few that courts and agencies could require others to pay for.

Thus where the commission recommended "a comprehensive approach designed to reconstruct the ghetto child's social and intellectual environment, compensate for disadvantages already suffered and provide necessary tools for development of essential literary skills," courts could only try to contribute racially integrated schools—the educational advantages of which were already seen, by 1968, as marginal at best. Where the commission recommended massive job creation, including subsidized jobs for the "hard-core unemployed," the civil rights agencies and the courts—through an aggressive interpretation of the laws against employment discrimination—could only impose racial preferences in the zero-sum game of allocating existing jobs. The benefit of those preferences, moreover, went not to the "hard-core unemployed" but to the best qualified of the favored group. Government policy on race continues to be associated overwhelmingly with judicial and agency *enforcement,* producing a persistent emphasis (in the politics and rhetoric of contemporary civil rights) on the illegal discrimination that is the necessary predicate of an enforcement-based policy. This is not because illegal discrimination is central to the nation's profoundest racial problems—it is not—but because these are the only policies that courts and agencies can carry out by themselves.

The political coalition that formed or reformed in support of these policies paid a substantial price for the results that were achieved. One part of the price was the surrender of the antidiscrimination principle, with its unifying power and the moral claim associated with it. Another was the fact that in choosing policies by their capacity to produce a successful racial tally, the country lost sight of the crisis it originally set out to confront. The racial crisis described by Rustin, Moynihan, and the Kerner Commission stems from the unacceptable conditions of life for residents of the black ghetto. In the last twenty-five years those conditions have changed markedly for the worse. Yet it has proved possible to palliate the demands of the 1960s with policies of racial preference, from which the black ghetto poor benefit remotely if at all.

The idea of the color-blind Constitution was largely eclipsed after 1968 because those who make national policy came to the view, contrary to the earlier beliefs of many of them, that race-specific measures were necessary means to imperative political ends. Subsequent developments in the law of race have constituted, in one sense, merely an extended epilogue to the history of the color-blind idea. The central initiatives of the new race-conscious policies—the racial balancing of public schools; the economic preferences known as "affirmative action"; and the utilization of "voting rights" to encourage proportional representation by race—remain the highly visible subjects of present-day controversy; and it may be perceived without commentary that such policies are inconsistent with a color-blind Constitution, a color-blind reading of the relevant statutes, or both.[14]

It is pertinent nevertheless to review the role of the federal courts in the post-1968 revolution in civil rights policy. Here two themes, at least, connect with longer strands of the color-blind history. One of these is the inability or unwillingness of the Supreme Court, in its decisions of the 1970s and 1980s, to enunciate any constitutional rule on the legality of racial classifications that may usefully be distinguished from the Court's views on the policy of the enactment in question. What has changed since

Plessy v. Ferguson is the political outlook of the justices, not constitutional law. Another is the extraordinary policymaking latitude, even by modern standards, that the judiciary has allowed itself in the area of post-1968 civil rights.

The tendency toward judicial legislation is less pronounced in connection with those issues (such as school desegregation) that have turned primarily on constitutional grounds, since the law that is made and unmade in such cases derives, in any event, merely from the judges' reshaping and reconsidering their own prior views. It has been particularly marked, by contrast, in the cases involving statutory interpretation. To accommodate the most prominent aspects of present-day affirmative action, the Civil Rights Act of 1964 has been interpreted to permit and even to require the contrary of what its terms provide and what its authors plainly intended. The Voting Rights Act of 1965 and even the Civil Rights Act of 1866[15] have been interpreted to authorize initiatives in civil rights policy that, while they do not contradict them, are equally foreign to the historical objectives of those statutes. Congress, to be sure, has been willing to claim territory originally staked out for it by judges—as in the 1982 amendments to the Voting Rights Act, or the Civil Rights Act of 1991. Yet the political impetus that is sufficient to bring about ratification in such circumstances falls well short of what would presumably be necessary, were Congress obliged to identify and defend the same policy choices as an original proposition.

Post-1968 civil rights law has been notably imposed on American democracy from the top down. Little disposed to reclaim the burden of self-government in an area offering only hard choices, the nation has largely acquiesced in policies chosen by administrators and judges. But the crucial issues of race still facing the country have yet to be resolved; and their genuine resolution will require the stronger ratification of affirmative political consensus.

School Desegregation

Of the new race-specific policies pursued by the federal government in the 1970s, the effort to require racial balance in the public schools was most distinctively the work of the federal judiciary. Authority for a policy of racial balancing was found in a constitutional rule, rather than a statute; and the policy was carried out almost entirely by the judges themselves, in the face of both executive and legislative opposition. A simple but pervasive civic function—the assignment of pupils to public schools—was the issue on which American judges had first considered the legality of classifying citizens by race (in *Roberts v. City of Boston*) and on which the Supreme Court had founded not only the modern constitutional law of that question but its own unprecedented role in American political life. As the government establishment pondered the recommendations of the Kerner Commission at the end of the 1960s, the most notable achievement in the area of race relations on the part of any branch of the federal government had been the triumph of the judiciary over old-style segregation in recalcitrant southern school districts. There was thus every reason for judges to feel that the racial composition of the nation's public schools was a matter within their special charge. Given in addition the institutional momentum from the victorious fight against segregated southern schools, and the logical impossibility of drawing a clear distinction between racial assignments for the purpose of ending segregation, on the one hand, and for the purpose of achieving racial balance, on the other, we may already have a sufficient explanation of the single-minded judicial campaign evolving after 1968 to integrate the nation's public schools.

The social benefit that was sought through this massive expenditure of the judges' political capital is less easily stated. The contention that racially mixed schools afford substantial educational advantages to their formerly isolated black pupils receives, at best, only modest support from modern social science. The ambitious empirical study giving rise to the Coleman Report of 1966 found that the overwhelming determinant of educational achievement was the family background of the student; in comparison with this single factor, *all* differences between one school and another—student body characteristics, facilities, curriculum, teacher characteristics—were relatively insignificant.[16] Even today there appears to be no conclusive evidence supporting the famous "social science" premise of the *Brown* decision in 1954, that racially isolated education (whether *de facto* or *de jure*) generates a feeling of inferiority in black pupils, reducing their motivation to learn and their "educational and mental development."[17]

Following publication of the Coleman Report, the standard academic justification for racially mixed schools shifted perceptibly. A report by the U.S. Commission on Civil Rights, *Racial Isolation in the Public Schools,* published in February 1967, stressed the positive correlation between the educational performance of black students and the "social class level of a student's classmates," a finding that was permissible though not compelled on the basis of the Coleman data.[18] But commonsense considerations, independent of social science findings, were equally if not more important to the liberal conviction that racially isolated schools must be socially harmful. The Civil Rights Commission argued that schools in which disadvantaged pupils were dispersed among classmates from more favored backgrounds must be better schools, with better and more motivated teachers, than schools in which the least advantaged children were concentrated; that all-Negro schools were regarded by the community as inferior, producing an adverse influence on student achievement; and finally, that the interracial contact afforded by integrated schools was an essential step toward changing racial attitudes so as to achieve a racially integrated society.[19] The new emphasis is plainly visible in the report of the Kerner Commission, which declared school integration to be "vital to the well-being of this country" even as it acknowledged the Coleman findings that the purely educational benefits of integration might be only marginal:

> We support integration as the priority education strategy because it is essential to the future of American society. We have seen in this last summer's disorders the consequences of racial isolation, at all levels, and of attitudes toward race, on both sides, produced by three centuries of myth, ignorance and bias. It is indispensable that opportunities for interaction between the races be expanded.[20]

The extraordinary judicial energy devoted to the desegregation enterprise is finally to be explained by this political and moral conviction, as well as by the unique attributes of the public school among all social institutions. "Positive interracial contact" might also occur in racially integrated families, or in neighborhoods, or in private associations such as churches; but the legal system has no effective means to alter the racial composition of these institutions. The state enjoys relatively few opportunities to encourage the regular association of persons, and of those it has—military service, prisons, state employment—the matching of pupils to schools in a system of compulsory education affects by far the greatest proportion of the population and permits the highest degree of discretion in assignment. The successful fight against southern segregation taught the federal courts that they could, as a practical matter, compel school boards to operate racially integrated schools. The mandate of the Kerner Commission was that they put this power to work more broadly.

The 1967 report of the Civil Rights Commission had recommended a statutory solution: federal legislation, effective nationwide, to require the elimination of racial isolation in public schools.[21] No such law was going to be passed. The judicial alternative to an impossible legislative task was to announce a constitutional requirement that schools be integrated.

The invisible line between a court order requiring racial assignment as a remedy for legal segregation, and an order requiring racial assignment as a means of achieving racial balance, lies somewhere between the Supreme Court's 1968 decision in *Green v. County School Board*[22] and its 1971 decision in *Swann v. Charlotte-Mecklenburg Board of Education.*[23] The earlier decision considered a court-ordered "freedom of choice" plan that had resulted, in practice, in little change in the racial composition of a rural district's historically segregated schools; the Court found the remedy inadequate to convert a formerly segregated school district to "a unitary system in which racial discrimination would be eliminated root and branch." The opinion was seen by many to presage a new constitutional standard for race-conscious pupil assignment, ratifying the change in emphasis from desegregation to integration previously signaled by Judge Wisdom in *United States v. Jefferson County.*

Seen in its immediate context, the decision in *Green* did not necessarily go so far. In a rural county with no significant residential segregation, whose two schools were located at the eastern and western ends of the district, the assignment of pupils by "freedom of choice" rather than by ordinary geographic zoning—with the attendant increase in administrative and transportation costs—looked like a device to resist the ordinary consequences of nonracial assignment. When it further appeared that all the white students, and the vast majority of black students, exercised their freedom of choice to attend the school to which members of their race had been assigned under legal segregation, the inference was irresistible. On these particular facts it was natural for the Supreme Court, persuaded of the defendants' intransigence, to speak of a constitutional requirement that the school board abolish "its dual, segregated system," of the board's "affirmative duty to take whatever·steps might be necessary to convert to a unitary system in which racial discrimination would be eliminated root and branch," of its burden "to come forward with a [desegregation] plan that promises realistically to work, and promises realistically to work *now.*"[24] An affirmative duty to achieve racial balance, regardless of the causes of racial isolation, was not (on the facts of the case) necessarily implied; but the Court's vigorous language portended a more general application. Desegregation plaintiffs and district court judges understood *Green* to say that *any* school district previously segregated by law was henceforth under a constitutional obligation to assign pupils in such manner as to achieve an appropriate degree of racial balance. Those who read the decision this way read it correctly.[25]

Three years later, the decision in *Swann* approved a district court order imposing the modern panoply of desegregation remedies—gerrymandered districts, "pairing" and "clustering" of schools, racial assignment of pupils, and massive, involuntary busing—to "disestablish" a very different kind of segregation. In 1969 the Charlotte-Mecklenburg Board of Education administered 107 schools in an area of 550 square miles, comprising the city of Charlotte, North Carolina, and surrounding Mecklenburg County. (City and county school districts had been consolidated in 1961 on "economic and administrative grounds not connected with questions of segregation.") The district had operated since 1965, with court approval, under a desegregation plan whose principal provisions included the closing of certain previously all-black schools; a primary system of pupil assignment based on neighborhood zoning; and a "free transfer" provision permitting any pupil to attend any school in the district in preference to his neighborhood school. Correctly assessing the implications of the Supreme Court decision in *Green,* the plaintiffs from Charlotte's earlier desegregation proceedings returned to court in 1968 to seek a more stringent desegregation order. A district judge newly assigned to the case, James McMillan, found that the Charlotte-Mecklenburg schools were "not yet desegregated."

The basis of Judge McMillan's conclusion was the fact that the racial composition of the schools in the city of Charlotte, its suburbs, and the surrounding rural areas reflected the population of the neighborhoods in which they were located:

> Approximately 14,000 of the 24,000 Negro students still attend schools that are all black, or very nearly all black, and most of the 24,000 have no white teachers. As a group Negro students score quite low on school achievement tests (the most objective method now in use for measuring educational progress); and the results are not improving under present conditions. The system of assigning pupils by "neighborhoods," with "freedom of choice" for both pupils and faculty, superimposed on an urban population pattern where Negro residents have become concentrated almost entirely in one quadrant of a city of 270,000, is racially discriminatory. This discrimination discourages initiative and makes quality education impossible. The quality of public education should not depend on the economic or racial accident of the neighborhood in which a child's parents have chosen to live—or find they must live—nor on

the color of his skin. The neighborhood school concept never *prevented* statutory racial segregation; it may not now be validly used to *perpetuate* segregation.[26]

The premise of the unusually far-reaching desegregation measures ultimately ordered by Judge McMillan was his assumption that each school in a "unitary" Charlotte-Mecklenburg school system should ideally reflect the racial balance of the district as a whole (71 percent white, 29 percent black), subject to "unavoidable" variations from that "norm." Although the Supreme Court ostensibly disapproved the view that there might be a constitutional right to "any particular degree of racial balance or mixing," it affirmed the district court order without modification.[27]

Judge McMillan was clear about what he was doing, why he was doing it, and his authority for doing so. The Charlotte-Mecklenburg schools were "not yet desegregated," despite compliance with "a court order which reflected the general understanding of 1965 about the law regarding desegregation," because "the rules of the game [had] changed."[28] Although the local school board—in contrast to the situation in *Green*—had "achieved a degree and volume of desegregation apparently unsurpassed in these parts," operating schools that "in many respects [were] models for others," its school populations reflected the racial concentration of the area's housing patterns. This was "racial discrimination" which according to *Green* had to be eliminated "root and branch." A predominantly black school was "discriminatory" because, in the view of the court, de facto segregation "produced its inevitable results in the retarded educational achievement and capacity of segregated school children." The fault lay with "the 'neighborhood school' theory," which the court found questionable as a "philosophy of education" and which had in any event "no standing to override the Constitution."[29]

The confidence and candor shown by Judge McMillan are missing in the opinion by which the Supreme Court upheld his desegregation order. The opacity of the Supreme Court opinion in *Swann* is due in part, no doubt, to the Court's desire to paper over some fundamental disagreements. The unanimous opinion contains discordant passages; it was widely reported that Chief Justice Warren Burger, after losing the votes necessary for an opinion disapproving busing to achieve racial balance, changed his vote in the case so that he might still write the opinion for the Court.[30] A majority of the justices were plainly unwilling to criticize a district judge who had taken a courageous stand on what he thought to be the implications of *Green.* Yet the same majority could not—at least without provoking dissent—enjoy the district judge's freedom to explain and justify the course the law was taking. The opinions for the Supreme Court, in *Swann* and every major desegregation case that followed, refused to acknowledge that the "rules of the game" had changed since *Brown* in any respect other than the timetable for compliance. They accordingly offered no justification for the different constitutional rules that were now being enforced by the district courts. Opinions written under these limitations could do little to elucidate policy or to promote its popular acceptance.

The stultifying premise of the Supreme Court's opinion in *Swann* was thus that the question presented was the same as in 1954, but with the necessity "of defining in more precise terms than heretofore the scope of the duty of school authorities and district courts in implementing *Brown I* and the mandate to eliminate dual systems and establish unitary systems at once." Rather than justify the new course of desegregation, the Court attempted to suggest that the only issue was one of enforcing compliance with established law:

> The objective today remains to eliminate from the public schools all vestiges of state-imposed segregation. Segregation was the evil struck down by *Brown I* as contrary to the equal protection guarantees of the Constitution. That was the violation sought to be corrected by the remedial measures of *Brown II.* That was the basis for the holding in *Green* that school authorities are "clearly charged with the affirmative duty to take whatever steps might be necessary to convert to a unitary system in which racial discrimination would be eliminated root and branch."[31]

In reality, the vital contention of the district court was that the dispersion of minority schoolchildren throughout a school district was a crucial goal of educational policy, so significant to the providing of equal educational opportunities as to be constitutionally compelled. That contention was tacitly approved, and the constitutional claim upheld, by a rhetorical expedient: the Court's use of the words "eliminate dual systems" and "convert to a unitary system" to refer indiscriminately to the varied circumstances of *Brown, Green,* and *Swann.* The transformation of the constitutional law of school segregation was thus made to turn on the fulcrum of a verbal equivocation.

The formal application of the Supreme Court's decision in *Swann* was limited to southern school districts—its avowed objective the "dismantling" of the "state-enforced dual school system"—but its logic could not be so confined. The wrong addressed by the judicial remedy in *Charlotte-Mecklenburg* was the disproportionate concentration of black pupils in inner-city schools, and this condition was more pronounced in the North than in the South. If black schoolchildren were harmed by attending a predominantly black school, moreover, the resulting problem of equal protection was independent of whether the schools in the community had ever been segregated by law. It was accordingly a foregone conclusion, after *Swann,* that the new constitutional mandate of dispersing minority pupils should extend as well to northern cities.

This conclusion was announced in 1973 in the Denver desegregation case, *Keyes v. School District No. 1.*[32] The mechanism employed to reach the result, in *Keyes* and subsequent cases, was to attribute existing patterns of residential segregation to past actions of school authorities in the administration of a neighborhood school policy—selecting sites for school construction, drawing of attendance boundaries, and so forth—alleged to have reinforced or encouraged the residential concentration of minority groups. If such a showing could be made for any part of a school district, the whole of a city's neighborhood school system might be shown to be a "dual system," segregated by state action, and as such a candidate for "root and branch" desegregation.[33] Because those elements of such a demonstration that were impossible of proof were normally resolved by presumption against school officials, the result was to make virtually every urban area in the country potentially subject to such desegregation remedies as a district judge might see fit to impose.[34]

The significance of this judicial device, for present purposes, is that it allowed the Supreme Court to extend to the whole country a new constitutional rule—requiring the dispersion of minority pupils within a school district—that it was never obliged candidly to acknowledge or to justify. Remedies were imposed on the pretext that "racially identifiable schools" in Denver, Detroit, or Columbus presented variations of the constitutional issue decided in 1954. Experience had shown that the Court's ability to enforce its mandate (in racial cases at least) did not depend to any significant extent on its willingness to state a rationale.

Justice Lewis F. Powell, a former president of the school board in Richmond, Virginia, had just joined the Court at the time of *Keyes.* Powell felt that the new desegregation policy deserved a more forthright defense. His concurring opinion displayed refreshing candor in acknowledging that the constitutional law being enforced in 1973 was something different from the rule announced in 1954 and 1955:

> [T]he doctrine of *Brown I,* as amplified by *Brown II,* did not retain its original meaning. In a series of decisions extending from 1954 to 1971 the concept of state neutrality was transformed into the present constitutional doctrine requiring affirmative state action to desegregate school systems. . . .

Having acknowledged that the Court was applying a new rule, Justice Powell (unlike the other members of the majority) was free to inquire openly into its constitutional basis:

> At the outset, one must try to identify the constitutional right which is being enforced. This is not easy, as the precedents have been far from explicit. . . . Although nowhere expressly articulated in these terms, I would now define it as the right, derived from the Equal Protection Clause, to expect that once the State has assumed responsibility for education, local school boards will operate *integrated school systems* within their respective districts. This means that school authorities, consistent with the generally accepted educational goal of attaining quality education for all pupils, must make and implement their customary decisions with a view toward enhancing integrated school opportunities.[35]

By avoiding any definition of the constitutional right being enforced, the Supreme Court retained for itself the greatest possible discretion to determine its contours. Later cases drew back from the course announced in *Keyes;* the reason can only be that a majority of the justices sensed that the political authority of the Court would not carry its mandate so far. If we acknowledge a constitutional right to attend a public school in which minority pupils are not unduly concentrated—and some such right was plainly given expression in the Denver case—it is difficult to see how that right could be ever relinquished with the passage of time, or why the scope of necessary desegregation remedies should be confined by existing school district boundaries. Reversing the decisions of district courts that had drawn these logical conclusions, the Court ruled that Pasadena need not perpetually readjust attendance zones to avoid "resegregation" resulting from white flight;[36] and that city and suburban school districts in metropolitan Detroit could not be consolidated by judicial order, even when consolidation was shown to be the sole means of ending racial isolation.[37]

The results were incoherent as constitutional law, but the policy limits established by the Court in this difficult area were no more arbitrary than the comparable lines necessarily drawn by the overtly political branches of government.

Economic Preferences

The most direct means available to government to foster a greater "equality of results" among racial or ethnic groups is to allocate economic benefits to members of those groups that are relatively less successful. Post-1968 civil rights policy has fostered an array of preferences, known collectively as "affirmative action," designed to enhance the relative economic position of blacks as a group: preferential treatment in hiring, in university admissions, in the awarding of government contracts and licenses. Originally justified in remedial terms, as a rough-justice corrective either for persistent discrimination or for the lingering effects of past discrimination, these preferences came increasingly to be defended in terms that imply a system of proportional economic entitlements for racial and ethnic groups.

Policies of economic preference have been the initiative, most notably, of administrative agencies charged with the enforcement of laws and regulations imposing a rule of nondiscrimination. The initiative of the civil rights agencies would have been substantially frustrated had the courts either enforced the Civil Rights Act of 1964 as written or interpreted the Fourteenth Amendment to prohibit the government's use of racial classifications to allocate economic benefits. The judiciary's essential contribution to affirmative action was that it did neither.

"Affirmative action," like "desegregation," acquired a new meaning in the late 1960s by the redefinition of a preexisting legal requirement. Beginning with a wartime order of Franklin Roosevelt affecting defense contractors, a series of executive orders required employers doing business with the federal government to undertake not to discriminate against any worker because of race, creed, color, or national origin.[38] By an order of President Kennedy signed in March 1961, the pledge of nondiscrimination already required to appear in each contract subject to the order—a statement that "the contractor agrees not to discriminate against any employee or applicant for employment because of race, religion, color, or national origin"—was supplemented by a clause restating the prohibition in positive terms: "The contractor will take affirmative action to ensure that applicants are employed, and that employees are treated during employment, without regard to their race, creed, color, or national origin."[39] As late as 1968, the published regulations of the secretary of labor still contained no suggestion that the requirement of "affirmative action" imposed any obligation beyond good-faith adherence to nondiscriminatory practices.[40]

Beginning in 1967, however, the Department of Labor had begun to experiment with more direct methods of increasing black employment. The celebrated "Philadelphia Plan," justified as a drastic remedy for obdurate racial discrimination in the building trades, imposed proportional hiring quotas on Philadelphia's construction industry; the plan had been "hammered out," as Hugh Davis Graham remarks, "while Detroit burned from the ghetto rioting."[41] New Labor Department regulations, published in May 1968, suggested that "affirmative action" would henceforth be interpreted to require hiring by race wherever protected groups were not proportionally represented. Larger contractors were obliged to develop written "affirmative action compliance programs," setting forth "specific steps to guarantee equal employment opportunity keyed to the problems and needs of members of minority groups, including, when there are deficiencies, the development of specific goals and time tables for the prompt achievement of full and equal employment opportunity."[42]

The evident implications of this language were bluntly spelled out in November 1969, when a further set of regulations, known as "Order No. 4," stated flatly: "The rate of minority applicants recruited should approximate or equal the rate of minorities to the applicant population in each location."[43] These quota provisions, revealed in Congress before the official publication of the order, caused some brief controversy;[44] but the order eventually issued by the Labor Department in February 1970 made no significant compromise. "Revised Order No. 4" described the "affirmative action program" required of government contractors as "a set of specific and result-oriented procedures," warning that "[p]rocedures without effort to make them work are meaningless; and effort, undirected by specific and meaningful procedures, is inadequate":

> An acceptable affirmative action program must include an analysis of areas within which the contractor is deficient in the utilization of minority groups and, further, goals and timetables to which the contractor's good faith efforts must be directed to correct the deficiencies, and thus to increase materially the utilization of minorities at all levels and in all segments of his work force where deficiencies exist.[45]

The references to "deficiency" and "utilization" expressed, in bureaucratic jargon, the inescapable logic of the new "equality of results." An executive order whose language required nondiscrimination—its literal command was still that government contractors "ensure that applicants are employed . . . without regard to their race"—had been formally interpreted by the Labor Department to require the contrary.

It might be questioned whether the government may constitutionally oblige those who do business with it to adopt racial quotas in hiring. A more immediate difficulty, at the time of the Labor Department's shift to "hard" affirmative action, was that the government was now compelling employers to do what the 1964 Civil Rights Act had made illegal. Title VII of the Act made it an unlawful employment practice for an employer

(1) to fail or refuse to hire . . . any individual . . . because of such individual's race, color, religion, sex or national origin; or

(2) to . . . classify his employees . . . in any way which would deprive or tend to deprive any individual of employment opportunities . . . because of such individual's race, color, religion, sex, or national origin.[46]

The force of this language to prohibit preferential or quota hiring, designed to correct imbalance or "underutilization," was fully understood in 1964. Responding to charges by southern senators that Title VII would require preferential treatment and "racial balancing" by employers, proponents insisted that the law would prohibit race altogether as a factor in employment and promotion decisions. An "Interpretive Memorandum of Title VII," presented to the Senate in April by the floor managers of the bill, Joseph Clark of Pennsylvania and Clifford Case of New Jersey, assured conservative opponents:

There is no requirement in title VII that an employer maintain a racial balance in his work force. On the contrary, any deliberate attempt to maintain a racial balance, whatever such a balance may be, would involve a violation of title VII because maintaining such a balance would require an employer to hire or to refuse to hire on the basis of race. It must be emphasized that discrimination is prohibited as to any individual.[47]

The "Dirksen-Mansfield substitute," negotiated during the extended Senate debate and introduced in early June, included a clarifying amendment that put the Clark/Case interpretation into the text of the law:

Nothing contained in this title shall be interpreted to require any employer . . . to grant preferential treatment to any individual or to any group because of the race . . . of such individual or group on account of an imbalance which may exist with respect to the total number or percentage of persons of any race . . . employed by any employer . . .

in comparison with the total number or percentage of persons of such race . . . in any community . . . or in the available work force in any community. . . .[48]

The policy of the U.S. Department of Labor by 1969 was thus to require what Congress had prohibited scarcely five years before. In those five years, both the outlook and the agenda for black equality had changed almost beyond recognition. When the issue came before the courts, in a suit by contractors challenging the Philadelphia Plan, it met a widespread judicial conviction that policies designed to address the new racial crisis should not be hindered by laws written before the present crisis was understood. Congress, it was said, could not have intended the consequences that would follow were the act to be enforced as written: in the case of the Philadelphia Plan, "to freeze the status quo and to foreclose remedial action under other authority [that is, the executive order] designed to overcome existing evils." The Philadelphia Plan was held not to violate the Civil Rights Act of 1964, and the Supreme Court declined to hear the case.[49]

Contemporaneous developments at the Equal Employment Opportunities Commission contributed even more importantly to the historic shift in the underlying premises guiding civil rights policy. When the Labor Department moved to encourage hiring quotas, the government acted by fiat—scarcely bothering, after the eventual success of the Philadelphia Plan, to justify its requirements as a remedy for identifiable discrimination.[50] At the EEOC, by contrast, analogous policies were advanced by successfully redefining the concept of discrimination itself. The political consequences have been profound: the revised definition both altered the essence of the wrong condemned as "discrimination" and reallocated the central entitlement of civil rights (that of protection against "discrimination") from the individual to the racial or ethnic group.

The object of the professional staff of the EEOC was to make Title VII of the Civil Rights Act an effective vehicle for increasing black employment. A statute prohibiting employment discrimination, particularly when it embodies the compromises exacted by the opponents of Title VII, is not the natural means to that end. Discrimination, where it exists, is often difficult to prove. A more fundamental difficulty is the fact that black applicants for employment are disproportionately excluded by what were traditionally viewed as nondiscriminatory selection criteria, such as aptitude tests.

Given the language of its authorizing statute, the EEOC was limited to seeking remedies for "discrimination." That being the case, its ambitious goals for increasing black employment required that "discrimination" be redefined.[51] The logic of the situation was summarized with admirable clarity by Alfred Blumrosen, a Rutgers law professor who served as an early EEOC administrator, writing in 1970 at the end of the agency's formative period:

> If discrimination is narrowly defined, for example, by requiring an evil intent to injure minorities, then it will be difficult to find that it exists. If it does not exist, then the plight of racial and ethnic minorities must be attributable to some more generalized failures in society, in the fields of basic education, housing, family relations, and the like. The search for efforts to improve the condition of minorities must then focus in these general and difficult areas, and the answers can come only gradually as basic institutions, attitudes, customs, and practices are changed.
>
> But if discrimination is broadly defined, as, for example, by including all conduct which adversely affects minority group employment opportunities . . . then the prospects for rapid improvement in minority employment opportunities are greatly increased. Industrial relations systems are flexible. . . . If discrimination exists within these institutions, the solution lies within our immediate grasp. It is not embedded in the complications of fundamental sociology but can be sharply influenced by intelligent, effective, and aggressive legal action.
>
> This is the optimistic view of the racial problem in our nation. This view finds discrimination at every turn where minorities are adversely affected by institutional decisions, which are subject to legal regulation. In this view, we are in control of our own history.[52]

This new conception of what should be held to constitute "discrimination," repudiating the traditional and very different view that informed the 1964 statute, was ratified by the Supreme Court when it decided *Griggs v. Duke Power Co.* in 1971.[53] The defendant in *Griggs* required either a high school diploma or a passing score on a standardized general intelligence test as a prerequisite to employment in certain positions at its power plant. Substantially fewer black than white applicants met this requirement. Plaintiffs argued, and it was found by the Court, that "neither the high school completion requirement nor the general intelligence test [bore] a demonstrable relationship to successful performance of the jobs for which it was used." Plaintiffs further argued, and the Supreme Court held, that under these circumstances the educational or intelligence-test requirement constituted employment discrimination prohibited by Title VII of the Civil

Rights Act: that is, discrimination "against any individual . . . because of such individual's race." As Chief Justice Burger concluded, "If an employment practice which operates to exclude Negroes cannot be shown to be related to job performance, the practice is prohibited."

Reading these words for the first time, it is easy to suppose that the Court saw superfluous employment requirements as a means of covert discrimination—like the "freedom of choice" desegregation plan condemned in *Green v. County School Board.* Other facts in the case, including the history of segregated employment at Duke Power, made it hard to resist the inference that the requirements in question (adopted on the effective date of the 1964 Civil Rights Act) were motivated by discriminatory intent. If this could be established, the use of the test was illegal under Title VII as enacted. As with *Green* in the context of school desegregation, however, the Court ignored evidence of discrimination in order to state a legal rule in which wrongful intent was no longer a necessary element. Approving a finding that the employer in *Griggs* had no "intention to discriminate against Negro employees," the Supreme Court held flatly that "good intent or absence of discriminatory intent" was irrelevant to the existence of an unlawful employment practice under Title VII.[54]

As is clear both from the language of the statute and from some particularly unambiguous legislative history, the Court derived from Title VII a legal requirement that the proponents of the law had expressly disclaimed.[55] The Clark/Case "Interpretive Memorandum of Title VII" assured the Senate that nondiscriminatory testing (which the procedures in *Griggs* were presumed to be) would not be affected:

> There is no requirement in title VII that employers abandon bona fide qualification tests where, because of differences in background and education, members of some groups are able to perform better on these tests than members of other groups. An employer may set his qualifications as high as he likes, he may test to determine which applicants have these qualifications, and he may hire, assign, and promote on the basis of test performance.[56]

Persistent fears that Title VII might nevertheless be construed to prohibit the use of employment tests on which whites performed better than blacks led, after extended debate, to the adoption of another clarifying amendment:

> Notwithstanding any other provision of this title, it shall not be an unlawful employment practice for an employer . . . to give and to act

upon the results of any professionally developed ability test provided that such test, its administration or action upon the results is not designed, intended or used to discriminate because of race, color, religion, sex or national origin.[57]

The amendment was deprived of its intended effect because the Supreme Court now acquiesced in the EEOC's redefinition of the word *discrimination*—bringing any test that yielded a "disparate impact" within the proviso to the amendment.

Under the rule of *Griggs,* an aptitude test (or any other qualification for employment) yielding a racially disproportionate result became prima facie evidence of employment discrimination; such a test was permissible only if "validated" as a predictor of job-related ability. Although validation to the satisfaction of the civil rights enforcement agencies was predictably difficult to achieve, many valid tests of mental ability and general aptitude (in that they are demonstrably useful as predictors of employee performance) select white applicants disproportionately over blacks and Hispanics. The agencies' goal of proportional outcomes was necessarily in conflict with the ordinary assumption that an employer should hire for predicted success on the job.

The federal civil rights agencies offered a practical compromise when they openly endorsed, in published regulations issued in 1978, the so-called bottom line rule. The essence of the "bottom-line" approach to employment discrimination was that employers might be allowed to adopt any selection procedures they wished so long as the "total selection process" for a job showed no "adverse impact" on minorities. "Adverse impact" was avoided if the rate of selection for any protected group of applicants was not less than 80 percent of the rate for the most successful group.[58] The invitation to employers was thus to use any tests they liked, saving the expense and annoyance of EEOC "validation" for job relatedness, but to use them to compile separate lists by race, ethnicity, and sex; then to hire the best-qualified applicants from each list in the desired proportion. The "bottom-line" approach visibly turned nondiscrimination on its head: it was disapproved by the Supreme Court[59] and disavowed by the agencies that promulgated it. It is, however, the efficient means of achieving proportional outcomes wherever valid criteria for merit selection exist; and as such it remains an inevitable affirmative action strategy.[60]

In the celebrated *Bakke* case of 1978,[61] and in the *Weber* decision a year later,[62] the Supreme Court confirmed its willingness to amend or ignore those provisions of the 1964 Civil Rights Act that would otherwise inhibit important initiatives of the new civil rights. *Bakke* considered a challenge to a system of preferential admissions for minority applicants to a University of California medical school. If the words meant what they said, a system of preferential admissions for minority applicants to the University of California violated Title VI of the Civil Rights Act, which provided that "[n]o person in the United States shall, on the ground of race, color, or national origin, be excluded from participation in, be denied the benefits of, or be subjected to discrimination under any program or activity receiving Federal financial assistance."[63] Voting five to four, the Supreme Court held that the language quoted "prohibits only those uses of racial criteria that would violate the Fourteenth Amendment if employed by a State or its agencies."[64] As judicially revised in the context of *Bakke,* Title VI thus provided that the use of racial criteria to determine admission to federally assisted programs would be regulated by standards of reasonableness devised by the federal courts.

In *Weber,* a white steelworker had sought admission to a craft training program, jointly sponsored by his employer and his union, from which he was excluded by a racial quota. *Weber* presented the strongest "reverse discrimination" challenge ever heard by the Supreme Court, because Brian Weber's precise complaint had seemingly been anticipated, debated, and resolved in his favor by the 1964 act.[65] One specific provision of Title VII might almost have been written to cover the facts of the case:

> It shall be an unlawful employment practice for any employer, labor organization, or joint labor-management committee . . . to discriminate against any individual because of his race, color, religion, sex, or national origin in admission to, or employment in, any program established to provide apprenticeship or other training.[66]

Justice William J. Brennan, writing for a five-to-two majority, could not and did not controvert Justice William H. Rehnquist's demonstration that Congress in 1964 had intended, by this and other language in Title VII, to prohibit the quota that excluded Brian Weber. His central contention was rather that the color-blind means chosen at the time did not serve the underlying congressional objective, which he identified as the desire to improve the economic position of black workers. It followed that the statute's true purpose would be served by refusing it enforcement.[67]

In the constitutional cases on affirmative action, as distinct from those based on statute, the Court has produced—at enormous length—a record of its inability to agree on any decisive legal principle. The constitutional holding in the *Bakke* case was typically ambivalent. Justice Powell joined one group of four justices to make five votes for the constitutionality, under some circumstances, of racial preferences in university admissions; he then joined the opposing group of four justices to make five votes upholding a judgment that the system of preferences employed at UC Davis was unconstitutional.[68] The most notable opinion in *Bakke* is the one signed by Brennan, White, Marshall, and Blackmun, who would have approved the University's quota admissions without modification. "The position that . . . 'Our Constitution is color-blind,'" they observed, "has never been adopted by this Court as the proper meaning of the Equal Protection Clause."[69]

No clear authority, to be sure—only a tendency of the old decisions and the expectations they had once created—stood as a constitutional obstacle to government-sponsored racial preferences. Justice Powell's opinion in *Bakke* set the pattern for the decisions that followed, reviving the familiar rule that racial classifications were permissible so long as they were properly used for good ends. *Fullilove v. Klutznick,*[70] a 1980 decision upholding the constitutionality of "minority set-asides" in a federal public works appropriation, was in one sense merely another application of the same proposition. Yet *Fullilove* is historically noteworthy. The law in question was the first federal statute in well over a century to provide expressly that citizens of different races be treated differently by the government.[71] And with the extraordinary exception of the wartime Japanese Relocation Cases, no statute or regulation (state or federal) providing explicitly unequal treatment to citizens on the basis of race or ancestry had ever been upheld by the Supreme Court.[72]

The law challenged in *Fullilove* was in other respects mundane. The Public Works Employment Act of 1977, authorizing $4 billion in grants to state and local governments for local public works projects, had been amended on the floor of the House by the addition of the following provision:

> Except to the extent that the Secretary [of Commerce] determines otherwise, no grant shall be made under this Act for any local public works project unless the applicant gives satisfactory assurance to the Secretary that at least 10 per centum of the amount of each grant shall be expended for minority business enterprises. For purposes of this paragraph, the term "minority business enterprise" means a business at least 50 per centum of which is owned by minority group members or,

in the case of a publicly owned business, at least 51 per centum of the stock of which is owned by minority group members. For the purposes of the preceding sentence, minority group members are citizens of the United States who are Negroes, Spanish-speaking, Orientals, Indians, Eskimos, and Aleuts.[73]

The minority business enterprise ("MBE") provision challenged in *Fullilove* was a crude example of pork-barrel politics. The beginning and the end of the argument for it in debate was the assertion that less than 1 percent of federal procurement was concluded with minority business enterprises; and that minority businesses were entitled, in the words of its sponsor, to "get a fair share of the action from this public works legislation."[74] The specifics of the provision had received no attention from Congress: its arbitrary 10 percent quota and equally arbitrary definition of the preferred class would have made it unacceptable under even a moderately rigorous version of the equal protection "scrutiny" normally applied to legislation employing classifications deemed "suspect."

Six justices voted to uphold the MBE provision, though no more than three joined any single opinion. Justices Marshall, Brennan, and Blackmun adhered to their position (previously announced in *Bakke*) that "racial classifications that provide benefits to minorities" were subject to a different constitutional standard, one more easily satisfied, from that applicable to "racial classifications that stigmatize." While the latter were simply invalid, the test for "racial classifications designed to further remedial purposes" was whether they "serve important governmental objectives and are substantially related to achievement of those objectives." Judged by this standard, the MBE provision in *Fullilove* was "plainly constitutional."[75] Because they were unwilling to endorse the view that "good" and "bad" racial classifications should be judged by different standards, the other members of the majority (Chief Justice Burger, joined by Justices White and Powell) were obliged to defend the MBE provision by implying that it was something it was not: a "limited and properly tailored remedy to cure the effects of prior discrimination," a program "narrowly tailored to achieve its objectives, subject to continuing evaluation and reassessment."[76] The chief justice's disingenuous apology revealed more than Justice Marshall's candid partisanship about the Court's disinclination to countermand this modest congressional experiment in racial reparations.

The Court's inability to muster a majority vote for any view of a case in which the constitutional issue was so clearly drawn revealed that we had, in truth, no constitutional law on the subject of affirmative action. The rule applied by the Court, if a rule must be stated, is that those racial preferences are permissible that strike a majority of the justices, for whatever combination of reasons, as reasonable under the circumstances. State and local governments, it was later held, might undertake racial preferences in employment, at least if justified by a "compelling state purpose" to which the means chosen were "narrowly tailored." A plan under which white schoolteachers with greater seniority were laid off ahead of black teachers with less was approved by four justices but seemed inappropriate to five, who stated their different reasons in three separate opinions.[77] Six justices agreed that the city of Richmond, Virginia, might not constitutionally adopt a minority set-aside program much like the one the Court had approved in *Fullilove:* a full tally of their different reasons for coming to this conclusion required six separate opinions and parts of opinions.[78] The decision in the Richmond case was widely viewed as a threat to the future of racial preferences; but one year later, a new grouping of five justices held that the Federal Communications Commission might continue to prefer women and minorities in the award of broadcast licenses.[79]

While it ostensibly debated the arid distinctions between a "compelling governmental interest" and an "important governmental objective," between a remedy that is "narrowly tailored" and one that is "substantially related to the interests it seeks to serve," the Court in each of these cases was really addressing a more practical issue: whether a given racial classification in its particular context was an appropriate exercise of government power. But the result of such deliberations is "constitutional law" only by default.

Voting Rights

Among the new, race-conscious means of achieving "equality of results" adopted after 1968, the most radical innovation in terms of traditional American principles has inspired the least public controversy. Since 1970, a combined effort by the three branches of the federal government has required states and municipalities to alter election districts and systems of representation so as to facilitate the election of black and Hispanic candidates. The vehicle of this political revolution, the Voting Rights Act of 1965, was originally enacted for very different purposes. Its provisions were transformed, in practice, by the determination of the Justice Department and the federal courts to pursue a policy of affirmative action in matters touching political representation.

The reality of political representation is difficult to measure, but the racial or ethnic composition of a representative body is easily compared to that of its constituent population. Counting in this fashion, "equality of results" for black voters was visibly lacking in 1968: not just in the South—where access to the ballot had only just been won—but in the legislatures and city councils of northern states where the black franchise had been unimpeded for at least a hundred years. Because voting rights were demonstrably not the problem, voting rights alone could not be the answer. The hypothesis that black citizens needed black representation could be found between the lines of the report of the Kerner Commission:

> It is beyond the scope of this Report to consider in detail the many problems presented by the existing distribution of political power within city governments. But it is plain that the Negro ghetto resident feels deeply that he is not represented fairly and adequately under the arrangements which prevail in many cities. This condition strikes at major democratic values.
>
> To meet this problem, city government and the majority community should revitalize the political system to encourage fuller participation by all segments of the community. Whether this requires adoption of any one system of representation, we are not prepared to say. But it is clear that at-large representation, currently the practice in many American cities, does not give members of the minority community a feeling of involvement or stake in city government. Further, this form of representation dilutes the normal political impact of pressures generated by a particular neighborhood or district.[80]

A federal law requiring states and municipalities to facilitate the election of minority candidates could not conceivably have been enacted in 1968. As in the case of economic preferences, however, the executive and judicial branches were able to advance a controversial policy initiative without recourse to the legislative process, by finding new meaning in a preexisting rule.

The statutory means, the Voting Rights Act of 1965,[81] had been adopted (as its title declared) "to enforce the fifteenth amendment to the Constitution of the United States" in those states that had so far ignored it. In the formerly segregated South, the principal instrument of black disfranchisement was the discriminatory administration of literacy tests. Case-by-case proof of discrimination was an interminable task. To cut it short, the Voting Rights Act prohibited altogether the use of "tests or devices" as prerequisites to voting in "covered" jurisdictions: states or counties in which the use of a literacy test, combined with low voter turnout in the 1964 presidential election, gave rise to a presumption (created by the statute) that the literacy test had been used to discriminate. The jurisdictions that were violating the Fifteenth Amendment were well known to the Justice Department, and the statistical threshold was selected so that the southern states and counties at which the law was directed would be the only ones covered. Finally, to guard against the ingenuity of southern election officials in devising new exclusionary devices not covered by the language of the act, a further section prohibited covered jurisdictions from instituting any new or different "voting qualification or prerequisite to voting, or standard, practice or procedure with respect to voting," without prior approval from the U.S. District Court for the District of Columbia or the Department of Justice.[82]

The statutory language was unambiguous. "To assure that the right of citizens of the United States to vote is not denied or abridged on account of race or color"—this was the prohibition of the Fifteenth Amendment— section 4 provided that "no citizen shall be denied the right to vote . . . because of his failure to comply with any test or device in any [covered jurisdiction]. . . ." A jurisdiction caught by the statutory presumption could escape coverage if it could persuade the district court in Washington that no "test or device" had, in fact, been used for the past five years "for the purpose or with the effect of denying or abridging the right to vote on account of race or color." "Test or device" was defined as any requirement that a person as a prerequisite for voting or registration for voting (1) demonstrate the ability to read, write, understand, or interpret any matter, (2) demonstrate any educational achievement or knowledge of any particular subject, (3) possess good moral character, or (4) prove his qualifications by the voucher of registered voters or members of any other class.

No list of prohibited requirements could be made exhaustive. Given the southern states' history of "contriving new rules of various kinds for the sole purpose of perpetrating voting discrimination in the face of adverse federal court decrees," as the Supreme Court explained in its decision upholding the constitutionality of the Voting Rights Act, "Congress had reason to suppose that these States might try similar maneuvers in the future in order to evade the remedies for voting discrimination contained in the [Voting Rights] Act itself."[83] Section 5 accordingly required covered jurisdictions to obtain the approval of federal authorities before instituting *any* change in their voting procedures:

> Whenever a [covered jurisdiction] shall enact or seek to administer any voting qualification or prerequisite to voting, or standard, practice, or procedure with respect to voting different from that in force or effect on November 1, 1964, such State or subdivision may institute an action . . . for a declaratory judgment that such qualification, prerequisite, standard, practice, or procedure does not have the purpose and will not have the effect of denying or abridging the right to vote on account of race or color, and unless and until the court enters such judgment no person shall be denied the right to vote for failure to comply with such qualification, prerequisite, standard, practice, or procedure. . . .

Alternatively, a state or county might apply to the Department of Justice for "preclearance" of the new voting procedure. The relative expense of pursuing a declaratory judgment action in the federal district court in Washington has made Justice Department preclearance the principal vehicle of section 5 enforcement.[84]

The pertinent provisions of the Voting Rights Act have been quoted at some length as the best means of illustrating both the dilemma that soon confronted the Supreme Court and the gravity of the course it took. The clear import of the statutory language—amply reinforced by its legislative history[85]—is that the prophylactic rule of section 5 was intended to safeguard section 4's prohibition of literacy tests and other prerequisites for *voting;* and that the whole concern of the act was to ensure nondiscriminatory access to the ballot. The question of the ballot's "effectiveness"— the political consequences for southern blacks of different systems of representation or the drawing of district boundaries—appeared nowhere in the statute or its legislative history. On the contrary, the traditional claim for Negro suffrage, unvarying since its enunciation by Wendell Phillips a hundred years earlier, was that access to the ballot would enable southern blacks to assert political power on the same terms as everyone else. Neither in 1865 nor in 1965 was it suggested that the full and "undiluted" exercise of the franchise required a district in which blacks formed a majority.

The revolution in southern politics over the last twenty-five years—producing white southern Democrats beholden to black constituents for reelection—has proved Phillips correct. But in the immediate aftermath of the Voting Rights Act there were southern politicians who attempted, while complying with its terms, to delay its effects. Of the varied stratagems that came before the Supreme Court in 1969, in a series of cases reported as *Allen v. State Board of Elections*,[86] the crux of the legal problem was most distinctly presented by an act of the Mississippi legislature. Mississippi had authorized its county boards of supervisors, in their discretion, to shift their basis of representation from the single-member districts previously mandated by law to elections at large. The irresistible inference was that the purpose and effect of the change was to postpone indefinitely the day when the boards of supervisors in certain Mississippi counties would seat their first black members.

Congress had not made such conduct illegal in 1965 and was unlikely to do so even in 1969. Yet the case was one—like *Green v. County School Board*, or the legal challenge to the Philadelphia Plan—in which a decision that was faithful to existing law would acquiesce in a result the Court considered intolerable. The Supreme Court held by a vote of seven to two (Justices Harlan and Black dissenting) that the change from single-member districts to at-large elections was a change in a "standard, practice or procedure with respect to voting," subject to preclearance under section 5 of the Voting Rights Act.

Assuming, as seems likely, that the Mississippi election law could be shown to have been enacted with both the purpose and the effect of frustrating the political prospects of black candidates, the Warren Court in 1969 would surely have had no hesitation in finding such action unconstitutional under both the Fourteenth and the Fifteenth Amendments. But the whole point of the suit in *Allen* was to reach discriminatory redistricting (as opposed to voting procedures) with the extraordinary remedies of the Voting Rights Act; and the force of those remedies would have been largely dissipated had plaintiffs been required to establish defendants' discriminatory purpose. The opinion by Chief Justice Warren based the decision instead on the idea—drawn from *Reynolds v. Sims*,[87] the "one man, one vote" decision of 1964—that some votes count more than others:

> [The case] involves a change from district to at-large voting for county supervisors. The right to vote can be affected by a dilution of voting power as well as by an absolute prohibition on casting a ballot. Voters who are members of a racial minority might well be in the majority in one district, but in a decided minority in the county as a whole. This type of change could therefore nullify their ability to elect the candidate of their choice just as would prohibiting some of them from voting.[88]

The reference to "dilution" in this new context carried significant implications. "One man, one vote" applies just as well to at-large as to district voting; so the only "dilution" in the hypothesis of the chief justice was the dilution of the influence of a racial bloc. The quoted passage is nonsense without certain powerful assumptions that were left unstated. In the view of the chief justice, the political influence of black voters depended on their being able to elect a black candidate by a black majority; and a system of representation in which black voters were unable to elect black candidates was one in which they were effectively disfranchised, at least in part. These assumptions led, in turn, to a view of "voting rights" in which the "discriminatory" treatment proscribed by the act had no necessary connection with discriminatory intent. The radical transformation of the meaning of "discrimination" is the same one that has been observed in the case of school assignments and employment practices. In the new context of "voting rights," the ultimate standard of a nondiscriminatory electoral system became the degree to which blacks in a given jurisdiction were elected to office.[89]

The Voting Rights Act was interpreted in *Allen* to reach what was undoubtedly discriminatory conduct, but of a kind to which the terms of the act did not apply, and by a rationale that excluded any reference to discrimination. Given the basis of the decision, the act could henceforth be employed affirmatively: to protect and enhance the opportunities for black candidates to be elected to office. The old-fashioned denial of the right to vote that was the target of the Voting Rights Act in 1965 had been effectively eliminated when the act's extraordinary, temporary provisions were due to expire in 1970. The act was extended by Congress, and its coverage enlarged, as the instrument of a new federal policy to promote minority officeholding.

An appendage to the original legislative scheme now became its central provision. Section 5 required covered jurisdictions to obtain the consent of either the district court for the District of Columbia or the Department of Justice to any change in a "procedure with respect to voting." Decisions in the wake of *Allen* that both municipal annexations and reapportionments were "procedures with respect to voting" placed covered jurisdictions under the necessity of periodic negotiations with federal officials over the system of representation and districting required to avoid "denying or abridging the right to vote on account of race." The price of a Justice Department finding or court ruling that the new apportionment would not have the prohibited discriminatory effect was frequently the submission of a districting plan calculated to produce the greatest feasible number of "safe" seats for black candidates.[90] There is of course no reason in principle why a policy favoring minority officeholding, recognized for what it is, should be limited to particular areas of the country; nor why its most effective enforcement mechanism should be triggered only when a jurisdiction seeks to alter some established practice. These eccentricities of modern "voting rights" are a reminder of the law's origin in legislation having a distinctly different purpose.

By the early 1970s the federal government was thus in the anomalous position, by the standards of a decade before, of requiring state and local governments to gerrymander their election districts on racial lines. How the new policy worked in practice is readily seen in *United Jewish Organizations v. Carey,*[91] the Supreme Court decision upholding its constitutionality. Because of decreased voter participation in the 1968 presidential election, the New York counties of Bronx, Kings (Brooklyn), and New York (Manhattan) were brought within the scope of the Voting Rights Act as amended in 1970.[92] Because a judge held that New York City's failure to produce Spanish-language election materials constituted a prohibited literacy test, the three counties were unable to escape coverage by the affirmative demonstration of innocence contemplated by the statute.[93] New York's 1972 reapportionment statute, redrawing the boundaries of its congressional, state assembly, and state senate districts in accordance with the 1970 census, was accordingly submitted to the Department of Justice for preclearance under section 5. After review, the attorney general notified state officials that with respect to "parts of the plans in Kings and New York Counties," the state had not met its burden of proving that the proposed reapportionment would not have "the purpose nor the effect of abridging the right to vote because of race or color."[94]

More specifically, with respect to certain senate and assembly districts in the Bedford-Stuyvesant area of Brooklyn, the Justice Department felt that the available nonwhite population had not been used to best advantage. A simple nonwhite majority was not considered sufficiently likely to elect a nonwhite candidate. New York's original plan for Kings County included some districts with nonwhite majorities as high as 85 and 95 percent, while the lowest stood at 52 and 53 percent. In the ensuing negotiations with Justice Department officials, state officials "got the feeling" that the minimum acceptable figure for a nonwhite majority district would be 65 percent. Pressured by impending deadlines for the 1974 elections, the staff of New York's legislative committee on reapportionment hastily revised the challenged districts to meet the 65 percent standard. The attorney general's objections were withdrawn.

Under the original 1972 apportionment plan, the 30,000 Hasidic Jews concentrated in the Williamsburgh neighborhood of Brooklyn had been located entirely within a single assembly district that was 61 percent nonwhite. To attain the 65 percent standard, the 1974 gerrymander moved a portion of the Hasidic community to one of the adjoining districts, containing the even more concentrated nonwhite population to which the Justice Department had objected. Representatives of the Hasidic community sued to enjoin application of the revised plan, arguing that the legislative apportionment solely on the basis of race violated their rights under the Fourteenth and Fifteenth Amendments.[95]

The opinions in *United Jewish Organizations v. Carey,* written a year before *Bakke,* reveal the depth to which the race-conscious assumptions of the 1970s had already been assimilated by the justices. The context was the one in which, perhaps more than any other, the liberal convictions of the previous decade had taught that distinctions of race were to be treated as irrelevant: by fiat, if necessary. The older view is seen in Judge Wisdom's stated reason, in 1962, for overturning the Louisiana law requiring a racial identification on the ballot: "The vice in the law is the State's placing its power and prestige behind a policy of racial classification inconsistent with the elective processes. . . . If there is one area above all others where the Constitution is color-blind, it is the area of state action with respect to the ballot and the voting booth."[96] Until *Allen v. State Board of Elections,* the proposition that the Constitution required electoral districts to be drawn in color-blind fashion had been plausible at the very least. A gerrymander designed to isolate a racial minority had been held unconstitutional in 1960;[97] in 1964 the Court suggested more broadly that districts drawn "on the basis of race or place of origin" might be vulnerable to constitutional challenge.[98] The suggestion was a natural one under the color-blind assumptions then prevailing, but it was fatally inconsistent with the implications of *Allen* five years later.

The constitutional claim in *United Jewish Organizations* had not previously been addressed; but the Supreme Court's plurality opinion disposed of it by observing that it had been rejected, by implication, in *Allen* and the subsequent decisions approving the use of the Voting Rights Act to compel the creation of "safe" electoral districts for blacks and Hispanics. The Court was correct about the implications of the prior cases. "Voting rights," as redefined in *Allen,* is a zero-sum game. If a line is drawn to enhance the voting strength of one racial or ethnic group, another group is necessarily disadvantaged in the same terms, necessarily on the basis of ethnicity or race. What would have seemed in 1964 to be a vital constitutional issue had already been decided by default.

United Jewish Organizations brought to light another implication of

Allen. Not only had section 5 been effectively amended to regulate election laws as well as voting procedures; but its original, color-blind conception had been displaced when the Voting Rights Act was made an instrument to win political influence for protected groups. Were it not so, the Williamsburgh Hasidim might have been thought to assert a valid claim under section 5 itself. That is, the state of New York had instituted a new procedure with respect to voting, the purpose *and* the effect of which was to abridge (by "dilution"), on account of race, the plaintiffs' right to vote: it was because the Hasidim were of one race rather than another that they had been split between two districts. Such a claim must obviously fail, but it was necessary to explain why.

One approach, adopted by the Civil Rights Division of the Department of Justice, was to determine—on the basis of a "review of the circumstances surrounding the adoption of the Fifteenth Amendment, the passage of the Voting Rights Act and its Amendments," and so forth—that "nothing . . . indicates that Hasidic Jews or persons of Irish, Polish or Italian descent are within the scope of the special protections defined by the Congress in the Voting Rights Act."[99] The essential speciousness of this response lay in the fact that Congress in 1965, motivated by the denial of the ballot to southern blacks, enacted a standard of nondiscrimination that was color-blind in both outlook and language. As originally conceived, section 5 gave no "special protections" to anyone. The Civil Rights Division was describing section 5 as subsequently interpreted by those responsible for its enforcement, notably including itself.

The Court's answer to the same question is more interesting. The Williamsburgh Jews could not claim "a cognizable discrimination against whites or an abridgment of their right to vote on the grounds of race" so long as "whites in King County, as a group, were provided with fair representation":

> As the Court of Appeals observed, the plan left white majorities in approximately 70% of the assembly and senate districts in Kings County, which had a countywide population that was 65% white. Thus, even if voting in the county occurred strictly according to race, whites would not be underrepresented relative to their share of the population.[100]

The base line for assessing racial discrimination in electoral districting—the question of who wins and who loses in the zero-sum game—was thus explicitly identified with a standard of proportional representation by race. Even more striking is the matter-of-fact way in which the political interests of the Williamsburgh Hasidim, one of the most "discrete and insular minorities"[101] it is possible to imagine, were identified with those of the other white residents of Brooklyn. Of the innumerable factors that might cause different groups to share interests and sentiments—political beliefs, wealth, occupation, geographic proximity, religion—the formerly proscribed category of race was now accorded paramount importance.

One week before announcing the decision in *United Jewish Organizations,* the Court had agreed to hear the *Bakke* case; and its seeming reticence about the constitutional implications of racial redistricting may have reflected a feeling that the great issue of "reverse discrimination" should be reserved for the following term. Justice Brennan was less reluctant to state his views. His concurring opinion in *United Jewish Organizations* began by acknowledging that, had the Hasidim been of another race, their treatment at the hands of the state of New York would in all likelihood have been unconstitutional. "It follows," he wrote, "that if the racial redistricting involved here . . . is not similarly to be prohibited, the distinctiveness that avoids this prohibition must arise from either or both of two considerations: the permissibility of affording preferential treatment to disadvantaged nonwhites generally, or the particularized application of the Voting Rights Act in this instance." Brennan found both distinctions pertinent; and his exposition of the former alternative provided a candid and concise summary of the contemporary constitutional law of racial preferences.

Just as the argument for the color-blind Constitution need not assert that the effect of a racial classification must in every instance be bad, the contrary argument need not deny that a race-based remedial policy may impose significant costs. Brennan indicated what, to his mind, such costs might be. There was, first, the difficulty of ascertaining "whether a given race classification truly furthers benign rather than illicit objectives" and of arbitrating the competing claims to the benefits of a racial preference: in the context of the Brooklyn redistricting, for instance, Puerto Rican groups (lumped together with blacks as "nonwhite") protested that the result of the Justice Department's intervention had been to reduce their political strength from what it would have been under the state's initial plan. Second, "even in the pursuit of remedial objectives, an explicit policy of assignment by race may serve to stimulate our society's latent race consciousness, suggesting the utility and propriety of basing decisions on a factor that ideally bears no relationship to an individual's worth or needs." Finally, according to Brennan, "we cannot well ignore the social reality that even a benign policy of assignment by race is viewed as unjust by many in our society, especially by those individuals who are adversely affected by a given classification. This impression of injustice may be heightened by the natural consequence of our governing processes that the most 'discrete and insular' of whites often will be called upon to bear the immediate, direct costs of benign discrimination." There were indications of "just such decisionmaking" in the case at hand, where officials "chose to localize the burden of race reassignment upon the petitioners rather than to redistribute a more varied and diffused range of whites into predominantly nonwhite districts."

The solution to this dilemma was to require that courts, agencies, and legislatures make reasonable choices:

> In my view, if and when a decisionmaker embarks on a policy of benign racial sorting, he must weigh the concerns that I have discussed against the need for effective social policies promoting racial justice in a society beset by deep-rooted racial inequities. But I believe that Congress here adequately struck that balance in enacting the carefully conceived remedial scheme embodied in the Voting Rights Act. However the Court ultimately decides the constitutional legitimacy of "reverse discrimination" pure and simple, I am convinced that the application of the Voting Rights Act substantially minimizes the objections to preferential treatment, and legitimates the use of even overt, numerical racial devices in electoral redistricting.[102]

A policy of "benign racial sorting," in other words, should be designed so as to maximize its benefits while minimizing its costs. If the balance is "adequately struck" (in the judgment of a Supreme Court majority), the test of constitutionality is met. The utter banality of the conclusion does not alter the fact that it accurately states present-day constitutional law.

The liberal conviction of the early 1960s, memorably expressed by Alexander Bickel, was that for the government to treat persons differently on the basis of race was "illegal, immoral, unconstitutional, inherently wrong, and destructive of democratic society."[103] For the past generation the U.S. government has asserted the contrary. Taught with the most powerful instruments at the government's disposal, the new lesson has been readily accepted. Racial and ethnic classifications, with the underlying premise of entitlements for groups, are seen as presumptively relevant to an unprecedented range of social transactions. These include not only every distribution of benefits and burdens, public or private, but areas of intellectual activity to which the belief in a transcendent individualism once seemed central. The former lesson, the insistence that race was an "irrelevance," was the harder, counterintuitive one; and it has proved very easy to unlearn.

The national habit of counting by race will be more difficult to eradicate than it was to instill. It is easier to confer an entitlement, or to inspire a claim to one, than to withdraw it. The ease with which the benefits from racial or ethnic preferences may be identified by their recipients, set against the diffuse nature of the corresponding injury, affords the proponents of preferences a decisive political advantage. The difficulty of harnessing the latent popular support for nondiscrimination suggests that the federal government will not be restored to a color-blind posture by the political branches.

Part of the future argument for the color-blind Constitution will thus be that the Supreme Court, alone among American institutions, retains the power to deflect what will otherwise become an irreversible tendency toward the convenient and destructive practice of allocating social resources by racial and ethnic groups. Whether the Court in fact has that power will not be seen unless and until it makes the attempt. The likelihood that a future Supreme Court will attempt to reinstate a constitutional rule of color blindness depends, obviously enough, on the view of political and social developments taken by the members of the Court over the next generation. As a minimum precondition to any announcement that the Constitution is color-blind, a majority of the Supreme Court would have to be persuaded that the racial preferences associated with school desegregation, affirmative action, and voting rights are not indispensable to the nation's discharge of its obligations to black citizens; and that such policies carry social costs that outweigh their benefits.

The heaviest costs are likely to be perceived, not in the injustice to individual victims of reverse discrimination such as Alan Bakke or Brian Weber, but in certain unintended consequences of the policies of preference. One such consequence is that visible and controversial affirmative action policies spend the limited political capital available for "programs to help blacks" on measures that do little or nothing to improve the condition of those black Americans in whose name the modern civil rights agenda is consistently advanced. The strategy of explaining every incidence of "disparate impact" as the result of "discrimination" was, as Alfred Blumrosen perceptively wrote in 1970, "the optimistic view of the racial problem in our nation," permitting us to avoid the conclusion that "the plight of ethnic minorities must be attributable to some more generalized failures in society, in the fields of basic education, housing, family relations, and the like."[104] Precisely this had been the unwelcome conclusion of the Moynihan Report in 1965, and for more than two decades affirmative action has helped us to ignore it. The "optimistic view" was a concession to political reality: a choice forced on judges and administrators who were determined to achieve visible results in the short term and who lacked the power to commit real resources to social change. Remedial policies directed not at race but at disadvantage, promising disproportionate benefits to blacks despite a racially neutral allocation, remain the costly alternative.

Another consequence, surely unintended at the outset, is the threat that a theory of proportional entitlements by race and ethnicity will become the American political model. Wherever the proportional allocation of social benefits among competing groups becomes the political line of least resistance, we may expect to see the argument that such allocation is equitable. Thus a bill introduced in the California legislature in 1989 would have required the state's colleges and universities to "strive to approximate by the year 2000 a diverse student body which mirrors the composition of recent high school graduates . . . for individuals from historically and currently underrepresented or economically disadvantaged groups."[105] University administrators in California and elsewhere have already moved aggressively in this direction, defending racial and ethnic proportionality in admissions as the only equitable system.[106] Because an explicitly proportional allocation of public resources on racial and ethnic lines merely formalizes the logic of "disparate impact," there is no reason why the technique should be restricted to university admissions. The distribution of the more visible benefits and burdens of citizenship—such as public employment or military service—is already routinely scrutinized for conformity to the racial and ethnic composition of the relevant populations; the presumption is widespread that any significant deviation from proportional representation in these areas is an evil to be corrected. Laws or policies mandating a proportional allocation represent but a short further step.

A scrupulous nondiscrimination may yet prove, because of the limitations of human justice, to be the most effective contribution that *law* (as distinct from political action) can make to the achievement of racial equality in this country. No one will contend, however, that a strict legal equality can of itself settle the score between the United States of America and the descendants of her slaves. Where race-specific measures direct benefits to persons whose ancestors were brought to this country in slavery, the sense that this discrimination works rough justice—unjust, but less unjust than doing nothing—cannot easily be dismissed.

No other racial or ethnic group among America's immigrants has a comparable claim to special treatment, and the moral awkwardness of asking black Americans to be content with nondiscrimination should not stop us from giving that answer to everyone else. Yet the breach in the antidiscrimination principle made in favor of African-Americans has led to a multiplicity of government-sponsored preferences for groups defined by race, ethnicity, or status as a "language minority." The expanded claims to group entitlements could not rest on the unique circumstances of slavery and its aftermath. The necessity of a more broadly applicable justification has led to the wide currency of a profoundly different rationale: a variety of arguments whose common core is the idea that a distribution of social benefits is presumptively just when made to racial and ethnic groups in proportion to their numbers. Yet to the extent that a system of proportional entitlements becomes acceptable as an avowed premise of equality, the aspirations of American democracy will be profoundly altered.

The Constitution does not contain the solution to every political or social dilemma, and even our urgent need for an answer does not mean that the Constitution must supply it. Rules that many would regard as the bedrock of constitutional liberties—stemming from the application to the states of the federal Bill of Rights—are part of the Constitution only because we have chosen to see them in the document. So it is with the color-blind proposition. The Constitution as written does not necessarily contain *any* special rule about the government's use of racial classifications (other than as grounds for denying the right to vote). That much was settled in 1866 with the rejection of Wendell Phillips's Fourteenth Amendment.

A constitutional rule actually capable of constraining political results, not merely subjecting them to judicial oversight, must either require the government to classify its citizens by race[107] or else forbid the practice: there is no middle ground. The alternative is to treat a racial classification like any other (age, sex, occupation, income), with the result that such use of it will be made as the political process approves. If we regard the Supreme Court's legislative oversight as part of the political process, such is the choice that was made when the constitutionality of racial classifications first came before the Court in *Plessy v. Ferguson* and that the Supreme Court majority has never been disposed to alter.

The advocates of a color-blind Constitution have at every stage been those who were unwilling to leave the proper use of racial classifications to be settled by the political process, and who sought therefore to put such distinctions beyond the reach of legislators and judges alike. The nineteenth-century argument as distilled by Harlan, at a time when the political objection to racial classifications was their use in the systematic oppression of black citizens, was careful to place the legal objection on racially neutral grounds. However we appraise the strength of Harlan's argument today, it applies with equal force to circumstances in which racial classifications may be thought to work a different harm:

> The sure guarantee of the peace and security of each race is the clear, distinct, unconditional recognition by our governments, National and State, of every right that inheres in civil freedom, and of the equality before the law of all citizens of the United States without regard to race.[108]

Harlan's prescription gains in force if for "each race"—by which he meant the black and the white—we substitute a reference to the present components of a diverse, multiracial, multiethnic society. His statement is more a political judgment than a constitutional reading. The judgment is essentially pessimistic: that tools of government we know to be capable of much harm, and that we cannot confidently use for good, should be abjured altogether. The experience of the intervening century has not yet proved Harlan wrong.

Notes

Index

Notes

1. A Glorious Liberty Document

1. Mass. Const. art. I, §1 (1780).
2. Va. Declaration of Rights art. I (1776).
3. For a moderate appraisal of the framers' accommodation with slavery, emphasizing the difference between the constitutional text and its interpretation by the federal government from 1787 to 1860, see Don E. Fehrenbacher, "Slavery, the Framers, and the Living Constitution," in *Slavery and Its Consequences: The Constitution, Equality, and Race* 1 (Robert A. Goldwin & Art Kaufman eds., 1988). The darker, neo-Garrisonian view appears in William M. Wiecek, *The Sources of Antislavery Constitutionalism in America, 1760–1848,* ch. 3 (1977), and Paul Finkelman, "Slavery and the Constitutional Convention: Making a Covenant with Death," in *Beyond Confederation* 188 (Richard Beeman, Stephen Botein, & Edward C. Carter II eds., 1987).
4. "What to the Slave Is the Fourth of July?: An Address Delivered in Rochester, New York, on 5 July 1852," 2 *The Frederick Douglass Papers* 359, 385 (John W. Blassingame ed., 1982). Douglass himself had only recently renounced the Garrisonian view of the pro-slavery character of the Constitution, and this well-known passage reflects the enthusiasm of the convert. See id. at 331; Douglass, *Life and Times of Frederick Douglass* 260–262 (reprinted 1962).
5. *Cong. Globe,* 39th Cong., 1st Sess. 673 (1866).
6. Id. at 536–537. Stevens overcame his scruples and voted for a Fourteenth Amendment whose second section contained the word "male," when his preferred reform of the basis of representation proved politically unfeasible.
7. "The better to secure and perpetuate mutual friendship and intercourse among the people of the different states in this union, the free inhabitants of each of these states, paupers, vagabonds and fugitives from justice excepted, shall be entitled to all privileges and immunities of free citizens in the several states. . . ." Articles of Confederation art. IV, cl. 1. The privileges and immunities clause was not debated at the Constitutional Convention. According to the contemporary explanation of Charles Pinckney, "The 4th article, respecting the extending the rights of the Citizens of each State, throughout the United States . . . is formed

exactly upon the principles of the 4th article of the present Confederation. . . ." Pinckney in 1821 would declare that "at the time I drew that constitution, I perfectly knew that there did not then exist such a thing in the Union as a black or colored citizen . . . ; nor, notwithstanding all that has been said on the subject, do I believe one does exist in it." 3 *Records of the Federal Convention* 112, 446 (Max Farrand ed., 1911).

8. 11 *Journals of the Continental Congress* 652–656 (1908) (proceedings of June 25, 1778); 1 *Documentary History of the Ratification of the Constitution* 126–127 (Merrill Jensen ed., 1976).

9. Don E. Fehrenbacher, *The Dred Scott Case* 66 & n. 62 (1978).

10. Dred Scott v. Sandford, 60 U.S. (19 How.) 393, 575–576 (1857) (Curtis, J., dissenting). The reference by Curtis to this piece of history plainly influenced contemporary views as to the racial inclusiveness of the comity clause. In Smith v. Moody, 26 Ind. 299 (1866), the postwar Indiana Supreme Court reversed its earlier decisions and held that the state's constitutional and statutory ban on immigration or sojourn by "any negro or mulatto" was void, as to foreign-state citizens, under the guarantee of article IV. (The Fourteenth Amendment had not yet been adopted.) The court adopted as its own Curtis's analysis of the pertinent history. Id. at 304–305.

11. *Liberator,* Dec. 29, 1832, at 207, col. 1.

12. William L. Garrison, *An Address, Delivered before the Free People of Colour* 15–16 (1831).

13. Act of Dec. 21, 1822, ch. 3, 1822 S.C. Acts 11.

14. In 1829 the Georgia legislature moved quickly to strengthen existing laws restricting the entry of free black seamen following the discovery at Savannah of an incendiary pamphlet, *Walker's Appeal . . . to the Coloured Citizens of the World,* published in Boston by the black abolitionist David Walker. (Excerpts appear in 1 *A Documentary History of the Negro People in the United States* 93–97 [Herbert Aptheker ed., 1951].) *Walker's Appeal* contained passages that hinted at violent slave rebellion, and its appearance in the slave states caused understandable excitement. The circumstances of its discovery in Georgia are recorded in a letter dated Dec. 16, 1829, from the Mayor of Savannah, William T. Williams, to Governor George R. Gilmer:

"I send by this days mail a pamphlet addressed to the negroes of which a parcel containing 60 was seized by the police a few days since—the parcel came from Boston in charge of the Steward, a white man and [was] delivered to a negro preacher named Cunningham, who immediately returned it on ascertaining the character of its contents. As attempts to introduce into the ports of the South similar dangerous publications will no doubt be made, and there is every probab[il]ity that their dissemination through the State may be effected, I have deemed it my duty to communicate to you the facts in my possession that you may adopt such measures as you may deem necessary to detect or defeat these destructive efforts. Immediately after their seizure I sent one of the pamphlets to the Intendant of Charleston and another to the Mayor of Boston accompanied with a letter to apprize the one of the probability of similar attempts being made there, and to request of the other, that the parties concerned in the publication might be properly dealt with." Mayor's Letter Book, Georgia Historical Society Library, Savannah.

Governor Gilmer communicated this discovery to the legislature with a recommendation for vigorous action:

"This is a subject about which, less should be said than done. The imagination of each one is sufficiently prompt to portray the horrors of negro insurrection. The plots devised some years ago in Charleston, and very lately in Georgetown South Carolina—the late fires in Augusta and Savannah, have shewn us the danger to be apprehended in the cities from negroes. The information communicated presents this danger in a new shape; it is the duty of those who have the power to meet it promptly and efficiently. For this purpose I would recommend to the Legislature the passage of a law prohibiting the entry of vessels into the ports of Georgia navigated in any manner by negroes; such vessels should be subjected to quarantine so severe as to prevent all intercourse between them and the shore. We are aware that our right to pass such laws has been questioned. When the torch is ready to be applied to our houses and the assassins dirk drawn upon our breast is not a time when we can stop in our defence to dispute with casuists about the rights of other states—the fact of a vessel not belonging to the state having negroes on board, ought to be made itself sufficient evidence that it carries contagion dangerous to our people.

"I would further respectfully recommend to the Legislature, the passage of a law prohibiting under severe penalties the further introduction of slaves into the state." 1829 *Ga. Senate J.* 326–327 (message dated Dec. 21, 1829). The recommendation to enact stricter quarantine laws was adopted the next day. By further provisions of the Act of Dec. 22, 1829, the importation or circulation of writings "for the purposes of exciting to insurrection . . . the slaves, negroes, or free persons of colour, of this state" was made a capital offense; teaching any such person "to read or write either written or printed characters" was made punishable by fine or, in the case of nonwhite offenders, by whipping. 1829 Ga. Laws 168, 171.

15. Elkison v. Deliesseline, 8 Fed. Cas. 493 (C.C.S.C. 1823) (No. 4,366).

16. S. Res. of Dec. 22, 1823, 1823 Ga. Acts 231.

17. S. Res. of Dec. 8, 1824 (No. 8), Records of the General Assembly, Resolutions (1824), South Carolina Department of Archives and History, Columbia. The resolution, which does not appear in the official printed compilation, may be found at 27 *Niles' Weekly Reg.* 264 (Dec. 25, 1824).

18. The language is quoted from the Resolves of March 3, 1842, ch. 82, 1842 Mass. Acts 568. Compare the earlier Resolves of April 8, 1839, ch. 66, 1839 Mass. Acts 105.

19. S. Res. of Dec. 24, 1842, 1842 Ga. Acts 181–182.

20. Resolves of March 24, 1843, ch. 67, 1843 Mass. Acts 81; Resolve of March 16, 1844, ch. 111, 1844 Mass. Acts 330.

21. For the career of Samuel Hoar see 9 *Dictionary of American Biography* 89 (1932).

22. H. Res. of Dec. 5, 1844, 1844 S.C. House J. 65–66 (bound with 1844 S.C. Gen. Assembly Reports & Resolutions); reprinted 67 *Niles' Nat'l Reg.* 226–227 (Dec. 14, 1844). The resolutions occasioned by Hoar's visit were promptly codified in an act providing for the punishment and banishment of any person entering South Carolina, "in virtue of any commission or authority from any State" or otherwise, "with intent to disturb, counteract or hinder the operation of [laws and regulations] in relation to slaves or free persons of color." Act of Dec. 18, 1844, No. 2925, 1844 S.C. Acts 292.

23. Hoar's official report of his Charleston expedition was published in *Liberator,* Jan. 17, 1845, at 9, col. 4, and in 67 *Niles' Nat'l Reg.* 315–317 (Jan. 18, 1845). Hubbard's report of his mission to New Orleans appears in *Liberator,* Feb. 14, 1845, at 25, col. 1, and in 67 *Niles' Nat'l Reg.* 398–399 (Feb. 22, 1845).

24. The argument based on the comity clause was unsuccessfully raised in state court challenges to a variety of statutes that discriminated, in terms, against nonresident free Negroes. For representative cases see Amy (a woman of colour) v. Smith, 11 Ky. (1 Litt.) 326 (1822) (free status of certain former slaves, made citizens of Pennsylvania by that state's abolition act, jeopardized by Kentucky's special statute of limitations); State v. Claiborne, 19 Tenn. (Meigs) 331 (1838) (sojourn prohibited); Pendleton v. State, 6 Ark. 509 (1844) (free Negro or mulatto immigrant required to post bond).

    An Indiana statute of 1831, requiring every "black or mulatto person coming or brought into this state" to post a bond in the amount of $500, and punishing failure to do so with "hiring out" for a term of six months "for the best price in cash that can be had," was held "not unconstitutional" on three occasions. While the Indiana Supreme Court did not bother to state its reasons, the established terms of the argument leave little doubt that these decisions, too, stood as judicial authority against the possibility of constitutional citizenship for Negroes. Act of Feb. 10, 1831, codified as ch. 66, 1831 Ind. Rev. Laws 375; State v. Cooper, 5 Blackf. 258 (Ind. 1839); Baptiste v. State, 5 Blackf. 283 (Ind. 1840); Hickland v. State, 8 Blackf. 365 (Ind. 1847).

25. Crandall v. State, 10 Conn. 339 (1834). Contemporary pamphlets containing accounts of the trial and arguments of counsel are reprinted in *Abolitionists in Northern Courts* 79–206 (Paul Finkelman ed., 1988).

26. 60 U.S. (19 How.) 393 (1857).

27. Fehrenbacher, supra note 9, at 287, 278–279. Field's view of the potential significance of the diversity jurisdiction as an obstacle to the enforcement of the Fugitive Slave Law of 1850 is supported by Harold M. Hyman & William M. Wiecek, *Equal Justice under Law* 176–177 (1982).

28. The defendant's name was misspelled as *Sandford* in the report of the Supreme Court decision.

29. 60 U.S. (19 How.) at 403, 406.

30. Id. at 416–417.

31. Id. at 407.

32. "'A House Divided': Speech at Springfield, Illinois" (June 16, 1858), 2 *Collected Works of Abraham Lincoln* 461, 464 (Roy P. Basler ed., 1953).

33. See generally Philip M. Hamer, "Great Britain, the United States, and the Negro Seamen Acts, 1822–1848," and "British Consuls and the Negro Seamen Acts, 1850–1860," 1 *J. S. Hist.* 3, 138 (1935).

34. Quoted in Carl Brent Swisher, *Roger B. Taney* 154 (1935). Taney's opinion on this occasion, addressed to Secretary of State Edward Livingston, was omitted from the published collection of the opinions of the attorneys general. On the history of the opinion, see generally id. at 147–159; Fehrenbacher, supra note 9, at 70 & nn. 76–77.

2. The Lynn Petition

1. This large and active organization was founded as the Female Anti-Slavery Society of Lynn in May 1835; the Quaker schoolteacher Abigail Kelley (later Abigail Kelley Foster, one of the ultras of the American Anti-Slavery Society and a prominent advocate of women's rights) served as its corresponding secretary. A single volume of the Society's minutes and records, covering the years 1836–1838, is preserved at the Lynn Historical Society.

2. *Liberator,* Jan. 11, 1839, at 7, col. 3. The description of the fair was contributed by Maria Weston Chapman (1806–1885), the leading woman among the Garrisonian abolitionists, at times editor of the *Liberty Bell,* the *Liberator,* and the *National Anti-Slavery Standard.* Mrs. Chapman was the presiding genius behind the institution of antislavery fairs: her description for the *Liberator* of the "Massachusetts Anti-Slavery Fair and Soiree," held in Boston during Christmas week, 1840, offers a detailed picture of this popular fund-raising activity. *Liberator,* Jan. 1, 1841, at 3, col. 2.

3. *Liberator,* Jan. 11, 1839, at 7, col. 3; Feb. 1, 1839, at 19, col. 3. Garrison was accused (with reason) of hindering the cause of abolition, and dissipating the influence of the *Liberator,* by making the paper a vehicle for his personal religious views and for extraneous radical causes. One of the latter was "non-Resistance," a theory of pacifism devised by Garrison that involved the renunciation of "any human government," with the consequence (among many others) that to hold office, to vote, or to institute a lawsuit were alike held sinful; another was "the woman question," the question just then being whether women should be allowed not only to attend antislavery meetings but also to speak and to vote. These and numerous other grievances led in January 1839 to a schism within the Massachusetts Anti-Slavery Society and, a year later, to a breach between the Garrisonians and the New York-based American Anti-Slavery Society: Garrison and his followers prevailed in both factional disputes, the dissidents being left to start their own antislavery organizations and newspapers. The bitter controversies of the period are summarized in Walter M. Merrill, *Against Wind and Tide,* ch. 12 (1963). For a more detailed, documentary, and partisan account, see 2 Wendell

Phillips Garrison & Francis Jackson Garrison, *William Lloyd Garrison*, chs. 3–6 (1885).

4. This is the text published in *Lynn Record*, Jan. 23, 1839, at 3, col. 3, reprinted in *Liberator*, March 1, 1839, at 36, col. 4. The editor of the *Lynn Record* was Daniel Henshaw; Deborah S. Henshaw was president of the Lynn Society. The original text of the Lynn Petition was edited for publication by substituting the word "ladies" for the word "Women." See note 12 infra.

5. Mass. Rev. Stat. ch. 75, §5 (1836) (interracial marriage forbidden); ch. 76, §1 (such marriage void, if solemnized within the state); ch. 76, §21 (issue of such marriage, upon its dissolution, deemed illegitimate).

6. *Report on Sundry Petitions Respecting Distinctions of Color*, Mass. H.R. Doc. No. 28, 1839 Sess., reprinted in *Liberator*, March 15, 1839, at 41, col. 4.

7. Docket No. 577/12, Legislative Packets (House Unpassed [1839]), Mass. State Archives; reprinted (with emended spelling) in *Liberator*, Feb. 22, 1839, at 30, col. 2.

8. Reprinted in *Liberator*, Feb. 8, 1839, at 23, col. 6.

9. *Liberator*, Feb. 8, 1839, at 21, col. 1; April 19, 1839, at 61, col. 1. Compare the favorable comments reprinted Feb. 22, 1839, at 30, col. 1 (letter from John Greenleaf Whittier); May 10, 1839, at 75, col. 2.

10. The Revised Statutes of 1836 contained only two other racial distinctions, both relatively unimportant. A provision limiting enrollment in the militia to "[e]very able bodied white citizen," Mass. Rev. Stat. ch. 12, §5 (1836), had been faithfully copied from the federal statute directing the organization of the state militias; as late as 1859, the Supreme Judicial Court rendered an advisory opinion stating that Massachusetts might not constitutionally require the enrollment in its militia of persons other than those enumerated by Congress. Act of June 22, 1793, ch. 1 of May 1793 Sess., Mass. Acts & Laws 290 (1793), reprinted as ch. 14, 1793 Mass. Acts 381 (rev. ed. 1895); Act of May 8, 1792, ch. 33, §1, 1 Stat. 271; Opinion of the Justices, 80 Mass. (14 Gray) 614 (1859). A statute directed against slave-catchers, making it a crime to "sell, or in any manner transfer for any term the service or labor of any negro, mulatto, or other person of color, who shall have been unlawfully seized, taken, inveigled or kidnapped from this state, to any other state, place or country," drew a distinction on account of color but would scarcely have been a target of the abolitionists. Mass. Rev. Stat. ch. 125, §20 (1836).

11. For the disavowal of the Dorchester petition by some of its signers see *Report on the Petition of S. P. Sanford and Others, Concerning Distinctions of Color*, Mass. H.R. Doc. No. 74, 1839 Sess. (April 3, 1839). The debate in the House over the reception of this report is transcribed at length in *Liberator*, April 19, 1839, at 62, col. 1.

Other influences (beyond the bare fact that such a petition was being circulated) led many antislavery sympathizers to suppose that the laws of Massachusetts included various discriminatory statutes. In a book first published in 1833, the popular author Lydia Maria Child denounced a Massachusetts law of 1788 providing that "no person being an African or negroe, other than a subject of the Emperor of *Morocco,* or a citizen of some one of the United States . . . shall tarry within this Commonwealth, for a longer time than two months"; violations were punishable, upon complaint to any justice of the peace, by commitment to the local workhouse at hard labor and, upon conviction at the following sessions, by whipping. Mrs. [Lydia Maria] Child, *An Appeal in Favor of That Class of Americans Called Africans* 197 (1836 ed.); Act of March 26, 1788, ch. 21 of Feb. 1788 Sess., Mass. Acts & Laws 680, 682 (1788); reprinted as ch. 54, 1787 Mass. Acts 626 (rev. ed. 1893). The old statute was repealed in 1834, in the course of a general revision of the law of correctional institutions. Act of March 29, 1834, ch. 151, §22, 1834 Mass. Acts 206. But the 1836 edition of Mrs. Child's book retained both the reference to the 1788 statute and the statement, no longer correct, that the forgotten law "still remains to disgrace the statutes of this Commonwealth"; and the work's success apparently contributed to an impression that some unspecified number of racially discriminatory laws still awaited repeal. Thus the Women's Anti-Slavery Conference, meeting in Haverhill in January 1840, resolved "[t]hat we consider all laws making a distinction on account of color, as a disgrace to the Statute-Book of this Commonwealth." *Liberator,* Jan. 31, 1840, at 19, col. 4.

12. The original Lynn Petition is preserved in the Massachusetts State Archives under Docket No. 577/11, Legislative Packets (House Unpassed [1839]). The signatures fill numerous pages glued end to end. The text is set forth on a narrow printed slip, glued to the head of the first page, reading as follows (handwritten insertions in brackets):

    To the Legislature of the State of [Massachusetts]

    The undersigned, [Women] of [Lynn] in the County of [Essex], respectfully pray you immediately to repeal all laws in this State, which make any distinction among its inhabitants, on account of COLOR.

    Identical printed slips (except for the handwritten insertions) were used to create the petitions submitted in 1839 from Cambridge, Dorchester, Fairhaven, and Plymouth; while in others the same text was manually transcribed.

    The source of the preprinted headings was the American Anti-Slavery Society, the form being one of eleven recommended to the use of local antislavery societies as part of the expanded petition campaign launched in mid-1837: see the following note. Printed forms setting forth the proposed texts were widely circulated by agents of the Society. Some nine months into the new campaign, Henry B. Stanton (one of the Society's corresponding secretaries) reported that "[w]e have incurred an enormous expense this year in printing and circulating petitions; many thousands (probably 100,000) have been printed and sent out from this office, into every part of every free State." *National Enquirer* (Philadelphia), March 8, 1838, at 103, col. 6.

13. Following its fourth annual meeting in May 1837, the American Anti-Slavery Society undertook to coordinate the efforts of local antislavery societies in circulating petitions for presentation both to Congress and to state legislatures,

proposing uniform texts and standardized procedures. See American Anti-Slavery Society, *Fifth Annual Report of the Executive Committee* 48–49 (1838); Gilbert Hobbs Barnes, *The Antislavery Impulse, 1830–1844* 133–145 (1933). Barnes's classic account of "The Petition Flood" omits any mention of the petitions that were concurrently being circulated and submitted, by the same antislavery organizations, to the various state legislatures. The consequence of this omission, which the deserved influence of Barnes's work has magnified, is that an interesting historical episode has been left in near-total obscurity: a petition campaign conducted throughout the free states, from 1837 to 1840, on behalf of color-blind state legislation.

The July 1837 issue of the American Anti-Slavery Society's monthly *Human Rights* (vol. 3, no. 1, whole no. 25) offers a valuable synoptic view of the national petition campaign at its inception. On the back page of the paper were printed "several forms of petitions to Congress and the State Legislatures, which, after the paper is read, may be cut out and pasted on a blank half sheet of foolscap, to be immediately circulated." The first six petitions, addressed to Congress, prayed respectively (1) for the abolition of slavery in the District of Columbia; (2) for the abolition of slavery in the territories; (3) for the abolition of the domestic slave trade, in exercise of the commerce power; (4) against the admission to the Union of any new slave state (Florida, though not named, was principally intended); (5) against the annexation of Texas (long form); and (6) against the annexation of Texas (short form). The remaining five forms, to be sent to state legislatures rather than to Congress, asked them (7) to submit resolutions to Congress on the subjects of petitions 1, 2, and 3; (8) to repeal all laws making a distinction on account of color, in the language already quoted; (9) to pass a law securing a trial by jury to any person accused of being a fugitive slave; (10) to submit resolutions to Congress opposing the admission of new slave states; and (11) to submit resolutions to Congress opposing the annexation of Texas.

The same issue of *Human Rights* reprinted a circular letter to local agents from the Society's petition committee, explaining in minute detail how the petition forms were to be completed, pasted together, circulated, and justified to skeptical recipients. (The committee's letter of instructions to agents, with the text of the proposed petitions, was also reprinted in Benjamin Lundy's *National Enquirer* [Philadelphia], July 1, 1837, at 62, cols. 3–5.) The petition respecting distinctions of color was explained as follows: "No. 8, prays for the repeal of all laws which make *distinctions* among our citizens, *on account of color.* This applies to the anti-republican and unchristian statutes of Ohio, New York, &c. &c. There is scarcely a State where such laws do not disgrace the statute book. If there be any such State, this petition need not be circulated there."

"We suggest," added the committee, "that all the petitions should be circulated at the same time. This will be an economy of labor; and, generally, those who would sign one, would sign all." Either this advice was ignored, or its prediction proved erroneous. A tally made in 1838 of antislavery petitions submitted to the

House of Representatives showed a total of 182,392 signatures against the annexation of Texas; 130,248 signatures for abolition in the District of Columbia; and no more than 32,000 signatures for any of the other propositions. See *Correspondence between the Hon. F. H. Elmore . . . and James G. Birney*, app. G [*Anti-Slavery Examiner*, No. 8] (1838).

14. Article IV of the Ohio constitution, adopted in 1802, limited the franchise to white males. An "Act to regulate black and mulatto persons," dating from 1804, required that any black or mulatto immigrant to Ohio post a bond of $500 to secure his good behavior and support; made it a crime to employ any such person who had not posted the necessary bond; and made black or mulatto persons incompetent to testify in any civil or criminal proceeding to which a white person was a party. Act of Jan. 5, 1804, amended by Act of Jan. 25, 1807, 1 Salmon P. Chase, *Statutes of Ohio* 393, 555 (1833). The contemporary version of Ohio's public school statute, establishing "common schools, for the instruction of the white youth of every class and grade, without distinction," was the Act of March 10, 1831, 3 Chase, *Statutes of Ohio* 1867 (1835).

15. Shortly before leaving the Western Reserve in September 1833, Elizur Wright appears to have instigated a petition campaign requesting the Ohio legislature "to repeal all laws now existing in this state, which make a distinction between white and colored men in the enjoyment of rights and privileges." Wright became corresponding secretary of the American Anti-Slavery Society upon its formation in December of that year, and his experience in Ohio presumably influenced the Society's subsequent adoption of a standard petition for repeal of state laws making a racial distinction. For Wright's activities in connection with the 1833 Ohio petitions, see *Observer and Telegraph* (Hudson, Ohio), Sept. 5, 1833, at 3, col. 2; *Ohio Observer*, Oct. 12, 1833, at 3, col. 2; Nov. 9, 1833, at 3, col. 4. The next session of the Ohio legislature received numerous petitions, principally from the Western Reserve counties, praying (in varying formulas) the repeal of all laws making a distinction between white and black inhabitants. The petitions were reported unfavorably by the House and Senate judiciary committees, the central justification offered for Ohio's "black laws" being that they discouraged the immigration of free persons of color. Report of the Standing Committee on the Judiciary (Jan. 27, 1834), 1833–34 *Ohio Senate J.* 504–507; House committee report (Jan. 20, 1834), 1833–34 *Ohio House J.* 435–436. On the career of Elizur Wright, Jr., "reformer, actuary" (1804–1885), see the article (by Gilbert H. Barnes) in 20 *Dictionary of American Biography* 548 (1936).

16. In the publications of the American Anti-Slavery Society, the laws of Ohio are repeatedly invoked as the ultimate example of racially discriminatory enactments:
"Says the delegated wisdom of Ohio, in general assembly convened, with a magnanimity which occupies absolutely no space whatsoever, we have no wish to favor the escape of your slaves. Far from it. We have 15 or 20,000 colored people of our own. Though they were counted to make up the 60,000 people to entitle us to a State Constitution, we refused them the right of suffrage in that instrument; we have refused them their oath in our courts; loaded them with all

manner of disabilities; shut our school house doors in their faces; refused to give them acts of incorporation for their own schools; have trampled on their petitions; and in all manner of ways we have brow-beaten them and spit in their faces, in short, we hate them, and *we wonder so many of them are in our jails and penitentiaries.*" American Anti-Slavery Society, *Sixth Annual Report of the Executive Committee* 92–93 (1839).

And, in the same year: "But among all the free States, OHIO stands pre-eminent for the wickedness of her statutes against this class of our population. These statutes are not merely infamous outrages on every principle of justice and humanity, but are gross and palpable violations of the State constitution, and manifest an absence of moral sentiment in the Ohio legislature as deplorable as it is alarming." [William Jay], *On the Condition of the Free People of Color of the United States* 7 [*Anti-Slavery Examiner,* No. 13] (1839).

17. As might be expected, the appeal published by the American Anti-Slavery Society in 1837, in circular letters and in the pages of *Human Rights* (see note 13 supra), found a ready response in Massachusetts. All the proposed state petitions were submitted to the Massachusetts legislature at its 1838 session: the text of many of them was supplied by a form clipped from *Human Rights* in the manner the paper had recommended. Docket No. 10,274 of Legislative Packets (Senate Unpassed [1838]), Mass. State Archives, contains no fewer than nineteen "No. 8" petitions, identical in wording with the Lynn Petition of the following year, together with a formal committee report finding it inexpedient to legislate thereon.

This initial call for a general repeal of Massachusetts laws "making a distinction between the inhabitants, on account of color" provoked no controversy—indeed, it made no impression whatsoever on the public mind—for the simple reason that it was never reported. The existence of petitions to this effect was not mentioned in the Boston newspapers. Readers might have inferred, instead, that "Charlotte F. Thompson and fifteen other ladies of Rehoboth" had submitted a petition to the legislature seeking the repeal of the prohibition of interracial marriage, because some editors reported the answering petitions by which the ladies of Rehoboth were being lampooned: the joke (as in the case of the Lynn ladies a year later) was that "Charlotte F. Thompson and her associates" were hoping to find black husbands. Submitted in Massachusetts, the actual thrust of the "no distinctions" petition was so radical that it was initially misread. Thus in the House and Senate journals themselves, the Rehoboth petition was recorded as one of a group "severally relating to Slavery"; it was later referred to as seeking "repeal of the law which interdicts marriage between white people, & persons of color." *Evening Gazette* (Boston), Jan. 27, 1838, at 2, col. 5; Feb. 17, 1838, at 2, col. 4; *Atlas* (Boston), March 6, 1838, at 2, col. 4; 1838 Mass. Senate J. 92 (proceedings of Jan. 23, 1838), 114–115 (Jan. 27, 1838); cf. 1838 Mass. House J. 97 (Jan. 22, 1838).

In reality, the Rehoboth petition that attained this mild notoriety in early 1838 was apparently another "No. 8," seeking the repeal of all laws making a racial distinction. But the only outsiders who ever realized this were those who happened to see a pseudonymous letter (signed "Cosmopolite") published after the fact in the *Liberator:*

"The ladies, to whom the *printed* copy was sent by the Agent of the American Anti-Slavery Society, well knew, that in many of the non-slaveholding States, some of the inhabitants were deprived of important rights and privileges, on account of their *color. . . .* They felt no hesitation in giving their names to a petition, which—instead of praying for 'a repeal of the law against intermarrying with negroes,' as reported in the papers—simply asks for 'the repeal of all laws making a distinction between the inhabitants, on account of color.' I believe these are the *precise* words of the petition. There is nothing *said,* and I presume nothing *thought,* by those benevolent ladies, respecting any *particular* law." *Liberator,* April 6, 1838, at 55, col. 2. A year later, the members of the Lynn Women's Anti-Slavery Society were widely credited with the authorship of the American Anti-Slavery Society's "No. 8" petition, because their copy of it was the first whose substance was accurately reported in a newspaper of general circulation.

18. *Lynn Record,* April 3, 1839, at 3, col. 2, reprinted in *Liberator,* April 12, 1839, at 57, col. 5; *Lynn Record,* June 26, 1839, at 2, col. 3, reprinted with minor variations in *Liberator,* June 28, 1839, at 103, col. 5.

19. See the interesting letter of Theodore Dwight Weld to Lewis Tappan, written in February 1836, in which Weld inquires, "ought not the American [Anti-Slavery] Society to turn more of its attention to the Education and elevation of the *free colored* population?" Weld proceeds to list ten arguments in favor of "free colored Elevation at the north," referring to this goal (for the most part) not as an end in itself but as a source of strategic advantage for the antislavery cause. Where he does advert to the interests of the free Negroes themselves, arguing that "[i]t would remove the great difficulty in the way of their enjoying in every respect civil rights," Weld seems to imply that "education and elevation" were preconditions, in a practical sense at least, of any campaign to repeal discriminatory laws. 1 *Letters of Theodore Dwight Weld, Angelina Grimké Weld, and Sarah Grimké, 1822–1844* 262 (Gilbert H. Barnes & Dwight L. Dumond eds., 1934).

20. Id. at 256 (James A. Thome to Theodore Weld, Feb. 9, 1836).

21. See Barnes, supra note 13, chs. 6–10.

22. William Lloyd Garrison, *Thoughts on African Colonization* 80 (1832).

23. The phrase "protection and equal laws," identified by Howard Jay Graham as one of the important sources of John Bingham's equal protection clause, derives from William Ellsworth's 1834 argument on behalf of Prudence Crandall, reprinted in *Abolitionists in Northern Courts* 173, 179 (Paul Finkelman ed., 1988). See Howard Jay Graham, "The Early Antislavery Backgrounds of the Fourteenth Amendment" (Part I), 1950 *Wis. L. Rev.* 479, 498–506.

24. Charles Olcott, *Two Lectures on the Subjects of Slavery and Abolition* (1838). On Olcott and the significance of his *Lectures,* see Howard Jay Graham, "The Early Antislavery Backgrounds of the Fourteenth Amendment" (Part II), 1950 *Wis. L. Rev.* 610, 626 & nn. 156–157.

25. Olcott, supra note 24, at 44, 45, 48, 116.

26. 59 Mass. (5 Cush.) 198 (1850). Sumner's argument and the *Roberts* case are discussed in Chapter 3.

27. Quoted in David Donald, *Charles Sumner and the Coming of the Civil War* 233–234 & n. 2 (1960).

28. For an overview of the Garrisonian civil rights campaigns of the 1840s and 1850s, particularly useful for its extensive references to contemporary sources, see J. Morgan Kousser, "'The Supremacy of Equal Rights': The Struggle against Racial Discrimination in Antebellum Massachusetts and the Foundations of the Fourteenth Amendment," 82 *Nw. L. Rev.* 941 (1988).

29. *Liberator,* Jan. 8, 1831, at 7, col. 1; May 7, 1831, at 75, col. 3. A representative early petition for repeal of the marriage law is reprinted in *Liberator,* Jan. 28, 1832, at 15, col. 1.

30. The racial distinctions in the marriage laws were repealed by Act of Feb. 25, 1843, ch. 5, 1843 Mass. Acts 4. See Louis Ruchames, "Race, Marriage, and Abolition in Massachusetts," 40 *J. Negro Hist.* 250 (1955).

31. *Liberator,* Feb. 5, 1841, at 23, col. 4.

32. See, e.g., *Liberator,* Feb. 24, 1843, at 31, col. 3.

33. Mass. H.R. Doc. No. 7, 1841 Sess., 7, 9; reprinted in *Liberator,* Jan. 29, 1841, at 18, col. 3.

34. *Liberator,* Feb. 18, 1842, at 26, col. 4 (proceedings of Feb. 10, 1842).

35. Mass. S. Doc. No. 63, 1842 Sess., 4.

36. Mass. S. Doc. No. 9, 1843 Sess.

37. See Louis Ruchames, "Jim Crow Railroads in Massachusetts," 8 *Am. Q.* 61 (1956).

38. A campaign of petitions and boycotts by Nantucket's black families led to a series of hotly contested school board elections. Abolitionist candidates obtained a majority in 1843, lost it in 1844, lost again in 1845, and regained a narrow majority in 1846: mandatory segregation was abolished, reinstated, and abolished accordingly. In 1849 Nantucket still had "a separate Colored School" attended by 35 pupils, but this appears to have been an instance of de facto segregation. See Kousser, supra note 28, at 960–961; Boston City Document No. 42 (1849) at 57, reprinted in *Jim Crow in Boston* (Leonard W. Levy & Douglas L. Jones eds., 1974) at 81, 134. The Nantucket School Committee's defense of its decision to desegregate in 1843, originally published in its *Annual Report* for that year, was reprinted (in the context of the subsequent desegregation controversy at Salem) in the *Salem Register,* March 7, 1844, at 2, col. 3.

39. *Salem Gazette,* March 5, 1844, at 2, col. 6; *Salem Register,* March 14, 1844, at 2, col. 3. The petition to the School Committee from colored citizens of Salem (received Jan. 15, 1844) is preserved in a folder headed "Town of Salem, School Committee, Reports on Blacks in Schools," in the Essex County Collection, Essex Institute, Salem, Mass.

40. Legal opinions on school segregation dated [1831?] and 1834 by Leverett Saltonstall, in his capacity as town solicitor of Salem, are in the Essex Institute "School Committee" folder, supra note 39. Saltonstall (1783–1845) served several terms in the Massachusetts legislature; was mayor of Salem from 1836 to

1838; and was Essex County's member of Congress from 1838 to 1843. For his career see 1 *The Papers of Leverett Saltonstall, 1816–1845* xi–lix (Robert E. Moody ed., 1978).

41. Stephen Clarendon Phillips (1801–1857), a wealthy shipowner and philanthropist, represented Essex County in Congress from 1834 to 1838. Resigning his seat in favor of Leverett Saltonstall, Phillips then served as mayor of Salem from 1838 to 1842.

42. Richard Fletcher (1788–1869) served single terms as a representative in the Massachusetts legislature and in the Twenty-fifth Congress (1837–1839); he sat on the Massachusetts Supreme Judicial Court from 1848 to 1853. Fletcher was chiefly known, however, for his accomplishments as a trial lawyer, including his triumph in the famous case of Charles River Bridge v. Warren Bridge, 23 Mass. (6 Pick.) 376 (1828), 24 Mass. (7 Pick.) 344 (1829), in which he was opposed by Daniel Webster, Lemuel Shaw, Leverett Saltonstall, and "the almost unanimous opinion of the Boston bar." "Throughout his life [Fletcher] was a devout member of the Baptist Church, and an unusually acute sense of religious responsibility pervaded all his social and professional contacts." 6 *Dictionary of American Biography* 466 (1931). A memorial of Fletcher's career at the bar appears at 4 *Am. L. Rev.* 182 (1869).

43. *Salem Gazette,* March 22, 1844, at 2, col. 5; a more accessible source is 6 *Common School Journal* 326 (Oct. 15, 1844).

44. 6 *Common School Journal* at 327–328.

45. In its broadside form (undated), Fletcher's opinion is headed "The Hon. Richard Fletcher's Opinion / As to whether the school committee can lawfully exclude colored children from the public free schools, and confine them to separate schools established exclusively for them." The opinion is prefaced by the notation "[From the Morning Telegraph]" and by an extract from a letter "received from the Hon. Stephen C. Phillips, late Mayor of the city of Salem, forwarding the annexed opinion." The copy in the collection of the Massachusetts Historical Society bears, on the verso, the manuscript date of June 1845. A *Morning Telegraph* of "Independent Whig" and antislavery sympathies was published at Nantucket in 1844 and 1845, and it seems likely that the broadside publication of Fletcher's Salem opinion occurred in connection with the campaign of Nantucket abolitionists in the school board elections of the latter year. See note 38 supra.

46. *Roberts,* 59 Mass. (5 Cush.) at 200. On the origins of Boston's segregated schools see Boston City Document No. 23 (1846) at 15–19, reprinted in *Jim Crow in Boston,* supra note 38, at 3, 17–21; Stanley K. Schultz, *The Culture Factory: Boston Public Schools, 1789–1860,* ch. 7 (1973). The segregation controversy of the 1840s was limited to Boston's primary and grammar schools, black students being admitted without discrimination to Boston's English and Latin High Schools. See *Jim Crow in Boston* at xi.

47. The successive stages of the controversy over the educational facilities provided to Boston's black population are described in Schultz, supra note 46, ch. 8. Within Boston's black community, a militant faction supported the abolitionist attack on

separate schools while others favored the continuation of the schools and the appointment of black teachers. See Kousser, supra note 28, at 993–999.

48. See Schultz, supra note 46, at 203–206; Kousser, supra note 28, at 988–992; Act of April 28, 1855, ch. 256, 1855 Mass. Acts 674. By the time the 1855 statute was enacted, segregated schools had already been discontinued in all cities and towns in Massachusetts other than Boston. Mass. H.R. Doc. No. 167, 1855 Sess., at 3, reprinted in *Jim Crow in Boston*, supra note 38, at 247, 249.

49. *Report of the Minority of the Committee of the Primary School Board, on the Caste Schools of the City of Boston; With Some Remarks on the City Solicitor's Opinion* (1846). The *Minority Report (1846)* is reprinted in *Jim Crow in Boston* at 43–78; it may also be found (minus its appendices) in *Liberator,* Aug. 21, 1846, at 133, col. 3.

From 1818 to 1855 Boston's primary schools, offering free public education to children aged four to seven, were administered by the Primary School Committee, a self-perpetuating body of private citizens. The Committee normally had as many members as there were schools, each member acting in the role of superintendent to one school. The extent of the oversight exercised by the publicly elected School Committee (also known as the Grammar School Board) over the gentlemen of the Primary School Committee was much contested by the latter. On the primary schools and the Primary School Committee see Joseph M. Wightman, *Annals of the Boston Primary School Committee, from Its First Establishment in 1818, to Its Dissolution in 1855* (1860); Schultz, supra note 46.

50. Several points at which Sumner obviously borrowed from the school committee minority reports of 1846 and 1849 are noted in the discussion of Sumner's argument in Chapter 3.

51. The official opinion by Chandler and the unofficial reply by Phillips were reprinted in *Liberator,* Aug. 28, 1846, at 137, cols. 2–6.

52. *Minority Report (1846)* at 4–7, reprinted in *Jim Crow in Boston,* supra note 38, at 46–49.

53. *Majority Report (1846)* at 35, 37, reprinted in *Jim Crow in Boston* at 37, 39.

54. *Minority Report (1846)* at 30–31, reprinted in *Jim Crow in Boston* at 72–73; *Liberator,* Aug. 28, 1846, at 137, col. 4.

55. *Minority Report (1846)* at 7–8, 11, 13, reprinted in *Jim Crow in Boston* at 49–50, 53, 55.

56. Edmund Jackson served on the Primary School Committee from 1835 to 1851, Bowditch from 1837 to 1850. Wightman, supra note 49, at 295, 298. In 1846 (and for many years thereafter) Jackson was auditor of the Massachusetts Anti-Slavery Society; Bowditch regularly served on its "Council" or board of trustees.

57. Henry Ingersoll Bowditch (1808–1892), son of the mathematician Nathaniel Bowditch, was a distinguished physician and professor of medicine. The fullest account of his career, including his activities in the Garrisonian cause, is the memorial by C. F. Folsom appearing at 28 *Proc. Am. Acad. of Arts & Sci.* 310 (1893). See also Vincent Y. Bowditch, *Life and Correspondence of Henry Ingersoll Bowditch* (1902).

58. The arrest in Boston of the fugitive slave George Latimer, in October 1842, and his imprisonment (by order of Justice Story, on circuit) pending trial of the claim of ownership, galvanized northern resistance to the Fugitive Slave Law of 1793. To abolitionists like Wendell Phillips, the events were proof of the moral imperative of Disunion. On October 30, a tumultuous meeting at Faneuil Hall heard Phillips declare that when he saw his neighbors "trample on their consciences and the rights of their fellow-men, at the bidding of a piece of parchment, I say, my CURSE be on the Constitution of these U. States!" *Liberator,* Nov. 11, 1842, at 178, col. 4. A "Latimer Committee," formed by Bowditch with two friends, published seven issues of an ad hoc newspaper, the *Latimer Journal and North Star,* and gathered signatures for two "monster petitions" to the state and federal legislatures. Bowditch and other sympathizers eventually purchased Latimer's freedom.

    The petition to the Massachusetts legislature produced results of some consequence, notably the enactment of the "Latimer Law," quickly copied by a number of northern states, prohibiting state officials from cooperating in the arrest or detention of persons claimed as fugitive slaves. Act of March 24, 1843, ch. 69, 1843 Mass. Acts 33; see the elaborate legislative report (written by Charles Francis Adams) reprinted in *Liberator,* March 3, 1843, at 34–35. The federal version of the "monster petition"—its pages, glued end to end, were wound on a wooden reel "of the diameter of a common flour barrel"—caused a satisfying sensation in the House of Representatives when John Quincy Adams attempted, in vain, to present it in the teeth of the gag rule. See *Cong. Globe,* 27th Cong., 3d Sess. 317 (1843). For modern discussions of the Latimer case see Leonard W. Levy, *The Law of the Commonwealth and Chief Justice Shaw* 78–85 (1957); Thomas D. Morris, *Free Men All: The Personal Liberty Laws of the North, 1780–1861* 109–117 (1974); William M. Wiecek, "Latimer: Lawyers, Abolitionists, and the Problem of Unjust Laws," in *Antislavery Reconsidered: New Perspectives on the Abolitionists* 219 (Lewis Perry and Michael Fellman eds., 1979). On the role of Henry I. Bowditch see the first volume of his *Life and Correspondence,* supra note 57, at 133–141.

59. Francis Jackson (1789–1861) served as president of the Massachusetts Anti-Slavery Society from 1837 until his death. His bequest of $10,000 to trustees charged with encouraging antislavery sentiment produced, after ratification of the Thirteenth Amendment, a serious breach between Garrison and Phillips: the former wanted the funds devoted to freedmen's relief, the latter to support the *National Anti-Slavery Standard.* The lawsuit by which the dispute was eventually resolved occasioned an elaborate opinion on the legal doctrine of charitable trusts and *cy pres.* See Jackson v. Phillips, 96 Mass. (14 Allen) 539, 596–599 (1867).

60. The extensive collection of abolitionist correspondence in the Boston Public Library contains only two letters from Edmund Jackson (1795–1875). In an undated letter to Maria Weston Chapman, who edited the antislavery annual *Liberty Bell* from 1839 to 1846, Jackson regrets that it is not in his power "to offer other than pecuniary aid to the Liberty Bell," pleading "a better conscious-

ness of my deficiencies, than others possess, to tell a story or pen an essay." A letter of December 1848 to Mrs. Chapman's sister, Ann Warren Weston, reads in its entirety: "Miss Weston, I send for the Fair 50 Boxes Soap which should not be sold at less than 2 dolls per Box."

61. Edmund Jackson appears to have been the principal author of a published letter to the Rev. John Pierpont, embattled pastor of the Hollis Street Meeting House, on behalf of those parishioners who supported Pierpont "in the bitter conflict with the rum-selling and pro-slavery element of the congregation." *A Letter from the Pastor of Hollis Street Society to His Parochial Friends, with Their Reply to the Same* (1841); 1 Garrison & Garrison, supra note 3, at 454 n. 3 (1885). A rather plodding editorial signed "E. J.," upholding "no union with slaveholders," appears in the *Liberator* for June 28, 1844, at 102, col. 6.

62. Wendell Phillips to Edmund Quincy, Aug. 8, 1846, Quincy Papers, Massachusetts Historical Society.

63. Edmund Quincy to Wendell Phillips, Aug. 10, 1846, Blagden Papers, Houghton Library, Harvard University.

64. *Liberator,* Aug. 21, 1846, at 134, col. 6.

65. Wendell Phillips to Edmund Quincy, Aug. 30, 1846, Quincy Papers, Massachusetts Historical Society.

66. *National Anti-Slavery Standard,* Aug. 27, 1846, at 49, col. 1. Edmund Quincy's letters to the *Standard* as its "Boston Correspondent" carried the cryptic signature "D. Y."

67. [Abner Forbes & J. W. Greene,] *The Rich Men of Massachusetts: Containing a Statement of the Reputed Wealth of about Two Thousand Persons, with Brief Sketches of Nearly Fifteen Hundred Characters* 37 (2d ed. 1852). The book's principal author, Abner Forbes, was for ten years the (white) headmaster of Boston's segregated Smith School; he resigned amid controversy in 1844, when militant black parents threatened to boycott the school unless Forbes were dismissed. On Forbes and the Smith School boycott, see Kousser, supra note 28, at 963–964; Donald M. Jacobs, *A History of the Boston Negro from the Revolution to the Civil War* 127–129, 146–149, 230–237 (1968). Resolutions voted at a meeting of "colored citizens" during the Smith School controversy, critical of Forbes, are reproduced in 1 *A Documentary History of the Negro People in the United States* 243 (Herbert Aptheker ed., 1951).

3. Sumner and Shaw

1. Roberts v. City of Boston, 59 Mass. (5 Cush.) 198, 200–201 (1850); Act of March 24, 1845, ch. 214, 1845 Mass. Acts 545.

2. Sumner's oral argument of December 4, 1849, was published as a pamphlet by Sarah's father, Benjamin F. Roberts. *Argument of Charles Sumner, Esq. against the Constitutionality of Separate Colored Schools, in the Case of Sarah C. Roberts vs. The City of Boston* (1849), reproduced in *Abolitionists in Northern Courts* 493 (Paul Finkelman ed., 1988). The argument was later revised for publication, and it is the revised version that appears in the various editions of

Sumner's collected works. References in these notes to *Argument* are to the 1849 pamphlet.

3. See Mass. H.R. Doc. No. 167, 1855 Sess., at 10, reproduced in *Jim Crow in Boston* (Leonard W. Levy and Douglas L. Jones eds., 1974) at 247, 256.

4. *Argument,* supra note 2, at 3.

5. Id. at 8–10.

6. Id. at 14–16. Sarah was assigned to a school 2,100 feet from her home. The primary school nearest to the Roberts home was 900 feet distant. 59 Mass. at 200–201.

7. *Argument,* supra note 2, at 16–20.

8. Id. at 21–23. Sumner's demonstration that the black citizen might be governor or school committee member was drawn from Charles Theodore Russell's 1849 minority report on that year's petitions (addressed this time to the Boston School Committee) for the abolition of the Smith School. The relevant portion of Russell's report is reproduced in *Jim Crow in Boston,* supra note 3, at 151, 157. For Russell's role on the School Committee see J. Morgan Kousser, " 'The Supremacy of Equal Rights': The Struggle against Racial Discrimination in Antebellum Massachusetts and the Foundations of the Fourteenth Amendment," 82 *Nw. L. Rev.* 941, 969 & n. 141 (1988).

9. *Argument,* supra note 2, at 23.

10. Id. at 23–24.

11. Finding no reference to racial distinctions in the Massachusetts statutes regarding the maintenance of "public schools," Sumner had argued at an earlier stage that a "public school" within the meaning of the statute could only be "the general Public School, free to all the inhabitants." Id. at 12. From this he now concluded that "[t]he separate school for colored children is not one of the schools established by the law relating to Public Schools. (Revised Statutes, chap. 23.) It is not a Public School. As such, it has no legal existence, and, therefore cannot be a legal equivalent." Id. at 24. Sumner's definition of a statutory "public school" was tendentious to begin with, and he seemed to overlook the fact that by this definition the schools for white children were not "public schools" either.

12. Id. at 24–25. The notion of the free public school as the institution in which "all classes meet together in equality" is drawn from a passage (quoted in Chapter 2) of the opinion delivered by Richard Fletcher in 1844 to the Salem School Committee.

13. Sweatt v. Painter, 339 U.S. 629, 634 (1950).

14. *Argument,* supra note 2, at 25. The idea that relegation to "equivalent" facilities constitutes an illegal forced exchange was plainly inspired by another passage of Judge Fletcher's Salem opinion.

15. Id. at 25–26.

16. 35 Mass. (18 Pick.) 193, 210 (1836). *Aves* (also known as *Med's Case*) presented the question whether a slave in one jurisdiction retained his status as such during a mere sojourn (not constituting residence) in a nonslavery jurisdiction. Shaw held that a six-year-old slave girl from Louisiana, brought to Boston by her mistress on a vacation trip, could not be removed from the state against her will

and thus might obtain her freedom by petition for habeas corpus. *Aves* was a New World version of *Somerset's Case* (Somerset v. Stewart, Lofft 1, 98 Eng. Rep. 499 [K.B. 1772]), in which Lord Mansfield held that the law of England did not permit a sojourning slave to be removed from the jurisdiction against his will. The underlying issues of interstate comity and conflict of laws would persist in subsequent American cases, becoming an important theme of the Dred Scott controversy. See Leonard W. Levy, *The Law of the Commonwealth and Chief Justice Shaw* 62–68 (1957); Don E. Fehrenbacher, *The Dred Scott Case* 51–61, 260–265, 396–399, 411–413 (1978); Paul Finkelman, *An Imperfect Union: Slavery, Federalism, and Comity* (1981).

17. *Argument,* supra note 2, at 26.

18. 109 U.S. 3 (1883).

19. *Argument,* supra note 2, at 31.

20. Id. at 29. Cf. Brown v. Board of Educ. of Topeka, 347 U.S. 483, 493–494 (1954).

21. "With the law as their monitor, they are taught to regard a portion of the human family . . . as a separate and degraded class. . . . Their characters are debased, and they become less fit for the magnanimous duties of a good citizen." *Argument* at 28–29.

22. Id. at 30.

23. Id. Compare the passage from the *Minority Report (1846)* reproduced in *Jim Crow in Boston,* supra note 3, at 55.

24. *Liberator,* Dec. 7, 1849, at 195, col. 1.

25. Justice Fletcher, whose views on the illegality of segregation had been set forth in his 1844 opinion to the Salem School Committee, did not participate in the decision. Sumner, noting Fletcher's absence, appealed in argument to the authority of the "extensively published" Salem opinion. *Argument,* supra note 2, at 24. It is assumed that Fletcher recused himself because of his public identification with the desegregation cause. See Kousser, supra note 8, at 987 & n. 217.

26. 59 Mass. at 205, 209.

27. Id. at 205–206.

28. "[A]re the Committee, having the superintendence of the public schools of Boston, entrusted with the *power,* under the constitution and laws of Massachusetts, to exclude colored children from these schools . . . ?" *Argument,* supra note 2, at 3.

29. 59 Mass. at 206.

30. Shaw's biographer accuses him of making "an assumption—in itself, sufficient to decide the case—that all individuals did not possess the same legal rights," and of defending it in language that, "stripped of its rhetoric," could be summarized in the cynical statement that all animals are equal but some animals are more equal than others. Levy, supra note 16, at 114–115. The remark misconceives the sense of Shaw's discussion. All individuals do not in fact "possess the same legal rights," if that phrase means an entitlement to identity of treatment at the hands of the law. The question Shaw addresses is how this evident disparity of treatment is to be reconciled with the principle of legal equality.

31. 59 Mass. at 208–209.

32. Id. at 209–210.

33. In the new chapters he added to Story's *Commentaries* to explicate the newly ratified Reconstruction Amendments, Thomas M. Cooley—the foremost authority on American constitutional theory in the latter half of the nineteenth century— cited the key passage from *Roberts* (the quotation accompanying note 29 supra) as the *locus classicus* for the principle of "equal protection of the laws" in its true application. 2 Joseph Story, *Commentaries on the Constitution of the United States* §1960, at 677 (Thomas M. Cooley 4th ed. 1873).

4. The Reconstruction Amendments of Wendell Phillips

1. See James M. McPherson, *The Struggle for Equality: Abolitionists and the Negro in the Civil War and Reconstruction* 120–133 (1964). McPherson's book is an invaluable resource for any study of the activities of the abolitionists during this period.

2. 6 *Collected Works of Abraham Lincoln* 29 (Roy P. Basler ed., 1953). Lincoln's prospective emancipation proclamation of Sept. 22, 1862, had promised, in effect, that those portions of the Confederacy no longer in rebellion on Jan. 1, 1863, would be exempted from emancipation.

3. *National Anti-Slavery Standard,* June 6, 1863, at 2, col. 3.

4. *Liberator,* Oct. 24, 1863, at 170, col. 3.

5. See, e.g., *National Anti-Slavery Standard,* Sept. 26, 1863, at 2, col. 3 ("Constitution as it now stands will cover the necessities of the country; but it will mean something very different from what Courts have ruled it to mean"); Dec. 26, 1863, at 3, col. 2 (proposed amendment "unlikely, if not impossible, of success," while proposed emancipation bill "satisfies everything that the anti-slavery public, North and South, have ventured to hope or to ask for").

6. The famous phrases appear in a resolution introduced by Garrison, adopted at the annual meeting of the Massachusetts Anti-Slavery Society in January 1843. *Liberator,* Feb. 3, 1843, at 19, col. 4.

7. *New York Times,* July 3, 1863, at 4, col. 3. Missouri's emancipation ordinance of July 1, 1863, appears at 4 *Federal and State Constitutions* 2190 (Francis N. Thorpe ed., 1909).

8. *New York Times,* Sept. 2, 1863, at 5, col. 1–2. See Bill R. Lee, "Missouri's Fight over Emancipation in 1863," 45 *Mo. Hist. Rev.* 256 (1951).

9. *National Anti-Slavery Standard,* Oct. 10, 1863, at 1, col. 4 (describing the delegates' reception in Washington, September 30).

10. *New York Times,* Oct. 3, 1863, at 1, cols. 5–6.

11. *Liberator,* Nov. 20, 1863, at 186, col. 5. Contemporary editorials in the *Liberator* signed by C[harles] K. W[hipple], Garrison's assistant editor, supported the idea of an antislavery amendment. *Liberator,* Nov. 13, 1863, at 182, col. 5; Dec. 11, 1863, at 198, col. 4.

12. *National Anti-Slavery Standard,* Dec. 26, 1863, at 4, col. 4.

13. *Cong. Globe,* 38th Cong., 1st Sess., at 19, 21. The joint resolution proposing the Thirteenth Amendment was adopted by the Senate on April 8, 1864, and by the House (after an initial defeat and the intervening presidential election) on Jan. 31, 1865. Id. at 1490, 2995; id., 2d Sess., at 531. Ratification was declared completed, following approval by Georgia, on Dec. 18, 1865. 13 Stat. 774.

14. *Liberator,* Jan. 1, 1864, at 4, col. 4 (Stanton); March 11, 1864, at 42, col. 5 (Smith). The revised form of petition with which the American Anti-Slavery Association joined the call for a constitutional amendment appears in the *Liberator* for Jan. 15, 1864, at 10, col. 3. The Women's Loyal League amended its petition some weeks thereafter. *Liberator,* March 11, 1864, at 43, col. 2.

15. On Phillips's recanting of Disunion and his resulting political transformation, see McPherson, supra note 1, at 40–51, 82–86.

16. 7 *Collected Works of Abraham Lincoln,* supra note 2, at 36, 51–52, 54–55.

17. Phillips and his followers were not the only observers to understand Lincoln in this sense. Given a draft of the Reconstruction Proclamation and asked to comment, Salmon P. Chase (then Lincoln's secretary of the Treasury) recommended "that in the Proclamation you now propose to put forth,—virtually inviting the people of the rebel states to reorganize their political institutions on the basis of free labor,—no suggestion be made of any apprenticeship of the freedmen or other special legislation for them." (Chase to Lincoln, Nov. 25, 1863, Abraham Lincoln Papers, Library of Congress.) After Lincoln ignored his advice, Chase wrote to Henry Ward Beecher that he had been disappointed by the president's determination "to retain the suggestion of qualified involuntary servitude in the form of apprenticeship of the freed people." (Chase to Beecher, Dec. 26, 1863, Beecher Family Papers, Manuscripts and Archives, Yale University Library.)

18. *National Anti-Slavery Standard,* Jan. 9, 1864, at 1, cols. 3–4.

19. Id. at 1, col. 6. Phillips concluded with a call for the distribution to the freedmen of confiscated southern lands. "This nation owes to the negro not merely freedom; it owes him land, and it owes him education also. It is a debt which will disgrace us before the peoples if we do not pay it." Id. This seemingly radical proposal was in fact the least original of the propositions put forward by Phillips in his speech of Dec. 22. Abolitionist views on confiscation and redistribution of land are described in McPherson, supra note 1, at 246–259.

20. The historiographical tradition for a broad interpretation of the Thirteenth Amendment derives largely from Jacobus tenBroek, *The Antislavery Origins of the Fourteenth Amendment* (1951); it is continued by Harold M. Hyman & William M. Wiecek, *Equal Justice under Law* (1982). In a legal context, the argument was already fully developed by Justice Harlan's dissenting opinion in *The Civil Rights Cases,* 109 U.S. 3 (1883).

21. See, e.g., Mark DeWolfe Howe, "Federalism and Civil Rights," 77 *Proc. Mass. Hist. Soc'y* 15 (1965).

22. Hyman & Wiecek, supra note 20, at 389.

23. Early appeals for Negro suffrage appear in the *National Anti-Slavery Standard,*

May 23, 1863, at 1, col. 6 (Phillips' speech of May 12, 1863); 3 *The Frederick Douglass Papers* 570, 575–579 (John W. Blassingame ed., 1985) (speech of May 15, 1863). Differences within the abolitionist ranks over the wisdom of immediate suffrage for the freedmen continued through 1864 into 1865. See McPherson, supra note 1, at 294–303.

24. *National Anti-Slavery Standard,* May 23, 1863, at 1, col. 6; id. at 2, col. 2 (speech to American Anti-Slavery Society, May 12, 1863).

25. *National Anti-Slavery Standard,* July 11, 1863, at 3, col. 2.

26. *New York Times,* Feb. 18, 1864, at 4, col. 3.

27. *National Anti-Slavery Standard,* Feb. 6, 1864, at 2, col. 6.

28. See, e.g., *National Anti-Slavery Standard,* Feb. 13, 1864, at 1, col. 4 ("I would have a clause in the Constitution of the United States, that no State shall make a law which recognizes any distinction of race"); *New York Times,* Feb. 17, 1864, at 8, col. 1 ("We want to provide that no State shall have Slavery or be permitted to make any law that makes a distinction among its citizens on account of race"). In April, signaling his adherence to the fledgling movement to challenge the renomination of Lincoln under the banner of John C. Frémont, Phillips summarized his current proposals for national policy:

"Subdue the South as rapidly as possible. The moment territory comes under our flag, reconstruct States thus: confiscate and divide the lands of rebels; extend the right of suffrage as broadly as possible to whites and blacks; let the Federal Constitution prohibit Slavery throughout the Union, and forbid the States to make any distinction among their citizens on account of color or race." *New York Times,* May 8, 1864, at 6, col. 4 (letter dated April 21, 1864). On the Frémont movement and the split it occasioned within the abolitionist ranks, see McPherson, supra note 1, at 264–286.

29. Robert Dale Owen, *The Wrong of Slavery, the Right of Emancipation, and the Future of the African Race in the United States* 197–198 (1864). Owen's early advocacy of the color-blind principle is significant in light of his role in the framing of the Fourteenth Amendment by the Joint Committee on Reconstruction. On his career see the interesting article (by Broadus Mitchell) at 14 *Dictionary of American Biography* 118 (1934).

30. *National Anti-Slavery Standard,* Feb. 11, 1865, at 2, col. 4 (speech to Mass. Anti-Slavery Society, Jan. 26, 1865). See also Phillips' speeches reported in *National Anti-Slavery Standard,* Nov. 5, 1864, at 1, col. 2 (speech of Oct. 20, 1864) ("let the Federal government . . . ignore the difference between white and black, be blind to color"); Dec. 17, 1864, at 4, col. 1 (speech of Dec. 6, 1864) (necessity of "no distinction" amendment).

31. *National Anti-Slavery Standard,* Feb. 11, 1865, at 1, cols. 1, 6.

32. *National Anti-Slavery Standard,* March 4, 1865, at 2, col. 2.

33. *National Anti-Slavery Standard,* Feb. 7, 1863, at 3, col. 1 (Garrison's speech of Jan. 29, 1863).

34. On the final schism within the abolitionist ranks see McPherson, supra note 1, at 287–307; 4 Wendell Phillips Garrison & Francis Jackson Garrison, *William*

Lloyd Garrison 153–162 (1889). The critical debates at the annual meetings of the Massachusetts and American Anti-Slavery Societies (in January and May 1865) are reported in the *Liberator* and the *Standard.*

35. *National Anti-Slavery Standard,* June 3, 1865, at 3, col. 5 (speech of May 12, 1865). Phillips had earlier explained the revised wording of his color-blind amendment: "I therefore want an amendment—not that a State shall make no distinction among her *citizens*—that leaves her to say who is a citizen, and she might say that no son of a slave shall be a citizen—but that she shall make no distinction among persons born on her soil, heretofore or hereafter, of parents permanently resident there, on account of race, color or descent." *National Anti-Slavery Standard,* May 13, 1865, at 2, col. 3 (speech of May 9, 1865). At the close of the rancorous meeting that afternoon, which witnessed Garrison's departure from the American Anti-Slavery Society, a resolution in the sense proposed by Phillips was voted by the remaining members. *National Anti-Slavery Standard,* May 20, 1865, passim; May 27, 1865, at 3, cols. 1, 3; June 17, 1865, at 3, col. 4.

36. Oliver Johnson's bitter valedictory as editor appears in the *Standard* for May 20, 1865, at 3, col. 3. He was succeeded as editor by Parker Pillsbury, one of the Anti-Slavery Society's ultras; Pillsbury was succeeded less than a year later by Aaron Powell. From June 1865 until the Society's dissolution in April 1870, the views of the *Standard* did not differ appreciably from those of its "Special Editorial Contributor," Wendell Phillips. See McPherson, supra note 1, at 305–307; Irving H. Bartlett, *Wendell Phillips: Brahmin Radical* 289–292 (1961).

37. *National Anti-Slavery Standard,* July 22, 1865, at 2, col. 2.

38. On the mobilization of abolitionist sentiment in opposition to Johnson and in favor of Negro suffrage as a minimum condition of reconstruction, see McPherson, supra note 1, at 308–356.

39. *National Anti-Slavery Standard,* May 27, 1865, at 2, col. 3.

40. See Michael Les Benedict, *A Compromise of Principle: Congressional Republicans and Reconstruction, 1863–1869* 100–133 (1974).

41. Civil Rights Act of 1866, §1, 14 Stat. 27.

42. The presidential veto message appears at *Cong. Globe,* 39th Cong., 1st Sess. 1679–81 (1866). On Johnson's decision to veto the civil rights bill see LaWanda Cox & John H. Cox, *Politics, Principle, and Prejudice, 1865–1866* 195–232 (1963).

43. The words are taken from Stevens's final speech on the proposed Fourteenth Amendment, immediately before the House vote on the text as revised in the Senate. *Cong. Globe,* 39th Cong., 1st Sess. 3148 (June 13, 1866).

44. Phillips to Stevens, April 30, 1866, Thaddeus Stevens Papers, Library of Congress; *National Anti-Slavery Standard,* July 16, 1866, at 1, col. 1 (speech at the Framingham picnic, July 4, 1866).

45. *National Anti-Slavery Standard,* May 26, 1866, at 2, col. 2; June 23, 1866, at 2, col. 3 (calling the first section of the proposed amendment "unexceptional, with the ordinary rules of interpretation" and its second section "a license offered by

Congress to rebels and unrepentant slaveholders . . . to disfranchise, and practically to re-enslave millions of the colored citizens of the nation"); Sept. 22, 1866, at 2, col. 3; Feb. 2, 1867, at 1, col. 4 (Phillips's testimony before the legislative committee).

46. For occasional instances, see *National Anti-Slavery Standard,* April 4, 1868, at 2, col. 2 ("we claim a Constitutional Amendment which shall forbid any State to make distinctions among its citizens, in civil or political rights, on account of race, color or previous condition"); April 18, 1868, at 2, col. 3 (amendment should be proposed "forbidding any distinction in any State, among its citizens . . . on account of color").

47. *National Anti-Slavery Standard,* April 13, 1867, at 2, col. 2.

48. The Senate version of the Fifteenth Amendment, proposed by Henry Wilson of Massachusetts, would have prohibited any discrimination in the elective franchise or the qualifications for office on the basis of "race, color, nativity, property, education, or religious creed." *Cong. Globe,* 40th Cong., 3d Sess., 1035, 1040, 1044 (1869). The House refused to concur in the Senate version. Id. at 1226.

49. *National Anti-Slavery Standard,* Feb. 20, 1869, at 2, col. 2.

50. 2 George Boutwell, *Reminiscences of Sixty Years in Public Affairs* 46, 48–50 (1902), quoted in McPherson, supra note 1, at 426. On the role of Phillips in the passage for the Fifteenth Amendment, see generally id. at 424–427.

51. *National Anti-Slavery Standard,* May 25, 1867, at 1, col. 3.

52. *National Anti-Slavery Standard,* June 8, 1867, at 1, col. 2 (speech of May 29, 1867).

53. *National Anti-Slavery Standard,* Dec. 28, 1867, at 1, col. 1 (speech of Dec. 19, 1867).

54. *National Anti-Slavery Standard,* May 22, 1869, at 1, col. 2 (speech of May 11, 1869).

5. The Thirty-ninth Congress

1. *Cong. Globe,* 39th Cong., 1st Sess. 10 (1865). (In the notes to this chapter, the *Congressional Globe* for the first session of the 39th Congress is cited as *Globe,* its *Appendix* as *Globe App.*)

2. *Globe* at 14.

3. On the Black Codes and their significance to the politics of Reconstruction see Eric Foner, *Reconstruction: America's Unfinished Revolution, 1863–1877* (1988); Theodore B. Wilson, *The Black Codes of the South* (1965).

4. William Nelson, *The Fourteenth Amendment: From Political Principle to Judicial Doctrine* 80 (1988).

5. See, e.g., W. R. Brock, *An American Crisis: Congress and Reconstruction, 1865–1867* (1963); LaWanda Cox and John H. Cox, *Politics, Principle, and Prejudice, 1865–1866* (1963); Michael Les Benedict, *A Compromise of Principle: Congressional Republicans and Reconstruction, 1863–1869* (1974).

6. Alfred H. Kelly, "Comment on Harold M. Hyman's Paper," in *New Frontiers of*

the American Reconstruction 40 (Harold M. Hyman ed., 1966); Herman Belz, *A New Birth of Freedom: The Republican Party and Freedmen's Rights, 1861 to 1866* 157–182 (1976); Foner, supra note 3, at 242–243; Nelson, supra note 4, at 27–39; and Earl M. Maltz, *Civil Rights, the Constitution, and Congress, 1863–1869* (1990), all emphasize the extent to which Radical Reconstruction was conceived by its proponents within the political constraints of traditional federalism.

7. See C. Vann Woodward, "Seeds of Failure in Radical Race Policy," in Woodward, *American Counterpoint: Slavery and Racism in the North-South Dialogue* 163 (1971).

8. The long-standing debate has traditionally centered on the question whether, or to what extent, the first section of the Fourteenth Amendment was understood or intended to "incorporate" (as restrictions on the states) the limitations on the federal government set forth in the Bill of Rights. The extreme positions on this question are currently occupied by Raoul Berger, *Government by Judiciary: The Transformation of the Fourteenth Amendment* (1977) (no incorporation), and Michael Kent Curtis, *No State Shall Abridge* (1986) (full incorporation). Charles Fairman, "Does the Fourteenth Amendment Incorporate the Bill of Rights?" 2 *Stan. L. Rev.* 5 (1949), still represents an influential moderate position. The controversy over the "original understanding" of the Fourteenth Amendment guarantees resists resolution by customary standards of legal and historical interpretation because the authors and sponsors of the amendment's first section were themselves visibly unsure of its meaning. (As William Nelson has noted, "history can never tell us how the framing generation would have resolved inconsistencies that it did not, in fact, resolve." Nelson, supra note 4, at 6.) Reverdy Johnson of Maryland, a member of the Joint Committee on Reconstruction and the man regarded both by contemporaries and by modern commentators as the most reliable constitutional lawyer in the Thirty-ninth Congress, moved at the close of debate in the Senate to strike the "privileges or immunities" clause from the final version of the Fourteenth Amendment because, he explained, he did not understand what its effect would be. *Globe* at 3041. The Republican majority that rejected the motion assuredly had no clearer understanding than did Johnson.

9. See Alexander Bickel, "The Original Understanding and the Segregation Decision," 69 *Harv. L. Rev.* 1 (1955).

10. See generally Joseph B. James, *The Framing of the Fourteenth Amendment* 3–33 (1956); Benedict, supra note 5, at 100–133.

11. See Paul Finkelman, "Prelude to the Fourteenth Amendment: Black Legal Rights in the Antebellum North," 17 *Rutgers L.J.* 415, 425 (1986).

12. See [1865] *Appleton's Annual Cyclopedia* at 304 (Connecticut), 577 (Minnesota), and 823 (Wisconsin).

13. "From 1865 through 1869 eleven referendum votes were held in eight Northern states on constitutional changes to provide Negroes with the ballot; only two were successful—those held during the fall of 1868 in Iowa and Minnesota. The

Minnesota victory, gained after two previous defeats, has been attributed to trickery in labeling the amendment. The issue was never placed before the white voters of Illinois, Indiana, Pennsylvania, or New Jersey; and this fact probably indicated a higher intensity of race prejudice than in Connecticut, New York, and Ohio, where equal suffrage was defeated. These seven were marginal states of critical importance to the Republicans in national elections." LaWanda Cox & John H. Cox, "Negro Suffrage and Republican Politics: The Problem of Motivation in Reconstruction Historiography," 33 *J. S. Hist.* 303, 318–319 (1967).

14. "Representatives . . . shall be apportioned among the several States . . . according to their respective Numbers, which shall be determined by adding to the whole Number of free Persons . . . three fifths of all other Persons." U.S. Const. art. I, §2. One widely accepted estimate suggested that, in the absence of an amendment (and assuming no increase in the membership of the House, then fixed at 241), reapportionment would give the restored southern states nine House seats at the expense of other sections. By contrast, the exclusion of the black population, North and South, from the basis of federal representation would reallocate to the North and West twelve southern seats from the prewar House. *Globe* at 357 (tabulation of Rep. Conkling).

15. See James, supra note 10, at 22–23. Stevens proposed a constitutional amendment to this effect on Dec. 5, 1865. *Globe* at 10.

16. See *Globe* at 141 (remarks of Rep. Blaine) (Jan. 8, 1866).

17. Pursuant to a resolution introduced in the House by Thaddeus Stevens on the first day of the session, the Thirty-ninth Congress created a Joint Committee on Reconstruction, consisting of nine members from the House and six from the Senate, with instructions to "inquire into the condition of the States which formed the so-called confederate States of America, and report whether they or any of them are entitled to be represented in either House of Congress." Proposals for constitutional amendments intended as the basis for Reconstruction were thereafter referred to the Joint Committee. Stevens himself served as chairman of the House delegation; his counterpart from the Senate was William Pitt Fessenden of Maine, a conservative Republican. (Sumner, who had sought the chairmanship, was not appointed to the committee.) The fullest account of the origins and activities of the Joint Committee is the historical essay that accompanies the committee's journal in Benjamin B. Kendrick, *The Journal of the Joint Committee of Fifteen on Reconstruction* (1914). For a more modern analysis of the political orientation of its members see Benedict, supra note 5.

18. Kendrick, supra note 17, at 43–47.

19. Id. at 50–51.

20. Id. at 51–52. As cochairman of the Joint Committee, Stevens exercised pragmatic leadership. He moved the adoption of Bingham's Article B and voted for his own motion. The three "nays" were cast by Fessenden, Sen. Jacob Howard of Michigan (a radical) and Rep. Henry Grider of Kentucky (a Democrat). Grider's vote is presumably explained by a desire that the report of the committee be as offensive as possible. Counting Stevens with the "nays," there were on January

20 only three votes on the Joint Committee (out of twelve Republican members) in favor of immediate Negro suffrage and a constitutional rule of nondiscrimination.

21. *Globe* at 537.

22. Sumner opened the Senate debate on the Blaine Amendment on February 5 (Fessenden being apparently indisposed) by attacking the "defilement" that it would introduce into the Constitution, whose text had theretofore been kept "blameless" by the framers' refusal to admit "the idea that man could hold property in man." "And now, after generations have passed, . . . it is proposed to admit in the Constitution the twin idea of Inequality in Rights, and thus openly set at naught the first principles of the Declaration of Independence and the guarantee of a republican government itself, while you blot out a whole race politically." *Globe* at 673.

23. Id. at 703–704 (Feb. 7, 1866).

24. Id. at 705.

25. Id. at 1224–25. An hour or so later, Sumner reproached his colleagues that "you imitate Judas who betrayed the Saviour for thirty pieces of silver . . . in offering fellow-citizens to be sacrificed, in betraying them for less than 'thirty' Representatives in Congress. . . ." Id. at 1228.

26. Id. at 1275–81.

27. Sumner's measure, unartfully drafted, seemingly proposed to amend the Constitution by means of a joint resolution of Congress. After a "Whereas" clause of 150 words, locating the necessary constitutional authority alternatively in the Guarantee Clause and in section 2 of the Thirteenth Amendment, the resolution provided:

"*Be it resolved by the Senate and House of Representatives of the United States of America in Congress assembled,* That there shall be no Oligarchy, Aristocracy, Caste, or Monopoly invested with peculiar privileges and powers, and there shall be no denial of rights, civil or political, on account of color or race anywhere within the limits of the United States or the jurisdiction thereof; but all persons therein shall be equal before the law, whether in the court-room or at the ballot-box. And this statute, made in pursuance of the Constitution, shall be the supreme law of the land, anything in the Constitution or laws of any State to the contrary notwithstanding." Id. at 674. Before the vote in the Senate, Sumner amended his proposed resolution to restrict its application to "all States lately declared to be in rebellion." Id. at 1287.

28. Yates, who argued that the Joint Committee's constitutional amendments "cannot be adopted" (presumably because they were politically unacceptable to the country at large), *Globe App.* at 98, had offered his color-blind proposal as an ordinary statute on January 29:

"*Be it enacted, &c.,* That no State or Territory of the United States shall, by any constitution, law, or other regulation whatever, heretofore in force or hereafter to be adopted, make or enforce, or in any manner recognize, any distinction between citizens of the United States, or of any State or Territory, on account of race, color, or condition; and that hereafter all citizens of the United States, without distinction of race, color, or condition, shall be protected in the full and equal enjoyment of all their civil and political rights, including the right of suffrage." *Globe* at 472. Yates offered the same proposition (in the form of a joint resolution) as a substitute for the Blaine Amendment, and in this form it was rejected 7–38 (5 absent). Id. at 1287.

29. Id. at 1288.
30. Id. at 2459.
31. The final vote was 25–22 (3 absent). Id. at 1289.
32. Id. at 2459.
33. "Section 2. Representatives shall be apportioned among the several States according to their respective numbers, counting the whole number of persons in each State, excluding Indians not taxed. But when the right to vote at any election for the choice of electors for President and Vice President of the United States, Representatives in Congress, the Executive and Judicial officers of a State, or the members of the Legislature thereof, is denied to any of the male inhabitants of such State, being twenty-one years of age, and citizens of the United States, or in any way abridged, except for participation in rebellion, or other crime, the basis of representation therein shall be reduced in the proportion which the number of such male citizens shall bear to the whole number of male citizens twenty-one years of age in such State." U.S. Const. amend. XIV.

The complex and potentially controversial enumerations required by this provision, which theoretically eliminated from the basis of representation adult white males disfranchised for failure to meet property, literacy, or poll-tax requirements, doomed it to disuse even in the absence of the Fifteenth Amendment. By contrast, the Blaine Amendment would have been easily applied on the basis of the decennial census, which already recorded the race of respondents.

34. "The materials of enlightened constitutional interpretation permit us, I think, to treat the Constitution as repudiating the propriety of regulating people by race . . . but they do not compel that conclusion. It is oddly a matter of what we might wish to make of it." William Van Alstyne, "Rites of Passage: Race, the Supreme Court, and the Constitution," 46 *U. Chi. L. Rev.* 775, 776–777 (1979).

35. 14 Stat. 27 (1866). The relevant portion of the Civil Rights Act of 1866 is presently codified at 42 U.S.C. §§1981 & 1982 (1982).

36. *Globe* at 474 (emphasis added).

37. Id. at 475–476 (language of the bill defines "civil rights," bill has nothing to do with political rights) (remarks of Sen. Trumbull); id. at 1117 ("suffrage is a political right which has been left under the control of the several States") (Rep. Wilson); id. at 1151 (bill cannot "by any possibility, or by any forced construction" affect laws regulating suffrage) (Rep. Thayer). See generally Bickel, supra note 9, at 11–29.

38. "This measure is called for because these reconstructed Legislatures, in defiance of the rights of the freedmen and the will of the nation embodied in the [thirteenth] amendment to the Constitution, have enacted laws nearly as iniqui-

tous as the old slave codes that darkened the legislation of other days. The needs of more than four million colored men imperatively call for its enactment." *Globe* at 603 (remarks of Sen. Wilson of Massachusetts). Comparable statements explaining the need for the civil rights bill by reference to the Black Codes include, *inter alia,* id. at 475 (Sen. Trumbull); id. at 1124 (Rep. Cook); id. at 1153 (Rep. Thayer); id. at 1160 (Rep. Windom). Cf. The Slaughter-House Cases, 83 U.S. (16 Wall.) 36, 70–71, 81 (1873), where Justice Miller identifies the Black Codes as the primary motivation for congressional enactment of §1.

39. *Globe* at 477–478.

40. Id. at 505–506.

41. The vote was 33–12 (5 absent). Id. at 606–607.

42. Id. at 1117 (rights to vote, to sit on juries, to attend integrated schools "not civil rights or immunities") (Rep. Wilson); id. at 1151 ("in order to avoid any misapprehension [the civil rights guaranteed] are stated in the bill") (Rep. Thayer); id. at 1121–22 (bill would compel states to allow interracial marriage, Negro suffrage) (Rep. Rogers).

43. Id. at 1266.

44. *Globe* at 1291.

45. Compare Bickel, supra note 9, at 23–27 & n. 54, with Alfred H. Kelly, "The Fourteenth Amendment Reconsidered: The Segregation Question," 54 *Mich. L. Rev.* 1049, 1067–68 & n. 73 (1956).

46. *Globe* at 1291, 1293.

47. Id. at 1296.

48. Id. at 1366.

49. Bingham voted against the amended bill and was paired against in the vote to override the presidential veto. Id. at 1367, 1861.

50. *Globe* at 1034. The proposal is the subcommittee's "Article C," as modified at subsequent meetings of the Joint Committee. Kendrick, supra note 17, at 54–58, 60–62. Bingham's proposal was debated for three days in the House (Feb. 26–28), then postponed until "the second Tuesday in April." *Globe* at 1095. It was not heard from again. In modified form, it would reappear in section 1 of the Fourteenth Amendment as reported by the Joint Committee.

51. See, e.g., *Globe App.* at 135 (no right of the citizen not included in the words "life, liberty, property, privileges, and immunities") (Rep. Rogers); *Globe* at 1094 (amendment would confer "general power of legislation" for the protection of life, liberty, and property) (Rep. Hale); id. at 1095 (amendment would "authorize Congress to establish uniform laws throughout the United States upon the subject named, the protection of life, liberty and property") (Rep. Hotchkiss).

52. *Globe* at 1095.

53. Id. at 1063.

54. Id. at 1064.

55. Id. at 1063.

56. Stewart's amendment, introduced April 12, included the following provision: "Sec. 1. All discriminations among the people because of race, color, or previous

condition of servitude, either in civil rights or the right of suffrage, are prohibited; but the States may exempt persons now voters from restrictions on suffrage hereafter imposed." Id. at 1906. The chief obstacle facing any antidiscrimination amendment was the issue of Negro suffrage. Stewart's amendment, like the Owen proposal shortly to be considered, attempted to gain acceptance for the principle of antidiscrimination by delaying its effectiveness with respect to suffrage. Stewart would have invited the states to regulate suffrage by literacy tests and similar devices sufficiently stringent to exclude most blacks, while protecting the existing generation of white voters from disfranchisement by means of grandfather provisions. Similar "grandfather clause" statutes enacted in response to the Fifteenth Amendment were held unconstitutional in Guinn v. United States, 238 U.S. 347 (1915).

57. James, supra note 10, at 102.

58. Kendrick, supra note 17, at 83.

59. The circumstances of Owen's proposal to Stevens are recounted in Robert Dale Owen, "Political Results from the Varioloid," 35 *Atlantic Monthly* 660 (June 1875).

60. Kendrick, supra note 17, at 83–84.

61. Owen recalled that Stevens, speaking of the proposed delay in granting suffrage, exclaimed "I hate to delay full justice so long." Owen, supra note 59, at 662. But Stevens himself, on other occasions, expressed doubts as to the freedmen's qualifications for voting. See Fawn M. Brodie, *Thaddeus Stevens: Scourge of the South* 211 (1959).

62. Owen recalled Stevens's praise of the proposal: "Stevens picked up my manuscript, looked it carefully over, and then, in his impulsive way, said: 'I'll be plain with you, Owen. We've had nothing before us that comes anywhere near being as good as this, or as complete. It would be likely to pass, too; that's the best of it. We haven't a majority, either in our committee or in Congress, for immediate suffrage; and I don't believe the States have yet advanced so far that they would be willing to ratify it. I'll lay that amendment of yours before our committee to-morrow, if you say so; and I'll do my best to put it through.'" Owen, supra note 59, at 663.

63. Kendrick, supra note 17, at 85.

64. Id. at 87–88.

65. Id. at 98–99. Four members of the committee (Howard, Johnson, Williams, and Boutwell) voted on April 21 to insert Bingham's §5 and on April 25 to delete it. Howard and Boutwell were radicals, Williams a conservative, Johnson an ex–Whig Democrat.

66. Id. at 99. The vote was 4–8 (3 absent), Bingham being joined only by the committee's three Democrats. On April 25, all members of the Joint Committee (other than Bingham) appear to have been in agreement that submission of Bingham's language as a separate amendment would somehow procure partisan advantage to the Democrats.

67. Owen, supra note 59, at 665.

68. Kendrick, supra note 17, at 100.
69. Id. at 101–106.
70. Id. at 106–107. The vote was 10–3, Fessenden and Harris not voting. Stevens voted for the motion, as did all the Democrats. The votes against were cast by three Republican senators: Howard of Michigan, Morrill of Vermont, and Grimes of Iowa. The latter two are usually classified as moderates.
71. Owen, supra note 59, at 666.
72. Quoted in James, supra note 10, at 109.
73. Id. at 109–110, 117–122.
74. Writing to Wendell Phillips just three days after the committee's action, Chief Justice Salmon P. Chase put a more statesmanlike gloss on events:
    "It has become clear that no measure securing immediate universal suffrage, whether in the form of a constitutional amendment or act of Congress, can now be carried. For such an amendment the requisite three fourths of the States cannot be hoped for, even if the requisite two thirds could be obtained in Congress; and besides, its desirableness, unless sure of ratification, may be questioned, because of its implied negation of legislative power in Congress over the subject. . . . The opinion therefore is almost universal among our friends, & I agree with them, that the best that can now be done is to propose amendments to the constitution which will smooth the path to future state legislation & contain no implied rejection of the power of Congress. . . ." Chase to Phillips, May 1, 1866, Blagden Papers, Houghton Library. Chase's apology for the radicals confirms the committee's apparent calculation: that Negro suffrage and, by extension, broad-based antidiscrimination measures were incapable of ratification.
75. *Globe* at 1291.

6. The Judicial Assessment

1. Jay to Chase, Jan. 5, 1867, Salmon P. Chase Papers, Library of Congress. Jay's deletions (clearly legible in the manuscript) reflect the lesson taught by Wendell Phillips: *racial* equality was only to be achieved by a prohibition of *racial* distinctions.
2. *Boston Daily Advertiser,* Jan. 11, 1875, at 2, col. 4; quoted in James Brewer Stewart, *Wendell Phillips: Liberty's Hero* 308 (1986). The bill that would become the Civil Rights Act of 1875 (18 Stat. 335), then awaiting action in the House, had been explained in the Senate as securing to both races equal, but not necessarily integrated, school facilities: it was to this omission that Phillips objected. The bill was subsequently amended to delete the reference to schools altogether. For the legislative history of the Civil Rights Act of 1875 see Charles Fairman, *Reconstruction and Reunion 1864–88, Part Two* [7 *Oliver Wendell Holmes Devise History of the Supreme Court of the United States*] 156–184 (1987). On Sumner's successive attempts to obtain federal legislation to require "mixed schools" see Alfred Kelly, "The Congressional Controversy over School Segregation 1867–1875," 64 *Am. Hist. Rev.* 537 (1959).

3. See, e.g., Act of May 13, 1869, ch. xvi, 1869 Ind. Acts Spec. Sess. 41; Act of April 4, 1870, ch. 556, §56, 1869–70 Cal. Stat. 824, 839.

4. See, e.g., Claybrook v. City of Owensboro, 16 F. 297 (D. Ky. 1883); cf. Puitt v. Commissioners of Gaston County, 94 N.C. 709 (1886) (analogous state constitutional grounds).

5. See Minor v. Happersett, 88 U.S. (21 Wall.) 162 (1875) (denying that Fourteenth Amendment confers right of suffrage on women). The Court's most controversial decisions on the scope of the Reconstruction Amendments were those that held unconstitutional, for want of adequate legislative authority, civil rights laws passed by the Reconstruction Congress in exercise of the enforcement authority conferred by the new amendments. See United States v. Reese, 92 U.S. 214 (1876) (§§3 & 4 of the Enforcement Act of 1870, punishing interference with the right to vote, unconstitutional because not limited to the racially motivated interference proscribed by the Fifteenth Amendment); United States v. Harris, 106 U.S. 629 (1883) (§2 of the Ku-Klux Act of 1871 unconstitutional because not directed at state action proscribed by Fourteenth Amendment); Civil Rights Cases, 109 U.S. 3 (1883) (public accommodations provisions of Civil Rights Act of 1875 unconstitutional as to their operation within the states, because not authorized by either Thirteenth or Fourteenth Amendment).

6. 83 U.S. (16 Wall.) 36 (1873).

7. 100 U.S. 303 (1880).

8. For a brilliant account of the legal context and factual background of the *Slaughter-House Cases,* see Charles Fairman, *Reconstruction and Reunion 1864–88, Part One* [6 *Oliver Wendell Holmes Devise History of the Supreme Court of the United States*] 1301–1349 (1971).

9. 83 U.S. at 71–72.

10. The Court did so, overtly, in 1954. See Brown v. Board of Educ. of Topeka, 347 U.S. 483, 490 & n. 5.

11. Washington, A. & G. R.R. v. Brown, 84 U.S. (17 Wall.) 445 (1873).

12. Id. at 451.

13. See the authorities cited infra note 28.

14. 12 Stat. 805 (1863).

15. The background of the suit is recounted in John P. Frank & Robert F. Munro, "The Original Understanding of 'Equal Protection of the Laws,'" 50 *Col. L. Rev.* 131, 150–152 (1950), reprinted as revised in 1972 *Wash. U. L. Q.* 421.

16. 84 U.S. at 452–453.

17. *Cong. Globe,* 37th Cong., 3d Sess. 1329 (1863). Sumner subsequently obtained the addition of "no exclusion" provisos to the charters of other railroads, and in these latter instances there is evidence—in the different wording of the provision, in the Senate debate, or both—that his objective was indeed to put an end to segregated accommodations. See Earl M. Maltz, "'Separate but Equal' and the Law of Common Carriers in the Era of the Fourteenth Amendment," 17 *Rutgers L.J.* 553, 558–565 (1986). It is not clear whether Sumner expanded his aims or merely became more candid about them.

18. 84 U.S. at 447.
19. 100 U.S. 303 (1880).
20. The companion cases are Virginia v. Rives, 100 U.S. 313 (1880), and Ex parte Virginia, 100 U.S. 339 (1880).
21. 100 U.S. at 307–308.
22. Civil Rights Cases, 109 U.S. 3, 25.
23. State ex rel. Garnes v. McCann, 21 Ohio St. 198, 211 (1871).
24. Usually cited were laws passed by the Thirty-ninth Congress a few weeks following the passage of the Fourteenth Amendment, guaranteeing a proportionate share of school funds to the trustees of "colored schools" in Washington and Georgetown, Act of July 23, 1866, 14 Stat. 216, and granting certain city lots "for the sole use of schools for colored children," Act of July 28, 1866, 14 Stat. 343.
25. Cory v. Carter, 48 Ind. 327, 364–365 (1874).
26. The Supreme Court's order for reargument in the School Segregation Cases, directing counsel to discuss the evidence "that the Congress which submitted and the State legislatures and conventions which ratified the Fourteenth Amendment contemplated or did not contemplate, understood or did not understand, that it would abolish segregation in public schools," 345 U.S. 972 (1953), naturally elicited contradictory responses from the parties; but the "original understanding" on the issue of school segregation is not genuinely in doubt. The classic answer is the article by Alexander Bickel, "The Original Understanding and the Segregation Decision," 69 *Harv. L. Rev.* 1 (1955).

    In the continuing debate over the "original understanding," the proponents of a broad interpretation of the guarantees of the Reconstruction Amendments no longer trouble themselves to argue that the Thirty-ninth Congress contemplated or understood that the amended Constitution would prohibit segregated schools. See, e.g., Judith A. Baer, *Equality under the Constitution: Reclaiming the Fourteenth Amendment* (1983); Robert Kaczorowski, "Revolutionary Constitutionalism in the Era of the Civil War and Reconstruction," 61 *N.Y.U. L. Rev.* 863 (1986). The old fight against the evidence (on a point where the evidence is particularly clear) has been made unnecessary by the broad acceptance, among both lawyers and historians, of the view advanced in Bickel's article that the Republican consensus responsible for the Fourteenth Amendment understood and intended that the rights of national citizenship it guaranteed would to some extent be left to future determination; that "the catalog of rights" would be left to posterity "to make specific in nondiscriminatory terms." Harold M. Hyman & William M. Wiecek, *Equal Justice under Law* 507 (1982). At the same time, the Supreme Court's repeated demonstration since *Brown* that it will not be deterred by history from a constitutional interpretation it conceives to be beneficial has encouraged historical candor by lowering the political stakes.
27. In addition to *State ex rel. Garnes v. McCann* and *Cory v. Carter,* leading nineteenth-century decisions holding explicitly that separate but equal school facilities did not violate the constitutional guarantees of the Fourteenth Amend-

ment include State ex rel. Stoutmeyer v. Duffy, 7 Nev. 342 (1872); Ward v. Flood, 48 Cal. 36 (1874); United States v. Buntin, 10 F. 730 (C.C.S.D. Ohio 1882); and People ex. rel. King v. Gallagher, 93 N.Y. 438 (1883) (discussed in the text).

28. Leading cases include Day v. Owen, 5 Mich. 520 (1858); West Chester & P. R.R. v. Miles, 55 Pa. 209 (1867); Chicago & N.W. R.R. v. Williams, 55 Ill. 185 (1870); The Sue, 22 F. 843 (D. Md. 1885); cf. Hall v. DeCuir, 95 U.S. 485, 500–06 (1878) (Clifford, J., concurring). For a contemporary summary of the case law see 2 H. G. Wood, *Treatise on the Law of Railroads* §297, at 1199 n. 3 (H. D. Minor 2d ed. 1894).

29. See, e.g., The Sue, 22 F. 843, 846 (D. Md. 1885); Chilton v. St. Louis & I. M. R.R., 114 Mo. 88, 21 S.W. 457 (1893). A notable exception is Coger v. North West. Union Packet Co., 37 Iowa 145 (1873), discussed in the text. Referring to segregation of railroad passengers in the 1873 edition of his respected treatise, Chief Justice Isaac Redfield of Vermont suggested hopefully that "[t]he recent amendments of the United States Constitution, have been supposed by some to settle this question." 1 Isaac F. Redfield, *The Law of Railways* §28(15), at 115 (5th ed. 1873). But the decision in *Coger* was the only one to suggest that the Constitution restricted the right of private companies to regulate passengers on racial lines.

30. See, e.g., Thomas M. Cooley, *A Treatise on the Law of Torts* 283–284, 287–288 (1880); Cooley, *General Principles of Constitutional Law* 230–231 (1880); Note (by J. C. Harper), 10 F. 736 (1882); E. Irving Smith, "The Legal Aspect of the Southern Question," 2 *Harv. L. Rev.* 358, 360–363 (1889); D. H. Pingrey, "A Legal View of Racial Discrimination," 30 *Am. L. Reg.* 69, 86–93 (1891); Owen Wister, "A Note of the Line of Cases in Which the Discrimination Is Made Not between the Sex but the Color of Citizens," 32 *Am. L. Reg.* 748 (1893).

In the foregoing sampling of opinion the views of Thomas M. Cooley are of particular interest. Cooley, a liberal Republican, was chief justice of the Supreme Court of Michigan; during the period in question he was the nation's most influential commentator on constitutional law. See Phillip S. Paludan, *A Covenant with Death* 249–273 (1975). While the treatises by Cooley cited in the preceding paragraph explain the law of "separate but equal" without apparent criticism, an earlier work—the analysis of the Reconstruction Amendments that Cooley prepared for the 1873 edition of Story's *Commentaries*—contains a statement that has sometimes been read as reflecting a more radical position: "And now that it has become a settled rule of constitutional law that color or race is no badge of inferiority and no test of capacity to participate in the government, we doubt if any distinction whatever, either in right or in privilege, which has color or race for its sole basis, can either be established in the law or enforced where it had been previously established." 2 Joseph Story, *Commentaries on the Constitution of the United States* §1961, at 677 (Thomas M. Cooley 4th ed. 1873).

These are arresting words. But to read them with modern eyes, as an assertion that the Constitution has been rendered color-blind, is to overlook what in the 1870s was the principal question: whether or not (if equal facilities were provided) segregation imposed a "distinction . . . in right or in privilege." Applied to schools, the more likely meaning of Cooley's statement was merely that states could no longer provide public education for white children only. The third edition of Cooley's own *Constitutional Limitations,* which he must have prepared almost simultaneously with the fourth edition of Story's *Commentaries,* described the current state of the law as follows: "It is also said [that, notwithstanding the provisions of the new amendments to the federal Constitution] colored children may be required to attend separate schools, if impartial provision is made for their instruction. . . . But some States forbid this. And *when separate schools are not established for colored children,* they are entitled to admission to the other public schools." Thomas M. Cooley, *A Treatise on the Constitutional Limitations Which Rest upon the Legislative Power of the States of the American Union* 391, n. 1, at 458 (3d ed. 1874) (emphasis added).

In 1880 Cooley expanded this statement and gave it on his own authority:

"So long as slavery existed, it was customary, in establishing and providing for the support of schools, to discriminate in the advantages given, throwing open some schools to children generally, but denying admission to colored children. . . . Since then the fourteenth amendment to the federal Constitution has been adopted, and it is now held that when the provision is made for education, it must be impartial. . . . [T]o single out a certain portion [of the people] by the arbitrary standard of color, and say that these shall not have rights which are possessed by others is said to deny to them 'the equal protection of the laws' and is consequently forbidden. But no right is violated when colored pupils are merely placed in different schools, provided the schools are equal, and the same measure of privilege and justice is given in each." Thomas M. Cooley, *A Treatise on the Law of Torts* 287–288 (1880).

31. 24 Iowa 266 (1868).

32. Id. at 269, 270–274, 276–277.

33. See, e.g., Chase v. Stephenson, 71 Ill. 383 (1874); Board of Educ. v. Tinnon, 26 Kan. 1 (1881) (discussed in the text).

34. Cases that apply state statutes prohibiting segregation include People ex rel. Workman v. Board of Educ., 18 Mich. 399 (1869); Kaine v. Commonwealth ex rel. Manaway, 101 Pa. 490 (1882); People ex rel. Longress v. Board of Educ., 101 Ill. 308 (1882); State ex rel. Pierce v. Union Dist. School Trustees, 46 N.J.L. 76 (1884); Wysinger v. Crookshank, 82 Cal. 588 (1890).

35. For a revisionist view of the tendency of state court decisions prior to *Plessy,* stressing the existence of a current of "racially liberal" judicial opinion that was prepared to hold school segregation illegal, see J. Morgan Kousser, *Dead End: The Development of Nineteenth-Century Litigation on Racial Discrimination in Schools* (1986).

36. 37 Iowa 145 (1873).

37. Id. at 149.

38. Id. at 153–154.

39. Id. at 154–155, quoting Iowa Const. art. I, §1.

40. 37 Iowa at 155–156.

41. 427 U.S. 160 (1976).

42. See, e.g., Wister, supra note 30, at 754 (distinguishing *Coger* because "the accommodations set apart for blacks were obviously inferior").

43. Board of Educ. of the City of Ottawa v. Tinnon, 26 Kan. 1 (1881).

44. *Records of the Board of Education, City of Ottawa,* minutes of meetings Sept. 4 and 11, 1876. The minute book for this period, retitled "Minute Book No. 2, Origin and History of School District No. 30, June 2, 1873, to September 22, 1884," is in the archives of Unified School District No. 290, Ottawa, Kansas.

45. Id., minutes of meetings Sept. 11 and 12, 1876.

46. Id., minutes of meetings May 19 and June 7, 1880. A more accessible source is the statement of facts published with the Kansas Supreme Court opinion in the subsequent litigation, 26 Kan. 1, 2–4.

47. A concerted protest against the new segregation policy turned to litigation when the Board of Education refused to reconsider its decision. See *Ottawa Republican* (weekly ed.), Sept. 16, 1880, at 3, col. 3; *Daily Republican* (Ottawa, Kans.), Sept. 21, 1880, at 4, col. 2.

48. The most informative account of the black migration to Kansas in 1879–1880 is Robert G. Athearn, *In Search of Canaan: Black Migration to Kansas, 1879–80* (1978). See also Nell Irvin Painter, *Exodusters: Black Migration to Kansas after Reconstruction* (1977).

49. See Painter, supra note 48, at 184; Athearn, supra note 48, at 261–262.

50. [1880] *Appleton's Annual Cyclopedia* 412.

51. Elijah Tinnen [*sic*] appears as a resident of Ottawa in the state census conducted by the Kansas Board of Agriculture as of March 1, 1875 (vol. 21, p. 22), Kansas State Historical Society, Topeka. According to the census report, Tinnon, age thirty-one, was a laborer and the owner of real estate worth $200; he had been born in Arkansas and had moved from that state to Kansas. His wife, Mary, also thirty-one, had moved to Kansas from Indian Territory (Oklahoma). Elijah and Mary were both illiterate. They had four sons in 1875, the eldest being ten years old, the youngest four. All the children had been born in Kansas (thus placing their parents' arrival in Kansas not later than 1865); all four were listed as having "[a]ttended school within the year."

52. Ottawa's newspapers during this period contain a good deal of comment about the Exodus in general, without providing specific indications as to the number of Exodusters present in the city itself. As the Exodus got under way in the spring of 1879, the *Ottawa Republican* was optimistic about the forthcoming migration and ridiculed Democrats for their fears. At the high point of its enthusiasm, on May 8, the paper ran an editorial decrying the conditions of peonage from which the Exodusters were escaping and concluding, "Come along to Kansas, Sambo. . . . Kansas is ready for you." By August 21, an editorial suggested more soberly that "Kansas is no place for southern colored agriculturalists, unless they have means to support themselves till they can get a start." *Ottawa Republican* (weekly ed.), May 8, 1879, at 2, cols. 1–2; Aug. 21, 1879, at 2, col. 1.

53. A newspaper account of conditions at the Central School Building in November 1879 described the perennial overcrowding of the primary classrooms and hinted at the uneasy racial accommodation that had taken place. "Imagine, kind reader," the author wrote of the second-grade classroom, "70 little pupils of two shades of color. . . ." The author noted that "A class of twelve colored pupils read very well, with a word frequently pronounced in a way characteristic of the race." Given the organization of the school in 1879, the reference to a "class of twelve colored pupils" can only mean that the teacher had assembled her twelve black pupils (among the seventy pupils assigned to her room) and was teaching them as a group apart from the others. *Ottawa Republican* (weekly ed.), Nov. 13, 1879, at 2, col. 5.

54. Tinnon v. Wheeler, *Daily Republican* (Ottawa, Kan.), Jan. 19, 1881, at 2, col. 1 (Dist. Ct. Franklin Co. Jan. 18, 1881). The opinion was reprinted in the paper's weekly edition the following day.

55. Id. col. 2.

56. Board of Educ. of the City of Ottawa v. Tinnon, 26 Kan. at 16–18.

57. Id. at 18–20.

58. Id. at 23.

59. The official report of the decision carries no date, but the case was described on Sept. 23, 1881, as having been "recently decided by the Supreme Court." *Daily Republican* (Ottawa, Kan.), Sept. 23, 1881, at 4, col. 2

60. *Records of the Board of Education,* supra note 44, meetings of Oct. 3, 1881; Dec. 5, 1881; May 1, 1882; June 7, 1882.

61. Id., meetings of June 4, 1883; Sept. 22, 1884.

62. 10 *Weekly Notes of Cases* 156 (C.P. Crawford County, Pa. 1881).

63. Obscure even in the last century, *Commonwealth ex rel. Allen v. Davis* has been rescued from oblivion by J. Morgan Kousser, whose paper includes interesting background notes on the case and on Judge Church. See Kousser, supra note 35, at 21–22 & n. 73.

64. Act of June 8, 1881, No. 83, 1881 Pa. Sess. Laws 76. Judge Church's opinion appeared in *Weekly Notes of Cases* for June 16, 1881.

65. Act of May 2, 1864, ch. 555, 1864 N.Y. Laws 1211, 1281.

66. Consolidated School Law of 1894, ch. 556, tit. 15, art. 11, §28, 1894 N.Y. Laws 1181, 1288; repealed by Act of April 18, 1900, ch. 492, 1900 N.Y. Laws 1173.

67. See Dallas v. Fosdick, 40 How. Pr. 249 (N.Y. Sup. Ct. 1869) (Buffalo); People ex rel. Dietz v. Easton, 13 Abb. Pr. (n.s.) 159 (N.Y. Sup. Ct. 1872) (Albany); People ex rel. Cisco v. School Bd. of Borough of Queens, 44 App. Div. 469, 61 N.Y.S. 330 (1899), aff'd, 161 N.Y. 598, 56 N.E. 81 (1900).

68. 93 N.Y. 438, 441 (1883).

69. Act of April 9, 1873, ch. 186, 1873 N.Y. Laws 303. New York's statute was a replica, at the state level, of the civil rights bills being urged on Congress at the same period by Charles Sumner. Sumner's supplementary civil rights bill, from which the first section of the New York statute was derived, appears at *Cong. Globe,* 42d Cong., 2d Sess. 244 (1872).

70. Act of May 2, 1864, ch. 555, 1864 N.Y. Laws 1211, 1250.

71. 93 N.Y. at 458, 460.

72. Id. at 460–462, 465.

73. Id. at 442.

74. Id. at 450; cf. Plessy v. Ferguson, 163 U.S. 537, 551 (1896).

75. 93 N.Y. at 448–449.

76. Id. at 455.

77. Id. at 452–453.

78. Id. at 454.

79. Russel B. Nye, "Comment on C. Vann Woodward's Paper," in *New Frontiers of the American Reconstruction* 148, 152 (Harold M. Hyman ed., 1966).

80. Charles Lofgren has devoted a chapter of his recent book on *Plessy v. Ferguson* to a convenient and pertinent summary of "The Intellectual Environment: Racist Thought in the Late Nineteenth Century." Charles A. Lofgren, *The Plessy Case: A Legal-Historical Interpretation,* ch. 5 (1987).

7. *Plessy v. Ferguson*

1. 163 U.S. 537 (1896).

2. The decision was reported on an inside page of the *New York Times,* in a regular column on railway news, "sandwiched between reports of another Supreme Court railway decision, which overturned an Illinois law ordering minor re-routing of interstate passenger trains, and a request by the receivers of the Baltimore and Ohio for authority to issue new improvement bonds." Charles A. Lofgren, *The Plessy Case: A Legal-Historical Interpretation* 197 (1987). Although the decision was emphatically condemned by the Negro press and some religious publications, "the most common press response was simply routine notice of the case, or no mention at all." Id. at 196. A limited selection of press commentary is collected in *The Thin Disguise: Turning Point in Negro History: Plessy v. Ferguson, a Documentary Presentation* 123–130 (Otto H. Olsen ed., 1967).

3. Act of July 10, 1890, No. 111, 1890 La. Acts 152.

4. The vote was 7 to 1, Justice Brewer not participating because of ill health. In view of Brewer's opinion in *Board of Education v. Tinnon* (discussed in Chapter 6), where he "dissent[ed] entirely from the suggestion that under the fourteenth amendment of the federal constitution, the state has no power to provide for separate schools for white and colored children," 26 Kan. 1, 23 (1881), there is no doubt that Brewer would have voted with the majority in *Plessy.*

5. Commentators who see in *Plessy* the fountainhead of legally imposed racial segregation have often disparaged Justice Brown's opinion, calling it "irrational," "absurd," "overtly racist," and (most quotably) "a compound of bad logic, bad history, bad sociology, and bad constitutional law." These and similar characterizations are collected, with citations, in Lofgren, supra note 2, at 3–4 & nn. 2–4.

6. 83 U.S. (16 Wall.) 36, 81 (1873).

7. Racial restrictions on the franchise, which would otherwise meet this definition

of a discriminatory statute, were by consensus excluded from the original scope of "equal protection." The ratification of the Fifteenth Amendment in 1870 foreclosed judicial consideration of the point.

8. *Cong. Globe,* 39th Cong., 1st Sess. 2459 (1866). In the Senate, Jacob Howard of Michigan explained the equal protection clause in substantially identical terms. Id. at 2766.

9. In Bradwell v. Illinois, 83 U.S. (16 Wall.) 130 (1873), decided the day after the *Slaughter-House Cases,* the Court found no constitutional objection to a rule of the Illinois Supreme Court by which the practice of law was restricted to men.

10. Strauder v. West Virginia, 100 U.S. 303, 310 (1880).

11. Most of the race-specific provisions of the Black Codes had been repealed by the end of 1866; any that remained were supplanted by the Reconstruction constitutions that the southern states were required to adopt as a condition of readmission to the Union. See Eric Foner, *Reconstruction: America's Unfinished Revolution, 1863–1877* 209, 320 (1988).

12. 320 U.S. 81 (1943) (upholding wartime reporting and curfew requirements, imposed by military order, applicable to persons of Japanese ancestry).

13. 448 U.S. 448 (1980) (upholding "minority set-asides" in federal public works expenditure).

14. For an illuminating discussion of the process by which the nineteenth-century Supreme Court came to choose "unjustifiable classifications" rather than "impermissible classifications" as its "model" for the meaning of the equal protection clause, see Richard S. Kay, "The Equal Protection Clause in the Supreme Court, 1873–1903," 29 *Buffalo L. Rev.* 667 (1980).

15. 106 U.S. 583 (1883).

16. It is possible to analyze laws of the kind considered in *Pace,* like laws prohibiting interracial marriage, as denying equal treatment to members of racially determined classes: cf. McLaughlin v. Florida, 379 U.S. 184, 188 (1964) (distinct penalty for cohabitation by interracial couples). The logical awkwardness of identifying the classes, however, is a clue to the fact that the real objection to such laws is not racial "inequality" but the bare racial motive underlying the legislation. A strong demonstration of their unconstitutionality—meaning one that does not depend on agreement about the policy of the statutes—requires an appeal to a rule of near-absolute color blindness. The holding in Palmore v. Sidoti, 466 U.S. 429 (1984), overturning a child-custody decision based on the adverse consequences to the child of residing in a racially mixed household, resists conventional equal protection analysis for the same reasons. See David A. Strauss, "The Myth of Colorblindness," 1986 *Sup. Ct. Rev.* 99.

17. 163 U.S. at 549–550.

18. The broad standard of "reasonableness" to which racial classifications were remitted by the opinions in *Roberts* and *Plessy* is not, of course, the "reasonable relationship" test of modern equal protection analysis. (Where economic regulations are concerned, a "reasonable relationship" between legislative ends and means is ordinarily enough to satisfy the constitutional requirement of equal

protection of the laws; whereas laws deemed more constitutionally sensitive must satisfy judges as to both the appropriateness of the means employed and the desirability of the ends in view.) The argument in the text is that even the Court's strictest judicial "scrutiny" may be logically comprehended within a broad legal requirement of "reasonableness." That the reasonableness of a course of action depends both on the end to be achieved and the means proposed to achieve it is, in ordinary usage, the essence of the idea.

19. Regents of the Univ. of Calif. v. Bakke, 438 U.S. 265, 355 (1978) (Brennan, White, Marshall & Blackmun, JJ., concurring in the judgment in part).

20. *National Anti-Slavery Standard,* Nov. 5, 1864, at 1, col. 2.

21. Letter from Theodore Tilton to Lydia Maria Child (Jan. 22, 1865), published in *Liberator,* March 3, 1865, at 33, col. 4.

22. A native of Ohio and a Civil War veteran, Tourgée emigrated in 1865 to North Carolina, where he became active in Reconstruction politics and served for six years as an elected judge of the Superior Court. With the decline of Republican fortunes and the loss of his judgeship, Tourgée turned increasingly to writing and lecturing. *A Fool's Errand, by One of the Fools,* a story of Reconstruction that was his best-known work, was published shortly after Tourgée left the South in 1879. The novel's most exciting scenes were drawn from Tourgée's real-life confrontations with the Ku-Klux Klan; it possesses considerable historical interest as a description of the failure of Reconstruction by an observer who managed to combine northern and southern sympathies. For the facts of Tourgée's career, see the biography by Otto H. Olsen, *Carpetbagger's Crusade: The Life of Albion Winegar Tourgée* (1965). The most influential modern appreciation of Tourgée's literary work is Edmund Wilson, *Patriotic Gore: Studies in the Literature of the American Civil War* 529–548 (1962).

23. Brief for Plaintiff in Error [by Albion W. Tourgée & Jas. C. Walker] at 19, Plessy v. Ferguson (No. 210, Oct. Term 1895), reprinted in 13 *Landmark Briefs and Arguments of the Supreme Court of the United States: Constitutional Law* (Philip B. Kurland & Gerhard Casper eds., 1975) at 27, 46. Two briefs were submitted to the Supreme Court on behalf of Plessy, both styled "Brief For Plaintiff in Error." The submission hereinafter referred to as the "Tourgée Brief" was signed by Tourgée and his New Orleans counsel, James C. Walker. The second brief for Plessy was signed by S. F. Phillips and F. D. McKenney. Samuel F. Phillips, who as solicitor general had argued the *Civil Rights Cases* for the government, was retained by Tourgée as co-counsel when *Plessy* reached the Supreme Court; McKenney was Phillips's partner in private practice in Washington. See Lofgren, supra note 2, at 30–31, 148–151.

24. 163 U.S. at 559.

25. 109 U.S. 3 (1883). On the circumstances surrounding the preparation and publication of the dissenting opinion and Harlan's resulting celebrity, see Alan F. Westin, "John Marshall Harlan and the Constitutional Rights of Negroes: The Transformation of a Southerner," 66 *Yale L.J.* 637, 674–685 (1957).

26. For the background and early stages of the litigation culminating in *Plessy,* see

Lofgren, supra note 2, at 28–43; C. Vann Woodward, "The National Decision against Equality," in Woodward, *American Counterpoint: Slavery and Racism in the North-South Dialogue* 212 (1971).

27. The fiercely partisan *Inter Ocean*—its supposed motto "Republican in everything, independent in nothing"—had an extensive national circulation, and Tourgée's "Bystander" column was frequently reprinted by sympathetic Negro papers. On this phase of Tourgée's activities see generally Olsen, supra note 22, at 281–311; Otto H. Olsen, "Albion W. Tourgée and Negro Militants of the 1890's: A Documentary Selection," 28 *Sci. & Soc'y* 183 (1964).

28. *Daily Inter Ocean* (Chicago), Aug. 15, 1891, at 4, col. 4; Lofgren, supra note 2, at 30. Tourgée returned to the subject of "the 'Jim Crow Car' infamy," urging boycotts and praising the movement to obtain a test of the laws' constitutionality, in his *Inter Ocean* columns for Sept. 5, 1891, at 4, col. 7; Sept. 26, 1891, at 4, col. 4; Oct. 3, 1891, at 4, col. 6; Oct. 17, 1891, at 4, col. 7.

29. *Daily Inter Ocean,* June 10, 1893, at 12, col. 6.

30. Of the brief's twenty-three numbered sections, for example, the first five make the following points: (I) that Louisiana's separate car law denies a claim for damages to a person assigned to the wrong car because of a bona fide error as to his race (although the Louisiana Supreme Court had expressly determined that the act had no such effect), thereby denying to such person the equal protection of the laws; (II) that the "reputation of belonging to the dominant race" constitutes property, of which Plessy was deprived, without due process of law, by his assignment to the Jim Crow car; (III) that by authorizing railroads to refuse to carry passengers who refuse to travel in the cars to which they are assigned, the act legalizes the deprivation of liberty and property without due process of law; (IV) that in requiring the separation of passengers who might (legally, under the laws of Louisiana at the time) be husband and wife or mother and child, the act constitutes "authority to interfere with natural, domestic rights of the most sacred character"; and (V) that the determination of a person's race cannot be made "equitably and justly . . . without evidence, investigation on responsibility," and thus should not be left to railway conductors. Tourgée Brief, supra note 23, at 7–10, 13 *Landmark Briefs* at 34–37. None of these arguments is inconsistent with the propriety of legally required racial discrimination, provided only that it be properly administered.

31. Tourgée Brief, supra note 23, at 19, 35–36, 13 *Landmark Briefs* at 46, 62–63.

32. 163 U.S. at 551. Reviewing *Plessy* after Harlan's death and his own retirement from the bench, Justice Brown came close to conceding the injustice of this sophistry, noting that Harlan "assumed what is probably the fact, that the statute had its origin in the purpose, not so much to exclude white persons from railroad cars occupied by blacks, as to exclude colored people from coaches occupied [by] or assigned to white persons." H. B. Brown, "The Dissenting Opinions of Mr. Justice Harlan," 46 *Am. L. Rev.* 321, 338 (1912).

33. 163 U.S. at 563.

34. "The white race deems itself to be the dominant race in this country. And so it

is, in prestige, in achievements, in education, in wealth and in power. So, I doubt not, it will continue to be for all time, if it remains true to its great heritage and holds fast to the principles of constitutional liberty." Id. at 559.

35. Id. at 558–559.

36. 123 U.S. 623 (1887).

37. 118 U.S. 356 (1886). The condemnation of San Francisco's "unjust and illegal discriminations" against the Chinese owners of wooden laundry buildings turned on the finding that the classifications established by the ordinance bore no discernible relation to the ostensible objects of fire prevention and public health. Id. at 374.

38. 163 U.S. at 559.

39. Id. at 559, 560.

40. The fullest source of information on Harlan's career before his appointment to the Supreme Court is the well-known article by Alan Westin, supra note 25. On Harlan's early opposition to emancipation and his subsequent political conversion, see id. at 640–662 as well as Louis Hartz, "John M. Harlan in Kentucky, 1855–1877: The Story of His Pre-Court Political Career," 14 *Filson Club Hist. Q.* 17 (1940). See also Document, "The Appointment of Mr. Justice Harlan," 29 *Ind. L.J.* 46 (1953).

41. Thus Laurence H. Tribe writes that "for this late nineteenth-century proponent of white dominance [i.e., Harlan], the color-blind ideal, it turns out, was only shorthand for the concept that the Fourteenth Amendment prevents our law from enshrining and perpetuating white supremacy." Tribe, "In What Vision of the Constitution Must the Law Be Color-Blind?," 20 *John Marshall L. Rev.* 201, 203 (1986).

42. 175 U.S. 528 (1899).

43. C. Vann Woodward reads Harlan's opinion in *Cumming* as indicating that "even" Harlan "saw nothing unconstitutional in segregated public schools." Woodward, supra note 26, at 231–232. Benno Schmidt finds it "reasonably clear after *Cumming* that even Justice Harlan took for granted the authority of the state to segregate public schools." Alexander M. Bickel & Benno C. Schmidt, Jr., *The Judiciary and Responsible Government, 1910–21* [9 *Holmes Devise History of the Supreme Court of the United States*] 759 (1984).

44. United States v. Clark, 96 U.S. 37 (1878).

45. See, merely as one famous example, Chief Justice John Marshall's protestation in *McCulloch v. Maryland* that where an act of Congress "is not prohibited, and is really calculated to effect any of the objects intrusted to the government, to undertake here to inquire into the degree of its necessity, would be to pass the line which circumscribes the judicial department, and to tread on legislative ground. This court disclaims all pretensions to such a power." 17 U.S. (4 Wheat.) 316, 423 (1819).

46. See, e.g., Civil Rights Cases, 109 U.S. 3, 51 (1883) ("But it is for Congress, not the judiciary, to say that legislation is appropriate—that is—best adapted to the end to be attained"); Mugler v. Kansas, 123 U.S. 623, 662 (1887) (courts "have

nothing to do with the mere policy of legislation"); Pollock v. Farmers' Loan & Trust Co., 158 U.S. 601, 674 (1895) ("With the policy of legislation of this character, this court has nothing to do"); United States v. Union Pac. Ry., 160 U.S. 1, 35 (1895) ("We have nothing to do with the wisdom or policy of legislation"); Plessy v. Ferguson, 163 U.S. 537, 558 (1896) ("But I do not understand that the courts have anything to do with the policy or expediency of legislation"); Booth v. Illinois, 184 U.S. 425, 432 (1902) ("The courts have nothing to do with the mere policy of legislation"); Northern Securities Co. v. United States, 193 U.S. 197, 352 (1904) ("These . . . questions as to the policy of [the Sherman Act] belong to another department, and this court has no function to supervise such legislation from the standpoint of wisdom or policy"); Lochner v. New York, 198 U.S. 45, 69 (1905) ("Under our systems of government the courts are not concerned with the wisdom or policy of legislation"); Standard Oil Co. v. United States, 221 U.S. 1, 106 (1911) ("the courts, under our constitutional system, have no rightful concern with the wisdom or policy of legislation enacted by that branch of the government which alone can make laws").

47. It is notoriously difficult to square Harlan's enthusiastic exposition of the freedom-of-contract aspect of substantive due process in Adair v. United States, 208 U.S. 161 (1908) (invalidating congressional prohibition of "yellow dog contract" for railroad workers), with his dissent three years before in *Lochner,* supra note 46. In the earlier case Harlan had stated that New York might properly infringe the liberty of contract of bakery workers so long as "the means devised by the State are germane to an end which may be lawfully accomplished and have a real or substantial relation to the protection of health. . . ." 198 U.S. at 69.

48. In a stump speech delivered as Kentucky's Republican candidate for governor in 1871, in which he criticized the Democratic legislature for exempting black taxpayers from the school tax and simultaneously cutting off public funds for Negro schools, Harlan observed that "[s]o far as keeping whites and blacks separated, I think it was right and proper." *Cincinnati Daily Gazette,* June 3, 1871 (supplement), at 5, col. 5.

49. 109 U.S. at 36, 48.

50. See note 43 supra.

51. For a wealth of information on the factual background of the *Cumming* litigation and a view of Harlan's opinion diametrically opposed to the one here suggested, see J. Morgan Kousser, "Separate but *Not* Equal: The Supreme Court's First Decision on Racial Discrimination in Schools," 46 *J. S. Hist.* 17 (1980).

52. Board of Educ. v. Cumming, 103 Ga. 641, 29 S.E. 488 (1898).

53. Cumming v. Richmond County Bd. of Educ., 175 U.S. 528 (1899).

54. Id. at 539–540 (argument of George F. Edmunds for the plaintiff in error).

55. Id. at 543–544.

56. Civil rights plaintiffs thereafter, and the Supreme Court itself in 1954, were thus enabled to distinguish *Cumming,* correctly, as a case constituting no authority for the legality of segregated schools. "In *Cumming* . . . the validity of the ['separate but equal'] doctrine itself was not challenged." Brown v. Board of Educ., 347 U.S. 483, 491 (1954).

57. 175 U.S. at 545.
58. Kousser, supra note 51, at 18.
59. Kay, supra note 14, at 721.
60. For an extensive discussion of the freedmen's education missions of the three Protestant denominations operating secondary schools in Augusta at this time, see James M. McPherson, *The Abolitionist Legacy* 143–243 (1975).
61. The foregoing facts are drawn variously from 175 U.S. at 529–535, 542–543 and from the Transcript of Record before the Supreme Court (No. 621, Oct. Term 1898) at 10–33.
62. Kousser, supra note 51, at 43.
63. Transcript of Record, supra note 61, at 2.

8. Separate but Equal

1. C. Vann Woodward, "The National Decision against Equality," in Woodward, *American Counterpoint: Slavery and Racism in the North-South Dialogue* 212 (1971).
2. Alexander M. Bickel & Benno C. Schmidt, Jr., *The Judiciary and Responsible Government, 1910–21* [9 *Oliver Wendell Holmes Devise History of the Supreme Court of the United States*] 819 (1984).
3. 252 U.S. 399 (1920); see Bickel & Schmidt, supra note 2, at 785–789.
4. 275 U.S. 78 (1927).
5. 211 U.S. 45 (1908). On the background and historical significance of *Berea College v. Kentucky, McCabe v. Atchison, T. & S.F. Ry.* (1914), and *Buchanan v. Warley* (1917), see the invaluable discussion in Bickel & Schmidt, supra note 2, at 729–819 (1984).
6. Act of March 22, 1904, ch. 85, 1904 Ky. Acts 181.
7. For the contrasting rationales of the decisions compare Berea College v. Commonwealth, 123 Ky. 209, 220–221, 94 S.W. 623, 626 (1906), with Berea College v. Kentucky, 211 U.S. 45, 54–58 (1908).
8. 211 U.S. at 65–70 (Harlan, J., dissenting). Justice Day also noted his dissent.
9. 235 U.S. 151 (1914).
10. Act of Dec. 18, 1907, ch. 15, 1907 Okla. Laws 201.
11. McCabe v. Atchison, T. & S.F. Ry., 186 F. 966, 970–971 (8th Cir. 1911). This holding by the majority of the circuit court provoked a vigorous dissent by Judge Walter Sanborn, in which the influence of Harlan's *Plessy* dissent is clearly evident. Id. at 977–989.
12. Justices White, Holmes, Lamar, and McReynolds concurred in the result only, thereby dissociating themselves from Hughes's advisory opinion as to the requirements of "separate but equal."
13. Holmes Papers, Library of Congress; quoted in Bickel & Schmidt, supra note 2, at 780. (The same work includes a photographic reproduction of Hughes's letter.)
14. 235 U.S. at 161–162.
15. 334 U.S. 1, 22 (1948) (holding that a racially restrictive covenant in a deed to real property might not constitutionally be enforced).

16. 245 U.S. 60 (1917).

17. For the background of the Baltimore ordinance (the work of a progressive, reform-minded municipal administration) see Garrett Power, "Apartheid Baltimore Style: The Residential Segregation Ordinances of 1910–1913," 42 *Md. L. Rev.* 289 (1983).

18. For the background of the Louisville litigation see Bickel & Schmidt, supra note 2, at 789–798.

19. 245 U.S. at 72–73. The measurable interference with property rights that could be found on the facts of the case might be thought too frail a reed on which to rest the decision, and was in fact so regarded by contemporary critics. See Bickel & Schmidt, supra note 2, at 802–804. So far as the plaintiff was concerned, it amounted to no more than the marginal difference in price resulting from the lost opportunity to sell to a larger class of buyers. Interference of this magnitude was trivial when compared with the effect of restrictions on land use such as those recently approved in Hadacheck v. Sebastian, 239 U.S. 394 (1915), where the Court upheld a zoning ordinance that prohibited the further operation of a brickyard, thereby destroying the greater part of its value.

20. 245 U.S. at 75–79.

21. Id. at 81.

22. On the origins of the NAACP's litigation strategy as a means of fighting segregation, as outlined in a report (by Nathan Margold) sponsored by the left-wing philanthropic foundation known as the Garland Fund, see Richard Kluger, *Simple Justice* 132–137 (1976); Mark V. Tushnet, *The NAACP's Legal Strategy against Segregated Education, 1925–1950,* chs. 1 & 2 (1987).

23. 305 U.S. 337 (1938). For the events surrounding the litigation in *Gaines* see Kluger, supra note 22, at 186–194, 202–204, 212–213; Tushnet, supra note 22, at 70–77.

24. 305 U.S. at 349–350.

25. 320 U.S. 81 (1943).

26. 323 U.S. 214 (1944). The history of the relocation program and of the ensuing litigation is detailed in Peter Irons, *Justice at War* (1983).

27. 320 U.S. at 100–101.

28. Id. at 110–111.

29. 323 U.S. at 242.

30. Id. at 216.

31. The postwar cases on graduate education are Sipuel v. Board of Regents, 332 U.S. 631 (1948); Sweatt v. Painter, 339 U.S. 629 (1950); and McLaurin v. Oklahoma State Regents, 339 U.S. 637 (1950). The latter two, decided together with Henderson v. United States, 339 U.S. 816 (1950), a case involving segregation in railroad dining cars, comprise what is sometimes called the "1950 Trilogy." On the litigation background of all these cases see Jonathan Entin, "*Sweatt v. Painter,* the End of Segregation, and the Transformation of Education Law," 5 *Rev. Litigation* 3 (1986). The dilemma posed for the Supreme Court in deciding how to handle the cases of the 1950 Trilogy—their outcome, narrowly

defined, being a foregone conclusion—is explored in Dennis Hutchinson, "Unanimity and Desegregation: Decisionmaking and the Supreme Court, 1948–1958," 68 *Georgetown L.J.* 1 (1979).

32. 314 U.S. 160, 184–185 (1941) (Jackson, J., concurring). *Edwards* considered a California statute making it a misdemeanor to bring into the state any nonresident "indigent person." The law was held to be an unconstitutional interference with interstate commerce.

33. Kotch v. Board of River Port Pilot Comm'rs, 330 U.S. 552, 565–566 (1947) (Rutledge, J., dissenting).

34. Brief for Petitioner, Sipuel v. Board of Regents of the Univ. of Okla. (No. 369, Oct. Term 1947), at 27. Marshall signed the brief as principal author on behalf of the NAACP Legal Defense and Educational Fund Inc.

35. 339 U.S. 629 (1950).

36. See Kluger, supra note 22, at 274–276.

37. Motion and Brief of Amicus Curiae [Committee of Law Teachers Against Segregation in Legal Education] in Support of Petition for Certiorari, Sweatt v. Painter (No. 44, Oct. Term 1949), at 8–9, 19. The brief, signed by Thomas Emerson, John Frank, Alexander Frey, Robert Hale, Harold Havighurst, and Edward Levi, was actually written by Emerson, Frank, and a younger colleague at the Yale Law School, David Haber. Kluger, supra note 22, at 275. The brief is reprinted as "Segregation and the Equal Protection Clause: Brief for the Committee of Law Teachers Against Segregation in Legal Education," 34 *Minn. L. Rev.* 289 (1950).

38. 339 U.S. 816 (1950).

39. Brief for the United States, Henderson v. United States (No. 25, Oct. Term 1949), at 14–15, 16–18. An *amicus* brief submitted in the case by the NAACP also contained the argument, though only as a subsidiary point, that "[t]he government is powerless under the Constitution to make, sanction, or enforce, any distinctions or classifications based upon race or color." Motion and Brief for the National Association for the Advancement of Colored People as *Amicus Curiae, Henderson v. United States,* at 21.

40. See note 31 supra.

41. Statement as to Jurisdiction, McLaurin v. Oklahoma State Regents (No. 34, Oct. Term 1949), at 13 (citations omitted).

42. Id. at 21–22.

43. 339 U.S. 629, 631 (1950).

44. The justices' determination in 1950 to avoid anticipating the future course of desegregation was conscious and explicit; it is the principal theme of the materials documenting their deliberations on these cases, as compiled by Dennis Hutchinson. The point was made with particular emphasis in a memorandum to the Supreme Court conference by Felix Frankfurter, criticizing a passage in a draft of the Court's opinion in *Henderson* that referred to the division between the tables of a segregated dining car as "symbolic":

"[F]or this Court to indicate objection to the division at tables as being 'symbolic' is to introduce legal objection to separateness as such. 'Symbolic' is an anti-segregation slogan. That is precisely the social objection to segregation, namely, that it represents a symbol of inferiority. We cannot introduce it into an opinion without giving just ground to the notion that we have ruled out segregation as such. . . .

"Even in the opinions dealing with graduate education we should not give currency to the term 'symbolic.' I cannot put too strongly my conviction that if we put the Court behind that term we have opened the door to the very thing which, at least for the moment, we have agreed to keep out—passing on segregation as such—reaching down to primary instruction. Indeed it would affect not only the whole question of education but all other aspects of segregation. It seems to me we ought to avoid language which will do the very thing we have decided not to adjudicate." Frankfurter, Memorandum to the Conference (May 31, 1950), Felix Frankfurter Papers, Library of Congress, quoted in Hutchinson, supra note 31, at 29.

9. *Brown v. Board of Education*

1. The decision announced as *Brown v. Board of Education* covered separate school segregation cases from four states (Kansas, South Carolina, Virginia, and Delaware) that had been consolidated, together with a fifth case arising in the District of Columbia, for argument in the Supreme Court. In the order they were placed on the Supreme Court's docket, the cases were Brown v. Board of Education of Topeka, 98 F. Supp. 797 (D. Kan. 1951); Briggs v. Elliott, 98 F. Supp. 529 (E.D.S.C. 1951), vacated and remanded, 342 U.S. 350 (1952), 103 F. Supp. 920 (E.D.S.C. 1952); Davis v. County School Bd. of Prince Edward County, 103 F. Supp. 337 (E.D. Va. 1952); Bolling v. Sharpe, Civ. No. 4949–50 (D.D.C. April 9, 1951); and Gebhart v. Belton, 33 Del. Ch. 144, 91 A.2d 137 (Del. 1952), aff'g 32 Del. Ch. 343, 87 A.2d 862 (Del. Ch. 1952).

The first round of Supreme Court argument in the consolidated cases took place in December 1952. The Court issued an order in June 1953 directing that the cases be held for further briefing and reargument the following term. Brown v. Board of Educ. of Topeka, 345 U.S. 972 (1953). A second round of argument took place in December 1953. The famous opinions prohibiting school segregation, frequently designated as *"Brown I,"* were issued on May 17, 1954: Brown v. Board of Educ. of Topeka, 347 U.S. 483 (1954), and Bolling v. Sharpe, 347 U.S. 497 (1954). *Brown I* ordered a third round of briefing and argument, limited this time to the question of implementing the 1954 decision. The final arguments took place in April 1955, and the Court's implementation order, known as *"Brown II,"* was issued in May 1955. Brown v. Board of Educ. of Topeka, 349 U.S. 294 (1955).

Richard Kluger's indispensable history of the school desegregation litigation, *Simple Justice* (1976), provides a detailed account of each of the cases from its inception through the lower courts and of their consideration by the Supreme Court at each stage of the proceedings.

2. *New York Times,* May 23, 1954, §4, at 10E, col. 1.

3. See Kluger, supra note 1, at 609.

4. Alexander M. Bickel, "The Original Understanding and the Segregation Decision," 69 *Harv. L. Rev.* 1, 2 (1955).

5. Kluger, supra note 1, at 696.

6. 345 U.S. 972.

7. See Kluger, supra note 1, at 614–615.

8. The research undertaken by the parties in response to the order for reargument is described in Kluger, supra note 1, at 617–646. Bickel's research, which formed the basis for his well-known article, supra note 4, had been prepared as a memorandum for Justice Frankfurter and in that form circulated to the Court.

    The historical materials collected by the parties are set forth in Brief for Appellants in Nos. 1, 2, and 4 and for Respondents in No. 10 on Reargument, Brown v. Board of Educ. et al. (Oct. Term 1953), reprinted in 49 *Landmark Briefs and Arguments of the Supreme Court of the United States: Constitutional Law* 481 (Philip B. Kurland & Gerhard Casper eds., 1975); Supplemental Brief for the United States on Reargument, Brown v. Board of Educ. et al. (Nos. 1, 2, 4, 8 & 10, Oct. Term 1953), 49 *Landmark Briefs* 853; Brief for Appellees on Reargument, Briggs v. Elliott (No. 2, Oct. Term 1953). The briefs for the South Carolina defendants in *Briggs v. Elliott,* written by John W. Davis, contain what is incomparably the most skillful argument for the losing side in the School Segregation Cases; and it is unfortunate that they are not included in the admirable *Landmark Briefs* reprint.

9. 347 U.S. at 489, 492.

10. Brief for the United States as Amicus Curiae, Brown v. Board of Educ. et al. (Nos. 8, 101, 191, 413 & 448, Oct. Term 1952), at 8–17, 49 *Landmark Briefs* 113, 123–132. The brief for the United States, whose principal author was Philip Elman, counseled the narrowest possible disposition of the cases: it stressed that the question of "separate but equal" need not be reached at all (though if it were, the government favored the overruling of *Plessy*). On the background of the government's brief see Elman, "The Solicitor General's Office, Justice Frankfurter, and Civil Rights Litigation, 1946–1960: An Oral History," 100 *Harv. L. Rev.* 817, 825–830 (1987).

11. 347 U.S. at 495.

12. Chief Justice Warren's opinion quoted factual findings by the trial court that "[s]egregation of white and colored children in public schools has a detrimental effect upon the colored children. The impact is greater when it has the sanction of the law; for the policy of separating the races is usually interpreted as denoting the inferiority of the negro group. A sense of inferiority affects the motivation of the child to learn. Segregation with the sanction of law, therefore, has a tendency to [retard] the educational and mental development of negro children and to deprive them of some of the benefits they would receive in a racial[ly] integrated school system." Id. at 494. The opinion added the comment, "Whatever may have been the extent of psychological knowledge at the time of Plessy v. Ferguson, this finding is amply supported by modern authority," citing seven

recent social science studies. Id. & n. 11. Legal Defense Fund lawyers had been sharply divided over the wisdom of using the social science evidence relied on by the Court. See Kluger, supra note 1, at 555–557.

13. See Harold B. Gerard, "School Desegregation: The Social Science Role," in *Eliminating Racism: Profiles in Controversy* 225 (Phyllis A. Katz & Dalmas A. Taylor eds., 1988). The city of Milwaukee announced in 1990 that it would create "African-American Immersion Schools," intended exclusively for black males, in "a pilot program that seeks to emphasize black culture, build self-esteem and promote the rewards of responsible male behavior." *New York Times,* Sept. 30, 1990, §1, at 1, col. 2.

14. Plessy v. Ferguson, 163 U.S. 537, 551 (1896).

15. See Kluger, supra note 1, at 582–616, 678–699; Dennis J. Hutchinson, "Unanimity and Desegregation: Decisionmaking in the Supreme Court, 1948–1958," 68 *Georgetown L.J.* 1 (1979).

16. Because the District of Columbia is not subject to the Fourteenth Amendment, the question of segregation in the District could be addressed without reference to *Plessy v. Ferguson.* For this reason the Court's separate opinion in the District of Columbia case, *Bolling v. Sharpe,* affords some idea of how the decision in *Brown* might have been explained had the chief justice not felt obliged to decide the Fourteenth Amendment issue in ostensible harmony with *Plessy.* The brief opinion hints at several themes more substantial than the discussion pursued in *Brown.* According to *Bolling v. Sharpe,* "Classifications based solely on race must be scrutinized with particular care, since they are contrary to our traditions and hence constitutionally suspect" (citing *Korematsu* and *Hirabayashi*); "'the Constitution . . . forbids . . . discrimination by the General Government, or by the States, against any citizen because of his race'" (quoting out of context the opinion of Justice Harlan in Gibson v. Mississippi, 162 U.S. 565, 591 (1896)); and "Segregation in public education is not reasonably related to any proper governmental objective." The apparently determining consideration in *Bolling v. Sharpe*—the highly practical argument that "[i]n view of our decision that the Constitution prohibits the states from maintaining racially segregated public schools, it would be unthinkable that the same Constitution would impose a lesser duty on the Federal Government"—cut short the development of these contentions and tended to obscure their potential relevance to *Brown.* 347 U.S. 497, 499–500. On the framing of the opinion in *Bolling v. Sharpe* see Hutchinson, supra note 15, at 44–50.

17. Noted civil rights lawyers who signed the numerous briefs on the desegregation side of the School Segregation Cases included, *inter alia,* Robert L. Carter, William T. Coleman, Jack Greenberg, Thurgood Marshall, Constance Baker Motley, James M. Nabrit, Jr., Spottswood W. Robinson III, and Jack B. Weinstein. Litigation strategy in the consolidated cases was jointly developed, largely under the auspices of the NAACP Legal Defense Fund. See Kluger, supra note 1.

18. An argument similar to that ultimately adopted by the Court—by which the illegality of segregation stemmed from its adverse psychological consequences

for Negro children and the resultant inequality of treatment—was included in the briefs in the Kansas and Delaware cases, where the trial courts had made factual findings lending that argument direct support. See Brief for Appellants, Brown v. Board of Educ. (No. 8, Oct. Term 1952), at 8–10, 49 *Landmark Briefs* 23, 34–36; Brief of Respondents and Appendix to Brief, Gebhart v. Belton (No. 448, Oct. Term 1952), at 11–12; cf. Brief for the United States as Amicus Curiae, Brown v. Board of Educ. et al. (Nos. 8, 101, 191, 413 & 448, Oct. Term. 1952), at 12–14, 49 *Landmark Briefs* 113, 127–129. Despite the favorable findings of the trial court, counsel in the Kansas case subordinated the argument based on psychological impact to the broader antidiscrimination position.

19. Brief for Appellants, Brown v. Board of Educ. (No. 8, Oct. Term 1952), at 5–7, 49 *Landmark Briefs* 23, 31–33.

20. Statement as to Jurisdiction, Briggs v. Elliott (No. 816, Oct. Term 1951), at 25, 26, 29.

21. Brief for Appellants, Briggs v. Elliott (No. 101, Oct. Term 1952), at 23.

22. Reply Brief for Appellants, Briggs v. Elliott (No. 101, Oct. Term 1952), at 2.

23. Statement as to Jurisdiction, Davis v. County School Bd. of Prince Edward County (No. 4, Oct. Term 1953), at 8.

24. See Kluger, supra note 1, at 520–523. The complaint in *Bolling v. Sharpe* appears in the Transcript of Record before the United States Supreme Court (No. 8, Oct. Term 1953), at 1–14.

25. Brief for Petitioners, Bolling v. Sharpe (No. 8, Oct. Term 1953), at 11.

26. Brief for Appellants in Nos. 1, 2, and 4 and for Respondents in No. 10 on Reargument, Brown v. Board of Educ. et al. (Oct. Term 1953), at 16–30, 49 *Landmark Briefs* 481, 529–543.

27. Naim v. Naim, 197 Va. 80, 87 S.E.2d 749, vacated and remanded, 350 U.S. 891 (1955), reinstated and aff'd, 197 Va. 734, 90 S.E.2d 849, app. dismissed, 350 U.S. 985 (1956). At the time of the Virginia decision, more than half the states had miscegenation statutes: see Andrew D. Weinberger, "A Reappraisal of the Constitutionality of Miscegenation Statutes," 42 *Cornell L.Q.* 208 (1957). Their constitutionality had been repeatedly upheld in state court decisions, the sole exception being Perez v. Sharp, 32 Cal. 2d 711, 198 P.2d 17 (1948). Pace v. Alabama, 106 U.S. 583 (1883), affirming the constitutionality of a statute that punished fornication more severely when the actors were of different races, was considered to provide cognate authority.

28. On the Supreme Court's handling of *Naim v. Naim,* see Hutchinson, supra note 15, at 62–67; Justice Frankfurter's memorandum (advising against hearing the appeal) is reprinted id. at 95. See also Elman, supra note 10, at 845–847.

29. So far as the evidence reveals, the key to resolving the impasse within the Supreme Court over the School Segregation Cases was not "inherently unequal" but "all deliberate speed": the idea, in other words, that the Court might declare that personal constitutional rights had been violated yet withhold immediate relief. The course ultimately followed was that counseled by the United States as *amicus curiae* in the first round of argument in 1952, when the brief submitted

by the solicitor general suggested that the Court need not overrule *Plessy* to find school segregation unconstitutional. See note 10 supra. The same brief went on to recommend that, should the Court rule against segregation, the cases be remanded to the district courts "with directions to devise and execute such program for relief as appears most likely to achieve orderly and expeditious transition to a non-segregated system." Brief for the United States as Amicus Curiae, Brown v. Board of Educ. et al. (Nos. 8, 101, 191, 413 & 448, Oct. Term 1952), at 27, 49 *Landmark Briefs* 113, 142. Between the second round of argument in December 1953 and the Court's formal vote to end school segregation, taken in February or March 1954, the theme was recalled in a memorandum from Justice Frankfurter to the Supreme Court conference: "When the wrong is a deeply rooted state policy the court does its duty if it decrees measures that reverse the direction of the unconstitutional policy so as to uproot it 'with all deliberate speed.' *Virginia* v. *West Virginia,* 222 U.S. 17, 20." The Frankfurter memorandum, dated Jan. 15, 1954, is quoted in Kluger, supra note 1, at 686, and in Hutchinson, supra note 15, at 41.

In May 1955, following a final round of argument on the question of implementation, *Brown II* remanded the several cases to the lower courts for such proceedings, orders, and decrees as might be "necessary and proper to admit to public schools on a racially nondiscriminatory basis with all deliberate speed the parties to these cases." Brown v. Board of Educ., 349 U.S. 294, 301 (1955).

Philip Elman, who claims credit for introducing the idea, argues forcefully that the judicial anomaly of *Brown*—the fact that the Supreme Court affirmed a constitutional right while denying immediate relief—was what "broke the logjam," making possible the unanimous decision of May 1954. Elman, supra note 10, at 827–830. In its emphasis on the practical importance of the deferred remedy to the Court's achievement of unanimity, Elman's account is consistent with the documentary evidence marshalled by Kluger, supra note 1, chs. 23 & 25, and Hutchinson, supra note 15, at 34–44.

30. Muir v. Louisville Park Theatrical Ass'n, 347 U.S. 971 (1954) (mem.), vacating and remanding 202 F.2d 275 (6th Cir. 1953).

31. Mayor & City Council of Baltimore v. Dawson, 350 U.S. 877 (mem.), aff'g 220 F.2d 386 (4th Cir. 1955) (public beaches and bathhouses); Holmes v. City of Atlanta, 350 U.S. 879 (mem.), rev'g 223 F.2d 93 (5th Cir. 1955) (municipal golf courses); Gayle v. Browder, 352 U.S. 903 (mem.), aff'g 142 F. Supp. 707 (M.D. Ala. 1956) (city buses). The affirmance in the Baltimore case cited no authority at all; the reversal in the Atlanta case directed the entry of a decree for petitioners in conformity with the affirmance in the Baltimore case; the affirmance in *Gayle v. Browder* (one of the cases arising from the Montgomery bus boycott) cited as authorities the Baltimore and Atlanta cases together with *Brown* itself.

32. Bailey v. Patterson, 369 U.S. 31, 33 (1962) (per curiam) (segregated transportation facilities). Cf. Turner v. City of Memphis, 369 U.S. 350, 353 (1962) (per curiam) ("our decisions have foreclosed any possible contention that such a statute or regulation [fostering segregation in public facilities] may stand consistently with the Fourteenth Amendment").

33. Johnson v. Virginia, 373 U.S. 61, 62 (1963) (per curiam).

34. Plessy v. Ferguson, 163 U.S. 537, 563 (1896) (Harlan, J., dissenting).

35. The well-known exchange inspired by Herbert Wechsler's criticism of *Brown* in terms of "neutral principles" was concerned with whether the decision in the School Segregation Cases could be explained in principled terms, not with identifying the contours of the broader rule that by then was being enforced. See Wechsler, "Toward Neutral Principles of Constitutional Law," 73 *Harv. L. Rev.* 1 (1959); Louis H. Pollak, "Racial Discrimination and Judicial Integrity: A Reply to Professor Wechsler," 108 *U. Pa. L. Rev.* 1 (1959); Charles L. Black, Jr., "The Lawfulness of the Segregation Decisions," 69 *Yale L.J.* 421 (1960).

36. Albert P. Blaustein & Clarence Clyde Ferguson, Jr., *Desegregation and the Law: The Meaning and Effect of the School Segregation Cases* 145 (1957).

37. Chief Justice Warren's opinion included the observation that "[i]n the first cases in this Court construing the Fourteenth Amendment, decided shortly after its adoption, the Court interpreted it as proscribing all state-imposed discriminations against the Negro race," with a footnote quoting the famous antidiscrimination passage from *Strauder.* 347 U.S. at 490 & n. 5. In context, the principal effect of this remark was to suggest (obliquely and somewhat disingenuously) that "separate but equal" was a judicial innovation at the time of *Plessy* in 1896.

38. Blaustein & Ferguson, supra note 36, at 157.

39. 168 F. Supp. 149 (E.D. La. 1958), aff'd mem., 359 U.S. 533 (1959).

40. Act of July 16, 1956, No. 579, 1956 La. Acts 1054.

41. 168 F. Supp. at 151 (Wisdom, J.).

42. 359 U.S. 533 (1959) (mem.).

10. The Road Not Taken

1. Goss v. Board of Educ. of Knoxville, 373 U.S. 683, 687–688 (1963), quoting Steele v. Louisville & N. R.R., 323 U.S. 192, 203 (1944). A "minority transfer rule" permitted a student to transfer from a school in which his race constituted a minority to a school in which his race was in the majority.

2. Abington School Dist. v. Schempp, 374 U.S. 203, 317 (1963) (Stewart, J., dissenting).

3. Bell v. Maryland, 378 U.S. 226, 287–288 (1964) (Goldberg, J., concurring).

4. 375 U.S. 399 (1964), rev'g 206 F. Supp. 700 (D. La. 1962).

5. In effect, the measure protected a narrow category of voters—those for whom race is a determining factor, yet who are so ill informed as to be mistaken about the race of a given candidate—against casting a vote in error. The net gain or loss to a given candidate resulting from better information on this point is probably trivial and, in any event, is incapable of proof.

6. 206 F. Supp. at 705 (Wisdom, J., dissenting).

7. Brief for Appellants, Anderson v. Martin (No. 51, Oct. Term 1963), at 7–8.

8. 375 U.S. at 401–402.

9. 230 F. Supp. 156 (E.D. Va.), aff'd mem., 379 U.S. 19 (1964).

10. Id. at 157.

11. That laws restricting intermarriage would eventually be found unconstitutional had been reasonably clear since 1955, when the Supreme Court—visibly embarrassed—declined to rule on the question. See the discussion of *Naim v. Naim* in Chapter 9.

12. 379 U.S. 184 (1964).

13. Brief for Appellants, McLaughlin v. Florida (No. 11, Oct. Term, 1964), at 12, 13.

14. 379 U.S. at 198 (Stewart & Douglas, JJ., concurring).

15. Id. at 191–192.

16. The logic of Pace v. Alabama, 106 U.S. 583 (1883), was that laws prohibiting sexual relations between persons of different races subjected all persons, regardless of race, to identical prohibitions and penalties; they did not therefore deny equality before the law. Writing in *McLaughlin,* Justice White explained *Pace* as the product of a "limited view of the Equal Protection Clause which has not withstood analysis in the subsequent decisions of this Court," a view that if a law merely "applied equally to those to whom it was applicable" it did not violate the equal protection clause. 379 U.S. at 188–190. But this characterization of the reasoning of *Pace* is clearly inaccurate. Had the Supreme Court in 1883 actually subscribed to the "limited view of the Equal Protection Clause" attributed to it by Justice White, it could not have explained how the Fourteenth Amendment prohibited the State of Alabama from subjecting all blacks to one criminal code and all whites to another.

17. When the decision in *McLaughlin* was announced, five months after the enactment of the Civil Rights Act of 1964, the United States Supreme Court (it would seem) would hardly have shrunk from an implication that miscegenation laws would eventually be held unconstitutional: *McLaughlin* itself merely underscored the handwriting that was already on the wall. Nor should the Court have been unduly embarrassed at this point to repudiate directly the racist assumptions behind the decision in *Pace v. Alabama*.

18. 388 U.S. 1 (1967).

19. Id. at 8–11.

20. Brown v. Board of Educ., 349 U.S. 294, 301 (1955).

21. Briggs v. Elliott, 132 F. Supp. 776, 777 (E.D.S.C. 1955) (Parker, Dobie & Timmerman, JJ.).

22. Circuit Judges Parker and Dobie, the senior members of the three-judge district court in *Briggs,* both sat on the unanimous Fourth Circuit panel that four months earlier had decided *Dawson v. Mayor and City Council of Baltimore* (discussed in Chapter 9).

23. 349 U.S. at 300–301.

24. Brown v. Board of Educ. of Topeka, 345 U.S. 972, 973 (1953).

25. Transcript of Argument (Dec. 9, 1952), Briggs v. Elliott (No. 101, Oct. Term 1952), 49 *Landmark Briefs and Arguments of the Supreme Court of the United States: Constitutional Law* 307, 321 (Philip B. Kurland & Gerhard Casper eds., 1975).

26. Jack Greenberg, *Race Relations and American Law* 240 (1959).

27. Id. at 249–255.

28. "The question arises whether the [New Jersey antidiscrimination] Law goes further and prohibits a board of education from permitting the existence of segregation-in-fact when it can reasonably be eliminated. We believe that the Law Against Discrimination should be so construed. . . .

    ". . . [T]he term 'discrimination on account of race' as used in the Law Against Discrimination . . . should not be narrowly confined to cases where a harmful division of the races has resulted from a deliberate purpose or intent to bring it about. . . .

    "The guiding principle, we submit, is that the Board of Education should establish, and where necessary alter, zones of attendance in such a manner as to eliminate racial segregation so far as possible consistently with due regard for physical and economic factors." Brief on Behalf of Complainants, Walker v. Board of Educ. of the City of Englewood, 1 Race Rel. L. Rep. 255 (N.J. Dept. of Educ., Division against Discrimination, 1955) (No. M-1268), quoted in Greenberg, supra note 26, at 251–252.

29. Greenberg, supra note 26, at 250.

30. Policy statements to this effect by state education officials are reviewed with citations in Robert L. Carter, "De Facto School Segregation: An Examination of the Legal and Constitutional Questions Presented," 16 *W. Res. L. Rev.* 502, 508–512 (1965).

31. The quoted statements are from J. Skelly Wright, "Public School Desegregation: Legal Remedies for De Facto Segregation," 40 *N.Y.U. L. Rev.* 285, 292 (1965).

32. Both arguments are clearly sketched in the perceptive article by Carter, supra note 30, at 512–519.

33. See Branche v. Board of Educ. of the Town of Hempstead, 204 F. Supp. 150, 153 (E.D.N.Y. 1962) ("The central constitutional fact is the inadequacy of segregated education"); Blocker v. Board of Educ. of Manhasset, 226 F. Supp. 208 (E.D.N.Y. 1964); Barksdale v. Springfield School Comm., 237 F. Supp. 543, 546 (D. Mass.), vacated, 348 F.2d 261 (1st Cir. 1965) ("The question is whether there is a constitutional duty to provide equal educational opportunities for all children within the system").

34. Act of Aug. 3, 1955, No. 201, §4, [1955] 1 Ala. Acts 492, 493–494. Section 8 of the act provided that "[a]ny other provisions of law notwithstanding, no child shall be compelled to attend any school in which the races are commingled when a written objection of the parent or guardian has been filed with the Board of Education." Id. at 495.

35. Shuttlesworth v. Birmingham Bd. of Educ., 162 F. Supp. 372 (N.D. Ala.), aff'd mem., 358 U.S. 101 (1958). The district court stressed that its judgment was on "the constitutionality of the law *upon its face*," 162 F. Supp. at 384, and the Supreme Court noted that "the judgment is affirmed upon the limited grounds on which the District Court rested its decision." But the purpose and effect of the pupil placement laws were alike transparent: the Supreme Court, in 1958,

was simply not prepared to involve itself in the day-to-day task of school desegregation. The Court's complacency toward this subterfuge should be compared with its reaction to overt defiance (by Governor Orval Faubus of Arkansas), as expressed two months earlier in Cooper v. Aaron, 358 U.S. 1 (1958).

36. See Dove v. Parham, 282 F.2d 256, 258 (8th Cir. 1960) ("standards of placement cannot be devised or given application to preserve an existing system of imposed segregation"); Dodson v. School Bd. of Charlottesville, 289 F.2d 439 (4th Cir. 1961); Bush v. Orleans Parish School Bd., 204 F. Supp. 568, 570 (E.D. La.), aff'd in part, 308 F.2d 491 (5th Cir. 1962) ("where a school system is segregated, there is no constitutional basis whatever for using a pupil placement law").

37. See Kelly v. Board of Educ. of Nashville, 159 F. Supp. 272 (M.D. Tenn. 1958); Houston Indep. School Dist. v. Ross, 282 F.2d 95 (5th Cir. 1960); Boson v. Rippy, 285 F.2d 43 (5th Cir. 1960).

38. Goss v. Board of Educ. of Knoxville, 373 U.S. 683 (1963). According to the opinion by Justice Clark, "The recognition of race as an absolute criterion for granting transfers . . . is no less unconstitutional than its use for original admission or subsequent assignment to public schools." 373 U.S. at 688. The constitutional use of race as an absolute criterion for pupil assignment—in order to achieve integration—was just over the horizon but (in June 1963) still invisible and unsuspected.

39. See, e.g., Gaines v. Dougherty County Bd. of Educ., 334 F.2d 983 (5th Cir. 1964); Bradley v. School Bd. of Richmond, 345 F.2d 310 (4th Cir.), vacated and remanded on other grounds, 382 U.S. 103 (1965); Kemp v. Beasley, 352 F.2d 14 (8th Cir. 1965).

40. For an excellent account of the several phases of southern resistance to school desegregation and the Supreme Court's uneasy role in the process between 1955 and 1968, see J. Harvie Wilkinson III, *From Brown to Bakke: The Supreme Court and School Integration, 1954–1978* ch. 5 (1979).

41. Civil Rights Act of 1964, Pub. L. No. 88–352, §§601–602, 78 Stat. 243, 252–253 (codified at 42 U.S.C. §§2000d-2000d-1 [1982]); Elementary and Secondary Education Act of 1965, Pub. L. No. 89–10, 79 Stat. 27.

42. The Department of Health, Education and Welfare (to which the determination was committed by statute) ruled that a segregated school system might meet the requirements of Title VI by submitting a plan of desegregation, determined to be adequate by the Commissioner of Education, with reasonable assurances that the plan would be carried out. 45 C.F.R. §80.4(c) (Supp. 1966).

43. U.S. Office of Education, Department of Health, Education and Welfare, *General Statement of Policies under Title VI of the Civil Rights Act of 1964 Respecting Desegregation of Elementary and Secondary Schools* (April 1965), 45 C.F.R. §181 (Supp. 1966). The 1965 guidelines are more readily accessible in Price v. Denison Indep. School Dist. Bd. of Educ., 348 F.2d 1010, 1015–20 (5th Cir. 1965), where they are reprinted in full.

44. United States Comm'n on Civil Rights, *Survey of School Desegregation in the Southern and Border States, 1965–66* (February 1966).

45. Id. at xi, 54.
46. U.S. Office of Education, Department of Health, Education and Welfare, *Revised Statement of Policies for School Desegregation Plans under Title VI of the Civil Rights Act of 1964,* 31 Fed. Reg. 5623 (April 9, 1966), codified at 45 C.F.R. §181 (1967); quoted sections are at 45 C.F.R. §§181.32, 181.33, 181.54(d), 181.54(f). For a contemporary discussion of the HEW guidelines see James R. Dunn, "Title VI, the Guidelines, and School Desegregation in the South," 53 *Va. L. Rev.* 42 (1967).
47. 372 F.2d 836 (5th Cir. 1966).
48. Id. at 845–847.
49. Id. at 861–866, 872, 878. The *Jefferson County* opinion was not Judge Wisdom's first venture onto this ground. See Singleton v. Jackson Mun. Separate School Dist. *(Singleton I),* 348 F.2d 729, 730 n. 5 (5th Cir. 1965); and Singleton v. Jackson Mun. Separate School Dist. *(Singleton II),* 355 F.2d 865, 869 (5th Cir. 1966), where he had already argued that the "oversimplified dictum that the constitution 'does not require integration'" should be "laid to rest."
50. 372 F.2d at 846, n. 5.
51. Judge Wisdom's revisionist history of *Brown* was ratified by the Supreme Court in the major desegregation cases that followed: *Green v. County School Bd.* in 1968 and *Swann v. Charlotte-Mecklenburg Bd. of Educ.* in 1971. (The latter cases are discussed in Chapter 11.) The virtual obliteration from the American language of the distinction—once perfectly clear—between "desegregation" and "integration" must be attributed at least in part to the opinion in *United States v. Jefferson County.* The significance of this linguistic evolution, as Judge Wisdom obviously realized, is by no means merely semantic.
52. Title IV of the Civil Rights Act of 1964 contained the express statement that "'desegregation' shall not mean the assignment of students to public schools in order to correct racial imbalance"; southern senators were assured by liberal proponents of the bill that Titles IV and VI were *in pari materia.* Judge Wisdom's contention that Congress was concerned only with de facto segregation in northern jurisdictions is not persuasive. See the legislative history presented in section IV of the *Jefferson County* opinion, 372 F.2d at 878–886.
53. Id. at 848, 858–859, 866–869, 874–875.
54. Id. at 869.
55. Wright, supra note 31, at 298.
56. 372 F.2d at 876.

11. Benign Racial Sorting

1. 110 *Cong. Rec.* 5423, 11848, 12723 (1964) (remarks of Sen. Humphrey).
2. The Civil Rights Act of 1964 prohibited discrimination "on the ground of race" or "against any individual . . . because of such individual's race" in public accommodations, in federally assisted programs, and in employment. Pub. L. 88–352, §201 (public accommodations), §601 (federally assisted programs), §703

(employment), 78 Stat. 241, 243, 252, 255; codified as 42 U.S.C. §§2000a(a), 2000d, 2000e-2 (1982).

3. On the early argument for compensatory racial preferences, advanced in 1962 and 1963 by Whitney Young, Jr., of the National Urban League, see Hugh Davis Graham, *The Civil Rights Era* 110–113 (1990). Chapter 5 of Graham's work provides a concise legislative history of the Civil Rights Act of 1964.

4. Bayard Rustin, "From Protest to Politics: The Future of the Civil Rights Movement," 39 *Commentary* 25–27 (Feb. 1965).

5. U.S. Department of Labor, Office of Policy Planning and Research, *The Negro Family: The Case for National Action* (March 1965). (The passage quoted appears in an unpaginated summary introduction.) The text of the Moynihan Report (as it came to be called) is reproduced in Lee Rainwater & William L. Yancey, *The Moynihan Report and the Politics of Controversy* (1967), where it is most readily accessible. The latter work presents a highly useful synopsis of the circumstances in which the Moynihan Report was produced and of the political and scholarly reaction it provoked.

6. Nathan Glazer, "Negroes and Jews: The New Challenge to Pluralism," 38 *Commentary* 29, 34 (Dec. 1964), reprinted in Glazer, *Ethnic Dilemmas, 1964–1982* 29 (1983).

7. *The Negro Family,* supra note 5, at 3–6.

8. The sociology of the Moynihan Report, with its emphasis on matriarchal family structure and the "tangle of pathology" of the ghetto community, was largely derived from well-known works by black sociologists: E. Franklin Frazier's *The Negro Family in the United States* (1939) and Kenneth B. Clark's *Dark Ghetto: Dilemmas of Social Power* (1965).

9. See William Julius Wilson, *The Truly Disadvantaged: The Inner City, the Underclass, and Public Policy,* ch. 1 (1987); Paul E. Peterson, "The Urban Underclass and the Poverty Paradox," in *The Urban Underclass* 3 (Christopher Jencks & Paul E. Peterson eds., 1991).

10. Rustin, supra note 4, at 28.

11. The Howard University speech, titled "To Fulfill These Rights," is reprinted in Rainwater & Yancey, supra note 5, at 125–132.

12. *New York Times,* June 6, 1965, §4, at 10, col. 2.

13. *Report of the National Advisory Comm'n on Civil Disorders* 282 (N.Y. Times ed. 1968).

14. On the subject of school desegregation, see the informative general account provided by J. Harvie Wilkinson III, *From Brown to Bakke: The Supreme Court and School Integration, 1954–1978* (1979). The most useful case-by-case study of the Supreme Court's role, despite its occasionally polemical tone, is Lino A. Graglia, *Disaster by Decree: The Supreme Court Decisions on Race and the Schools* (1976). Much of the same ground is covered more concisely by Philip B. Kurland, "The School Desegregation Cases in the United States Supreme Court: 1954–1979," 1979 *Wash. U. L. Q.* 309. Although Kurland studiously avoids any reference to Graglia's work, their views are largely in harmony.

The complex history of "voting rights" since the 1965 Act, and the process by which that law was made a vehicle of proportional representation for racial and ethnic groups, are brilliantly elucidated by Abigail M. Thernstrom, *Whose Votes Count? Affirmative Action and Minority Voting Rights* (1987).

An even more difficult subject—the bureaucratic and political process by which the civil rights agencies of the federal government came to enforce racial preferences in employment—receives masterly treatment in Graham, supra note 3. Graham's book, which makes intelligible and even compelling history out of the impenetrable workings of federal agencies, will stand as the definitive account of a historical episode that has been both extraordinarily important and (in the absence of Graham's work) peculiarly inaccessible.

15. In Jones v. Alfred H. Mayer Co., 392 U.S. 409 (1968), the Supreme Court held that the right "to make and enforce contracts" guaranteed by the Civil Rights Act of 1866 (now codified as 42 U.S.C. §1981 [1982]) conferred a private right to contract with an unwilling individual whose refusal was motivated by racial discrimination. The case involved discrimination in housing. The fact that the decision in *Jones v. Alfred H. Mayer Co.* was issued two months *after* the enactment of a comprehensive federal open housing statute (Title VIII of the Civil Rights Act of 1968, Pub. L. 90–284, 82 Stat. 81; codified as 42 U.S.C. §3601 et seq. [1982]) says much about the Supreme Court's conception of its political role at this period. On the fair housing legislation of 1968 see Graham, supra note 3, at 270–273.

16. James S. Coleman et al., *Equality of Educational Opportunity* 302–325 (1966). Concluding its discussion of the "relation of school factors to achievement," the Coleman Report stated: "Taking all these results together, one implication stands out above all: That schools bring little influence to bear on a child's achievement that is independent of his background and general social context; and that this very lack of an independent effect means that the inequalities imposed on children by their home, neighborhood, and peer environment are carried along to become the inequalities with which they confront adult life at the end of school." Id. at 325.

17. Brown v. Board of Educ. of Topeka, 347 U.S. 483, 494 (1954). Testing the effect of integration on minority children's "control of the environment" and "self-concept," the Coleman study found only minor, contradictory results that in any event seemed likely to be outweighed by the student's family background. Coleman et al., supra note 16, at 323–324. For a review of the post-Coleman literature see Harold B. Gerard, "School Desegregation: The Social Science Role," and Stuart W. Cook, "The 1954 Social Science Statement and School Desegregation: A Reply to Gerard," in *Eliminating Racism: Profiles in Controversy* 225, 237 (Phyllis A. Katz & Dalmas A. Taylor eds., 1988).

18. 1 U.S. Comm'n on Civil Rights, *Racial Isolation in the Public Schools* 81–91 (1967). While it found that "[i]n general, as the educational aspirations and backgrounds of fellow students increase, the achievement of minority group children increases," the Coleman Report cautioned that "[s]uch a result must be

subject to special scrutiny, because it may be confounded by the student's own educational background and aspirations, which will generally be similar to those of his own fellow students." Coleman et al., supra note 16, at 302–303. As Frank Goodman pointed out, it was impossible in the nonexperimental Coleman study to isolate the influence of school racial composition from the other variables thought relevant to educational achievement. "The stubborn fact would remain that black students who attend white middle-class schools do so in most cases because their parents have made a deliberate decision to send them there—a decision that bespeaks the strength of their commitment to educational values." Goodman, "De Facto School Segregation: A Constitutional and Empirical Analysis," 60 *Calif. L. Rev.* 275, 404, 406 (1972).

19. 1 *Racial Isolation in the Public Schools,* supra note 18, at 94–114. The contention that integrated schools promote racial tolerance and understanding is a principal justification offered by more recent social science investigation. See Willis D. Hawley & Mark A. Smylie, "The Contribution of School Desegregation to Academic Achievement and Racial Integration," in *Eliminating Racism,* supra note 17, at 281.

20. *Rep't of the National Advisory Comm'n,* supra note 13, at 438.

21. 1 *Racial Isolation in the Public Schools,* supra note 18, at 209–212.

22. Green v. County School Bd. of New Kent County, 391 U.S. 430 (1968).

23. Swann v. Charlotte-Mecklenburg Bd. of Educ., 402 U.S. 1 (1971).

24. 391 U.S. at 437–439.

25. The thrust of the opinion was not a mystery to those who sensed the Court's momentum on the issue. Shortly before the decision in *Green,* Judge Frank Johnson had ordered that teachers in Montgomery County, Alabama, be assigned to schools on the basis of a fixed racial quota. When the court of appeals modified this order to the extent of substituting a requirement that teacher assignments be made "substantially or approximately" in the desired racial proportions, the Supreme Court took the trouble to reverse. It reinstated "the more specific and expeditious order of Judge Johnson," which it praised as having been "adopted in the spirit of this Court's opinion in *Green* . . . in that [it] 'promises realistically to work, and promises realistically to work *now.*'" United States v. Montgomery County Bd. of Educ., 395 U.S. 225, 234, 235–236 (1969).

26. Swann v. Charlotte-Mecklenburg Bd. of Educ., 300 F. Supp. 1358, 1360 (W.D.N.C. 1969).

27. See 402 U.S. at 23–25. References to the desirability of a uniform racial ratio in all Charlotte-Mecklenburg schools appear in the published opinions of Judge McMillan at 300 F. Supp. 1358, 1371–72, 306 F. Supp. 1299, 1312 (W.D.N.C. 1969) and 311 F. Supp 265, 267–268 (W.D.N.C. 1970).

28. 300 F. Supp. at 1372.

29. 306 F. Supp. at 1296–1297; 300 F. Supp. at 1369.

30. See Graglia, supra note 14, at 312 n. 105; Bob Woodward & Scott Armstrong, *The Brethren* 95–112 (1979).

31. 402 U.S. at 6, 15.

32. Keyes v. School Dist. No. 1, Denver, Colo., 413 U.S. 189 (1973).

33. On the operation of this judicial technique see the dissenting opinions of Justice Rehnquist in *Keyes,* 413 U.S. at 254–265, and in Columbus Bd. of Educ. v. Penick, 443 U.S. 449, 489–525 (1979).

34. The nature and extent of the desegregation remedies to which a given school district is subject are frequently determined, in practice, in a three-cornered negotiation between civil rights plaintiffs (sometimes including the federal government), school officials, and the local district judge. For published materials (other than newspaper accounts) on desegregation plans in a sample of large school districts see the valuable bibliography in Finis Welch & Audrey Light, *New Evidence on School Desegregation* 115–176 (1987).

35. 413 U.S. at 220–221, 225–226.

36. Pasadena City Bd. of Educ. v. Spangler, 427 U.S. 424 (1976).

37. Milliken v. Bradley, 418 U.S. 717 (1974).

38. The succession of executive orders prohibiting employment discrimination by government contractors is conveniently summarized in Contractors Ass'n of Eastern Pa. v. Secretary of Labor, 442 F.2d 159, 168–171 (3d Cir. 1971).

39. Exec. Order No. 10,925 [March 6, 1961], 3 C.F.R. 86, 87–88 (1961 Supp.). The absence of any substantive change in the contractor's obligation becomes clear from a comparison of the successive versions of the Executive Order before and after the 1961 amendment: the earlier version is Exec. Order No. 10,557 [Sept. 3, 1954], 3 C.F.R. 69 (1954 Supp.). The pertinent language of the 1961 order was carried forward without alteration by President Johnson's Executive Order No. 11,246 of Sept. 24, 1965, 3 C.F.R. 567, 568–569 (1966), the current source of the authority of the Office of Federal Contract Compliance Programs of the Department of Labor. Executive Order No. 11,246 (as amended) is reprinted as a note to 42 U.S.C. §2000e (1982).

40. See 41 C.F.R. §60 (1968).

41. Graham, supra note 3, at 289. The story of the Philadelphia Plan under both the Johnson and Nixon administrations is described in detail in chapters 11 and 13 of Graham's study.

42. 41 C.F.R. §60–1.40(a) (1969).

43. *New York Times,* Jan. 16, 1970, at 15, col. 1.

44. See Graham, supra note 3, at 342.

45. 41 C.F.R. §60–2.10 (1971).

46. Civil Rights Act of 1964, §703(a); 42 U.S.C. §2000e-2(a) (1982).

47. 110 Cong. Rec. 7213 (1964).

48. Civil Rights Act of 1964, §703(j); 42 U.S.C. §2000e-2(j) (1982).

49. Contractor's Ass'n of Eastern Pa. v. Secretary of Labor, 442 F.2d 159, 173 (3d Cir.), cert. denied, 404 U.S. 854 (1971).

50. Testimony before a Senate committee in 1971 by Laurence Silberman, then under-secretary of labor, illustrated the rationale of the new affirmative action:

"One of the things interesting about the affirmative action concept, it is not antidiscrimination. It goes beyond that. We every day put pressure on—well, let me say it slightly differently.

"We and the compliance agencies put pressure on contractors to come up with commitments even though those contractors are not guilty of any discrimination, but because we think they are required under the Executive order to go beyond, to provide affirmative action. . . . [Y]ou say to that contractor, you have to make an extra effort beyond what the civil rights laws are in this country and go beyond that in order to get a Government contract. . . .

". . . [W]e have so much clout over government contract[ors] that very few of them are willing to or want to fight that through litigation. They usually come into compliance." *Equal Employment Opportunities Enforcement Act of 1971: Hearings on S. 2515 . . . before the Subcomm. on Labor of the Senate Comm. on Labor & Public Welfare,* 92d Cong., 1st Sess. 88–90 (1971).

51. The process by which the EEOC first came to this conclusion, then sought to impose it through its own interpretation of Title VII, is explored in detail by Graham, supra note 3, chs. 7 & 9.

52. Alfred W. Blumrosen, *Black Employment and the Law* vii–viii (1971).

53. 401 U.S. 424 (1971).

54. Id. at 431–432.

55. For a thorough account of the pertinent legislative history, highly critical of the decision in *Griggs,* see Richard A. Epstein, *Forbidden Grounds: The Case against Employment Discrimination Laws,* ch. 10 (1992).

56. 110 *Cong. Rec.* 7213 (1964).

57. Civil Rights Act of 1964, Title VII, §703(h); 42 U.S.C. §2000e-2(h) (1982).

58. *Uniform Guidelines on Employee Selection Procedures (1978),* 29 C.F.R. §1607.4 (1979). On the EEOC's "war against testing" and its eventual acquiescence in the "bottom-line rule" of 1978, see Herman Belz, *Equality Transformed: A Quarter-Century of Affirmative Action,* ch. 5 (1991).

59. See Connecticut v. Teal, 457 U.S. 440 (1982).

60. If applicants for a position can be usefully differentiated by ability, yet must be chosen in approximate proportion to their representation in the relevant population (or any other ratio), the most straightforward selection process is to rank the relevant groups separately and choose from the top of each list. Such is the inevitable process, for example, of race-conscious university admissions.

The "race-norming" of aptitude test scores is a particularly well-documented illustration of "bottom-line" selection procedures. Since 1981, the U.S. Employment Service of the Department of Labor has promoted the screening of all applicants for employment through state employment service agencies by means of a test known as the General Aptitude Test Battery (GATB). Technical studies performed for the Labor Department established the predictive validity of the GATB (with a degree of accuracy sufficient to make the test a useful tool in increasing productivity) for all jobs and all applicants handled by the Employment Service. They also revealed, as do virtually all standardized tests, "significant group differences in average test scores," such that a "strict top-down referral would adversely affect the employment chances of black and Hispanic applicants." The U.S. Employment Service accordingly recommended that the conversion of raw test scores to percentile rankings be done separately for black, Hispanic, and "other" applicants. "The resulting percentile scores reflect an applicant's standing with reference to his or her own racial or ethnic group, thus effectively erasing average group differences in test scores." National Research Council, Committee on the General Aptitude Test Battery, *Fairness in Employment Testing: Validity Generalization, Minority Issues, and the General Aptitude Test Battery* 17–21 (John A. Hartigan & Alexandra K. Wigdor eds., 1989). "Race-norming" is not a means of correcting the GATB for predictive error: the GATB Committee of the National Research Council (which favored race-norming) found that unadjusted scores were "somewhat more likely to overpredict than to underpredict the performance of black applicants." Id. at 188. On the committee's report see Jan H. Blits & Linda S. Gottfredson, "Equality or Lasting Inequality?" and Alexandra K. Wigdor & John A. Hartigan, "The Case for Fairness," *Society* (March/April 1990), at 4, 12.

61. Regents of the Univ. of Calif. v. Bakke, 438 U.S. 265 (1978).
62. United Steelworkers of America v. Weber, 443 U.S. 193 (1979).
63. Civil Rights Act of 1964, §601; codified as amended at 42 U.S.C. §2000d (1982).
64. 438 U.S. at 328 (Brennan, White, Marshall & Blackmun, JJ.). "Title VI must be held to proscribe only those racial classifications that would violate the Equal Protection Clause or the Fifth Amendment." Id. at 287 (Powell, J.).
65. The pertinent legislative history (marshaled by Justice Rehnquist in dissent) establishes this beyond dispute. 443 U.S. 193, 230–255. The essential commentary on the decision is Bernard D. Meltzer, "The *Weber* Case: The Judicial Abrogation of the Antidiscrimination Standard in Employment," 47 *U. Chi. L. Rev.* 423 (1980).
66. Civil Rights Act of 1964, §703(d); 42 U.S.C. §2000e-2(d) (1982).
67. See 443 U.S. at 204. Justice Brennan's opinion in *Weber* makes something of a litmus test for modern legal scholars favoring greater judicial latitude in statutory interpretation. For a representative defense see Cass R. Sunstein, *After the Rights Revolution: Reconceiving the Regulatory State* 201–205 (1990).
68. Justice Powell believed that the use of racial and ethnic criteria in the medical school's "special admissions program" was overly categorical. By contrast, "a properly devised admissions program involving the competitive consideration of race and ethnic origin"—along the lines, Justice Powell suggested, of those employed at Harvard and Princeton—could "legitimately" serve a "substantial" state interest and would accordingly be constitutional. 438 U.S. at 315–320.
69. Id. at 355.
70. 448 U.S. 448 (1980).
71. Prior to the 1977 public works appropriation considered in *Fullilove,* the most recent congressional legislation to impose an explicit racial distinction in the treatment accorded to citizens (racially discriminatory immigration laws being directed against aliens) appears to have been the act of July 22, 1854, donating lands to settlers in the Territory of New Mexico. The benefit of the donation was

extended to "every white male citizen of the United States, or every white male above the age of twenty-one years who has declared his intention to become a citizen," meeting a specified residence qualification. Acts of the 33d Cong., 1st Sess., ch. 103, §2, 10 Stat. 308. Reconstruction measures securing benefits to former slaves, while unquestionably a species of race-conscious legislation, afford no comparable example of a racial classification. The language of these statutes typically avoided racial qualifications, describing their beneficiaries as "freedmen" and "refugees."

For a survey of antebellum racial discrimination by the federal government, more frequently imposed by administrative action than by statute, see Leon F. Litwack, "The Federal Government and the Free Negro, 1790–1860," 43 *J. Negro Hist.* 261 (1958).

72. Discrimination against aliens on racial or ethnic grounds must again be distinguished. See the Chinese Exclusion Case, 130 U.S. 581 (1889). The most flagrant instances of legislation imposing explicitly unequal treatment on racial lines, such as state laws prohibiting the immigration or sojourn of free Negroes, antedated the Fourteenth Amendment; and no challenge to these laws based on the comity clause of article IV ever reached the Supreme Court.

73. Public Works Employment Act of 1977, Pub. L. 95–28, §103(f)(2), 91 Stat. 116, 117; 42 U.S.C. §6705(f)(2) (1982).

74. 123 *Cong. Rec.* 5327 (1977) (remarks of Rep. Mitchell).

75. 448 U.S. at 517–519.

76. Id. at 484, 490.

77. Wygant v. Jackson Bd. of Educ., 476 U.S. 267 (1986).

78. City of Richmond v. J. A. Croson Co., 488 U.S. 469 (1989).

79. Metro Broadcasting, Inc. v. Federal Communications Comm'n, 110 S. Ct. 2997 (1990).

80. *Report of the National Advisory Comm'n,* supra note 13, at 296.

81. Pub. L. 89–110, 79 Stat. 437; codified as amended at 42 U.S.C. §1973 et seq. (1982).

82. On the background, purpose, and operation of the Voting Rights Act of 1965, see South Carolina v. Katzenbach, 383 U.S. 301 (1966) (upholding its constitutionality); Thernstrom, supra note 14, at 11–22.

83. South Carolina v. Katzenbach, 383 U.S. at 335.

84. The passages quoted are from the Voting Rights Act of 1965, §§4(a), 4(c), and 5, 79 Stat. 437, 438–439; codified as amended at 42 U.S.C. §§1973b(a), 1973b(c) & 1973c (1982).

85. See Thernstrom, supra note 14, at 20–21; Allen v. State Bd. of Elections, 393 U.S. 544, 582–594 (1969) (Harlan, J., dissenting).

86. 393 U.S. 544 (1969).

87. 377 U.S. 533 (1964).

88. Allen v. State Bd. of Elections, 393 U.S. 544, 569.

89. The 1982 amendments to the Voting Rights Act added to §2 an express statement that "[t]he extent to which members of a protected class have been elected to

office" might be considered in establishing whether its members "have less opportunity than other members of the electorate to participate in the political process and to elect representatives of their choice." The latter circumstance was declared to constitute a violation of the act's central prohibition, namely, the "denial or abridgement of the right of any citizen of the United States to vote on account of race or color." Pub. L. No. 97–205, §3, 96 Stat. 134 (1982); 42 U.S.C. §1973(b) (1982).

90. The leading case on annexation is City of Richmond v. United States, 422 U.S. 358 (1975), holding that an extension of municipal boundaries that reduces overall percentage of black population has the proscribed "effect" of "denying or abridging the right to vote on account of race" unless a post-annexation districting plan "fairly reflects the strength of the Negro community as it exists after the annexation" and "would afford [it] representation reasonably equivalent to [its] political strength in the enlarged community." Id. at 370–371. "Given the widespread use of at-large electoral systems in the covered cities of the South and Southwest, [this] requirement has almost always meant a switch to ward voting and a consequent gain in the number of legislative seats held by blacks and Hispanics." Thernstrom, supra note 14, at 150. On the issue of reapportionment, Beer v. United States, 425 U.S. 130 (1976), held that §5 of the Voting Rights Act prohibits implementation of a plan that "would lead to a retrogression in the position of racial minorities with respect to their effective exercise of the electoral franchise." 425 U.S. at 141. The potential for "effective exercise of the electoral franchise" was measured in *Beer* by counting the number of electoral districts in which protected groups constitute a "safe" majority. While *Beer* announced a standard of "nonretrogression" in reapportionment cases, less stringent than the "fairly reflects" test for post-annexation electoral districting, the Justice Department and the District Court for the District of Columbia (the two tribunals that decide §5 cases) have in practice required the maximum number of "safe" minority districts, with proportional representation as the ultimate benchmark. See Thernstrom, supra note 14, at 137–191.

91. United Jewish Organizations of Williamsburgh, Inc. v. Carey, 430 U.S. 144 (1977).

92. On the 1970 amendments that brought New York City within the coverage of the Voting Rights Act see Thernstrom, supra note 14, ch. 2.

93. See United Jewish Organizations of Williamsburgh, Inc. v. Wilson, 510 F.2d 512, 515–516 (2d Cir. 1975); Torres v. Sachs, 381 F. Supp. 309 (S.D.N.Y. 1974).

94. 510 F.2d at 526.

95. The facts are drawn from 430 U.S. at 150–152; 510 F.2d at 517–518, 526–527.

96. Anderson v. Martin, 206 F. Supp. 700, 705 (D. La. 1962) (Wisdom, J., dissenting). The Supreme Court's decision invalidating the statute (Anderson v. Martin, 375 U.S. 399 (1964)) is discussed in Chapter 10.

97. Gomillion v. Lightfoot, 364 U.S. 339 (1960).

98. Wright v. Rockefeller, 376 U.S. 52, 57–58 (1964).

99. Department of Justice, Civil Rights Division, Memorandum of Decision, July 1,

1974 (announcing the absence of objections to New York's reapportionment as revised to meet the 65 percent standard), quoted in 510 F.2d at 528.

100. 430 U.S. at 166.

101. The phrase is from the famous "Carolene Products footnote," United States v. Carolene Products Co., 304 U.S. 144, 152 n. 4 (1938).

102. 430 U.S. at 170, 172–175.

103. Alexander M. Bickel, *The Morality of Consent* 133 (1975).

104. See note 52 supra and accompanying text.

105. Assembly Bill No. 462, §15, Calif. Legislature, 1989–90 Regular Sess. A joint committee of the legislature recommended in 1989 that "[e]ach segment of California public higher education shall strive to approximate by the year 2000 the general ethnic, gender, economic, and regional composition of recent high school graduates, both in first-year classes and subsequent college and university graduating classes." California Legislature, Joint Committee for Review of the Master Plan for Higher Education, *California Faces . . . California's Future: Education for Citizenship in a Multicultural Democracy* 20–21 [1989].

106. The most accessible account of the University of California's affirmative action policies is Dinesh D'Souza, *Illiberal Education: The Politics of Race and Sex on Campus,* ch. 2 (1991).

107. Article 153 of the constitution of Malaysia (1957) requires that the "special position of the Malays" (*sc.* as opposed to the Chinese population) be protected by proportional representation and by quotas for civil service positions and university places. Since its adoption, article 153 has been amended to add "natives of any of the States of Sabah and Sarawak" to the protected group. The constitution of India, arts. 330–342 (1950), provides "reserved" legislative seats for members of the scheduled castes and scheduled tribes and requires that their claims be recognized in civil service appointments. The guarantee of proportional representation, which by its original terms would have expired thirty years after the constitution's January 1950 effective date, has twice been amended to extend it for successive periods of ten years.

108. Plessy v. Ferguson, 163 U.S. 537, 560 (1896).

Index of Cases

General Index

Abolitionists: views on the Constitution, 7–8, 10–11, 53, 54, 55, 63, 241n58; factional disputes among, 22, 61–62, 231n3; Garrisonian, 22, 25, 28–29, 32, 37, 39, 58, 61, 160; on legal and civic equality, 26–28, 59, 119–120, 184, 237n19; on Thirteenth Amendment, 53, 55–56, 62; on Negro suffrage, 59, 61–62, 63. *See also* American Anti-Slavery Society; Garrison, William Lloyd; Massachusetts Anti-Slavery Society; Petitions; Phillips, Wendell

Adams, Charles Francis, 241n58

Adams, John Quincy, 24, 241n58

Affirmative action, 2, 5, 6, 120, 130, 187, 190, 200–201, 202, 206, 207, 209–211, 222, 285n50; origin of expression, 200–201. *See also* Racial preferences; Voting rights

American Anti-Slavery Society, 53, 55, 62, 65, 66, 231nn1,3, 235nn15,16; petition campaigns of, 24–25, 233nn12,13, 236n17, 246n14

Anthony, Susan B., 53

Articles of Confederation, 9, 10, 15, 20

Ashley, James M., 55

Augusta, Ga., segregated schools in, 126, 128–129

Bakke, Alan, 221

Barnes, Gilbert Hobbs, 233n13

Basis of representation. *See* Fourteenth Amendment

Beck, Joseph, 98–100

Berea College, 134

Bickel, Alexander M., 69, 152, 153, 220

Bingham, John: favors alternatives to nondiscrimination, 4, 66, 67–69, 72, 77–80, 82, 84, 85, 86–87; in Joint Committee on Reconstruction, 71, 72, 77, 79, 83–86; opposes civil rights bill, 75–76, 77–79, 86

Bingham Amendment. *See* Fourteenth Amendment

Black, Hugo, 145, 214

Black Codes, 68, 76, 79, 80, 81, 87, 113, 115, 117, 264n11

Blackmun, Harry A., 208, 209

Blaine, James G., 71

Blaine Amendment. *See* Fourteenth Amendment

Blaustein, Albert P., 161–162, 163

Blumrosen, Alfred W., 204, 221–222

Boston, Mass.: segregated schools in, 30, 32–33, 37, 40, 41, 42, 48–49; school committee reports on segregation, 33–39, 45, 46, 175, 243n8

Bottom-line rule, 206

Boutwell, George S., 65, 255n65

Bowditch, Henry Ingersoll, 33, 37, 240n57, 241n58

Bradburn, George, 29

Bradley, Joseph P., 94

Brennan, William J., 207, 208, 209, 219–220

Brewer, David, 105, 134, 263n4

Brooklyn, N.Y., 108, 216–219

Brown, Catharine, 91

Brown, Henry Billings, 46, 113, 116–117, 118, 121, 130, 131, 154–155

Burger, Warren, 196, 205, 209